Also by Nina Sankovitch

American Rebels: How the Hancock, Adams, and Quincy Families Fanned the Flames of Revolution

The Lowells of Massachusetts: An American Family

Signed, Sealed, Delivered: Celebrating the Joys of Letter Writing

Tolstoy and the Purple Chair: My Year of Magical Reading

How a Nonbinary Minister Became America's Most Radical Revolutionary

Not Your Founding Father

Nina Sankovitch

SIMON & SCHUSTER
New York Amsterdam/Antwerp London
Toronto Sydney/Melbourne New Delhi

Simon & Schuster
1230 Avenue of the Americas
New York, NY 10020

Copyright © 2026 by Nina Sankovitch

For more than 100 years, Simon & Schuster has championed authors and the stories they create. By respecting the copyright of an author's intellectual property, you enable Simon & Schuster and the author to continue publishing exceptional books for years to come. We thank you for supporting the author's copyright by purchasing an authorized edition of this book.

No amount of this book may be reproduced or stored in any format, nor may it be uploaded to any website, database, language-learning model, or other repository, retrieval, or artificial intelligence system without express permission. All rights reserved. Inquiries may be directed to Simon & Schuster, 1230 Avenue of the Americas, New York, NY 10020 or permissions@simonandschuster.com.

All rights reserved, including the right to reproduce this book or portions thereof in any form whatsoever. For information, address Simon & Schuster Subsidiary Rights Department, 1230 Avenue of the Americas, New York, NY 10020.

First Simon & Schuster hardcover edition January 2026

Simon & Schuster strongly believes in freedom of expression and stands against censorship in all its forms. For more information, visit BooksBelong.com.

SIMON & SCHUSTER and colophon are registered trademarks of Simon & Schuster, LLC

For information about special discounts for bulk purchases, please contact Simon & Schuster Special Sales at 1-866-506-1949 or business@simonandschuster.com.

The Simon & Schuster Speakers Bureau can bring authors to your live event. For more information or to book an event, contact the Simon & Schuster Speakers Bureau at 1-866-248-3049 or visit our website at www.simonspeakers.com.

Interior design by Lewelin Polanco

Manufactured in the United States of America

1 3 5 7 9 10 8 6 4 2

Library of Congress Cataloging-in-Publication Data is available.

ISBN 978-1-9821-7870-3
ISBN 978-1-9821-7872-7 (ebook)

Let's stay in touch! Scan here to get book recommendations, exclusive offers, and more delivered to your inbox.

For Jack Menz
Again, and always
1958–2024

"The Friend of Sinners began to serve
in the year 1777,
when this nation was all in arms
and . . . embroiled . . . in human blood,
the Messenger of peace going from city to city
and from village to village,
proclaiming news of salvation
to all that would repent. . . ."

—RUTH PRITCHARD

Contents

PART 2: FLIGHT (1788–93)

PART 3: FIGHT (1794–1819)

Not Your Founding Father

Introduction

"I will therefore so write here
that I may not Be ashamed to read hereafter. . . ."

—UNIVERSAL FRIEND

In the spring of 1776, Abigail Adams wrote to her husband, John, asking him to "Remember the Ladies" as he and the other (all male) representatives to the Continental Congress debated the path to American independence.[1] Abigail hoped that when the colonies achieved independence, women in America would join in the victory and finally have a say over their own lives without having to bow to the authority of men in managing their homes and property, and planning for their futures. But John Adams scoffed at Abigail's hopes, writing back to her, "I cannot but laugh. . . . Depend upon it, We know better than to repeal our Masculine systems."[2]

In October of that same year, a young woman from Rhode Island named Jemima Wilkinson claimed to have died and been reborn as a genderless messenger sent by God to save lost souls. Adopting the name "Universal Friend," within months the minister was preaching a message of universal salvation to crowds throughout New England. Universal Friend would become the first American-born founder of a religious sect, and the country's first nonbinary minister. But perhaps most importantly, in the decades following America's independence from England, Universal Friend established communities in which Abigail Adams's hopes were realized. Hundreds of followers from all walks of life, men and women, Black and white, lived as equals under the minister's leadership. Freed from constrictions based on race, class, or gender, they pursued dreams of social stability, economic prosperity, and shared piety—and made those dreams a reality.

What first drew me to the story of Universal Friend was the minister's refusal to be identified as either male or female, instead insisting, "I am that I am," and adopting a genderless name while also dressing in androgynous clothing.[3] But as I delved deeper, I became fascinated by how the story of Friend's life illustrated the story of the United States during the years of the American Revolution and the decades following independence. By looking closely at individual lives during specific times in history, we can learn so much about larger historical events and themes. The life of Universal Friend proved to be particularly illuminating, especially in how Friend established communities that embodied the ideals for which the American Revolution was fought, while elsewhere in the new nation of the United States those ideals fell woefully by the wayside.

Universal Friend did what men like Washington, Jefferson, and Adams had promised: created a society that valued equality, promoted opportunity, and fostered a flourishing economy based on individual enrichment while also emphasizing working for the common good. There is no denying that Friend was a religious zealot who had some very extreme ideas (which will be explored in this book). Nevertheless, the communities founded by Universal Friend are proof of just how impactful the American experiment could have been if the promises of the Revolution—Americans' inalienable rights to "Life, Liberty, and the pursuit of happiness"—had been kept.[4] Universal Friend, for example, required followers to manumit their enslaved workers. While the total number of persons emancipated under Friend's guidance remains unclear, just imagine what the United States would have looked like by the late eighteenth century if all the spiritual leaders in the country had required their congregants to manumit their enslaved laborers.

The writings left behind by Friend are sparse, consisting of fewer than a dozen letters written by the minister; journal entries (largely consisting of copied-out favorite texts); an undated sermon titled "An Answer to Roxbury People"; some notes scribbled on loose papers; an undated "Meditation"; a memorandum recording the alleged transformation from a dying woman to the reborn messenger of God; and a pamphlet of "Advice" setting out the rules of the sect (some of which are inspiring and some of which are just strange). There are also written records of Friend's dreams, which the minister viewed as direct communications with God. But most of what we know about Friend—how the minister looked and behaved, preached and loved, created a ministry and inspired followers—is from the observations of others. Some of these observers admired Friend very, very much, and some most definitely did not. These observations are found in newspaper articles, pamphlets, and journals, and in dozens of letters and diary and journal entries written by eyewitnesses to Friend's ministry.

Distilling the truth from the limited number of documents created by Friend and the often exaggerated or distorted tales recorded by others can be challenging. Throughout this book I use words like "likely," "perhaps," and "probably" to indicate where I cannot know something for sure, but as historian Paul Moyer points out in his biography of Friend (titled *The Public Universal Friend: Jemima Wilkinson and Religious Enthusiasm in Revolutionary America*), using "these terms is simply an act of honesty that reflects the reality that not much in history—or at least not much worth knowing—is known for certain."[5]

In writing the story of Friend's life, I have not put words into the mouth (or thoughts into the mind) of the minister, with one exception. Based on my readings of Friend's sermons and letters, I know that the minister drew inspiration from the Old Testament (heavy on warning and judgment) and also found solace and comfort in the

New Testament with Jesus's words about love and forgiveness. Where Friend's use of specific biblical texts is documented in conversations, letters, and sermons, I've noted it in the endnotes; excerpts that I *imagine* the minister to have chosen for a specific moment or event are endnoted by citation to the Bible itself.

Universal Friend adopted the name, uniform, and grooming of a nonspecific gender. While one may question whether it's appropriate to use the concept of nonbinary identity when discussing a person who lived over two hundred years ago, I believe there is no other accurate way to describe Friend's gender identity. Historians who have written about Universal Friend, as well as contemporary observers of the minister, largely conclude that Friend rejected identification by male or female gender: as reported in a Philadelphia newspaper following a visit of the minister to that city in 1787, Friend was not "supposed to be of either sex" and behaved and dressed in ways that underscored the state of "being neither man nor woman."[6] The LGBT Foundation defines as nonbinary "people [who] may identify as both male and female or neither male nor female. They may feel their gender is fluid, can change and fluctuate or perhaps they permanently don't identify with one particular gender."[7]

The question, then, is which pronoun to use when referring to Universal Friend. Two previous books, Moyer's biography and *Pioneer Prophetess: Jemima Wilkinson, the Publick Universal Friend* written by Herbert A. Wisbey, are both excellent studies of the life of Friend and proved very useful to me in writing this book. Neither, however, helped me in deciding which pronoun to use in referring to the reborn Jemima Wilkinson. Wisbey chose to use the female pronoun when talking about Universal Friend, while Moyer chose to use the male pronoun following the minister's transformation in 1776. In the times we live in now, the pronoun "they" might be appropriate. Letters and diary entries by devoted followers overwhelmingly refrain from using any pronouns in referring to the minister, and so I've chosen to respect what I believe was the practice of Friend's followers (perhaps at

Friend's explicit directive) to use no pronoun at all when referring to the minister.[8]

In addition to illustrating the times in which Universal Friend lived, the minister's story is compelling for how it relates to current debates over who we Americans are as a people and as a nation. In so many ways, Friend is an archetype of the American dream: a person who came from a modest background and managed to achieve widespread fame, influence, and prosperity. Universal Friend was independent, resolute, and brave—qualities that we Americans often claim as uniquely ours—but also stubborn and egotistical. The minister exhibited all those characteristics in a lifelong effort to resolve many of the same issues with which we Americans struggle today, including the role of religion in society; how to balance self-determination and freedom with civic responsibility; how to offer equal opportunities to diverse participants; and the politics of identity. Friend's underlying goal was one that Americans hold close to our hearts: How to create a practical, functioning utopia. A world in which all its citizens have hope.

Universal Friend believed that God had chosen Jemima Wilkinson's body to serve as the vessel to be his messenger of salvation. Whether or not we believe it doesn't matter; Friend did, and for forty-three years remained dedicated to the mission of salvation, while also challenging the status quo in just about every arena entered. How did a young Quaker woman from a sleepy village transition into an influential and charismatic force for change? From where did Friend's ideals of equality and liberty grow? What were the political and cultural circumstances that allowed Friend's sect to flourish? How did the minister find the strength to keep on going in the face of false accusations, slanderous press, treachery of trusted friends, deaths of beloved companions, the heavy burdens of natural disasters and decades-long legal proceedings, and against the tides of fickle public opinion and internecine dissent? I hope you find the answers to these questions—and the remarkable story of Universal Friend—as wonderfully interesting and inspiring as I do.

PART
1

Faith

1776–87

“We have it in our power
to begin the world over again.”

—THOMAS PAINE

1

Death at the Door

"If thou makes a good Use of the Blessings
thou hast already Received,
it will make way for yet Greater Enlargements . . ."

—UNIVERSAL FRIEND

In early October of 1776, a woman by the name of Jemima Wilkinson fell ill. She was twenty-three years old and lived with her father, Jeremiah, and a number of her siblings in the small village of Cumberland in the colony of Rhode Island and Providence Plantations. For five days, Jemima lay in her bed, feverish and restless, slipping in and out of troubled sleep.[1] Jeremiah rarely left her side, acting as both nurse and watchman over his daughter. From the window of the room where she lay, Jeremiah would have been able to see his cherry trees, row after row rising and falling over the gently sloping hills, their lobed leaves just starting to turn from summer green to autumn gold.

So many cherry trees had been planted by Jeremiah Wilkinson over the years that his nickname was Cherry Wilkinson. Cherry, not cheery, for he was a man of dour piety. Jeremiah was a Quaker and a member in good standing of the Smithfield Meeting, the congregation that met just four miles down the road from the Wilkinson home. His grandfather

Lawrence Wilkinson had arrived in Rhode Island from England in the 1640s. During the First Civil War in England, a religious war in which Puritan Roundheads battled the Anglican and royalist forces of King Charles I, Lawrence had fought for his king and was taken prisoner but later released. After the king's surrender in 1646, Lawrence found himself without property—his lands having been confiscated during his imprisonment—and without prospects. Rather than live under a government led by the Puritan Oliver Cromwell, Lawrence joined the "royalist emigration" and, along with hundreds of other Englishmen and -women, left his native country for the New World.[2]

He landed in the port town of Providence in what was then called the Providence Plantations (and would become in 1663 the colony of Rhode Island and Providence Plantations). The town had been named by the founder of the colony, Roger Williams, in honor of "God's merciful Providence," which led him there after he was banished in 1636 from the colony of Massachusetts for his nonconforming views of religious tolerance.[3] Granted a land patent for his Rhode Island colony in 1643 (around the time Lawrence Wilkinson arrived), in 1663 Williams was finally granted a charter for the colony (it had been held up by the civil wars going on in England). The charter was the first (and only) colonial charter that guaranteed religious freedom to all its citizens, ensuring that within its borders all spiritual practices would be tolerated and there would be no one prevailing state-mandated religion.

What a relief it must have been for Lawrence to find himself in a place where there'd be no need to take sides over religious affiliation. After witnessing the brutalities of a civil war fought in part over theological differences, he could surely appreciate just how precious peaceful coexistence was. While the records are unclear as to Lawrence's religious practices when he landed in America, within one generation the Wilkinsons of Rhode Island had become Quakers, joining the small congregations scattered throughout the colony.

Founded as the Society of Friends in England by George Fox in the late 1640s, the sect became known as "Quakers" due to its practitioners' tendency to tremble during moments of religious conviction. Under Fox's guidance, the Society of Friends emphasized both the importance of individual spiritual experience and the equality of all people before God: anyone, male or female, could receive God's wisdom through an intense personal communication known as "inner light."

Fox believed every person contained a carnal spirit that had to be subdued by removing oneself from worldly concerns and ambitions, including politics. This position led to problems for Fox and his followers in England, who refused to swear fealty or fight for their king, and was one reason the Quakers were persecuted. Fox himself was harassed, beaten, and imprisoned repeatedly for his religious beliefs.

Fleeing their persecution, Quakers traveled to America. What they found, however, was much of the same ill-treatment they had suffered in England, particularly in the colony of Massachusetts, where Quakers were subjected to whippings, mutilation, banishment, and even execution. Between 1659 and 1661, four Quakers were hanged in Massachusetts for attempting to proselytize in the colony. But the religiously tolerant colony of Rhode Island welcomed the Quakers (along with Jews, Presbyterians, Anglicans, and even a few Catholics). Those Quakers who settled in Rhode Island became active and prosperous members of its communities, and in 1672, Nicholas Easton, a Quaker who had been born in England but now hailed from Newport, was elected governor of the colony.

When Lawrence Wilkinson landed in Rhode Island, he found not only religious tolerance but also a new path to prosperity. Settlers from England in the 1640s were given parcels of land in return for promising to live in accordance with the laws of the colony, and to fence and till their lands with diligence. Wilkinson, having happily agreed to fence his plot of land, "pitched his tent and settled for life," as a nineteenth-century family genealogist so charmingly put it.[4] In the 1650s, he married Susannah Smith, only daughter of Christopher Smith, representative to the General Court (the governing body of the colony) and "a prominent man in the infancy of the colony."[5] In the years that followed, Wilkinson amassed over a thousand more acres of farming and grazing lands, became active in colonial government, and fathered a large family with Susannah.

The third child of Lawrence and Susannah was a boy named John, born in 1654. When he grew of age, John left home and made his own migration, traveling north through Rhode Island. He found his moorings along the Blackstone River and settled in the small but lively village of Smithfield. John became a property owner and a farmer, and in 1689, he married Deborah Whipple, a local Quaker (it may have been at this point that John became a practicing Quaker). In 1708, John died at the age of fifty-four, leaving behind his wife and six children.

Jeremiah, John's youngest son, was just a baby when his father died, having been born in April 1707. But he was not forgotten in his father's will: a parcel of property in the nearby village of Cumberland was left as his birthright. Like the region in England from which it took its name, Cumberland was rich with iron and other ore minerals, and the governments of Rhode Island and Massachusetts had been making rivaling claims to the area (and its riches) for years. In 1746, King George II at last interceded in the dispute and settled the issue: Cumberland belonged to Rhode Island. It made no difference to Jeremiah. He had always considered the land to be *his* free and clear, and he had been hard at work for years making the most of it.

Taking advantage of the land's ample stores of minerals, Jeremiah set up a successful ironmongering enterprise in his small village. But he wanted more than just metals to work with. Jeremiah wanted fruit trees, lots of them, to bring color to his springs and falls, and a bounty of delicious harvest every summer. He decided on cherries, and laid in row upon row of seedlings, bare roots, and grafts. How he managed to coax from the rock-flecked lands enough sustenance to support the growing stands of fruit trees, no one knows. But he did, and they flourished. Having built himself a sturdy farmhouse on a hilltop and planted the first of his cherry trees, Jeremiah went in search of a wife to share the views.

He was thirty years old when he married Amey Whipple and brought her to live in the house on the hill. Like Jeremiah, Amey was a Quaker and a member in good standing with the Smithfield Meeting. Jeremiah and Amey had twelve children together, including Jemima, born in 1752. Jemima had four older brothers, William, Jeremiah, Simon, and Benjamin; three older sisters, Amy, Patience, and Mercy (called Marcy); two younger brothers, Stephen and Jeptha; and two younger sisters, Elizabeth and Deborah.

Amey Wilkinson died giving birth to her last child. Bereft at the loss of his wife, Jeremiah was left with the task of naming the baby. Unlike the names of the other Wilkinson children, Deborah wasn't a family name. Perhaps Jeremiah picked it from the Bible, a reference to the Deborah of the Old Testament, who is both prophet and warrior for her people: without a mother to raise the girl, Jeremiah might have hoped the name would bless the infant with strength. Deborah was swaddled up and passed over to a wet nurse, and Jeremiah turned to the task of burying his wife. Following Quaker tradition, Amey was buried in a grave marked only by a rough fieldstone. And although it would have been in Quaker tradition to remarry, Jeremiah could not find another wife—or *would* not. Perhaps he found his duty in his children, and in his lands, and in his forge. In what he had produced and could produce: in what he could create that would last. In what he could protect, as best he could, from harm.

Jemima was eleven years old when her mother died. While losing a mother to childbirth was not uncommon in the eighteenth century, with as many as one in eight women dying as a consequence of giving birth, the grief would have been profound for the children left behind.[6] But work on the farm and in the home had to go on. Patience (age seventeen) and Marcy (age fourteen) stepped in to take charge of the household, and the younger boys and girls stepped up before their time to take on the many chores that needed doing. Jemima seemed to have imbibed lessons she learned at her mother's side in the garden; her prowess with plants and the medical acumen she exhibited later in life—which plants healed what ailments—stemmed from the tasks she took on as a girl in the motherless Wilkinson family.

Work around the farmhouse was not the only occupation of Jeremiah's children. As Quakers, education was important for the Wilkinson family, and Jemima and her siblings were schooled in a Quaker classroom. Using primers, they were taught their letters and numbers, and then they moved on to reading: the Bible, of course, and also other religious works, sticking to Protestant religious writings. They would have been discouraged from reading novels, which were prohibited by Quaker leaders as "profane and immoral writings," as were any texts that would "draw . . . affections to a love of the world, and desire after the rarities and evils that are therein. . . ."[7]

Education gave all the Wilkinson siblings, male and female, the confidence they needed to push themselves to achieve. Jeremiah Jr., who worked side by side with his father, would become famous for his ironwork—churning out everything from spoons to knifes, hinges to locks, carding tools and animal brushes—and also for his inventions. He was the first in America to make nails cut from a sheet of cold iron (versus hammering them by hand from bars of hot iron). He invented a method for pulling wire from iron, and during the Revolution came up with a machine to make darning needles. He charged a dollar per needle, a steep price, but well worth it, as the finely crafted needles lasted through the war and into the years of building—and clothing—a new nation. Simon became a mathematician and astronomer, and Stephen would follow in his father's footsteps, eventually planting acres upon acres of apple trees and building his own reputation as a bountiful grower of fruit.

Jemima's talents lay in her ability to memorize very long texts and to meaningfully integrate them into daily conversations. By her teens, she knew by heart entire sections of the Bible and would have been able to match any preacher verse for verse. While Jemima was never a great speller, such weakness did not deter the alacrity with which long letters were written, nor did it prevent the keeping of detailed notes on works written by others. With an excellent lending library located in Cumberland, Jemima would have found numerous books to read and the lifelong habit of copying out favorite texts likely started in youth.

Jemima copied out inspirational poems, essays, hymns, and quotations from sources as varied as Isaac Watts, an English minister and prolific hymn writer from the seventeenth century (his most famous hymn being "Joy to the World"); Johannes Tauler, a fourteenth-century German mystic; and Robert Dodsley, an Englishman whose writings were available in American bookshops. In 1750, Dodsley published *The Oeconomy of Human Life: An "Ancient Bramin" in Eighteenth-Century Tibet*. Dodsley claimed the book was a discovered translation of an ancient Indian text offering page after page of aphorisms for how to live a good and moral life. The book became an instant bestseller, with over two hundred editions published. Although it's not clear when Jemima Wilkinson first read *Oeconomy*, she wrote many of its maxims into a personal notebook found after her death.[8]

Jeremiah was sixty-nine years old when Jemima fell ill in the fall of 1776. The hands that smoothed the coverlet over his feverish child would have been worn and rough from years of working with metals and caring for his cherry trees, and his back, bent over her bed, would have ached from the labors his life had required. Now his heart, too, would have been heavy. The Wilkinson family had endured a hard year. But if his Jemima were to die, all the other hardships would pale by comparison.

The family troubles had started in March, when Jeremiah's sons Jeptha and Stephen were disciplined by the Smithfield Meeting of the Society of Friends because they had joined the local militia, which violated Quaker rules against participating in warfare. Or perhaps the troubles could be traced back further, to the year 1774, when the colony of Rhode Island first began to organize its men to fight for their rights under the British Constitution, setting up military exercises and procuring arms and ammunition. Or maybe the troubles could be traced all the way back to 1765, when Parliament passed the Stamp Act, which required that all sorts of printed products—newspapers, almanacs, pamphlets, broadsides, legal papers, wedding licenses, and playing cards—carry a stamp that had to be paid for, with all sums going to England to refill the coffers emptied in fighting the Seven Years' War (called the French and Indian War in America) and nothing remaining for the colonies themselves.

Or the troubles could be traced back further still, to the Seven Years' War itself, a global struggle fought across Europe, India, and America, which cost tens of thousands of American colonists their lives. When it was finally over in 1763, England had gained more lands but also incurred huge debts while also increasing its costs of maintaining an enlarged empire. Citizens in England couldn't be taxed enough to pay for it all, so Parliament turned to its American colonies to cover the difference. Having done their part in fighting for Britain, and having had for decades managed their economies without interference from Parliament, the colonists were outraged by the new taxes and duties. In the 1770s, British troops were sent to America to enforce compliance with the new regulations, and British ships patrolled the American coastline, inspecting local vessels with impunity and demanding payment on the cargoes they carried.

In Rhode Island, anger over Britain's attempted control of the colony's flourishing (and not always legal) trading economy led to colonists setting on fire (in 1769) a British customs ship docked in Newport Harbor; in 1772, Rhode Islanders descended with glee to loot and pillage, and then set afire, a British customs schooner that had run aground in the shallows off Newport. Throughout New England, colonists hung revolutionary symbols (such as effigies of hated English officials) from the branches of a prominent tree in a central location; the so-called liberty trees were gathering points for protests and rallies against English policies. In Rhode Island, an old buttonwood tree in Newport had been baptized for use as a "liberty tree" as early as 1766, its purpose to hold accountable, literally and figuratively, "offenders against the Liberties of their country, and Abettors and Approvers of such as would enslave her. . . ."[9]

By 1775, Stephen (age twenty) and Jeptha (age eighteen) were ready and willing to fight for freedom alongside their fellow Rhode Islanders. No matter that they had been raised Quakers; they could not stand by and watch their rights eroded by an oppressive king and Parliament who ruled from afar. Like their cousin Stephen Hopkins (who served as governor of Rhode Island three times and would serve as its representative to the Continental Congress in 1774), they must have believed that "Powder and ball will decide this question. The gun and bayonet alone will finish the contest in which we are engaged, and any of you who cannot bring your minds to this mode of adjusting the question had better retire in time."[10] In 1764, Hopkins had written a scathing indictment of English colonial policies in which he presented an exhaustive history of unjust governmental interference going all the way back to "the ancient commonwealths of Greece" and argued that citizens then and now had the right to engage in battle in order to maintain their freedom and dignity.[11] In the ten years since, Hopkins continued to support armed resistance—and his cousins Stephen and Jeptha sided with him all the way.

It seems likely that Jeptha and Stephen joined the local minutemen after news arrived in Rhode Island in April of 1775 that British troops had attacked American colonists in what became known as the Battles of Lexington and Concord. Three regiments of Rhode Island minutemen, numbering in the hundreds, immediately headed north to assist their New England compatriots in the Siege of Boston, during which British troops were isolated and contained within the city. That summer, the Rhode Island troops along with regiments from other New England colonies became the first soldiers of America's Continental army under the command of General George Washington.

Not only would the men of Rhode Island fight for freedom but its leaders would also take the bold step of being the very first colony to declare its independence from England. On May 4, 1776, Rhode Island's general assembly passed with almost unanimous support the Act of Renunciation, which officially repealed the colony's allegiance to King George. This bold declaration was made two months before representatives of all thirteen colonies followed suit and signed the Declaration of Independence in Philadelphia. Although there were those in Rhode Island who remained loyal to England, a greater number were ready to carry on the fight for what they viewed as their inherent rights to regulate and protect their economic, political, and private lives.

Despite the widespread support in Rhode Island for armed resistance to England, Quaker leaders in the colony opposed military activity of any kind, and also prohibited the taking of oaths—and an oath of allegiance was required by all men who joined the minutemen. In Cumberland, the leaders of the Smithfield Meeting delayed a bit in disciplining Stephen and Jeptha for joining the local militia, perhaps hoping the boys would drop out by themselves. But they did not drop out, and in March of 1776 Stephen and Jeptha were "brought under dealing," which is to say, castigated and warned by the Smithfield Meeting to forego any further participation in the militia. They both ignored the warning, and in July of 1776 they were "dismissed" (expelled) for having "frequented Trainings for military Service and Endeavor[ed] to Justify the Same."[12]

Perhaps it was a Wilkinson family trait to stubbornly do what conscience dictated rather than to follow the rules or orders of others; Jemima was also beginning to turn away from Quaker dictates as she tried to find her way forward in an increasingly chaotic world. She would have been influenced, as her brothers would have been, by the impassioned orations about freedom and rebellion made by fellow Rhode Islanders, including their cousin Stephen. It's also likely that the Wilkinson siblings would have heard about or even read for themselves Thomas Paine's *Common Sense*, which not only encouraged the use of force to secure liberty but also linked rebellion against Britain to God's will: "Even the distance at which the Almighty hath placed England and America, is a strong and natural proof, that the authority of the one, over the other, was never the design of Heaven."[13] Copies of *Common Sense* were circulating throughout New England, with an estimated 20 percent of colonists owning the pamphlet, making it America's first bestseller.[14] In the small village of Braintree, Massachusetts, Abigail Adams urged her husband to find a copy for her—and when he sent her the pamphlet, she read it through twice, and then, as she wrote to John, she "spread it as much as it lay in my power."[15]

Whatever the reasons may have been, sometime in the mid-1770s, Jemima had begun skipping attendance at her local Quaker Meeting in order to join the gatherings of a New Lights congregation that met at the Elder Miller Meeting House in nearby Abbott Run. The congregation at Abbott Run was one of many religious groups formed during the religious revivals inspired by the first Great Awakening. The Awakening began in the 1730s and was first led by established ministers looking to reinvigorate the religious practices of their flocks.

One such minister was Jonathan Edwards, who lived in Northampton, Massachusetts. Worried that his congregants had become lazy in their spiritual devotion, Edwards tried to revive their religious commitment by presenting them with vivid descriptions of the sufferings that non-repentant sinners could expect to endure in hell. "Your bodies," he preached, "which shall have been burning all this while in these glowing flames, shall not have been consumed, but will remain to roast through eternity. . . ."[16] Edwards's sermons proved effective in swelling church attendance among his own flock, and as news of the fiery rhetoric spread, hundreds more converts arrived at his church. When the sermons were published in pamphlet form, his influence spread even further, throughout the congregations and meeting halls of New England, and he became well known for his visions of hell and damnation.

The popularity of Jonathan Edwards was eventually eclipsed by a new kind of minister and a new way of preaching: itinerant Protestant preachers, not attached to any specific congregation, who traveled throughout the colonies spreading the word of the Lord in large outdoor meetings called "revivals." The meetings were called revivals because their purpose was to revive faith through rollicking events during which large crowds, often numbering in the thousands, were encouraged to loudly and exuberantly confess and repent their sins and then commit themselves heart and soul to God. While the itinerant preachers leading these revivals were by and large ordained clergy, non-ordained designated "evangelizers," male and female, also exhorted the crowds to repent. Claiming a special relationship with God, they spoke about the dangers of sin, and the need to confess and repent. As one pair of female evangelicals explained, they had "been to Heven [*sic*] . . . seen the Book of Life, [and] the Names of many Persons" written in it—and God had given them a "special Commission" to save what sinners they could.[17]

When the itinerant ministers traveled on after leading a revival, the men and women left behind often formed new religious organizations such as the congregation whose meetings Jemima attended at Abbott Run. Described as "separatists" for desiring a separation from existing congregations, these groups were also called "New Lights" because they believed God had brought new light into their spiritual lives by endowing them with rich emotional experiences of the divine. Most of the New Lights congregations welcomed women to speak publicly about their faith, reasoning that all true believers were believed capable of "the spirit of prophecy," regardless of sex, race, social class, or age.[18] The New Lights' exuberant professions of faith and equal-opportunity evangelizing were anathema to the Congregational churches of New England with their rigid rituals and strict hierarchy, and also to Quaker Meetings, which allowed women to speak when divinely inspired by the inner light of God, but emphasized silent worship and quiet exhortation by both men and women.

Why were the religious revivals and New Lights congregations so popular in the mid- to late eighteenth century? In part because colonists of the time were experiencing an excess of anxieties due to the many changes in their world. No longer did they inhabit small, insulated villages where everybody knew their neighbors; instead, towns were springing up, busy and diverse, where it was all too easy to become isolated. In 1700, about 260,000 settlers lived in the American colonies; by 1770, that number had risen to well over 2 million.[19] With the rise in population, new economic opportunities arose, but competition also increased, and the rift between rich and poor widened. Taxes and other burdens imposed by the British were increasing.

Revival meetings offered colonists relief from their anxieties by welcoming them into a shared community experience where they could freely vent their worries and frustrations, and channel their pent-up emotions into renewed spiritual devotion. By confessing their weaknesses and admitting their sins, they could find peace in the promise of salvation and purpose in their world. Itinerant ministers such as George Whitefield, a charismatic preacher from England, gave colonists hope even while warning them about the wages of sin. Whitefield was a homely man, cross-eyed and stunted in stature, and his sermons were neither original nor poetic. But there was something about the way he delivered his message—"come as poor, lost, undone, and wretched creatures"[20]—that made his audiences swoon. "[M]y hearing him preach gave me a heart wound," one attendee effused.[21] Whitefield spoke loudly on purpose: "I love those who thunder out the Word," he explained. "The Christian world is in a deep sleep! Nothing but a loud voice can awaken them out of it."[22] And awaken them he did. Everywhere he went, from England to Georgia to the Caribbean, crowds turned out in the thousands—and even tens of thousands—to hear him speak.

In 1770, Whitefield made his seventh and last tour through America, with stops in Providence and also in Attleboro (in Massachusetts) just six miles from the Wilkinson home. Whether or not Jemima participated in these outdoor revivals, she and the rest of her family certainly heard about them. No matter their own denomination, people turned out for Whitefield's sermons, talked about them, wrote about them, thought about them. Even Ben Franklin was impressed by Whitefield, writing in a letter to a friend about going to see the minister preach. Although Franklin had beforehand "silently resolved" that the minister "should get none from me," he was so taken by the sermon that he "emptied my pocket wholly into the collector's dish, gold and all."[23] Franklin became Whitefield's American publisher, and they kept up a correspondence for years.

Whitefield would have made an impression on Jemima. With her deep knowledge of the Bible, she would have recognized the spiritual quotes he used in his sermons, even the most obscure ("by rejecting conscience, certain persons have suffered shipwreck in the faith") and was likely interested in his interpretations of the texts.[24] She would have recognized in his preaching many of the ideas she heard at the New Lights meetings she attended, such as the need for a more emotional and active communion with God, a concept she seemed to welcome given the regularity with which she attended the meetings.

In the spring of 1776, Jemima Wilkinson was disciplined by the local Smithfield Meeting for failing to attend Society meetings (and attending the meetings of the New Lights congregation at Abbott Run).[25] Her sister Patience was also taken "under dealing" for having borne "an illegitimate child."[26] They were admonished to mend their ways or be expelled. While being disowned from their Quaker congregation would have no dire material consequences—they wouldn't be run out of town or deprived of their home and property—they would be shunned from the religious community they had lived in all their lives. But the sisters must have anticipated the disciplinary actions taken against them given that for the past ten years there had been stricter enforcements among Quaker congregations of sect rules. The enforcements were part of the Quaker Reformation, a movement to bring members back to the Society's original ideals of isolation from worldly concerns, such as economic or political ambitions (much like the first Great Awakening preachers had sought to bring wavering congregants back to strict Calvinist ideals).

The Quaker Reformation was driven by concerns, particularly

expressed by English Quakers visiting the colonies, that American Quakers were becoming alarmingly worldly and wealthy. The colony of Pennsylvania, founded by William Penn (a Quaker emigrant who arrived from England in 1682) offered huge economic opportunities due to its active ports and rich farmlands. There was money to be made in the colony, and thousands of the Quakers who arrived in the late seventeenth and eighteenth centuries became rich.

An unexpected outcome of this prosperity was that members of the Society in Pennsylvania, like Quakers in Rhode Island, became active in government, prominent in business circles, and very comfortable with outsiders. They also, according to critics, lost their commitment to Quaker ideals of separation and restraint. As Samuel Fothergill, an English Quaker minister who traveled to Pennsylvania in the 1750s, put it, "They settled in ease and affluence, and whilst they made the barren wilderness as a fruitful field, suffered the plantation of God to be as a field uncultivated and a desert."[27]

The participation of Society members in military actions also concerned reformers. American Quakers fought in the Seven Years' War and also in King Philip's War, a brutal and bloody conflict in the 1670s in which the English colonists defeated the Indigenous Wampanoag of New England. (Perhaps they had feared that the communities they'd established in America were at risk of being destroyed and fought to protect them.) There had been no punishment by their Quaker societies then, but now, under the dictates of the Quaker Reformation, military activity became a punishable offense for Society members.

The time had come, the reformers warned, for all Quakers to return their focus to spiritual practices, to reject worldly interests, such as politics and war, and to rededicate themselves to the fundamental Quaker belief that by practicing reverential silence, every individual can receive the inner light, i.e., messages directly delivered to them by God. Reformers also feared that their members, in becoming more secular, had abandoned Society standards regarding behavior (sober dress and speech, for example) and attending Meeting, they urged Society leaders to hold their members accountable for any transgressions. George Fox had advocated for equality among Quakers, yet in practice there were recognized Elders, "persons of strong character and judgment," who led congregations.[28] Elders now took responsibility to see that infractions, which had previously been punished with warnings and temporary probation, were punished by more dire discipline, including expulsion from the sect. In Rhode Island, local Quaker societies "saw dismissals grow from around ten a decade in the mid-eighteenth century to about *a hundred* a decade in the 1770s and '80s."[29]

There was some effort on the part of the Smithfield Meeting to avoid the final step of expelling the Wilkinson sisters from the Society. Lydia Wilkinson, an elder cousin to the family, was asked to "labor with [Patience and Jemima] for [their] offenses" and to report back on any progress achieved in returning the sisters into the fold.[30] But there would be no progress and no returning for the sisters. The threat of punishment could not force Jemima back to a spiritual practice she no longer found fulfilling, and Patience followed her sister's lead. In August of 1776, both Patience and Jemima were expelled by the Smithfield Quakers, joining their brothers in what must have been seen as a public humiliation for the family. Yet Jeremiah could hardly blame his children. The world was turning upside down, colonists were fighting the mother country, and everyone had to answer for themselves: rebel or loyalist? Decisions on religion were just as personal and felt just as dire. Perhaps Jeremiah understood that while his children trusted in God, they were also influenced by the times in which they lived.

At the age of twenty-three, Jemima Wilkinson sought a new path in life. So many ideas would have been circulating in her young brain: the plaintive and yet hopeful sermons of Whitefield and the New Lights preachers, the inspiring words of her cousin Stephen Hopkins and the famous Thomas Paine, the exhilaration of Watts's hymns, the inflammatory excitement of patriotic pamphleteers, the old wisdom of the Bible, the exhortations at Quaker Meetings to listen to one's inner light, perhaps even the translations of an allegedly ancient Indian spiritual text. . . .

And then in early October of 1776, Jemima fell deathly ill.

Of all the Wilkinson girls, Jemima seemed the least likely to succumb to the diseases that passed regularly through colonial towns and villages. Deborah had been the sickly one since birth, and Amy also suffered from bad health. But Jemima's health and outlook had always been good. When she lost her mother at eleven years old, she'd seemed to recover without any outward signs of trauma. She was strong enough, even at that age, to take over gardening chores. She was also good with horses and at ease in the saddle, able to ride for miles over the Cumberland hills. Jemima was robust and sturdy, and obstinate at times, insistent on doing things her way; she'd been so as a child and only grew more so as a young woman.

But now she lay on her sickbed, weakened and thin, her body barely raising a bump in the cloth that covered her. It was as if all the fat and muscle had burned off her bones, raising her temperature, clouding the usual clarity of her thoughts. Early in the morning of October 9, she seemed on the precipice of a crisis. Struggling to sit up, she looked wildly around. In a hoarse voice, she spoke of seeing "celestial beings floating by her bedside."[31] Her father must have been terrified, certain that his daughter was being called to the heavens.

A doctor, summoned from Attleboro, could only tell Jeremiah what his daughter's illness was *not*: not the bloody flux, not smallpox, not ague or camp fever. There were rumors going around that the American warship *Columbus*, which had arrived in Providence in September, brought into port not only prisoners but also typhus.[32] Perhaps the young woman had become exposed to that illness, as she seemed to exhibit its symptoms of fever, chills, loss of appetite, and fatigue.

As night fell that October 9, did Jeremiah begin to think about the funeral he would have to plan for his daughter? Another burial, another unmarked stone in the ground? Jemima's breath grew ever more shallow, low gasps coming out through dry, thin lips, slightly parted.

It was as if she were a vessel that had cracked open to allow her soul to escape. Soon she would be free to rise to heaven, where she would be saved from earthly concerns. It was what Jeremiah so fervently believed of the passage between life and death.

But a crack could also let the light in.

2

New Life

"I being the person who before the year
one thousand seven hundred & seventy seven
was known & called by the name Jemima Wilkinson
but since that time as the Universal Friend."

—UNIVERSAL FRIEND

On the morning of October 10, 1776, the patient who had been so close to death the night before sat up straight in bed. Jeptha, who had fallen asleep while watching over his sister through the night, was jolted awake by a whisper:

"There is room enough."[1]

Looking up, he would have been struck dumb by the sight of Jemima sitting up in bed unaided, eyes clear and cheeks glowing. And the surprise would have only deepened as she began to describe what had happened during the dark hours of the night to bring about the transformation he saw before him: "Archangels descending from the east, with golden crowns upon their heads" had brought to the dying young woman a message of universal salvation: "Room, Room, Room, in the Many mansions of eternal glory for Thee and for everyone. . . ."[2]

The angels told Jemima that she had been chosen by God to house a "Spirit of Life . . . [which] was waiting to assume the Body which God had prepared for the Spirit to dwell in. . . ." With Jemima's body serving as the "tabernacle" for the waiting spirit, the angels explained, the reborn Jemima would carry God's message of universal redemption to "the lost and the guilty, perishing dying world. . . ." When morning came, Jemima "dropt the dying flesh" and the Spirit then took "full possession of the body it now animates."[3] Jeptha must have called out to his father to quickly come, for his sister Jemima Wilkinson had been transformed into a messenger sent by God to save the world.

Looking at his child, brought back from the edge of death, was Jeremiah reminded of others who had undergone dramatic transformation by the hand of God? George Fox claimed to have experienced in the late 1640s a transformation wrought by God, which brought Fox into "the state of Adam, which he was in before he fell," in other words, into the state of innocence before Adam and Eve became aware of their sexuality and ashamed of the nakedness that revealed it.[4] From that point on, Fox traveled throughout England spreading the message that everyone could achieve redemption if they only listened for the word of God—their inner light—to instruct them.

There were other examples of spiritual transformation that would have been familiar to Jeremiah and his family. Margaret Brewster, a Quaker missionary who was persecuted in Boston in the late 1600s, had been lying in bed, feverish and weak from an unnamed illness, when she suddenly found herself "raised as one from the dead." She went straight from her "sick Bed to visit the bloody town of Boston," where she set about evangelizing to anyone who would stop and listen to what she had to say.[5] And George Whitefield famously preached about having experienced a kind of "New Birth," during which the Holy Spirit inhabits the soul in an act of—and as proof of—divine grace.[6] While Whitefield never claimed to have died and been reborn, he did describe a transformation in which a "new life imparts new principles, a new understanding, a new will, and new affections, a new conscience, a renewed memory, nay a renewed body. . . ."[7]

Americans in the eighteenth century lived close to death all their lives. Living was a dangerous occupation, with diseases and illnesses, accidents, famine and malnourishment all taking heavy tolls on population numbers. Smallpox alone decimated thousands, along with malaria, diphtheria, dysentery, measles, typhoid, influenza, and scarlet fever. War also led to early deaths, including the Seven Years' War and the many battles, massacres, and isolated ambushes of the Revolutionary War.[8] But while many people died from illnesses, wounds, and accidents, there were also those who, on the brink of death, seemingly miraculously recovered. Came back to life, as it were. And for those with deep faith, they could easily believe such recoveries were due to divine intervention. It wouldn't be hard for Jeremiah, who had seen his child so close to death and then seen that same child completely revived, to believe that Jemima had undergone death and then been transformed into a being full of divine grace.

In the days that followed, Jemima claimed to be a non-gendered messenger sent by God, rejecting the name given at birth and choosing to dress in genderless clothing, with the head bare of hat or scarf, and hair pulled back but loose on the shoulders. How easy would it have been for Jeremiah to accept that change? As Quakers, Jeremiah and his children were firm believers in the biblical prophecy that "there is neither male nor female, for ye are all one in Jesus Christ."[9] Quaker theology had as one of its primary principles that "in Souls there is no sex."[10] As George Fox wrote, spiritual "power was one in the male and in the female, one spirit, one light, one power, which brings forth the same witness."[11]

It was this belief in the equality of all souls that allowed women like Elizabeth Hooton to be welcomed as leaders inspiring the Quaker faithful from the very first days of the Society in England. Hooton led meetings in her home starting in the late 1640s and would be repeatedly imprisoned and physically persecuted both in England and in the colonies for her Quaker preaching over the next twenty-five years. When she traveled to Massachusetts to spread the word, she was arrested, stripped to the waist, tied to an oxcart, and then led through the streets to be beaten by onlookers.

Margaret Fell was another early convert to the Society of Friends, a member of the upper class who chose to devote herself to spreading the tenets of Quakerism—and was sentenced to life in prison for it. While imprisoned, Fell wrote a powerful text on the equality of the sexes and the importance of allowing women to preach the word of God, titled *Womens Speaking Justified*. When she was released from prison at the order of King Charles II (after serving four years in miserable conditions), she married George Fox and continued her proselytizing. By this time, Fox had already begun establishing schools (the first in 1668) to "instruct young lasses and maidens in whatsoever was civil and useful."[12] Women would go on to serve as Quaker leaders in the colonies as well; by the end of the eighteenth century, at least half of the Quaker ministers in Philadelphia were female.[13]

But even while preaching about the genderlessness of all souls before God, George Fox never claimed to be without gender himself and appears to have consistently identified as male. Margaret Brewster never disavowed the female gender as she went about her proselytizing mission, and certainly George Whitefield considered himself to be male: "after I am dead I desire no other epitaph than this, 'Here lies G.W. What sort of man he was the great day will discover."[14]

And yet here was Jeremiah's child, rejecting the name he had given her at birth—Jemima—and insisting that everyone use a new name for God's newly minted messenger: Universal Friend. A name that could encompass and embrace all possibilities, and that connoted neither male nor female gender. The concept of "friend" was an important tenet of Quakerism: Jesus had promised, "Ye are my friends, if ye do whatsoever I command you," and George Fox believed that it was through joined friendship (a Society of Friends) that one could foster receiving the inner light of God.[15] Those members of a Quaker Meeting who frequently spoke about messages received from God were acknowledged as "Public Friends" for sharing publicly the messages they received through inner light. The person who had previously been known as Jemima seemed to be adopting a Quaker practice but expanding it to a universal application; salvation was promised for all who would repent, and, as future events would show, Universal Friend hoped to speak to and for all those who wished to repent, no matter race, gender, or social status.

Followers of Universal Friend would come to rely on a variety of non-gendered names for describing the messenger, including "Publick Universal Friend," "Friend to all Mankind," "All-Friend," "Best-Friend," and simply, "Friend."[16] Friend also became known by the name of "Comforter," which, as one observer noted, meant that the minister and followers believed Friend had been "raised up by God to give comfort to his [God's] people."[17]

There is little record of how the Wilkinson family first adapted to living with a messenger in their midst. Patience was living in the family farmhouse at the time, along with sisters Elizabeth, Deborah, and Marcy (with no records of Patience's illegitimate child to be found, one might surmise that the child died in infancy; few records of infant deaths were kept at the time and infant mortality rates were high).[18] Their sister, who had been transformed into Universal Friend, was not so different from the person they had known before; as a girl Jemima had been "rather the ruler than the ruled" in the family home, and now as God's chosen messenger, Friend was proving to be just as assertive, obstinate, and confident in spreading the good news of universal salvation.[19]

All four of the Wilkinson sisters became devoted followers of the new minister, and in the months ahead, Elizabeth, Deborah, and Constance would be disowned from the Smithfield Meeting.[20] But just like Jemima and Patience before them, the sisters did not care. Along with their brothers Jeptha, Benjamin, and Stephen, they were bound to Friend through close-knit family ties; together they had endured early loss (the death of their mother) and the persistent demands of family forge and fruit trees. The bonds of family meant more to them than membership in the Quaker church.

In the autumn of 1776, all of them still single and living at home, the Wilkinson siblings remained each other's most constant companions. Family meals, with everyone gathered around the table, must have been noisy affairs. Dining on corn cakes and pumpkin bread, potatoes and turkey, turnips and trout, and sweets made of chocolate (Rhode Island was the chocolate-producing capital of the colonies), with plates clattering and voices chattering, it's easy to imagine dour old Jeremiah silently watching over his rowdy bunch voicing their opinions, arguing and agreeing, and testing and forging even further the bonds of family.

The siblings were likely initially responsible for spreading the story of Friend's transformation out to the wider world. When meeting a friend while visiting the market stalls, Patience might have shared the news or perhaps Marcy told the cobbler about Friend's transformation while getting measured for winter shoes (or having old shoes fitted with pattens—raised soles—for the slush and snow). The militia-enlisted brothers knew plenty of lads eager for a diversion and even Jeremiah might have passed on the story of his daughter's miraculous recovery to customers who came to his iron workshop.

From that point on, the flow of village gossip guaranteed that within days of Friend's death and rebirth everyone in Cumberland knew about the transformation. And from there, the story spread even farther, traveling on the wind to tap the news out at the window of every farmhouse in the surrounding countryside. When Universal Friend attended a New Lights meeting at the Elder Miller Meeting House just one week after the recovery, a crowd of people gathered round to see the transformed Jemima Wilkinson for themselves. The crowd was so large and so curious that Friend decided to seize the opportunity granted by God to deliver a message of salvation.

A wide step stool was set out on the autumn-browned grass underneath a large oak tree. The tree grew alongside the stone wall of the churchyard, and Friend's neighbors, family, and villagers from the area would have arranged themselves in a circle around the tree, some perching on the wall and others standing. Stepping up onto the stool,

Friend would have seen dozens of faces, young and old, male and female, looking up expectantly to hear what the gossiped-about Wilkinson had to say. Above Friend, the wide branches of the oak tree were like the beamed vault of a church, with weak sunlight filtering through its last hanging yellow leaves as if through stained glass.[21]

Friend spoke easily and calmly for a good hour, never shifting on the stool, eyes steady and chin raised. Drawing on memorized Bible passages, Friend spoke about the importance of living a moral life, the dangers of sin, and the urgency of repentance.[22] The sermon most likely would have ended, as most of Friend's sermons would end in the months and years to come, with a promise of eternal bliss for everyone who faithfully followed the minister's counsel: "What Great love God had . . . that all might come to the knowledge of the Truth and be Saved. . . ."[23]

There was nothing revelatory or new in Friend's first sermon, although the minister's remarkably wide knowledge of the gospels would have been impressive. What held the crowd's attention most that day, however, was likely not the message but the messenger. Everyone knew how ill the Wilkinson daughter had been, "render'd almost incapable of helping herself . . . [on the brink] of the Shock of Death. . . ."[24] The tall figure that appeared before them now was hale and full of life. The round face glowed with a calm energy; the broad shoulders, firmly squared, spoke of strength and resilience. Black hair, glossy in the rays of sun that came through the trees, and dark eyes, brilliant and clear, completed the picture of radiant health. The woman at death's door was gone and a powerful minister stood before them. It was a miracle of transformation.

From very early in the ministry, Universal Friend seemed to understand the importance of appearances. Not only the physical attributes of health and strength but the clothes themselves had to speak for the newly minted vessel of God: the long, dark robe, a white or purple cravat worn around the neck, and a silk skirt underneath the robe. Friend would continue in the years to come to go bareheaded (or in cold weather, sporting a white beaver hat) with the dark hair pulled back and falling in curls to the shoulders. While choice of hairstyle and dress was "singular and extraordinary," overall the minister presented "a very Agreeable aspect. . . ."[25] There were those who found Friend to be "perfectly beautiful"; they were charmed by the "arched black eyebrows and fierce looking black eyes . . . beautiful aquiline nose, handsome mouth and chin, all supported by a neck comfortable to the line of beauty and proportion."[26]

Perhaps Friend's bare head and long flowing hair can be understood as a message of rebellion. Not only rebellion against the Quaker custom of women always covering their hair but also a rejection of prevailing British fashion. As one observer noted, Friend's hairstyle of nature's ringlets was all the more remarkable, since the fashion of the day for ladies' head-dress consisted of frizzled hair, long wire pines, powder and pomatum. The late eighteenth-century trend of opulently styled and powdered hair was a direct import from the drawing rooms and salons of the English monarchy. Universal Friend's choice of a simple, unadorned, and uncovered hairstyle can therefore perhaps be seen as taking a stance that was anti-England, anti-Monarchy, and definitely revolutionary.

While there were those who understood Friend's "particular dress . . . to be a call to the people at large to come, see, and hear," there would always be critics who ascribed Friend's grooming and clothing to the minister's desire to appear masculine.[27] The Congregationalist minister Ezra Stiles, who saw Universal Friend in New Haven, stated bluntly that Friend "dressed like a man."[28] Another observer wrote that the minister had "so much like the dress and appearance of a man, that I conceived it to be very improper."[29] William Savery, a Quaker from Philadelphia, disapproved of Friend's "appearance of Immodesty in a woman [which] . . . would go far to Confound the Distinction of the Sexes [and] . . . be very Improper and of Pernicious Consequences to Society."[30]

Some modern historians believe Friend chose to appear masculine in order to be able to preach convincingly; these historians parrot the language of eighteenth-century critics, who also claimed Friend denied being female "in order to assert . . . religious authority."[31] These modern historians view Friend as an example of "female exhorters," who saw their "'femininity' as a burden. . . . In order to speak as God's prophets, they believed they had to lose their identities as women."[32] But just because Friend no longer wished to be perceived as a woman did not mean that the minister sought acceptance as a man.

Many contemporary observers understood Friend's uniform to be a deliberate rejection of gender altogether: the clothes Friend wore demonstrated "the idea . . . of . . . being neither male nor female."[33] After all, while the robe adopted by Friend was similar to what male ministers wore, the silk underskirt peeking out from underneath the robe and the long ringlets of hair curling around the neck were decidedly different. Perhaps the contrast was meant to indicate that for Friend, identification by gender had become meaningless.

When criticized for so-called "appearances as a man . . . which would excite many remarks, including some indecent ones," Friend replied, "There is nothing indecent or improper in my dress or appearance; I am not accountable to morals, I am that I am."[34] Friend was quoting from Exodus when God told Moses (another one of God's messengers), "I AM THAT I AM."[35] And yet the idea was also revolutionary: Friend asserting that a person could simply *be*, without being defined—or limited—by the opinions of others.

The simplest answer to the question of Friend's choice of uniform might be that the clothes were easy to put on, comfortable to wear, and, because the robe was similar to that worn by many ministers, also made a clear declaration as to Friend's spiritual status.[36] And just as many ministers strove to look like God's prophets, there is no doubt that Friend's bare head, flowing hair, and long robe may also have been chosen to conjure up widely shared images of Jesus Christ.[37]

Whether Friend intended to resemble Jesus Christ or not, looking like a prophet, or even the son of God himself, buttressed the claim of being sent directly by God to preach to the lost and the needy, just as God had previously sent prophets to deliver messages needed by the people on earth. According to Universal Friend, the angels that had transformed Jemima had told her "the time is at hand, when God will lift up his hand *a second time*, to recover the remnant of the lost sheep of the House of Israel."[38] The first coming was Christ; was Friend then the second coming?

In the years that followed, Friend would often be accused of blasphemy for having "professed to be Christ," but always denied the charge, explaining, one witness reported, to have been "sent by Jesus Christ and enlightened by his spirit to convert mankind."[39] Friend perhaps played the role both ways: as the second coming ordained by God *and* as the comforter sent by him to guide people safely to salvation. But there was no equivocating on the message: the minister consistently stated as fact that God and his angels had spoken directly to the dying Jemima and that in response, Friend had welcomed God's gift of transformation with vigor, determination, and conviction: "I have obeyed the words that are Spoken they are Spirit and they are Life. . . ."[40]

Why had God transformed Friend? And why now? The heavenly angels told the dying Jemima Wilkinson, "The time is at hand, when God will lift up his hand . . . to recover the remnant of his people . . ." and that the reborn messenger must "warn the lost and guilty . . . to flee from the wrath which is to come. . . ."[41] In other words, the transformed minister was charged with bringing the message of redemption to sinners everywhere before it was too late for them to repent and be saved. Unlike ministers like Jonathan Edwards, Friend believed that every single soul could achieve salvation and was worthy of redemption, and this belief in the equality of all souls before God would guide the minister for the next forty-three years.

"In the beginning was the word," Friend had learned as a child. Now Friend had taken the first step to spread the word of God, underneath the old oak tree and in front of a large crowd of onlookers. More steps would follow, one after another, like a child's first steps across the floor, words to follow words until an entire path forward was laid out and the mission of universal salvation was completed.

In late November of 1776, Friend accompanied Jeremiah Wilkinson to the weekly gathering of Quakers at the Smithfield Meeting House. Winter was approaching and the branches of the cherry trees on the hill were bare. The road into the village would have been hard with frost, and the air inside the hall damp and cold, even with a fire burning in the low brazier set against the far wall. As was customary at a Quaker Meeting, the faithful sat quietly on their hard benches, hands clasped and heads bowed in contemplation.

Meetings always began in silence and the quiet would continue until someone in the congregation found themselves moved to speak. They would rise up and give voice to the message they had received from God. Such was the respect for the inspiration of inner light that there would be no interruption from the rest of the congregation; the flow of words could continue as long as the moved member wanted to talk. Often, after one person had risen to give testimony, others would also rise, one by one, to offer their own simple words about hearkening to the inner light offered by God.

Perhaps no one paid attention when Jeremiah and his child first arrived, taking their places in the back. But when Universal Friend rose and began to speak about the message God had delivered to a dying Jemima Wilkinson, the congregants took notice. One after another, they demanded that Friend stop talking. Universal Friend, "not submitting," ignored them and continued to speak. Another member rose, and then another, until "no less than five" asked Friend to be silent.[42] What had Jeremiah been thinking, bringing one of his expelled brood to a meeting? He must have known that his fellow Quakers would never listen to what anyone from his disgraced family had to say about faith. Maybe he was as surprised as they were when his child rose to speak. And did Friend really expect that the same people who had condemned Jemima Wilkinson would now open their arms to a self-professed prophet sent by God?

Maybe Friend saw it as a challenge, to so move these people by this new incarnation of God's messenger that they would listen and be saved. Certainly Friend displayed neither hesitation nor fear in the face of their outrage, but instead plunged confidently on, declaring, according to an account, that "as it was the Lord who spoke by her she could not be silent unless they applied their hands to her mouth."[43] No one raised a hand to silence the aspiring messenger—it was a peaceful congregation, after all—but all eyes were averted and no hearts were moved nor minds changed. When the service was over, Friend left the Smithfield Meeting House and never returned.

Rejection by the local Quakers only spurred Universal Friend on in the search to find people willing to listen. God himself had ordered Friend's mission—"I have chosen you, and ordained you, that ye should go and bring forth fruit"—and there would be no shying away from the commandment borne by his heavenly angels.[44]

3

The Message

"But where, say some, is the King of America?
I'll tell you, friend, he reigns above,
and doth not make havoc of mankind. . . ."

—THOMAS PAINE

News of Friend's sermon under the wide oak tree spread throughout Rhode Island in the following weeks, and curious colonists made their way to the Wilkinson farmhouse to see and to hear the earnest young minister for themselves. Potential converts also began offering up their own homes in Cumberland and in the surrounding villages, inviting their friends to come listen to what this reborn messenger of God had to say. The fear of redcoats landing on the Rhode Island coastline (a very real threat) and the harsh winter conditions of snow and freezing temperatures (the Abbott Run river froze clear over) did not deter people—more and more every week—from coming to hear Friend speak.

The young minister was proving to be very good at preaching. From the start, Friend was described as a "very eloquent" speaker who spoke "with great Confidence and Boldness"; who spoke "with ease and facility"; who was "grave, manly, and reverent, recommending with a degree of power of a state of repentance"; and who had "a Good Voice of Utterance, and Captivating Powers of Oratory."[1] In other words, Universal Friend was a great communicator.

For some observers, this capacity to communicate was due to Friend's forceful expression and bold confidence, characteristics they deemed masculine and therefore inappropriate: Friend behaved "not in such a way as became a meek and good woman."[2] But Universal Friend had no desire to speak as a woman—or as a man. As Ruth Pritchard, a devoted follower, put it, the minister had "the Voice that spake as never Man spake."[3] Demanding obedience, as when Friend counseled audiences to "obey the Voice of the Lord by the Messenger of whom he hath sent," might have been viewed as an unseemly display of masculine authority, but it was meant to assure listeners of Friend's godsent status.[4] Much as Friend's manner of dress, so "singular and extraordinary," also viewed by critics as too masculine, served to draw attention to the message of salvation, along with the bare head and flowing tresses reminiscent of images of Jesus. There was an element of theatricality to Friend's style of preaching, not as emotionally turbulent as that of the itinerant preachers nor as blistering as Jonathan Edwards, but Friend seemed to instinctively know how to attract listeners.

The elements of show did not mean that Friend was faking the role of messenger. Like George Whitefield (who was also of a "singular" appearance, with his cross-eyes and gnomelike stature), Friend was a powerful preacher because Friend was a true believer. God had taken the body of Jemima Wilkinson and imbued it with a spirit charged to deliver the message of salvation to the world. This certainty in who and for what purpose Friend had been reborn proved to be very compelling to followers. The rumors—which proved to be true—that Friend never prepared notes for sermons but instead relied on in-the-moment inspiration from God further encouraged many observers to believe that God spoke directly through Friend.

There were those, of course, who viewed Friend not as a messenger or savior, but as "sadly demented."[5] New Englanders had seen their share of self-proclaimed prophets, such as the minister James Davenport, who in the 1740s organized public bonfires in Massachusetts to burn books, luxury goods, and even his own pants in protest of what he viewed as wanton and sinful materialism; or Bathsheba Kingsley, a neighbor of Jonathan Edwards who in 1743 stole a horse to travel from village to village delivering messages that she claimed God himself had delivered to her (Davenport was judged to be mentally deranged and sent back to his home parish on Long Island, and Kingsley was condemned as dangerous *and* crazy). Universal Friend's more skeptical observers were perhaps simply wary of taking the latest spiritual revivalist too seriously. Time would tell for these doubters whether Friend's message would have staying power in the turbulent years ahead.

As for Jeremiah, he kept his allegiance with the Smithfield Society of Friends, attending weekly meetings and keeping to himself his opinion as to whether his daughter had been transformed into God's messenger. He allowed Friend to hold meetings in his home, and seemed to accept the newfound faith of many members of his household. Perhaps he was just grateful to have his daughter restored to health after such severe illness and wanted only to continue to take care of all his children, while also staying on the right side of the local Quakers. It was a balancing act, but he managed—for a time.[6] Just as he had kept his fruit trees alive while also gathering the ore beneath their roots, he would do his best to keep his rebellious family safe and his Quaker faith unsullied.

The sermons that Friend delivered were typical in form to those of other preachers of the time: lessons drawn from the Bible and expounded upon. Relying heavily on texts from Revelation, Isaiah, Malachi, Psalms, and Acts of the Apostles (according to sect records kept throughout the life of the minister), Friend offered explanations for how to live according to God's wishes and warnings as to what happened to those who failed to do so.[7] For example, Friend used the story in Genesis of when "Jacob waked out of his sleep . . . and was afraid" to admonish listeners to wake up and see for themselves their sinful state: "if we were brought to a Sight and Sense of our State and Standing, we should be afraid as Jacob was to See how dreadful a State we was in."[8] Or, quoting from Revelation, "Blessed and holy is he that hath part in the first resurrection," Friend assured listeners that "God had provided for the Redemption of all that would Repent and Believe in him."[9]

Universal Friend also incorporated dreams into sermons and teachings. Like the Quakers, Friend viewed dreams to be "signals from God" meant to guide "the people of the world."[10] For example, when Friend dreamt about "a large pair of Scales let down to . . . way [weigh] all the inhabitants of the Earth," it was interpreted as a warning that Judgment Day was near and the need to repent was urgent.[11] Friend encouraged sect members to remember and interpret their own dreams (again, like the Quakers) and to share those interpretations with their minister; the shared dreams were recorded and preserved in what became known as the community's collective "Dream Journals."[12] Common themes of these dreams were perilous journeys, a guiding light leading the faithful, and the repetition of words, such as "tidings tidings tidings" and "victory, victory, victory."[13]

Friend's theology—the dogma that governed Friend's life and dominated the minister's sermons, letters, diaries, and journals—was clearly articulated in the early years of Friend's preaching and would remain constant in the decades that followed. In many ways, Friend's tenets of faith were similar to Quaker ideology and also to the beliefs of the New Lights congregations. But at the same time, there were significant differences in how Friend viewed both life on earth (and the duties of the faithful toward their God) and how to—and *who* could—fulfill the promise of eternal life in heaven. For example, unlike the Quakers, who valued the inner light for guidance from God, Friend insisted that "the Voice of the Lord by the Messenger . . . whom he hath sent" (i.e., Universal Friend) was paramount.[14]

Another difference can be seen in how Quakers focused on spiritual work devoted to making God's kingdom on earth a reality, as counseled by founder George Fox: "with the Light you will see the Kingdom of Heaven within. . . . And with this Light you will see the Field, which is the World, set in your hearts, where the Pearl is hid, and with what you may dig to find the Pearl. . . ."[15] Fox was more concerned with the new world to be created in the here and now (and for the good of all) rather than with the afterlife. Universal Friend, however, preached about God's promise to reward individuals of great piety with glory in the afterlife, a concept more in line with teachings of the New Lights, who took an individual's personal fate, whether to end up in heaven or in hell, very seriously.

Friend believed that eternal hell was the fate of those who did not repent of their sins, prophesying a bad end for those who "knew his Lord's will and prepared not himself, neither did according to his will. . . ."[16] And not only the unrepentant faced damnation: in the years to come, when sect followers were under threat from outsiders, the minister condemned those outsiders to "the Lake that Burns with fire and brimstone."[17] At least one disgruntled follower would later complain that the minister "preaches up terror very alarming . . . delivering the dreadful horror that will Seize them if they reject her counsel."[18]

But threats about damnation and punishment were secondary to Universal Friend's main message that anyone could be saved from eternal damnation. This was in stark contrast to ministers like Jonathan Edwards, who preached preordination, that is, that many people on earth were damned to suffer eternal punishment and wrath and there was nothing they could do about it. Friend seemed to understand that preordained damnation was not a very uplifting message to hear, and might have known about how Jonathan Edwards's sermons led to a wave of suicides in the Massachusetts countryside in the late 1730s (including that of Edwards's uncle Joseph Hawley) by people convinced that they had been damned to eternal hellfire with no hope of being saved from their fate.

Friend instead promised that salvation was available "*to all* who have . . . gone astray like Lost Sheep."[19] The minister believed that universal salvation was proof of God's love, and that it was important to replicate his love, mercy, and forgiveness here on earth: "For this is the message that ye heard from the beginning, that we should love one another. . . . Love is the fulfilling of God's law: and love is God."[20] Proclaiming early in the ministry, "I desire to Speak in Love," followers in the months and years to come frequently noted in their letters and journals that "Friend was all love."[21]

Love, however, was not enough. Sinners had to repent to be saved. What did Friend mean by "repent"? The minister seemed to see repentance as a self-cleansing that began with acknowledging thoughts or actions that would make God unhappy.[22] For example, if a person did something that contravened the teachings of Jesus, such as acting selfishly or maliciously, or being ungenerous or short-tempered, the acts had to be recognized as behavior that saddened and disappointed God. Once recognition had been made, then the repentant sinner could strive to never make those same mistakes again. This process of acknowledgment and commitment was similar to the famous nightly ritual of George Whitefield, a kind of self-excoriation in which he listed for himself all the ways in which he had failed that day to live by the word of God, and then committed himself to trying his hardest on the morrow. As he wrote in a letter in 1738, he prayed that "God give me a deep humility, a well-guided zeal, a burning love and a single eye, and then let men or devils do their worst!"[23]

Repentance was understood by Friend to be a personal commitment to reject evil for one's own good and also in order to please God: the minister preached often about how "The fear [of displeasing] the Lord is the beginning of wisdom; and to depart from evil is understanding."[24] The aim of repentance was not self-serving, i.e., rejecting evil only in order to be saved from damnation, but rather its purpose was to bring joy to God, thereby returning the gift of God's love—and such a deep love it was, that God promised "all might come to the Truth and be saved."[25]

Gratitude was another important component of repentance, and one that Friend frequently spoke about, as well as wrote about in a private diary: "O that My Whole Life Might Be one Continued Act of Gratitude and Obedience. . . ."[26] Gratitude was a commitment to appreciate the world; it was the expression of awe in the face of everyday happenings, not only the wondrous events but also the most commonplace. The best way to express awe and thanks for all of God's gifts was to be repentant, and the best way to demonstrate repentance was to be obedient to the word of the Lord. Gratitude and awe would motivate legions of Friend's followers to commit themselves to the message and the ministry of salvation—and when a follower's stores of either gratitude or awe were depleted, their devotion, too, would fade away and their commitment to Friend failed. But such defections were in the future, and in the first months and years of Friend's ministry, the number of followers only continued to grow.

Another central tenet of Friend's dogma was that the world was "dying."[27] Especially in the early years of the ministry, Friend warned that not only was the world "dying" but that it was quickly approaching its end: "the day of the Lord comes soon, cruel both with wrath and fierce anger, to lay the land desolate, and he shall destroy the sinners."[28] Sinners could not hesitate, but had to commit themselves, swiftly and with certainty, to live by the word of God before Judgment Day arrived and it was too late.

In offering universal salvation to all before it was too late, Friend consistently preached that "good and evil is set before all" and each person must choose for themselves, rejecting Christian orthodoxy that Adam and Eve had bestowed a legacy of damnation upon all mankind.[29] Perhaps even more significantly, Friend rejected the prevailing view that because Eve lured Adam to eat the apple, women were the ones primarily responsible for man's fall from grace. Friend instead proclaimed that "everyone has to Answer for his own Sins, by himself Committed"[30] and bears individual responsibility for ending up in either heaven or hell. Women were therefore empowered by Friend's teachings to make their own decisions—spiritual and, as later events would prove, material and political—in ways they had not been before.

Some historians argue that Universal Friend did not empower women because the minister personally chose to "repudiate" identification as a female "in order to assume the prophetic mantle" and that by rejecting "her feminine self . . . she implicitly sanctioned the cultural and institutional features that consigned her to a place of subordination and inferiority."[31] But Friend's assertion of a genderless identity served to underscore the non-importance of gender: "There is neither Jew nor Greek, there is neither bond nor free, there is neither male nor female; for ye are all one in Christ Jesus."[32] There was nothing inherently valuable in being a man or being a woman and Friend was neither, choosing not to have the appearance of either gender, but instead representing a nonbinary messenger.

Such historians also criticize Friend for having used vivid imagery that "embraced the misogynistic tradition of western Christianity that associated women with the fallen Eve."[33] The imagery used by Friend in sermons and in letters to followers, such as "sorcerers and Whoremongers," are texts that come directly from the Bible.[34] The vivid descriptions were used to describe all sinners and Friend never used such texts to blame women for the sins of men; nor did Friend ever preach on the inferiority of women or inherent sinfulness of women (as did many ministers of that era).[35] Female-specific terms from the Bible that Friend used in sermons and letters were used for the same purpose that vivid biblical imagery of destruction was employed (for example, "Beware for a severing time has come . . . the day is come that burneth like an oven and all that are proud and . . . do wickedly shall be as the stubble. . . ."): in order to make a strong point while preaching.[36] Friend didn't advocate violence nor did the minister ever accuse any followers of being sinners or sinful merely because they were female.

Friend's non-gendered appearance also worked to demonstrate that every human being had equal opportunity and agency before God. The outward vessel—the "tabernacle of flesh"—that housed one's soul was not important.[37] Gender, social status, the color of one's skin: these were all external manifestations that did not demonstrate the value of the soul within. God judged not by appearance but by acts, and the soul was the recorder of acts.

This belief in the inherently equal value of every single soul, and the corollary that every person had a unique and redeemable soul, would become crucial components of Friend's ministry of salvation, long before the concept of equality, especially in terms of gender and race, was accepted by other denominations, including the Congregationalists, Baptists, and Methodists. The ideal of equality before God was a message of possibility and of hope, and would inspire the followers of Universal Friend, male and female, to reach beyond what society had dictated to be their opportunities in life—and bring the sect further than the young minister could have ever predicted.

Friend's message of possibility and hope, and of the need to act decisively and swiftly (before the imminent arrival of Judgment Day), came at an opportune moment in American history. The year 1776 had proved eventful. War against England had been declared, and all thirteen colonies were unified in the battle for independence. The colonists, many of whom for years had been looking for a spiritual path that would bring them renewed feelings of faith and community—in other words, a spiritual transformation—were now also seeking a political transformation. On every level, they were ready to fight for control over their lives, their villages and towns, and their future.

Universal Friend had the formula for addressing both the spiritual and political concerns of the colonists. Self-empowerment. Agency. Choice. Friend's message about free will, intentionally or not, had political power: every colonist could save not only their souls, but they could also save their home here on earth and their place in it. Just as the Puritan preacher with his insistence on original sin no longer held sway over the state of their souls, England with its insistence on oppression no longer held sway over the state of its colonies. It was a revolutionary concept, the ability to choose one's own fate. And Friend, bold and strange and strong, embodied the concept. The banner had been raised. Now who would follow?

4

The Devil in Newport

"Work out your salvation
with fear and trembling,
redeeming your time,
because the days are evil."

—UNIVERSAL FRIEND

For Friend to gather more followers to the flock, the minister had to go out into the world and preach. But Rhode Island was becoming a dangerous place to be. On the morning of December 8, 1776, British troops took control of the town of Newport with barely a fight. Only seven hundred American soldiers had been deployed to guard the harbor town, and when the British troops, numbering in the thousands, landed on the streets of Newport, the American soldiers fled, taking as many cannons and other ammunition with them as they could while escaping across the water to the mainland of Rhode Island.

The British immediately began building fortifications to protect their position, while also sending out troops to patrol all of Aquidneck Island. The Colony House—where just six months earlier the colony of Rhode Island had renounced British rule—was retrofitted for barracks, most likely by an all-Black battalion called the Black Pioneers, made up of about sixty former enslaved workers from the South who had been recruited to serve as unarmed soldiers for England; they would be joined by runaways seeking any path to freedom they could find.

For the moment, the British were satisfied with securing themselves in Newport and had little interest in leaving Aquidneck Island to invade the mainland. Newport was a valuable-enough prize. By controlling the harbor and setting up a blockade to seal off Narragansett Bay, the British could block port deliveries throughout the Bay (including at the ports of Providence, Bristol, and Warren), thereby strangling all commerce and trade in the region and preventing both local militia and civilian colonists from getting much-needed supplies. And because the harbor at Newport was both deep and largely sheltered from harsh ocean gales and heavy seas, it was a good place for the British navy to spend the winter repairing their ships and readying themselves for further attacks against the colonies in the spring (winter conditions preventing assaults by sea).

Nevertheless, mainland Rhode Islanders feared the British would soon cross the water to invade their towns and villages. They knew how much the people of Boston had suffered under British occupation: lack of food and fuel; death by illness, injury, and assault; and the loss of their homes and belongings to purloining troops. Now they feared a similar fate not only for the residents of Newport but also for themselves. Accompanying the British troops were German mercenaries known as Hessians (because they hailed from the German principality of Hesse-Cassel) and stories of how these mercenaries conducted themselves in war—engaging in plunder and rape—struck fear into the hearts of Rhode Islanders. The German soldiers were viewed as monsters in uniform, capable of "cruelty, death and devastation as will fill those of us who survive the carnage, with indignation and horror. . . ."[1]

How long would it be before the redcoats and the Hessians struck out for the mainland in search of supplies? Winter was settling in and stockpiles of food and fuel in Newport would dwindle with the ports shut down. Town councils throughout the colony prepared to defend themselves against potential raids. Military exercises were ratcheted up and stores of guns and ammunition were hidden away from potential British spies. All the way north to Cumberland, anxieties deepened as winter wore on.

But nothing would stop Universal Friend from continuing with the mission of salvation, neither the news of Newport's miseries nor fears of what the British would inflict on the rest of Rhode Island. Venturing farther away from home and closing in on Newport fifty miles to the south, Friend tried to bring a message of hope to beleaguered colonists. Bundling up in a hat of felted beaver fur and a heavy wool cape, and riding a favored white mare, the young messenger rode through the countryside bearing no weapons other than a bold confidence. Accompanied by a sister or two, and maybe a brother (and at times even her father, Jeremiah), as well as by a growing cadre of followers, Friend's journey along the frosty roads was a sight to behold: the minister galloping at the front, family and supporters following behind. A promise of light amid a very dark winter.

The citizenry of Rhode Island seemed desperate for some good news and villagers opened their homes to Friend. In modest houses and grand halls, Friend preached the message of salvation. As one follower would later describe it, what could be more comforting when living in a country "all in arms . . . embroiled in human blood . . . [than seeing] the Messenger of Peace going from city to city, and from village to village proclaiming news of salvation . . ."?[2] After days of itinerant preaching, Friend and followers made their way back north to Cumberland. Universal Friend returned home weary but satisfied: the ministry of salvation was taking hold, embedding itself in the colony and spreading outward.

The winter was harsh that year. Up north in Massachusetts, Abigail Adams lamented in a letter to her husband, John (away at meetings of the Continental Congress in Philadelphia), that "the Season has been a continued cold"—and the frosty temperatures would continue all the way through to April—"we are yet hovering over a fire and shivering with the cold . . ." and on into May: "We have had a very long season of cold rainy weather, and the trees are not yet out in Blossome. . . ."[3] While John Adams commiserated with his wife, he felt most deeply for the sufferings of the poor "wretches at Newport."[4] The snow and rain, clouds and damp in the port town were made all the worse by living under the tyranny of the British occupiers, with every day spent in fear and uncertainty, and no end to the occupation in sight. Adams prayed that "the little Nest of Hornets in Rhode Island [be] crushed," but he lamented there were not enough troops available to do it: "The Honour of New England is concerned—if they are not crushed I will never again glory in being a N.E. man."[5]

Adams was right to be worried. The number of enlisted men in the Continental army was plunging dangerously low. Men like Stephen and Jeptha Wilkinson, and thousands of others, had eagerly joined up to fight the British in 1775. But when their terms of enlistment came to an end at the end of December 1776, close to half of the enlisted men (including Stephen and Jeptha) chose to return home to their farms or occupations rather than signing up for another term. Fighting the British was both horrific and dangerous (during the war close to seven thousand Americans, just under 5 percent of the total number of soldiers, would die from battle injuries, while the British claimed to have lost over six thousand men). More fatal than the battlefields were the army camps, prison camps, and prison ships, where smallpox and other diseases ran rampant. As one prisoner aboard HMS *Jersey* in Newport described it: "the bad quality of the provisions, the brutality of the guards, and the sick, pining for comforts they could not obtain, altogether furnished continually one of the greatest scenes of human distress and misery ever beheld. . . ."[6]

Soldiers received on average the low weekly pay of $6 a week, and, even worse, that salary was paid out in non-backed Continental currency or in paper certificates—and sometimes not paid at all. As one soldier wrote in his diary, "I received the six dollars and two thirds, till . . . the month of August 1777, when the paying ceased. And what was . . . this 'Continental currency' . . . worth? It was scarcely enough to procure a man a dinner."[7] The low salary could not make up for the the hardships, fears, and potential dangers of remaining in the army. In December of 1776, anticipating the dramatic falloff in enlisted soldiers, Thomas Paine wrote, "these are the times that try men's souls; the summer soldier and the sunshine patriot will, in this crisis, shrink from the service of their country. . . ."[8] But what could be done to bring the men back to fight?

Local town councils, charged by the Continental Congress to find more fighting men, wrestled with ideas for increasing recruitment numbers, including onetime cash and land bounties. Compulsory participation in colonial militias had been the norm in the sixteenth and seventeenth centuries, but now in the fight for independence, George Washington and the Continental Congress worried that a draft might prove unpopular. Not only because the fight for liberty should be a choice made voluntarily (and was stronger for its being freely made) but also because of the general distrust of standing armies given the thuggish behavior of British soldiers in the colonies.[9]

Before the compulsory draft was finally instituted in 1778, colonial leaders considered other possibilities for increasing the number of fighting men. While membership in the army had previously been limited to freeholders and property owners, now Washington and his generals widened the field to include apprentices, indentured and paid servants, artisans, laborers, convicted criminals, and, finally, free and enslaved Blacks. Enslaved Blacks were enticed with the promise of freedom if they fought in battle (their former master or mistress were promised reimbursement for the loss). About ninety enslaved men in Rhode Island enlisted in the army, along with free Black men and Native Americans, and together they formed what became known as the First Rhode Island Regiment. Rhode Island governor Nicholas Cooke observed that many of the white enslavers "are not pleased with it at all and grumble a great deal" about the freedom granted their former unpaid workers.[10] But the First Rhode Island Regiment was born out of desperate times and over the months to come, the regiment would be accepted and, as their mettle was proved, celebrated.

Having the devil in Newport (and baying at the mainland) was bad enough for the morale of all New Englanders. But when the "great pestilence of Bloody Flux" (dysentery) began to spread throughout the northern colonies in the summer of 1777, their miseries grew even worse.[11] Dysentery was called "the bloody flux" because it caused thick and bloody secretions to ooze from the rectum of the victim during long, painful bouts of diarrhea. Most of those afflicted with dysentery died from the disease, their bodies wasting away from the loss of fluids for days on end. Abigail Adams, describing a servant with dysentery, wrote that the girl was "the most ghastly object my Eyes ever beheld . . . [and] such a putrid mass" that no one could bear to come near her. . . ."[12]

Is it any wonder that Universal Friend began to invoke the end of times in sermons? God had warned of "a dying world" and the warnings were made darker by what the colonists could see happening all around them. Other ministers in New England also saw evidence of the coming judgment in the invading British troops, lurking German mercenaries, and now the bloody flux. Who could ignore the similarity of bloody flux to the plagues to be released by God's angels prior to the Day of Judgment? Two of the plagues prophesied in the Bible involved copious amounts of blood: "the second angel poured out his vial upon the sea; and it became as the blood of a dead man. . . . The third angel poured out his vial upon the rivers and fountains of waters, and they became blood."[13]

The timing of Judgment Day had been a common theme in Christian sermons for centuries, and the Puritans who came to America in the seventeenth century believed their New World settlements, so pious and faith-driven, would start the clock ticking toward the day when the Lord "cometh to judge the earth: he shall judge the world with righteousness and the people with his Truth" and the final cleansing of the world would begin.[14] (Revelation provides a series of events that have to occur before the Final Judgment Day arrives, when all people are judged, Satan is eventually subdued, and a new heaven and new earth are created.)

By the early eighteenth century, however, the colonists of New England, by and large, had come to believe that Judgment Day was far off in the future and nothing to worry about. Colonial economies were flourishing, and life was filled with new opportunities: Why worry about the end of times? Church attendance and community piety waned as earthly riches and comforts increased. During the first Great Awakening, preachers like Jonathan Edwards had tried to raise the specter of an imminent Judgment Day (along with the terrible torments of hell) in order to bring their wandering flocks back to church and pious living.

Now with war raging, influential ministers, especially in the northern colonies, were using the threat of Judgment Day in a new way: to encourage their congregations politically and urging them to revolt against the oppressor King George and Parliament. "The British Empire is ripe for destruction," preached Reverend Joseph Bellamy of Bethlehem, Connecticut, in 1776, beseeching the men of his flock to join the militia.[15] Chaplain Ebenezer Baldwin prophesied that the conditions were ripe for an independent America to become "the principal seat of the glorious kingdom, which Christ shall erect upon Earth in the latter days."[16] Presbyterian minister Abraham Keteltas preached that the Revolution was a righteous battle for the end of times: "it is the cause of heaven against hell" with the Americans facing off "against the prince of darkness, and the destroyer of the human race."[17]

In many villages, the local pastor was the man in charge of training local men for battle. On the morning of April 19, 1775, when the British marched toward Lexington, Massachusetts to begin what would become the first bloody battle of the Revolution, Reverend Jonas Clarke was asked by John Hancock if the men of Lexington were ready to fight. Clark replied, "I have trained them for this very hour!"[18] Jonathan Edwards (the second son of Jonathan Edwards Sr., and an acolyte of the war-whooping Reverend Bellamy) preached not only about useful war tactics that could defeat the enemy but also advocated "inflicting a capital punishment" on any and all traitors to the cause of independence.[19] Understanding just how powerful a role ministers played in promoting independence, King George supposedly called the Revolution "the Parson's Rebellion."[20]

Universal Friend had a different response to the war. The minister preached that piety and faith should lead to reconciliation: "if people had the love of God in them, there would be no warring, fighting, nor killing one another . . . but it would be all peace."[21] Unlike the other ministers, Friend urged audiences to "Pursue peace with *all* people."[22] In sermons, Friend never discussed the goals of the war nor offered strategies for winning it, and instead focused on individual redemption, one soul at a time, urging followers "to repent and pray to God for pardon . . . not only for the sin . . . but to be sincerely sorry to have grieved the heart of God."[23]

Friend did use the specter of an impending Judgment Day in sermons, but not as a trumpet for going to war against British enemies. The only enemy to fear was Satan himself, and Friend focused on how the colonists might survive the troubling times not by fighting but by piety, and not just with the goal of surviving the war but with reaching heaven. In other words, the steps that individuals could take toward making their villages (and the world) a better place for everyone in the here and now of wartime—compassion, honesty, faith—could also ensure their passage into the heavenly realm of God.

In one story that circulated New England in 1778, Universal Friend actually crossed enemy lines and went into occupied Newport to lecture British soldiers that God didn't care about rebellions against King George; George was, after all, only an earthly king. What concerned God, according to Friend (according to the story) was the great sin of engaging in war, because killing of any kind constituted rebelling against the "the great King of Heaven."[24] Reports of Friend's alleged visit across enemy lines spread as far as Connecticut, where Reverend Ezra Stiles, recently installed as president of Yale in New Haven, wrote in his diary: "I heard . . . she told them publickly in the streets that those they called Rebels were not so great rebels as those profane persons were. . . ."[25]

Quakers were harassed and punished by both the British and the Americans for refusing to fight in the Revolutionary War. The British sent Quakers, including many from Newport, to languish on prison ships. In 1777, the Continental Congress, warned by General John Sullivan that Quakers were "the most dangerous enemies America knows," expelled seventeen Quakers from Philadelphia and imprisoned them in a Virginia frontier town for one year.[26] Both British and American forces also confiscated goods and properties belonging to Quakers who failed to fight in the war.

Universal Friend, however, never seemed to have been punished by either side for the very anti-war stance promoted in the minister's sermons. Was it because Friend was viewed as unimportant and without influence? Perhaps. And yet Friend's bravery not only in preaching against war, but also in traveling widely during dangerous times, had certainly, as Ezra Stiles's diary entry indicated, merited attention. And there were increasingly large numbers of people who did notice Friend's ministry—and who found hope in Friend's actions and words.

In the spring of 1778, the war in Rhode Island escalated when the British forces began sending raiding parties onto the mainland in search of much-needed supplies; they looted and burned their way through villages, confiscating food, fodder, fuel, and weapons, and destroying everything else. One report sent to John Adams detailed how in Warren, Rhode Island, "the British . . . set Fire to the Baptist Meeting House, which with three or four other buildings were consumed . . . Rob'd and plundered . . . set Fire to the Episcopal Church and 22 of the best dwelling houses in the Town . . . and stealing Twenty respectable Inhabitants out of their beds, whom they took away, we suppose to Starve and Murder on board their Prison ships. . . ."[27] Adams was horrified: "Will America suffer such a Race of Tormentors so contemptible . . . to plague her much longer?"[28]

An attempt was made by the Americans in August of that year, with the help of the French (who had declared war against England in March), to seize control of Newport back from the British. France contributed its twelve warships to set up a blockade of western Narragansett Bay and the Americans approached from the mainland. But then a hurricane roared up the Eastern Seaboard, ravaging both the French and British fleets, and the French abandoned Newport to flee to Boston. The American troops fought valiantly while also retreating and the battle ended in their defeat, with almost two hundred soldiers suffering severe injuries or dying in the battle, many of them from heatstroke. Universal Friend's brother Stephen, who had reenlisted in the army sometime that year, was shot in the face, but survived. British casualties numbered even more than those of the Americans, with close to three hundred killed or injured, and many ships in their fleet were lost, destroyed in the hurricane (or deliberately scuttled to save them from falling into enemy hands). The British would hang on in Newport for another year, causing misery on Aquidneck Island and fear on the mainland.

Amid the hardships and anxieties of war, Universal Friend considered leaving America and going to England. Maybe the root cause of the "dying world" lay across the sea; maybe the Lord wanted his messenger to go to the lands from whence these rapacious, red-coated soldiers had come, and there, in the soil of the Old World, firmly plant the message of repentance and redemption. While there was little that Universal Friend could do to stem the tides of war—as the gospels stated, "with men this is impossible"—the minister was very sure of the path to repentance and salvation: "with God all things are possible."[29] The question now was: To fight the devil here in America or to bring the battle to England?

5

Gathering the Flock

"Remember that the surest way
to be happy, is to be good."

—ABNER BROWNELL,
FOLLOWER OF UNIVERSAL FRIEND

Universal Friend decided to stay in America. Perhaps the choice came down to the difficulty of arranging travel during wartime. Permission to leave Rhode Island had to be secured from both the American military and from the British forces holding Newport, and although Friend and sister Marcy secured the necessary approvals from the Americans, when the minister tried to get permission for a recent convert named William Aldrich (Marcy's future husband), concerns were raised about allowing a man of military age to pass into British territory. It's also possible that the British authorities refused to grant permission for the trip given its purpose: to proselytize on English soil.

Or perhaps Friend believed, in the end, that the Lord had rebirthed his messenger here in America for a reason. Americans were proving ripe for the message of salvation, with the number of followers increasing in New England—but who knew what waited across the sea? Not only were the spiritual meetings over which Universal Friend presided well-attended by all accounts, but many of the people who came to hear Friend preach were financially stable, and respected and influential in their communities. Friend must have realized that with the help of such impressive converts, the evangelizing net could be cast even wider, and even more Americans could be saved. Better to stay in the New World than try to convert the Old.

James Parker and his wife, Elizabeth, wealthy Rhode Island Quakers, first heard Friend preach in 1778. They lived in Little Rest, a prosperous village not far from Providence (and about forty-five miles south of Cumberland). James Parker was the kind of Quaker—a worldly man interested in secular affairs—the Quaker reformers worried about. In his thirties, ambitious and successful, he acted as a justice of the peace in Little Rest (adjudicating both criminal and civil cases) and was active in Rhode Island politics. Perhaps most worrisome to Quaker elders, Parker served as captain in the local colonial military forces.

The militia unit led by Parker was nicknamed the "Kingston Reds" due to their eagerness to fight. To promote their fierce reputation, the unit dressed in bright red jackets (which must have led to some confusion in battle due to the similarity in color worn by British forces).[1] Parker most likely would have been disowned from his local Society for his activities, but within months of hearing Friend preach, he threw off both his Quaker affiliations and his military ones; he "resigned as captain . . . and devoted his efforts to the cause of the Publick Universal Friend."[2] He retired his red uniform and began dressing in somber browns and grays. Together with Elizabeth, James Parker became instrumental to the growth of Friend's sect. They contributed funds and also encouraged "wise and learned Men of great parts," including family members such as Elizabeth's younger brother Ezekiel Shearman, and Parker's good friend William Potter, to join the ministry of salvation.[3]

Potter, ten years older than Parker, also lived in Little Rest. His father, John, had been one of the earliest settlers in southern Rhode Island, moving into an area named Narragansett for the Indigenous tribe that had lived there for generations. After the devastations of Native

American villages during King Philip's War, the Narragansett lands had been left wide open for development by incoming white settlers. Finding the soil rich and the growing conditions excellent, the incoming white farmers built up prosperous estates and grew wealthy off trade in crops and livestock. To work their fields, and raise their sheep, cattle, and horses, they relied heavily on slave labor, both Blacks and Native Americans. Large allotments of their harvests, especially grains such as corn, were exported to the South and to the West Indies as provisions for enslaved workers there, literally feeding a circle of slavery.[4]

The Narragansett estate owners lived lives of luxury: they drove black and gold coupé carriages stenciled with elaborate monograms or family crests and rode Narragansett Pacer horses (George Washington preferred them because of their comfortable gait and reliable endurance, and Paul Revere rode a Narragansett Pacer on his midnight ride to Lexington in April of 1775). The planters bought opulent silk textiles and elaborately carved dark oak furnishings for their homes, and hired French tutors for their children and English gardeners for their terraced yards. When John Potter died, he passed on considerable riches to his son.

William Potter built on that wealth through his own dairy and stock enterprises. Both were labor-intensive endeavors and Potter used paid and slave labor to keep his lucrative businesses humming. He and his wife, Penelope Hazard Potter (the Hazards were another wealthy planter family), lived in a mansion on a rise overlooking the village of Little Rest. Their estate included an "elegant garden with parterres, borders, shrubbery, summerhouse, fruit orchard," and included many outbuildings for housing servants and close to a dozen enslaved workers.[5]

Potter had served in the General Assembly of Rhode Island and was chief justice of the King's County Court. He was currently a member of the Anglican church, had a son at Harvard, and his daughters (Quakers like their mother) were known for their piety. Penelope's devotion to Quakerism (and later to Universal Friend) was driven by the heart, but nevertheless she had agreed to be married in an Anglican church. Perhaps she understood that William's religious affiliations were a practical choice that allowed him to conform to the expectations of his fellow planters and merchants, and she wanted to avoid rocking the boat that had lifted him so high in life.

Having built his wealth in a colony chartered and supported by the king, Potter remained loyal to England throughout the tumultuous years of the 1760s and early 1770s. In 1772, when the *Gaspé*, a British customs ship, ran aground in Narragansett Bay and was subsequently looted by locals and then set afire, Potter expressed outrage over the behavior of his fellow colonists. And in April of 1775, when Rhode Island mobilized their militia to go to Massachusetts after the Battles of Lexington and Concord, he publicly condemned them, professing his own "true allegiance to His Majesty King George the Third" in a letter addressed to the colony's General Assembly and printed in a local paper.[6] (The colony of Rhode Island had yet to make its declaration of renunciation of England; it was not until May of 1776 that it would officially choose independence from its king.)

After submitting his letter of allegiance, however, Potter found himself publicly criticized; as one observer put it, he was viewed as "obnoxious to his friends and the public in general."[7] Potter realized then that if he didn't join the rebel cause, his financial and political positions in Rhode Island were at risk, and on June 2, he wrote another letter addressed to the General Assembly claiming that his earlier letter had been "not so properly attended to as it might have been, and in . . . haste signed."[8] He avowed that "No man hath ever been more deeply impressed with the calamities to which America is reduced, by a most corrupt administration, than myself . . . no man hath held himself more ready to sacrifice his life and fortune in the arduous struggle now making throughout America for the preservation of our rights and liberties, and in these sentiments I am determined to live and die."[9] He added, a bit anxiously, the wish that "this public declaration ease the minds of friends, and the friends of liberty. . . ."[10]

Potter wanted to make it clear to everyone that he was no loyalist.

The properties of loyalists were being confiscated and they were subjected to heckling and abuse; loyalists in Rhode Island and the other colonies had been tarred and feathered, and paraded for abuse through the streets. But was Potter truly committed to the cause of independence? After years of having his hand steady on the tiller—knowing exactly which way the wind blew and where he was headed, did Potter now feel off-kilter, tottering like a ship without ballast?

In October of 1778, James Parker told his friend William Potter about a strikingly strange and interesting young minister, and Potter went to hear Universal Friend for himself. There are records of Friend speaking in the area that fall, outdoors on Tower Hill in nearby South Kingstown where both the Quakers and the Congregationalists had meetings houses, and on the hill in Little Rest itself, simply known as Little Rest Hill. Impressed by what he heard, Potter sent word to the preacher that he wished to meet in person, and arrangements were made between Friend and the Potter family.

Over the ensuing weeks, Potter found in the teachings of the young preacher a new star to follow. The question of loyalist or patriot meant nothing to Friend; instead, the minister instructed Potter that his first duty was to God and that all good things only came from God. By the end of the year, Potter; his wife, Penelope; and daughters, Alice and Susannah, became followers of the new sect. His son Arnold, away at college, would soon follow. Over the months to come, William Potter made big changes in his life under Friend's influence. He gave up his public positions and, loosening his grip on his sizable fortune, contributed large funds to support Friend's ministry of salvation. He left his church, and he would eventually release those he had enslaved from bondage, obeying Universal Friend's dictates against slavery as being a most grievous sin. It seemed as if he had finally firmed up his allegiances: not to country, or to money, or to power, but to the mission of repentance and salvation.

Not all of Friend's followers came from backgrounds as elevated as the Parkers and the Potters. Abner Brownell, a young man from

Dartmouth, Massachusetts, was an early convert who came from rather humble beginnings. Raised a Quaker, he nevertheless had volunteered with the local Dartmouth militia in the early months of 1776. He was only nineteen years old at the time and had been working for the past few years in his father's tailor shop. It's likely that Brownell joined the army with the hopes of finding something more exciting to do than cut and sew. As he admitted later, he joined the army less out of a desire for independence from England and more in the hopes of securing "the honor and applause of man."[11]

But such hopes for glory fell short when Brownell quit his regiment. It's not clear how long he lasted as a soldier nor why he left when he did. His only note on the subject is that once he left his regiment, he resolved "never to go on Such an occasion again."[12] Perhaps Brownell ran from army duty because, as he put it, he'd always suffered from "a weakly Constitution" and he feared the illnesses that ran rampant through the army camps. What bad luck for him then to find when he arrived back home in the summer of 1777 that the bloody flux was ravaging its way through his village and killing off many of his neighbors.

Brownell grew morbidly certain that "Soon it would be my turn" to die. He feared that having led a meaningless life, he had no hope of ever reaching heaven. He resolved to "Reform my life" and "live the Life of the Righteous" before it was too late. To do that, he would have to seek out "People of God" for guidance.[13] He was a desperate young man living in desperate times and he needed help.

In the spring of 1778, Brownell "heard of a Remarkable Female Preacher. . . . Very Eloquent in Speech . . . [who] spoke much of Repentance and Reformation and Living a Life of Holiness. . . ."[14] When Friend came to preach close to Dartmouth, he went to see for himself what the preacher had to say. He came away feeling optimistic for the first time in a very long time: after "feeling at times under great conviction of Sin . . . I was much Affected and Attach'd with her Doctrine and Set out to Live Uprightly."[15]

Brownell was captivated by the minister's origin story. As he explained later, "She heard an inquiry in heaven, 'who will go and preach to a dying world?' She answered and said, 'here I am, send me. . . .'"[16] The story—a simple request made by God, an immediate response from a dying Wilkinson, and then the transformation of that woman into a messenger of God—convinced Brownell to join the ministry. He had found the spiritual guidance he needed, and he reveled in absorbing the sermons of Friend, filled with so "much Resemblance to Holiness and the Truth. . . ."[17]

The twenty-two-year-old began accompanying Friend on missions throughout Rhode Island and into Massachusetts and Connecticut. Brownell and Friend followed a grueling schedule, riding on horseback from town to town, sleeping in beds offered by friendly hosts, but never for more than a night or two, and then they were off to the next town or village. Brownell kept copious notes of the places they visited together and of the sermons given by Friend. For example, during a visit to Swanzey in southern Massachusetts in the spring of 1778, the "35th Meeting" of the year, Friend preached to the gathered crowd of how "Necessary and Needful" was the rule of doing unto others as you would have them do unto you, for "if that was universally the rule . . . what a glorious day of peace and Joy it would be, and . . . how far different this rule was, to the present Conduct of People, both in Religion and State Affairs"—and how "Lamentable."[18]

At "the 37th Meeting" in Dartmouth—a full day's ride away from Swanzey, including crossing a river and skirting a pond—Friend preached about "the message that ye have heard from the Beginning, that we should love one another . . . he that Dwelleth in love, Dwelleth in God" and also warned listeners that "he that Says he loves God and hateth his Brother, is a liar. . . ." During a visit to Hopkinton, Rhode Island (a three days' ride from Dartmouth, but stops were made along the way), "being the 40th Meeting," Friend promised again that "God has provided for the Redemption of all that would Repent and Believe in him . . . and Death would have no power" over them.[19]

During missionary visits to central Connecticut (requiring days of travel over difficult roads, with many detours required due to the abundance of streams and rivers), new converts were recruited to the ministry of salvation. These Connecticut converts included Abraham and Abigail Dayton, prosperous farmers, mill owners, and active do-gooders in their community of New Milford, and also practicing Quakers. Why they left the Quakers for Friend's ministry is lost to history, but what is known is that after attending meetings of Friend in and around New Milford, they committed themselves to helping the ministry grow any way they could.

Another New Milford couple who joined Friend's mission was Sarah and Abraham Richards. Sarah grew up in nearby Southington, where her father, Henry Skilton, owned several businesses and properties, and also practiced medicine. Just as Abner Brownell had been desperately looking "amongst Several Sorts of Professors of Religion" to guide him to redemption, members of the Richards and Skilton families were also searching for someone or something new to help them find their way in a troubled world.[20] Sarah's father had been in the Continental army fighting at Bunker Hill in 1775 and later served as an army surgeon. All that he had seen while in the army, the injuries and diseases, the sufferings and miseries, likely led him to seek new assurances that God had not abandoned his flock, and upon returning home, he left the Congregational church and, taking "an active part in the religious controversies of his time," founded his own separatist church.[21]

But neither Sarah nor Abraham found what they were looking for in her father's church. Having heard the stories about Universal Friend—and about the crowds who came to see the minister throughout Connecticut—Sarah, Abraham, and his brother, Asa, were intrigued. When news arrived of a meeting to be held by Friend in Watertown, they decided to go. Twenty miles to the east of New Milford, the journey would have taken the trio a full day to walk or half a day on horseback, but they must have deemed the destination well worth the effort.[22]

Abner Brownell witnessed firsthand the effect Universal Friend had on audiences large and small. He understood that the minister's message of "Unity and Fellowship" was remarkably effective in drawing in those men and women desperate for guidance in a world turned upside down.[23] At their first meeting with Universal Friend, Sarah, Abraham, and Asa Richards each experienced the magnetic empathy that Brownell had also felt when meeting Friend (who had described himself as instantly "Affected and Attached").[24] Without hesitation, they committed themselves to the ministry of salvation and were welcomed as a family. Friend would always welcome families into the sect and celebrated the ties of kinship as one of God's gifts.

Sarah Richards may have been attracted to Universal Friend because she found the minister's origin story empowering, given her own personal struggles with epilepsy. The seizures that Sarah suffered often led to short periods of unconsciousness, which felt to her like little deaths. Her father, as both pastor of his Separatist congregation and practicing doctor, would have prayed for his daughter and also understood the malady to be a natural illness not caused by possession by the devil (as some people of the time thought it to be).[25] But he had no cure—divine or medical—to offer her.

Universal Friend's story presented another option for the young woman: that the illness needed no cure and instead could be seen as a gift from God. The minister's experience of falling into unconsciousness, dying, and being reborn could be viewed by Sarah as similar to what she herself suffered during seizures. She began to think that she, too, had been touched by God's hand, and that her epilepsy was not a curse but a blessing.[26] As Friend counseled, God was to be praised for every creation: "for I am fearfully and wonderfully made; marvelous are your works, and that my soul knows very well."[27]

As Friend's following increased, and the meetings convened by the minister became both talked about and anticipated, there were those in the Quaker community who wanted a reconciliation with the young preacher. Elijah Brown, a Quaker who began attending Universal Friend's meetings in early 1777, urged gratitude for this "messinger from God" who "wants a Wicked world to turne from thare Evel corsis and to Live A Life to God."[28] Friend's disownment did not matter to Elijah; all he cared about was the quality of the sermons and he described them as "sprung from the divine influence of God's holey spirit."[29]

In 1779, Elisha Brown (no close relation to Elijah), deputy governor of Rhode Island, consulted his nephew Moses Brown, a prominent businessman and Quaker, about how Universal Friend might be brought back into the Quaker fold. Elisha seemed to believe in the story of Friend's transformation and wrote to his nephew that the Smithfield Meeting had mistreated its former member when they failed to see that "God in his infinite wisdom . . . raised her as it were from the dead to declare his everlasting truth."[30] He hoped Friend could be convinced to become an "exhorter," a status conferred upon Quaker women (and men) who had special oratory skills. Elisha must have reasoned that, given the large crowds that gathered to hear Friend speak, the young minister had such skills in abundance.[31] Between 1700 and 1775, over 1,500 Quaker women traveled throughout the colonies (and farther afield in the British Empire) spreading the message of inner light and they were widely respected in the Quaker community for their efforts.[32] Why not invite the former Jemima Wilkinson to join them?

But Universal Friend was not interested in being granted "exhorter" status nor in reconciliation with the Smithfield Meeting. The mission with which God had charged the dying Jemima Wilkinson was dynamic and specific, and Friend would never, in all the years of the ministry of salvation, waiver from it. While the methods used to save souls would change in the future, Friend never expressed any doubt of having been entrusted by God himself with a clear mission and would never betray that trust. Friend's duty to God also meant that the minister answered to no one but God—and certainly not to the Quaker elders, who had disowned Jemima and siblings from the Smithfield Meeting.

Even if Friend had wanted to reconcile, neither Moses Brown nor the rigid Smithfield Meeting would have reversed the disownment of someone they still viewed as Jemima Wilkinson. Moses Brown never believed the story of rebirth: "how to reconcile her being actually dead and not the same body, I must confess I know not." He refused to condemn Universal Friend, however, because he believed the preacher "in general means well."[33] Nevertheless, the consensus among most influential Quakers in Rhode Island was that the ministry of Universal Friend was dangerous because it might attract too many Quakers away from the true path of faith. They warned members that they would be disciplined—even possibly expelled—just for attending a sermon given by Universal Friend, and in Connecticut to the south, Quaker leaders also warned their flocks away from Universal Friend.

But the warnings did little to deter a number of Rhode Island and Connecticut Quakers from finding out for themselves what this unusual preacher had to say. While Friend might appear strange to them, there were also things that were familiar: the long robe was plain and unadorned, as Quaker clothing was, and despite the uncovered head, Friend had a sober and serious demeanor befitting a Quaker. And because so many of Friend's practices were similar to Quaker Meetings, they felt comfortable in the ministry's meetings. Friend always began with a period of silence, just as the Quakers did. When Friend felt moved to speak, the words would flow, again very similar to practices in Quaker Meeting Houses (and Friend allowed others to share their God-inspired thoughts, just as the Quakers did). Because Quakers were used to accepting "spontaneous sermons" as carrying "great weight," they were open to what Friend had to say, and many found themselves especially inspired by the unorthodox preacher.[34]

Perhaps there were also those who saw Friend's ministry as blessedly free of the trappings of hierarchy and discipline that had come to define the Quaker reformation. There was no large organization behind Friend and no strict rules of conduct that had to be followed. Nor would there ever be strict rules regarding dress, behavior, or roles within Friend's ministry of salvation. Implicit in Friend's preaching was the trust that those who came to hear the words of God delivered through his messenger would be swayed by the truth and then would willingly conform their conduct to please God, demonstrating gratitude and awe for his works on earth: "good and evil is set before all" and each person is "Left to the Freedom of their choice . . . the manifestation of the Spirit is given unto all."[35]

As more followers joined the ministry, it became clear that they were not only looking for guidance on the state of their souls: they wanted help with all aspects of their lives. Abner Brownell witnessed how Universal Friend was routinely asked for advice on everything from "method of cooking" to "how they shall have their cloaths made"; and everything from "their farming business" to "such small things that one would think a rational man would blush at."[36]

In 1779, a woman by the name of Mehitable Smith came to hear Friend speak in Connecticut; it was likely at the meeting held in New London, where "more than three thousand people behav'd very Civil and gave very good attention" to what Friend had to say.[37] Mehitable Smith (known as "Hitty") had spent her life as an active member of the local Friends Meeting in Groton, Connecticut. However, in the past few years, she had grown increasingly dissatisfied with her role there. In her early thirties, unmarried, and confident of her abilities at channeling inward light, Hitty wanted to become an exhorter for the Quakers, to travel widely and preach about her faith to others. But the leaders of her local Meeting refused to give her exhorter status.

Claiming that they had "stultified" her oratory gifts and calling their actions "bigotry," Hitty looked elsewhere for spiritual satisfaction.[38] Both Hitty and members of her family began regularly attending gatherings led by Universal Friend, and in 1779, in punishment for attending those meetings, they were expelled from their local Quaker society. Hitty and her brother, Richard, then joined Friend's sect. Just like the Richards family from New Milford, the Smiths served as examples for other families to make the communal choice for change: to leave their old places of worship and follow the new ministry of Universal Friend.

It was around this time that William Potter offered Universal Friend his home in Little Rest to serve as headquarters for the growing ministry of salvation. The mansion was already large enough to accommodate Friend along with family members and a number of followers; nevertheless, Potter added an entire wing for the exclusive use of the sect. Composed of fourteen rooms, each with its own fireplace (a real luxury at the time, when more modest homes sufficed with heat from one central fireplace), the spacious and comfortable addition was nicknamed "the Abbey" by Potter's neighbors.[39]

Potter's generous offering of his renovated home, the financial support he gave Friend, his manumission of enslaved workers, and his resignation from civic life all demonstrated just how much he believed that Universal Friend could lead him to salvation. But Potter's actions were also motivated by another and perhaps even more heartfelt and desperate hope: that Universal Friend could save his son. Not his child Arnold, away at college in Cambridge, but William Jr., a boy in his early teens who spent his days locked up in the Potter mansion.

William was kept prisoner in his room because he suffered from a mental affliction with symptoms of violent and bizarre behavior; he had been described as "insane and raving."[40] Although Potter may have recognized that his son's behavior was a result of mental illness, he nevertheless feared for the boy's soul. And now a savior had appeared. Potter believed in the story of Universal Friend's rebirth. He believed that Friend had the power to save people from hell and damnation. And he also believed—or hoped—that the minister was empowered with the Christlike ability to heal the sick. William Potter invited the minister to come live with him in Little Rest for a very specific reason. He wanted Universal Friend to perform a miracle.

6

Miracles and Prophecies

"What I tell you in the dark, say in the light,
and what you hear whispered, proclaim on the housetops."

—MATTHEW 10:27

Universal Friend moved from Cumberland to Little Rest in the fall of 1779. Coming into the village, the minister encountered tall stands of goldenrod along the roads, through surrounding meadows, and up hillsides. The heavy blossoms billowing in the breeze like a conquering army waving its bright banners of victory. Residents of Little Rest would begin calling the plant "Jemima weed"—but they argued over whether it was because goldenrod bloomed "about the time [Universal Friend] came to the neighborhood" or because the weed was a "curse put upon the country for a repudiation of the doctrines of Jemimy Wilkinson."[1]

There was no argument over how the town itself had been named. In 1675, the small hamlet provided a safe place for colonial soldiers to hide during the Great Swamp Fight, one of the last and bloodiest battles of King Philip's War.[2] By the time Universal Friend arrived in Little Rest, the humble settlement had become a bustling county seat, humming with activity. The village had a post office, saddler, wheelwright, cooper, several forges, a selection of churches, at least three taverns, and a courthouse where the General Assembly of Rhode Island regularly met. As a local resident put it, Little Rest contained "all the conveniences of Life. . . ."[3]

Universal Friend arrived at Potter's mansion accompanied by a few Wilkinson siblings and several chosen followers, including Abner Brownell. They must have been happy to settle into the mansion. Little Rest was closer to the growing congregations of followers in Connecticut and Massachusetts, and living off the bounty of the Potters meant a freeing up of funds for proselyting activities. But Friend's household still had to care for itself and tasks were assigned not only for the spiritual duties of meeting, prayer, and missions to gather new members, but also for housekeeping, cooking, and the gathering of food supplies (not easy during wartime). Taking care of the sect's horses would have been another important chore. The animals, crucial to the evangelizing mission, had to be groomed, fed, and bedded both at home and wherever the group might travel (the number of horses that the ministry had attests to the financial support it received from wealthy followers, as horses were expensive to feed, stable, and saddle).

Friend encouraged the sharing of chores and duties, believing that such shared service would lead to "Happiness Exquisite, Unspeakable and Everlasting. . . ."[4] The principle of shared work would become as important in binding the community together as believing in Friend's transformation story. For the rest of the minister's life, Friend would always live in a communal setting of shared work and shared faith. Not only women shared (and worked in) Friend's home but also men; Abner Brownell, and one or two of the Wilkinson brothers, lived in the mansion at Little Rest, and in the future, men of all ages would live with the minister for long periods of time. Widows and single women, widowers and single men, young bucks and old mothers: all types of people made up the contributing members of Universal Friend's household, and they were called "family" by Friend, followers, and outsiders.[5]

William Potter's daughter Alice, known as Elsie, was eager to become part of that family, in part due to her unhappy marriage with Arnold Hazard. Arnold was the youngest son of George Hazard, deputy governor of Rhode Island (and a distant cousin of Penelope, Elsie's mother). Arnold's oldest brother, George, had inherited most of their father's property, including an island off the coast of Rhode Island. After the Revolution, George would become the first mayor of Newport, and Arnold's brother Carder would become a justice on the Rhode Island Supreme Court.

Arnold, however, dabbled in careers, including as an army captain, and Elsie seemed to have grown impatient with his lack of focus and drive. She herself was energetic and ambitious, and she began spending more and more time with Friend on the Abbey side of her parents' home. Elsie apparently told others (according to family acquaintance Reverend Ezra Stiles) that Friend had "anointed her to be a prophet. . . ."[6] She began to imitate the minister, dressing herself in long, dark robes, wearing her hair loose, and making a show of knowing Bible verses by heart.

Elsie and her father both hoped that Friend might be able to help young William Potter recover from his mental illness. By the late eighteenth century, the mental afflictions he suffered were no longer viewed as the work of a witch or Satan, or as a punishment levied by God for some sin.[7] But colonists still had no idea how to cure mental illness. They used terms like "distraction," "lunacy," "madness," and "insanity" to describe those afflicted: "distracted" for those suffering from nonviolent mental agitation; "lunacy" because it was believed by some that mental illness was connected to the phases of the moon; "madness" was used to describe a state of uncontrollable anger, wild behavior, and total absence of reason; and "insanity" literally meant unclean and unhealthy (the opposite of "sane").[8]

Treatments for mental illness included bloodletting and purging, and clergymen (who often acted as both spiritual and physical advisers due to their reputations for intelligence) also relied on the well-worn admonition to pray and fast, and then pray some more. Desperate families tried all sorts of folk medicines or so-called grandmother remedies, which included concoctions made up of jimson weed (which could actually bring on episodes of delirium), buckthorn and rhubarb (the latter introduced by Benjamin Franklin into the colonies, both of which induced purging), and bloodroot (as a relaxant).[9]

In general, the so-called distracted members of a community were largely tolerated and there are many village histories that mention people who behaved bizarrely or erratically but were allowed to move about freely. But if an afflicted person became violent (a "lunatic" or a "maniac"), the treatment was often very harsh, with the most extreme cases being "chained by their families in strong-rooms, cellars, and even in flimsy out-houses."[10] Young William Potter spent his days confined to his room, prevented from leaving not only by a locked door but also by a metal bracelet that encircled his ankle and was attached to a chain bolted to the floor.

Confinement and restraints were not a cure, however, and whatever purging or sedating, or prayer and fasting the Potter family might have undertaken, their efforts had not healed William. If William could not be cured, could he somehow be spared the agonies of his illness, the fear of being overcome by mania, the insecurity of never knowing when such fits might occur, and the physical and psychic pain of being locked away? The Potters would have been ready to try anything to help him find a measure of relief. Elsie Potter even tried to cure her brother herself. According to family friend Ezra Stiles, she went to his room and, finding "him asleep & chained . . . she prostrated herself upon him, putting her mouth to his face and prayed till he awoke and arose. . . ."[11] But Elsie's treatment failed to heal William.

At some point early in Universal Friend's residence in the Abbey, the minister attempted to help William. What Friend actually did for him is not recorded, but the minister's usual practice in meeting with both individuals and with groups of followers was to first observe a period of silence together and then Friend would speak for a while, offering counsel inspired by God. Perhaps Friend sat quietly with William and then talked about God's promise of love and forgiveness. An undated meditation written by the minister might have been inspired by efforts to help William, as the words seem especially appropriate to his situation: "If to your Soul your bodie will prove true / Your gardien angel then Will govern you / And All the powers of hell he will Subdue."[12]

Abner Brownell recorded in his diary that after meeting with the minister, William's condition improved; "by degrees he grew better of his disorder and got to be very still and steady . . . and there was great noise of a miracle."[13] William was allowed to leave his room and resume a normal life. The family's faith in Universal Friend deepened as the weeks passed and the boy seemed to be "as well as he was before" the manias began.[14]

But then he suffered a remission. In the months ahead, William would get better for a period, but then cycle back to madness and begin "to rave and tear about." Abner Brownell was given the duty of watching over the manic young man—and he complained mightily of the job in his diary: "a most tiresome piece of work it was, as he was exceeding troublesome."[15] William continued to suffer from mental illness until his death around 1800. Neither the administrations of Universal Friend nor the efforts of his sister could, in the end, save him.

Despite Friend's failure to heal William, the faith that the Potter family and other followers placed in their minister didn't waiver. Along with other followers, they continued to believe that Friend had special capabilities. Successful cures of the very ill were attributed to Friend, such as when an infirm woman was lifted from "her Sick bed and Restored her to a comfortable state of health," and offered as proof that the minister could channel God's "almighty power."[16] Ezra Stiles wrote in his diary about a healing in which "Jemima raised the Woman (who had great faith in her) from off her bed and led her across the room"—when suddenly an observer of the cure "began a warm Dispute with Jemima."[17] Disturbed by the argumentative woman, the minister stopped the healing process. The poor patient was returned to her bed, her useless "Limbs . . . as fixt as ever. . . ."[18]

This story seems strange for many reasons, including the allegation that the minister left a cure only half-completed. But Stiles's recording of the story demonstrates that people were fascinated by the idea of Friend being able to cure the sick, or eager to hear stories of failed cures. Although there were those during the Great Awakening who believed cures were possible through religious intervention, New Englanders in general were wary of such claims, seeing them as akin to Roman Catholic perversions; as one observer noted, "However such Miracles may go down in Popish Countries, I trust they will be but little regarded in this Land of Light."[19] George Whitefield expressly refuted claims of miracle healings and preached about the most important cure being the one in which the soul cleansed itself of sin: "As for you . . . who only mind your bodies, who are more afraid of a pimple in your faces, than of the rottenness of your hearts . . . if you neglect the prosperity of your souls what will become of you?"[20]

Did Universal Friend actually claim to have cured the physical afflictions of sinners? Brownell wrote in his diary about the minister's confidence when called to the bedsides of the infirm. But confidence in providing needed care was not the same as claiming curative powers granted by God. While rumormongers of the late eighteenth century exaggerated Friend's exceptional but earthly skills into otherworldly abilities, there is no evidence that the minister made claims of miracle cures nor that Friend ever intended to dupe anyone into joining the sect by performing alleged miracles.

Friend did attempt a different kind of fraud in the fall of 1779, when a religious tract purporting to be written by the minister, titled "Some Considerations Propounded to the Several Sorts and Sects of Professors of this Age," was published.[21] Moses Brown—one of the Rhode Island Quaker leaders who had refused to admit Friend back into the fold—was quick to point out that a number of the texts in the pamphlet had been plagiarized from the writings of two early Quakers, Isaac Pennington from England and William Sewell from Holland. Abner Brownell, who had arranged for the printing of the pamphlet, admitted that he knew the texts had been plagiarized. He explained that Universal Friend had condoned the copying of the texts, because the Quakers' ideas were very similar to what Friend preached about regularly, i.e., inner light, love, peace, and forgiveness, and that such ideas would have "the greatest effect upon people" if promoted by Universal Friend. Brownell claimed that to salve his conscience over the deception, he adjusted the title page to read "By *a* Universal Friend."[22]

Why would Friend have promoted the publication of a plagiarized document? And if the minister was capable of one form of fraud, were other fraudulent actions on the horizon? If deception would further the cause of salvation, did Friend therefore deem it acceptable, the means justifying the end?

Perhaps the minister felt pressure to publish when so many other ministers made it a practice to publish their sermons. Published tracts were not only a good source of revenue (George Whitefield largely funded his travels through his published writings) but they also provided wider audiences for a minister's teachings. With rates of literacy so high throughout New England, Friend might have seen publication as a way to reach more followers without having to endure a grueling and time-consuming travel schedule. But because Friend never wrote out sermons (preferring to rely on inspiration of the moment), it was difficult to re-create them for publication. Claiming the works of others (containing sentiments that coincided so fully with Friend's own) might have been seen as a shortcut solution to the problem.

Four years earlier, English theologian and founder of the Methodists John Wesley had published a diatribe against the American cause, titled *A Calm Address to Our American Colonies*, in which he stated that "the supreme power in England" had the clear right to tax American colonists.[23] Within weeks, a Baptist minister from Bristol pointed out that Wesley had stolen extensively and "verbatim, without acknowledgment," from a work by Samuel Johnson, titled *Taxation No Tyranny*, published just months earlier.[24] What was Wesley's response? That he had used "the chief arguments from that treatise" out of a "duty" to impart to others what it had taught him.[25] Wesley's reasoning was similar to an explanation offered by Friend, and later, one of Friend's followers would also argue, "Could not the spirit dictate the same words [to Universal Friend] as it did to Isaac?"[26] After all, the most important thing was the message, not the messenger.

English law provided that the taking of another's writing as one's own was a crime.[27] But given that property interest in writings lasted only for fourteen years and the writings plagiarized in Friend's pamphlet dated back one hundred years, neither the minister nor Abner Brownell would have been civilly liable for the plagiarized texts. In any event, the pamphlet never sold well, perhaps because Friend's popularity depended on actually seeing and hearing the sermons when the minister's charisma, dramatic looks, and oratory skills were on full display. Reading about the message, rather than experiencing its delivery, just didn't have the same magnetic effect.

The question remains: Would Friend utilize deception to further the cause of salvation? There is no indication in any of Friend's letters nor in anything written by people who knew the minister intimately that Universal Friend pretended to have been reborn in order to attract interest and gather followers. Stafford Cleveland, one of Friend's earliest biographers, who relied on eyewitnesses (three members of the Friends Society were still living at the time he wrote his biography, along with numerous neighbors of the Society) and carefully kept sect records, concluded that Universal Friend was a minister of "persevering fidelity . . . sincerity of heart and greatness of mind."[28] Not a liar, not a fraud, but a sincere practitioner of deep faith. But just how far would this practioner go to achieve success in the mission entrusted by God?

The war for independence raged on, although with the departure of the British from Newport in October of 1779, the battles would no longer occur on New England lands. When the British sailed off from Aquidneck Island, they left behind piles of filth and detritus in a town blighted with half-rotted buildings, treeless streets, empty warehouses, and broken piers. The residents that remained in Newport were only grateful that the redcoats didn't set their poor town ablaze before leaving. The British did, however, burn down the so-called Newport Light, a lighthouse at the entrance to Narragansett Bay, and the point would remain dark until after the war.

Amid the backdrop of war, disease, and want (food supplies were running low throughout the colonies), Universal Friend's sermons again focused on the theme of an imminent Judgment Day. Friend's warnings of doom contrasted dramatically with the religious convictions voiced by the political leaders of the time that Americans were not facing the end of times but rather the beginning of a new world. The signing of the Declaration of Independence had been the first step—as Samuel Adams (cousin to John Adams and fellow delegate from Massachusetts) described it, "We have this day restored the Sovereign to whom alone men ought to be obedient. . . . From the rising to the setting sun, may His kingdom come!"[29]

Friend predicted the coming of a different kind of kingdom, one that began with the judging of every person before God: when "the day of the LORD [shall be] darkness, and not light . . . even very dark, and no brightness in it."[30] And in the late fall of 1779, the minister prophesied an actual date for the arrival of the darkness. Relying on text from Revelation that Judgment Day would come "forty and two months"[31] after a significant event, and claiming such event was the date of Friend's rebirth, the minister prophesied that Judgment Day would be on or around April 1, 1780.[32] Friend's prophecy could have resulted in public humiliation for the minister, and the foundering, then fading away, of the sect, with both the messenger and the ministry becoming minor footnotes in history. But in May 1790, the dark day actually arrived—and it seemed that God's young messenger had been right all along.

7

A Dark Day

"But it is unbelievable to the poor soul
in its tortured state
that this unbearable darkness
could ever turn into light."

—JOHANNES TAULER

On the morning of May 19, 1780, Universal Friend woke from sleep to find a world turned vaporous and gloomy. Up and down the East Coast of America, "a thick smoaky atmosphere" blanketed fields and meadows, creating a dark fog that diluted the rays of the rising sun.[1] For the past few weeks, the weather had been sunny, hot, and dry. The road leading into Little Rest had turned to dust, and in the surrounding fields seedlings turned brown, spring beans withered on their vines, and herds of cows desperately congregated in the meager shade of border oaks. As the days passed, the skies turned hazy, and colonists noted how "the sun rises and sets *very* red."[2] And now this: a heavy gloom that seemed to cover the entire world.

Just as breakfast was being laid in the Potter mansion in Rhode Island and in Abigail Adams's farmhouse in Massachusetts, and in homesteads up and down the East Coast, the intensity of the gloom deepened until, as Abigail described in a letter, "such a darkness took place as appears in a total Eclipse."[3] It was as if evening had suddenly descended: "candles were light up in every House, the cattle retired to the Barns, the fowls to roost, and the frogs croaked."[4] Night birds came out, "cocks crowed to answer to each other . . . wood-cocks . . . whistled as they do only in the dark" and "whippoorwills sung their usual serenade."[5] The songs seemed to herald doom, for what night bird sings at midday? As a poet later described it, "Nineteenth of May, a gloomy day, When darkness veiled the sky; / The sun's decline may be a sign, Some great event is nigh. . . ."[6]

The darkness fell as far north as Maine and as far south as New Jersey. General George Washington was still camped out in Morristown, having endured there with his troops through a long, cold winter. He wrote in his diary of how the clouds blotting out the sun were "dark and at the same time a bright and reddish kind of light intermixed with them—brightening and darkening."[7] Not only did the skies shift between lighter and darker, but the air began to stink, with the spreading of "a strong, sooty smell," like fire and brimstone. It was as if giant fires were burning themselves out, then reigniting. The world looked—and smelled—like hell itself.[8]

In Massachusetts, one observer noted how the "smoke and vapor . . . never was darker since the children of Israel left the house of bondage," while a farmer, in despair over the "unusual darkness" and "dismal gloom which filled the beholder with fear and astonishment," concluded, "we may rationally conclude that some singular judgment will follow."[9] In New Jersey, a colonist recorded how the "the smoke and clouds . . . had given distress to thousands, and alarmed the brute creation,"[10] and in Connecticut, Reverend Timothy Dwight, who had succeeded Ezra Stiles as president of Yale, observed that "It was of the general opinion that the day of judgment was at hand."[11]

Although the next day dawned sunny and bright and the end of the world did not come, the Dark Day proved significant for Universal

Friend. It didn't matter that the darkness had not occurred on the day prophesied, nor did it matter that normalcy had returned the following day; as Abner Brownell explained it, "there wasn't much said about it afterwards, only that it would be in the Lord's own time. . . ."[12] It was enough that the Dark Day had happened and then a reprieve granted. Maybe followers believed that the reprieve was due to the intercessions of Friend, who was, after all, God's chosen messenger. The Shakers, another outlier religious group led by a compelling preacher (Ann Lee), also found itself welcoming new members after the Dark Day; as a Shaker historian put it, "Religious activity quickened."[13]

Cotton Tufts, Abigail Adams's uncle, wrote in a letter to John Adams that while there are those who "considered it . . . as portending great Calamities, [and] others as a Prelude to the general Dissolution of all Things . . . ," he believed that natural causes were the most likely reason for the Dark Day.[14] And what Tufts suspected turned out to be true: two centuries later, historians working off evidence of fire scarring in tree rings concluded that the Dark Day had been caused by heavy smoke from intense forest fires burning in northeastern America and parts of Canada. The smoke was driven by winds and barometric pressure into the upper atmosphere, where it led to the formation of dark, obscuring clouds that spread across New England and south into New York and New Jersey.[15] The fires had been started by farmers clearing trees and brush to create more land for planting, a widespread practice but with the high winds and dry conditions of the forestlands, the fires had burned especially long and hot.

For one follower of Universal Friend, the Dark Day did result in the Final Judgment: on May 19, Susannah Potter died "in the Arms of the Friend."[16] On her deathbed, the quiet young woman—so different from her bold sister Elsie—spoke about Friend's mission of salvation. Determined to leave "many worthy Instructions and admonitions" to those remaining "in time" (the phrase "in time" was how Universal Friend and followers referred to the state of living), she asked Abner

Brownell to write out her commands, including that Friend's followers "be steadfast in the faith, that we might live in love . . . and that we might So conduct [ourselves] as to meet again in the world of peace and Joy. . . ."[17]

Rumors circulated that Friend attempted to raise Susannah from the dead by removing "the lid of the coffin" and then kneeling down "in devout and fervent prayer for her restoration."[18] But there seems to be no truth to this story; an observer to the funeral, held three days later, noted only that "the publick friend preached to a very large ordi- tory [audience]."[19] As leader of the sect, it would not do for Friend to demonstrate any sort of weakness, including the demonstration of grief: "The Soul is the monarch of thy Frame. Suffer not its Subjects to rebel against it."[20] The death of a good person was a cause for joy, Friend reminded followers, and how wonderful it was that the gates of heaven had opened to allow entrance to yet another deserving soul.

Even with a scientific explanation offered for the Dark Day, its occurrence made both patriots and loyalists stop and think. General Washington, a man not known for superstitious suppositions, might nevertheless have seen the dark skies as a portent for the future of the army he led. Just days before gloom enveloped the Eastern Seaboard, British forces had captured Charleston in South Carolina. Close to 5,400 American soldiers (almost the entire southern army) had been forced to surrender and were then sent to rot—and many of them to die—aboard prison ships in Charleston Harbor. This would be the only surrender of American forces during the entire war and the worst defeat of its army.

American loyalists were feeling vindicated, including Jonathan Sewall, an old friend of John and Abigail Adams, and fellow lawyer to John. He wrote in a sarcastic letter to a friend that the Dark Day had been caused by "the Devil spreading his wings over Northern rebellious colonies—and if they do not repent, the next time he will certainly fly off with them all."[21] In his opinion, nothing could save the rebels from the "dying patriotic fire" and their ultimate defeat at the hands of the British.

But Jonathan Sewall and the other loyalists had backed the wrong horse, and in the fall of 1781 British commander George Cornwallis surrendered to General George Washington at Yorktown, Virginia. In the months to come, there would be further skirmishes between the two armies, and the cities of New York and Charleston would remain under British control until the peace treaty was signed in 1783. But the Revolutionary War was over. The Americans had won their independence.

Cannons were fired from the town green at Little Rest on October 27 to mark the American victory. Did Universal Friend join the Potter family on the wide lawn overlooking the village to watch the festivities? Five years earlier, on July 19, 1776, the Declaration of Independence had been read aloud to roaring approval. On this chilly day in late October 1781, the colonists roared again, cheering the blasts of the cannons and warming themselves by dancing jigs of victory. And yet the joy and relief brought by winning the war against Britain was not absolute. Victory would bring new anxieties for the colonists, and new fears to replace the old ones. They celebrated the creation of their new country—and at the same time, they wondered about its future, and their own.

The hopes that Universal Friend had for this new nation likely centered on the opportunities that peace offered to the salvation of ministry. Freedom of religion was one of the ideals for which the Americans had fought, and while Universal Friend had never faced government-imposed obstacles in preaching or gathering followers, the minister must now have assumed that the message of salvation could be spread without constraints. Longer evangelizing trips could be made more easily and safely, and Friend might also have hoped that victory had inspired in all Americans a renewed sense of gratitude for God's gifts, including the independence that they had won. Such gratitude would logically lead them to embrace a ministry based on expressing thanks and working toward repentance and redemption.

But new obstacles would arise for the sect in the new nation of the United States, and even worse, the minister would, for the first time, face dissension from within. From whom such dissension came, Friend never could have predicted—or prophesied.

8

Faith in a New Country

"For myself, I fully and conscientiously believe . . .
that there should be diversity of religious opinions among us:
It affords a larger field for our Christian kindness."

—THOMAS PAINE

Just after the victory of the Americans over the British at Yorktown, a Baptist minister by the name of Valentine Rathbun published a scathing condemnation of the Shakers and their leader, Ann Lee. He included in his pamphlet a denunciation of Universal Friend, while also implying that any ministries led by women were suspect. As a former follower of Ann Lee, Reverend Rathbun claimed special knowledge of the Shakers, who he claimed had turned his mind "wholly up-side down."[1] When he finally righted himself, Rathbun broke off his connection to Ann Lee and rejoined the Baptists. Claiming that he had been tricked by "the spirit of witchcraft . . . the most powerful of any delusion I ever heard or read of," Rathbun denounced "this new religion . . . led by a false spirit" and expressed gratitude that now "my eyes were wide open . . . as though I had come out of a dark cellar, into the brightest beams of the noon day sun."[2] He set out on a mission to dismantle not only the Shakers but also the ministry of Universal Friend: he viewed both as dangerous sects led by dangerous women.

In the pamphlet he wrote in 1781 titled *A Brief Account of a Religious Scheme, Taught and Propagated by a Number of Europeans, Who Lately Lived in a Place Called Nisqueunia*, Rathbun describes the Shakers as "the Principal Enemies of America," responsible for "the growing evils and dangerous errors that are prevailing in our land . . . [including] damnable heresies, abominable impieties, and horrible blasphemies. . . ." He condemned Lee and Universal Friend as being part of the devil's scheme to use women to deceive the good people of America: "As Satan first . . . made use of her to delude the man; so he is playing his old prank over again, sending one woman from the State of New-York, and another from the State of Rhode-Island, who vie with each other, and are as dangerous to the heedless passenger as Scilla and Charibides are to the unskilful mariner. . . ."[3]

The Shaker sect had started in England as an offshoot of the Quakers; they were first known as "Shaking Quakers" and then simply "Shakers" because of their habit of shaking their bodies while worshipping.[4] Ann Lee joined the sect as a teenager, but it was only after enduring harrowing experiences with childbirth (her deliveries were difficult and all four of her children died in infancy) that she became a Shaker minister and leader. She preached most vehemently against lust: Lee claimed to have received a message from Christ "that the root of human sin and misery was the illicit sexual intercourse committed by the first man and woman in the Garden of Eden."[5]

Much like Universal Friend, Lee believed herself to be commanded directly by God: "it is not I that speak, it is Christ who dwells in me."[6] But Lee went further and claimed to have the blood of Jesus Christ running through her veins, and told those who came to hear her speak, "I am Ann the Word."[7] Persecuted in England for her beliefs, Lee was subjected to verbal abuse, beatings, and even held captive for weeks in Bedlam, an insane asylum.

In 1774, Ann Lee left England to bring the Shaker movement to America. By 1776, she and her followers had settled in central New York in an area called "Niskayuna" by the local Native Americans. Lee traveled widely throughout New England to gain new followers. In addition to preaching against lust, Lee, like Universal Friend, urged followers to confess and repent before it was too late. When the Dark Day of May 1780 occurred, Lee seized on the event as proof of God's displeasure with the world. She held a large public meeting on that day and invited sinners to join her community or be damned.

Universal Friend preached in a sober and calm way, using a wide variety of biblical texts in sermons and stressing the importance of silence and repose in finding spiritual fulfillment. Ann Lee, who was illiterate, rarely quoted from the Bible and instead used emotional exhortations against lust and other sins when preaching to her followers, while also demanding they make exuberant physical demonstrations of faith, including shaking, singing, dancing, and speaking in tongues.

Friend's followers tended to be merchants, tradesmen, teachers, and farmers who came primarily from literate and financially stable backgrounds, but Ann Lee attracted many poor and largely uneducated members of the lower classes (as historian Herbert Wisbey put it, "poor farmers scrabbling for a living on a few acres of stony Berkshire land, bound girls, or hired hands").[8] Many of Lee's followers were former New Lights revivalists who found her preaching and spiritual practices exciting and inspiring. Reverend Rathbun was an exception for Lee; he was educated and influential, had been a member of the Pittsfield Committee of Inspection and Correspondence, representative to the General Court of the colony in 1779, and delegate to Massachusetts's Pittsfield State Constitutional Convention in 1780. Perhaps it was Rathbun's breadth of experience and status that led him to quickly reject Ann Lee and the Shakers.

While there were many differences between Ann Lee and Universal Friend (and their followers), what the two preachers shared was charisma and determination. They both exuded a personal magnetism that was based in part on their own internal convictions that God had directly charged them with the saving of souls, and in part on their striking appearances and demeanors. (With her bony face and fierce eyes, Lee was terrifying and intimidating.) They used their charisma to draw followers to their sects—but it also served to draw the consternation and condemnation of more traditional, and male, ministers. Rathbun attacked their preaching as the work of the devil himself, who was "manipulating "the whole artillery of . . . error, delusion, and blasphemy, attended with all the power of hellish fury" to bring damnation down on good men and women.[9] Reverend Ezra Stiles of New Haven didn't denounce Lee and Friend as being the emissaries of Satan but he did accuse them of being outright frauds: "it is remarkable that there should be two Women deceiving the public at the same time with two such . . . monstrous and sacrilegious systems. . . ."[10] Reverend John Pittman, a Baptist minister from Providence, described Universal Friend as an "Imposter" and Friend's followers as "Deluded Creatures."[11]

But even while Friend and followers were criticized, they enjoyed a protective imprint of respectability because many of them, like William Potter and James Parker, were men of status and means. Supporters like Stephen Hopkins, former governor of Rhode Island and signatory to the Declaration of Independence, and Joshua Babcock, prominent physician and friend to both Benjamin Franklin and George Washington, also lent propriety to the sect. Hopkins was a distant cousin who welcomed the minister "courteously" to his home, spent afternoons in long and "kindly" conversation with Friend, and "treated her with respect."[12] Babcock had at times invited the minister to stay with him and his family, and offered both advisory and material support to the growing sect. Quite simply, Friend and followers, with their higher social and economic status and more quiet mode of faith, were less scary than the working-class and religiously exuberant Shakers.

During the war, Lee and several followers were arrested for failing to sign oaths of allegiance to the American cause. After the war, they were subjected to beatings and harassment in the towns they visited, with Ann Lee suffering such severe beatings that "she was black and blue all over her body. . . ."[13] At one gathering, assailants tore off Lee's clothes in an attempt to verify "whether she was a woman or not"; the attackers were sure that a person with such power over an independent sect must be a man.[14]

Around the same time that Friend was being criticized by ministers from other congregations, a critic within the sect appeared. Abner Brownell was not happy with how the ministry of salvation was being managed, and he became convinced that the sect was devolving into a cult of personality. His greatest fear may have been that his own status in the organization was plummeting, as Friend increasingly relied on new members, especially women, to carry out spiritual and practical sect duties. His discontent perhaps was first sparked by the arrival of Hitty Smith in Little Rest sometime in 1781, and fed by how quickly Hitty became an integral part of the "family" community.

Both Abner and Hitty had aspirations to preach, and it must have irked Abner to see Friend encourage Hitty in her ambitions, while he seemed to be relegated to be Friend's constant helpmate, but without preaching duties of his own. He came to believe that Hitty had been rewarded not for her oratory abilities but because of her blind allegiance to Friend. He would later describe Hitty's devotion to Friend—and that of many of the other women followers—as a kind of mania. While he considered his own commitment to be based on rational acceptance of the minister's teachings, he found the women to be emotional hysterics in thrall to what he later alleged were Friend's manipulative promises that "she would be willing to suffer all Things for them that they might be happy, and then delivering the dreadful Horror that will seize them if they reject her Counsel. . . ."[15] The women's blind adoration of Friend was described by Brownell as "great ulcers and mortifications growing . . . within the community."[16]

The sermons that Hitty gave as a member of Friend's sect were never recorded, nor are there any journals or letters by which her spiritual beliefs can be judged. But all accounts of what she did for Friend throughout the many years of her membership in the sect indicate that she was a woman with her feet firmly planted on the ground and not "hysterical" in any way. (Women have been accused of "hysteria" since the time of the ancient Greeks, who took the phrase from their word for "uterus," believing that only those with a uterus could exhibit extreme symptoms of being overly emotional or irrational. Plato himself "attributed the disease to an impulse arising from the uterus . . . the sexual appetite impulse . . . which, frustrated in its natural aims, wanders around the body, and in its ruthless pressure for satisfaction distresses the woman, and causes hysterical somatic symptoms.")[17] Hitty was in fact so steady, reliable, and hardworking that Friend would often trust her with difficult (and thankless) tasks in the years to come. But her growing importance to Friend—and status in the community—rankled Brownell.

Brownell's frustrations can be understood. He wanted to preach the word of God, and he was being thwarted in his ambition, while a relative newcomer was being given all sorts of opportunities. In one last effort to distinguish himself from Hitty, in 1782 Brownell wrote a book of religious essays.[18] Mimicking Friend's origin story, he claimed that God had instructed him as "a Chosen Vessel . . . to bear testimony . . . on the Gospel & Proclaim Salvation to the Children of me. . . ." He titled his book *The Worship of God According to the True Christian Divinity*.[19]

But according to Brownell, Universal Friend was not pleased to hear about the manuscript he had written. James Parker and Hitty were sent to New London, Connecticut, where Brownell was meeting with his printer, to see what the book was all about. Parker admonished Brownell for not consulting with Friend first—no other followers had ever attempted to write or publish their own essays—and Hitty went even further; she absconded with the manuscript and traveled back to Little Rest, forty miles away, presumably to show it to Universal Friend. Brownell was thrown into a frenzy, but he didn't blame Hitty (much as he disliked her): "she was not the contriver of it but acted as an instrument to do it."[20] Brownell blamed Friend, and after Hitty made sure the manuscript was returned to the printer, Brownell demanded an apology from the minister for the worry it had caused him.

Instead of an apology, an entourage of Friend and followers arrived at Brownell's doorstep. They swarmed into his lodgings and, according to Brownell's account (the only record existing of the encounter), Friend ordered him to sit in a chair that had been placed in the center of the room. The minister then stood in front of him, while twenty followers surrounded him on every side, making him feel "like a criminal."[21] The purpose of their visit was clear: "to have talk'd and fear'd me out of" publishing the book.[22] Friend "said that her friends had heard I was writing about her . . . ," but Brownell replied that "it was for everyone to see and judge for themselves. . . ."[23] He explained the book was simply a book of religious essays (the text delivered directly to him by God) and that it was too late to stop its printing even if he wanted to.

Back and forth the dispute went, and finally Friend and followers departed, leaving Brownell alone, shaken and upset, in the gloom of late afternoon. He was now convinced that the sect no longer had anything to offer him—and that he had even less to give to them. It was time for him to leave Friend's ministry of salvation. But he would not go quietly: while the religious essays seemed never to have been published, a scathing account of his years with Universal Friend came out in 1782. He titled the book *Enthusiastical Errors*.

The parallels to Reverend Valentine Rathbun's actions regarding Ann Lee and the Shakers are striking: a man finds himself following the teachings of one he perceives as a woman, he becomes subservient to the female leader (and even worse, to other women in the sect) and eventually perceives his subservience as a demotion in status (and an attack on his masculinity), and he then reasserts his superiority by ascribing to the woman he previously adored the traits of witchery, enchantment, illusion, and other manipulative tools of Satan. Just as Rathbun had done, Brownell would use his book to attack the sect and the leader that had held him in such thrall—but in the end, left him unsatisfied and angry.

The very title of Brownell's book was a condemnation of Friend: the minister inspired deluded enthusiasm, and he had been one of the dupes. In his introduction, Brownell explained that he published the book in order to reveal "the discoveries I have made of . . . the religious Scheme . . . which has been, and is still propagated by an anonymous Person, who gives herself the Title of 'The Universal Friend.'"[24] His descriptions of Friend's fawning female followers and the inflated ego of their minister no doubt had a kernel of truth in them, as others would also describe in years to come of Friend making "many great and exalted Expressions in Allusion to Herself" and claiming to be the only one capable of carrying out God's "great and marvelous Mission" of universal salvation.[25] As for Brownell's claim that the female followers demonstrated "slavish devotion," it is certain that love for their minister and commitment to the sect would be hallmark characteristics of most of the female followers.

Did Brownell leave the sect because it had changed from the itinerant, folksy style of preaching to something larger, more organized, and more female-driven? Did he leave because he no longer enjoyed the intimate connections of their early days out on the road together or because Friend denied him the opportunity to preach? Brownell himself claims to have left because having "observed . . . [Friend]'s principle, practice, and conduct, and treatment of me, it gave me fully an occasion plainly and flatly to deny any further connexion with her. . . ."[26] If the account given by Brownell about his interrogation at the hands of Friend, while surrounded by somewhat threatening followers, is to be believed, then his decision to leave the sect is easily understood. Was Friend's theatricality, used to promote the message of salvation, now been used to control and manipulate a follower? If that was the case, then Brownell's abandonment of the sect makes perfect sense.

No matter the reason, Brownell's bitter departure was the first defection for Universal Friend, and it would have left the minister shaken. More than three years had been spent at the side of Abner Brownell, carrying out the mission of salvation (half the life of the ministry).

During those years, he had recorded every step the two of them took together: the perilous travels throughout New England, the sermons and meetings in strange homes and cold meetinghouses, the struggle to stay focused on the mission while a war raged all around them. Those early years of the ministry were heady and exhilarating. But then doubts had settled like a wall between them, and now Brownell had chosen to leave Friend and the sect behind.

Brownell set out in search of a new spiritual home and in 1784 he would join a Baptist congregation in Groton. Universal Friend never rebuked him for the choice he made—after all, Friend believed in free choice—nor was he criticized for publishing *Enthusiastical Errors*. But the breaking of faith must have felt like the betrayal in the garden, a defection from light to darkness. The minister's advice to stay "among good people, for there is no security in wicked Company, where the good are often made bad, and the bad always worse," was not always easy to follow.[27] Brownell had been good—but then he turned away from the ministry. How could Friend know which followers would stay true to the cause and whose head might be turned by new ideas or other opportunities?

In 1776, the newly reborn Friend had had a simple belief that in following the mission entrusted by God, success was assured: speak and they will come; when they come, they will hear; when they hear, they will follow the way of the Lord. Did Brownell's abandonment of Friend cause the minister to lose some of that early confidence? The attacks of men like Valentine Rathbun and the defection of Abner Brownell served as warnings. From this point on, the minister would have to guard against attacks from outside while also watching for signs of internal betrayals. But nothing would stop Friend from continuing the fight for lost American souls.

9

The Mission South

"If I can snatch a single one of you
from the danger which he runs,
I have not travelled too long
a road in seeking it. . . ."

—UNIVERSAL FRIEND

In the fall of 1782, Universal Friend set out for Philadelphia, the most populous city in America, renowned for its religious diversity and tolerance, and the hometown of hundreds of devout—but perhaps searching—Quakers. What better place to launch the next phase of the ministry of salvation? As the steamy summer of 1782 drew to a close and the fall harvests were brought in, Friend made plans for a different kind of harvest. The reaping of souls.

The city was larger and busier than any city Friend had ever seen, but at least it didn't stink, the way most big cities did at that time. Under Ben Franklin's direction, Philadelphia had been the first in America to institute public street cleaning, which was carried out by paid scavengers.[1] (Alas, in a bid to save money in January 1783 city leaders would fire the scavengers and instead offer "free manure" to any farmer who would come and clean the streets; the plan didn't work and residents were soon complaining about the mess of dead cats, dogs, and chickens, garbage, and animal waste that littered the city. By 1784, scavengers would resume their roles in clearing public roads of garbage, horse dung, and worse.)[2]

High Street ran from east to west through the center of Philadelphia; it was the widest street in town and the main thoroughfare; smaller streets and alleyways, lined with sooty red-bricked row houses, splayed out in an ordered maze to the north and south. Leading the horses down High Street, Friend would have been able to see Christ Church's white spire reaching high into the sky (making it the tallest building in America), while the more sober Quaker Meeting House stood staidly by on a tree-shaded corner. A market warren of vendors stretched two blocks inland from the waterfront on High Street ("Market" would soon replace "High" as the name of the street), where everything from food to furnishings to flowers was sold. The courthouse stood to the west (built in 1707 after colony justices complained of having to hear their cases in a rowdy alehouse), with the squat jailhouse conveniently set beside it.

A few passersby stopped to stare at the newly arrived travelers from the North, gawping openly at their long dark robes; an observer would later write in a letter to a local paper that their clothes were "singular and uncommon."[3] But attention to the new arrivals didn't last long. There was business to attend to and no time to waste. The Confederation Congress, previously known as the Continental Congress, was meeting daily under the tower and steeple of the Pennsylvania State House to debate the final peace terms with Britain and set the boundary lines between British Canada and the United States (the Treaty of Paris would finally be signed in 1783). Congress was also working on creating new American coinage, the copper "Fugio" cent (the Mint Act, however, wouldn't be passed until 1792, creating the United States dollar as the country's standard unit of money and establishing the U.S. Mint) and choosing the national bird (the bald eagle), which would be displayed across the officially adopted Great Seal of the United States.

Friend made the trip to Philadelphia with William Potter, his son

Arnold (home from college), and his daughter Elsie, along with recent Rhode Island converts Thomas Hathaway and William Turpin. In New London, Sarah Brown, a cousin of William Turpin, joined the travelers. Thomas Hathaway had been a successful shipbuilder before the war, and William Turpin was from a well-to-do family, just twenty-four years old, but with big dreams; Sarah's family in Groton was also prosperous, owning at least one slave (whom they freed upon becoming followers of Friend).

They made a striking group as they walked the streets of Philadelphia: in the lead, a tall, dark-robed minister with a scarf at the neck and flowing black hair, followed by "tall and handsome" congregants, also dressed in robes.[4] The robes, while plain, were made of well-cut quality cloth that, along with the fine horses they led and their richly grained saddles, signaled the group's comparative wealth and status.

Why did such well-to-do men and women give up the comfort and luxuries of their lives to follow Universal Friend? They were not searching for greater riches or fame or adventure. Not yet anyway. What they looked for in the young minister was an antidote to the unhappiness and uncertainty from which their riches had not protected them; they were recovering from the chaos of wartime, when so much had changed and questions of loyalty and duty had been turned upside down. With the war finally over, they were trying to find their footing again: "Thou, which has shewed me great and sore troubles, shalt quicken me again, and shalt bring up again from the depths of the earth."[5]

Thomas Hathaway had endured many difficulties in the past five years. During the war, he'd fled to Novia Scotia as a loyalist, leaving his family behind. He was sure they would be safe staying in a country farmhouse that he owned. But while he was away his wife was assaulted by British officers. Shortly after, Hathaway was finally reunited with his wife, she died, having "never recovered" from the "fright" given to her by the soldiers.[6] When Thomas's brother James introduced the grieving, guilt-ridden man to Universal Friend, he became a devoted follower and strove to become a trusted confidant as well.

What Friend offered men like Thomas and James Hathaway meant more to them than anything money could buy: a chance at repentance and hope for eternal bliss. A way to clean their souls and prepare the way for everlasting happiness as well as temporal happiness. Perhaps even a way to salve their guilt over surviving the war intact, while others had not.

Did Friend harbor any doubts as to how long and through what degree of hardships these followers, accustomed to comfort and influence, would remain devoted to the ministry? It would seem so, for while the early sermons of Universal Friend focused on elements of a moral life and the dangers of sin in general terms, the sermons delivered by Friend in the 1780s focused increasingly on the dangers of wealth and material goods and warned against feelings of superiority. Everyone was equal before God—"The rich and the poor meet together; the Lord is the Maker of them all"—but the minister also preached that "Better is the Poor that walketh in the integrity of his heart than he that is perverse in his way, 'tho he may be rich."[7]

On their journey south from Rhode Island, Friend and followers had easily found nightly lodgings. Everywhere they stopped, homes were opened and meals provided. The welcoming hosts knew of Universal Friend, perhaps even had written requesting a visit from the minister. All they asked in return for their hospitality was that Universal Friend lead a meeting and perhaps also provide a private session of shared advice and shared prayer. The minister had been treated with great respect and the followers with a kind of awe. But here in Philadelphia, Friend was unknown and unheralded, and the followers had trouble finding a place for their group to sleep.

Finally, a widow who lived on a narrow lane called Elfreth's Alley offered them a place to stay; her "heart and house . . . [were] open to their reception." But she may soon have regretted her kindness. Word had begun to spread that "a singular female preacher with two other women and four men as companions . . . arrived in this city in order . . . to publish and declare the glad tidings of salvation. . . ."[8] By noon of their second day in Philadelphia, a large crowd gathered in Elfreth's Alley to see "the innocent but majestic appearance of the woman preacher" who "struck wonder and amazement by her preaching and praying. . . ."[9] But then rabble-rousers arrived and stirred the crowd up into a mob: a "dreadful scene of outrage ensued: stones, brick-bats, etc. were thrown against the house. . . ."[10] Eventually the mob broke up and drifted away, leaving the travelers from Rhode Island—and their kindly hostess—safe but shaken behind the home's shuttered door and windows.

News of the attack spread throughout Philadelphia. Outraged by the reception shown Universal Friend, a group of Free Quakers sought out the travelers to offer them a warmer welcome to Philadelphia. The Religious Society of Free Quakers was formed in 1781, made up largely of men and women disowned from their local meetings for violating traditional Quaker rules of behavior, including the prohibition against involvement in politics and wars. Betsy Ross was a Free Quaker (disowned by her family and the Quakers after she eloped with an Episcopalian), as was Colonel Timothy Matlack, the man entrusted with copying onto parchment (animal skin) the Declaration of Independence that was then signed by representatives of all thirteen colonies in 1776.[11]

According to Samuel Wetherill, who founded the Society of Free Quakers, acting according to one's own conscience was paramount in all matters and "every man should enjoy his sentiments without being censured at [or] smote at."[12] These friendly Free Quakers now vowed their help to Universal Friend, along with their friendship. With their sponsorship, Friend was invited to hold prayer meetings at the Methodist Meeting House, a spacious and imposing brick church on Fourth Street.

Big as the church was, it was still too small to accommodate the many people who turned out to see this preacher that suddenly everyone was talking about. Crowds gathered not only because they were interested in what Friend had to say about religion but because they viewed the minister as a kind of curiosity or even a celebrity; as the prominent socialite Elizabeth Drinker wrote in her diary, the minister "has occasioned much talk in the City . . . her Dress and Behavior, remarkable."[13] The Marquis de Chastellux, a French aristocrat and exile traveling through the states, "made an attempt to hear her . . . but the crowd was so great and . . . so turbulent, that it was impossible to get near the place of worship."[14]

Another French traveler was more successful in his bid to enter the hall. François, Marquis de Barbé-Marbois was a statesman and diplomat who had come to the United States in 1779 to represent French interests in America and oversee aid to the colonists. He would eventually marry an American, and in 1803 he would negotiate the Louisiana Purchase with Thomas Jefferson, an old friend of his. But in 1782 he was still a man with a roving eye for beauty. Having heard rumors describing Friend's striking appearance, he was determined to judge for himself the appeal of the famed minister. He fought his way into the meetinghouse and found a seat as close as possible to the pulpit to get a good look. He liked what he saw: as he wrote in his diary, "This soul from heaven has chosen a rather beautiful body for its dwelling place. . . ."[15]

The marquis was annoyed when William Potter and Thomas Hathaway rose to speak, and he found both of their sermons to be quite boring. Finally, Universal Friend moved to the pulpit. At first, the marquis was not impressed, thinking that because Friend "enunciated so clearly though without elegance, that . . . she was reciting a prepared sermon." He found the sermon itself to be somewhat uninspired, full of "commonplaces about the Bible and the Fathers."[16]

But then the tenor and rhythm of the sermon changed. Friend launched into an indictment of those in the crowd who had come to hear the sermon only out of "curiosity" and out of their craven desire to "be able to tell of extraordinary things when they return to their own country." Friend went on to ask, "Do these strangers believe that their presence in the house of the Lord flatters me?" and then answered, "I disdain their honors, I scorn greatness and good fortune." Finally, in a voice that echoed through the hall (and displayed more than a touch of fiery temper), the minister commanded, "Do not seek me, do not listen to me, unless you are touched by grace. Go away, no longer profane this temple, if you are still in the snares of the infernal angel."[17]

It was as if the "soul from heaven" had read the Frenchman's mind. For a moment, he "believed her to be a prophetess or a fortune teller, and I expected her to speak of [the workings of] my diary. . . ."[18] But when Universal Friend took a handkerchief from the folds of the long robe and, as the marquis described it, dabbed at tears falling from wide eyes (he is the only one to report such dramatic sermonizing), then he found himself "hardened as before" against Friend's teachings. While impressed by the minister's beauty, he viewed with gallic cynicism Friend's dramatic plea for repentance.

Perhaps it was the widely shared reports of Friend's bold sermon that led Christopher Marshall to reach out to Universal Friend. Marshall was an Irish immigrant who, after arriving in Philadelphia in 1727, set up an apothecary shop, got married, joined the Quakers, and made his fortune as a chemist and pharmacist, providing medicines and other treatments for the people of Philadelphia. By the time the American Revolution began, he had already retired and was beginning to suffer from bad health. But he fired himself up in the fight for independence, and in 1776 he was appointed to serve on Pennsylvania's Provincial Conference (the governing body of the colony following its declaration of independence from England) and the Committee of Safety (which supervised the colony's military operations). He was disowned from the local Friends Society, but he, along with other so-called Fighting Quakers (Quakers disowned for actively supporting the American Revolution), happily joined the Society of Free Quakers.[19]

Marshall was a man with deep interests in all kinds of religion, and he was eager to talk with Universal Friend about the new sect's doctrines and practices. He invited the minister, along with Elsie Potter Hazard and Sarah Brown, to stay with him at his home, and arranged for the male travelers to stay at the homes of his sons. Over a period of days, the minister and host engaged in long conversations about faith, and although Marshall never became a convert (and always addressed Friend by the name "Jemimah"), he believed the sect's ambition of "true repentance" to be both sincere and worth supporting.[20] He wrote in his diary about how much he enjoyed the time spent in "Conversation with Jemimah," and in the months to come would describe the hours they shared talking "together in great freedom, simplicity, and affection. . . ."[21]

In one of their many discussions on faith, it's likely that Marshall brought up an outlier religious sect that interested him, and that he thought might interest Friend as well. The Ephrata sect shared some ideas in common with Universal Friend, such as the condemnation of war; the wearing of plain clothing; and mysticism, that is, the communication with God through dreams and visions. In 1736, the sect's founder, German mystic Conrad Beissel, established a cloistered community deep in the Pennsylvania wilderness, in a place he called "Ephrata" (a reference to an old name for Bethlehem, meaning "fruitful"). He had come to Pennsylvania in 1720 after being persecuted in Germany for his beliefs (and for his refusal to attend the state-mandated church); he was part of a migration of close to five thousand Germans drawn by the colony's reputation for tolerance. Beissel believed that too many supposedly religious people, including the Quakers of Pennsylvania, had become enthralled to the enticements of politics, commerce, and materialism, and he hoped that Ephrata's isolated location would protect his sect members from civilization's corrupting influences.

Celibacy was a principal rule of the Ephrata community, and men and women worked, ate, worshipped, and slept in separate and distinct spaces. The Sabbath was celebrated on Saturday (unlike Catholics, Quakers, and Protestants, who celebrated Sabbath on Sunday), and prayer meetings were often held at odd hours—late at night, for example, when all the world was asleep—to add to their mystical quality. Members lived without ownership of property or goods and submitted to a strict organizational structure that governed every aspect of their lives. Their one outlet of pure joy seemed to have been music. Beissel himself had composed over one thousand hymns, which were described as embodying a "softness and devotion almost superhuman" when performed. Those outsiders lucky enough to be granted an audience noted "the peculiar sweetness and weird beauty" of the "chorals and hymns" of the Ephrata community.[22]

Peter Miller, a leader of the Ephrata during the years of the American Revolution, became a correspondent of Christopher Marshall in the early 1770s. They exchanged numerous letters in which they discussed, among other things, the practices of the Ephrata, the texts of Conrad Beissel, and the musical compositions of the sect, and Marshall helped Miller publish many of Beissel's writings. By the early 1780s, the population of the Ephrata Community had dwindled from its peak of about three hundred people to a few dozen, in part due to its requirement of absolute celibacy. But its principles of isolation from civilization, commitment to communal work, and shared rituals of faith continued to interest Marshall, and based on future events, seemed to have interested Universal Friend as well.[23]

Christopher Marshall also introduced Friend to several potential followers, including the Wilson family and their cousins, the Malins, both well-to-do Philadelphia Quaker families. The daughters and sons of both the Wilsons and the Malins were beginning to question the practices of their local Societies, and to meet a minister who had moved beyond the traditional Quaker strictures interested them greatly. Sarah and Mary Wilson, daughters of George Wilson, in particular, took it upon themselves to ingratiate themselves with Friend, inviting the minister to their stately brick home on the corner of Walnut and Third (only a ten-minute walk from Elfreth's Alley, but a world away), where they plied Friend with tea and tidbits while asking about the ministry of salvation. In the years to come, both the Wilsons and the Malins—in very different ways—would play leading roles in the direction and fate of Universal Friend's mission and message.

But no members of the Malin or the Wilson family were ready to commit themselves to the ministry of salvation in 1782. Although there were many in Philadelphia curious to see and hear this non-gendered, reborn, and robust messenger from God, only one person in the entire city took the step of actually joining the sect: Jehu Eldridge, former Quaker and a member of the Free Quakers. Eldridge was an aspiring minister himself, and he hoped to find new avenues for preaching with the sect. When Friend decided to leave Philadelphia and look elsewhere in Pennsylvania for followers, he joined Friend's group as it headed out of the city.

Why had no one else from Philadelphia joined Friend's sect? In New England, gathering new followers had been easy. But here in Philadelphia, the curiosity that brought men and women out in droves to hear what Friend had to say had not converted into acceptance of Friend as spiritual adviser. There were—and always had been—so many avenues for faith in Philadelphia, with a variety of religions existing side by side and offering their own promises of rules to live by and a solid community within which to feel safe. While Friend seemed to have provided entertainment to Philadelphians, and certainly there were many who were fascinated by the visitors from Rhode Island, the fascination failed to evolve into religious commitment.

Christopher Marshall may have been the one to suggest to Universal Friend that Worcester, a lively village about thirty miles away, would be a good place to gather new followers. Worcester had been settled in the early 1700s by European immigrants, mostly from Germany, England, and Wales. The immigrants came for the fertile farmland and also to live in a place where they could practice their faiths in peace and in safety. Mennonite, Schwenkfelder, German Reformed, and other denominations laid down roots in the area. They built homes and churches and farms, and found security and prosperity in William Penn's colony. In early 1770, Hans Supplee, a prosperous farmer with deep faith but no religious affiliation, donated land and money for the building of a nondenominational chapel of worship; after he died, his was the first body to be buried in its churchyard. Three years later the congregation devoted itself to Methodism under the influence of Joseph Pilmoor, a traveling Methodist missionary from England. Supplee's Chapel then became known as Bethel Methodist Church, offering proof to Friend that the residents of Worcester were willing to change their religious devotions if something better came along.

Friend might also have been encouraged to travel to Worcester by David Wagener, a prosperous farmer from the village who had heard Friend preach in Philadelphia. He'd been captivated by Friend's sermon, "delivered with an agreeable sweetness and elegance, with propriety . . . and in such an awful and powerful manner" that all "the truths of the gospel" had been made clear to him.[24] Wagener convinced his brother-in-law and current minister of the Methodist chapel, Reverend Abraham Supplee (son of Hans), to open his church to Universal Friend. Wagener then invited Friend and all the travelers from Rhode Island to stay as guests in his home, a large and comfortable stone farmhouse set on a hill overlooking the Schuylkill Valley.

Surrounded by apple and pear trees alight with golden leaves under an autumn sky, the farmhouse must have reminded Friend of Cumberland in the fall. For the next few weeks, the minister stayed with the Wagener family and spent time getting to know not only David but also his wife, Rebecca; his brother, Jacob, and his sister, Anna. Just like the Potters and the Richards in Rhode Island, and Christopher Marshall, the Wilsons and the Malins in Philadelphia, the Wageners found Friend easy to talk to and easy to understand, both in sermons and in conversation. From the very beginning of the ministry, Friend had believed in the power of the word itself—"thy word is a lamp unto my feet, and a light unto my path"—and took it as a God-given duty to relay the word as clearly as possible, but also with the passion of one wholly committed to saving lost souls.[25]

Elsie Potter and her father and brother, Thomas Hathaway, William Turpin, Sarah Brown—all guests in the stone farmhouse—also impressed the Wagener family; David described them as "people who feared God and worked Righteousness, and had the living Gospel of Jesus Christ amongst them, to deliver to the inhabitants of the world." The Wageners became Friend's most enthusiastic supporters in Pennsylvania, and David himself never doubted that the minister was a messenger sent directly from God to save the world: "When I heard the Gospel's Trump sound, I knew it was the true sound, and that it was with great power from on high. . . ."[26]

Nor did David entertain any doubts as to Friend's messenger status. When questioned about Jemima Wilkinson, he replied there was no such person, explaining "that if a man lives in a house, and another person removes into it, it is . . . proper to call the house not by its first name, but by that of the person who removes into it."[27] Wagener firmly believed that while the vessel was still the body of the woman, the animating spirit of the minister was a messenger sent by God, non-gendered and all-knowing. Much as William Potter, wealthy and influential, had helped buoy Friend's standing in Rhode Island, David Wagener's support would encourage people from Worcester to join the sect; and Wagener, like Potter, would offer his stone farmhouse to Friend and followers to be their home away from home.

Despite (or maybe because of) David and his family's heartfelt support of Friend's ministry, Reverend Supplee's friendliness toward Friend turned frosty, and he closed the doors of his church to gatherings of the sect. But the Wagener farmhouse was large, and David happily allowed Friend to hold meetings there. Having experienced "[g]reat and powerful meetings to the communing and embellishing of my soul," David wanted everyone to hear the minister's sermons; they were, after all, "the truth and the whole counsel of the Lord declared," and no one should be denied the chance to hear the truth.[28] He also accompanied Friend on proselytizing missions to the nearby villages of Bethlehem and Easton, where he had numerous connections. Leaving his farming duties to others, he was proud to join the minister in spreading the word of God.

With the seeds of belief finally sown in the fields of Pennsylvania, Universal Friend turned for Rhode Island and home by the end of October 1782. The travelers returned along roads bordered by bare trees and brown fields, under skies that hung low with clouds. They had to be careful how they went, with rumors flying about the roving bands of British soldiers plundering what they could before being ordered home to England. But they traveled without incident, Friend boldly taking the lead and the faithful in dutiful lines, two by two, following behind.

After the minister left Pennsylvania, Christopher Marshall wrote in his diary, "I hope this Visitation from Heaven will not soon be forgotten by many who seemed not to be reached with it."[29] Marshall had no reason to worry. The journey south had been well worth the efforts taken; as Friend made clear when preaching in Philadelphia, "if you are disposed to enter in to the way of salvation, if my discourses have softened your hearts, if I can snatch a single one of you from the danger which he runs, I have not traveled too long a road. . . ."[30] Friend was confident that the sown seeds of faith would now grow and spread in Pennsylvania, creating fertile fields ripe for redemption.

10

Message in Return

"O! The arm on which I trust is strong
And in that hope I venture boldly
In having given the troops of hell a loud alarm. . . ."

—SARAH RICHARDS

In August of 1784, Universal Friend returned to Philadelphia. Only two years had passed, but so much had changed. Five meetinghouses dedicated to the sect had gone up in the past two years, solid buildings raised up on donated land and paid for out of the generous offerings of devoted sect members. In East Greenwich, Warwick, and South Kingstown, all in Rhode Island; and in Stonington and New Milford in Connecticut, the men and women who filled the rows of the new meetinghouses were established members of their communities, known to be "persons of very honorable and Christian character"—and now they were committed, heart and soul—and purse—to the teachings of Universal Friend.[1] As Abraham Dayton explained when he and his wife, Abigail, donated land for the meetinghouse in New Milford, they wanted to support "the increase and propagation of the everlasting Gospel of Jesus Christ" and relied wholeheartedly on "the particular care and direction of a person known by the name of Universal Friend" to do so.[2]

No longer did Friend's followers need to rely on borrowed spaces in private homes or in the churches and halls of other denominations; now the ministry of salvation had homes of its own. And the buildings looked like homes: unlike Congregational or Methodist churches, the sect's meetinghouses had neither steeple nor bell tower, no wide steps leading up to arched entrances, and no long aisle down the center of the meeting space. Instead, the buildings were square shaped with unadorned shingle roofs and narrow doorways that led straight into the indoor open space. Hard benches stood in rows inside, with rows of square windows to let in light and no paintings or murals to mar the plain, whitewashed walls. Inside and outside, everything was simple and unadorned. But there was beauty in the simplicity, and in the squares of light, and in the shine of the polished wide-planked floors and wooden benches.

The new meetinghouses were proof that the sect was stable, secure, solid: a ministry that members could trust, led by a minister whom they trusted. And when Friend was away, the followers did the best they could to follow their minister's spiritual practices. Meetings were largely conducted in silence, with the silence broken only when an individual felt inspired by God to speak or to share their dreams (dreams being an important way of receiving messages from God). There was no singing before, during, or after the meetings and no shared recitations of memorized prayers or ritual oaths. But praying—openly and with vigor—was a salient characteristic of the sect. As Abner Brownell had observed, "they will pray often in public and private, and when they get alone, some of them will have such a loud voice that they may be heard a great way. . . . I knew one of her adherents make above fifty public prayers in a day and evening. . . ."[3]

Despite the vigorous praying, in all other ways their practice of faith was unlike the highly emotional practices of the Shakers with their agitated dancing and their speaking in tongues, or the outdoor revivalists' dependency on communal declarations of sins and vehemently delivered vows to repent. Instead, Friend and followers preferred to keep things calm, quiet, and peaceful, in line with practices of the Quakers. And just like the Quakers, meetings of the followers always ended in the same way whether or not the minister was in attendance. The members turned from one to the other and shook hands with each other. A final act of fellowship: a touch of flesh to vouchsafe their shared fealty and piety.

Why had Friend's ministry of salvation flourished so much in just two years? One possible reason is that there were just too many influential men with money behind the ministry for it to fail. William Potter, James Parker, Thomas Hathaway, David Wagener: all were men who knew how to get things done. Even the Daytons, though not wealthy, were prosperous enough to donate land and determined enough to see the building of the New Milford meetinghouse through to its completion. Friend's charismatic appeal and majestic appearance, and the simplicity of the delivered message—repentance through gratitude and faith, salvation guaranteed for all—also contributed to the ministry's growth.

Just as the new meetinghouses supplied a framework of physical stability to the sect, its first public declaration of faith, published in 1783, provided the spiritual framework upon which Friend hoped to grow the ministry even further. The declaration began by explaining that "Universal Friend . . . hath for several years past Labored among us with Unvaryed Pains in Preaching the Everlasting Gospel . . . [offering] Instructions, Admonitions, & Invitations in the Demonstrations of the Spirit. . . ."[4] And Friend's labors had been fruitful: "numbers of People among us have been brought out of the Kingdom of Darkness into the Kingdom of Gods Dear Son." By "obeying . . . Dear Universal Friend of Friends . . . we are redeemed from the wrath to come & brought into Union with God."[5] The declaration ended with the announcement that the sect would henceforth be known as the "Society of Universal Friends."[6]

Ann Lee's Shaker sect was also thriving, despite the attacks it suffered in the early 1780s and the death of Lee. After her death, Joseph

Meacham, a former Baptist minister, took over its leadership and began proselytizing throughout New England. Instead of building up congregations within established communities as Friend had, under the guidance of Meacham and Lucy Wright (an acolyte of Ann Lee), isolated Shaker communities were set up in rural areas where the sect's mandates of celibacy, gender segregation, and ritualistic spiritual engagement could be more easily implemented (out of the public's eye). Membership in the sect would grow over the next decade into hundreds of men and women across a dozen communities and would peak in the mid-1800s with about five thousand people living in twenty-three settlements across ten states.

The Shakers' decision to establish isolated communities, separated from the rest of the world, not only allowed them to live by their own rules, but also gave them a safe place to live and worship, far from the haranguing and threatening mobs of the past. Friend would have heard about the new communities—and must have taken note of how they flourished in their rural isolation. But for now, the focus of the Society of Universal Friends would continue to be on converting citizens of existing towns and villages, and not on setting up a community far from civilization.

In the two years since Friend last visited Philadelphia, membership of the Society of Universal Friends had broadened to include not only the wealthy and the middle class, but also those without a stable economic foothold in society—and Friend gave them a place where they were accepted and respected. These followers included African Americans, some of them newly released from enslavement, such as Chloe Towerhill (manumitted by the Brown family in 1782 because, as followers of Friend, they had become "convinced by the spirit of truth that it is unjust for us to hold any of our fellow creatures in bondage").[7] At least three of William Potter's formerly enslaved people joined the Society, and other African Americans also made their way to the Friend's community, likely drawn by the ministry's promise and practice of equality: there was "room in the many Mansions of eternal glory . . . for everyone. . . . For everyone that will come, may come. . . ."[8]

Room was also made for single women, like Ruth Pritchard from Wallingford, Connecticut. Pritchard was a schoolteacher, and as she described herself, "sincerely a seeker," who traveled "about 7 miles to hear" Universal Friend preach. She was immediately enthralled: "Blessed be the day I went; O! Blessed be the Lord for giving me this great day of visitation: And I do testify unto thee . . . it was the voice . . . that which if obey'd will bring Light Life and Love Unto the Soul; That Peace that the world can neither give nor take away. And there is nothing below the sun shall tempt me back, the Lord helping me."[9]

Entire families had always been welcomed by Friend to join the Society (the Potters, Parkers, Richards, Daytons, Smiths, Browns, Briggs, Nichols, Hathaways, Botsfords, Dains, and Hartwells), and now new families were being created within the sect. These inter-Society marriages would serve the dual purpose of passing faith down through generations and binding the sect even closer together as a group. Four of Friend's sisters married followers: Patience married Thomas Potter (son of William Potter and seven years her junior) in 1781; Elizabeth married Samuel Hartwell in 1783; Marcy married William Aldrich in the 1780s; and Deborah would marry Benajah Botsford in 1785, the same year Sarah Brown married Arnold Potter, another son of William Potter. After Benajah died, Deborah would marry another follower, Elijah Malin. Benjamin Brown Jr. (brother to Sarah) married Penelope Potter, William Potter's daughter. Mary Botsford, sister of Benajah, married Thomas Hathaway Jr., and Friend's brother Stephen eventually married Lucy Botsford, another sister of Benajah.[10]

With the support of so many New England faithful, the minister must have had great hopes for the second mission to Pennsylvania. Accompanied by Sarah Richards and Abraham Dayton from New Milford (their spouses remained at home), along with Arnold Potter and Sarah Brown (not yet married), the minister arrived in Philadelphia at the height of summer. The city was sweltering in heat and humidity, and dank smells from the riverfront—rotting fish and vegetation, salt and brine—were carried inland on the shallowest of breezes. But Universal Friend, riding into town on a new sidesaddle of leather and blue velvet, with a bright white cap over cascading black curls and a white linen tippet tied neatly at the neck, would have seemed impervious to the heat, the damp, the smells. As a girl, Jemima had ridden sidesaddle, and now as a minister, the elegance of it added a touch of resplendence to the Society's return to Philadelphia.[11]

Hundreds of men and women fought for entrance into the three meetings Universal Friend held in Philadelphia that summer. But while many turned out to see Friend, few seemed ready to commit themselves to the minister's Society. Christopher Marshall still declined to join (he did host Friend during the weeks spent in the city), and members of the Malin and Wilson families hesitated on the precipice of commitment. Once again it was the village of Worcester that offered Friend the larger bounty of souls willing to be saved. When the minister arrived there at the end of August, David and Rebecca Wagener announced that they, along with David's siblings Jacob and Anna, and several other Worcester families, were ready to commit themselves to the Society. Thomas Hathaway, newly arrived from Rhode Island in the fall of 1784, took charge of fostering the village's burgeoning congregation, and from that point on, the center of Friend's ministry in Pennsylvania would be in Worcester, and David Wagener's stone farmhouse would be its headquarters.

A new tool for recruiting converts was a pamphlet titled *The Universal Friend's Advice to Those of the Same Religious Society, Recommended to Be Read in Their Public Meetings for Divine Worship*, written by Universal Friend in 1784.[12] It was an original work (no plagiarism from other writers) that nevertheless relied heavily on biblical texts in laying out the dictates of the Society according to Friend. The eight-page, densely worded pamphlet focused on the expression of repentance and faith through thoughtful actions ("be ye holy in all your conversation") and internal growth ("Gather in all your wandering thoughts, that you may sit down in solemn silence, to wait for the aid and assistance of the HOLY SPIRIT").[13] Universal Friend had experienced an *internal* transformation in 1776, not an external one, and it was what was *inside* a person that mattered.

In the *Advice*, just as in Friend's spoken ministry, redemption was presented as a choice ("the kingdom of GOD may begin with you") with every action taken having both meaning and consequence: "Take up your daily cross against all ungodliness and worldly lusts; and live as you would be willing to die, loving one another, forgiving one another, as ye desire to be forgiven by GOD and his HOLY ONE."[14] Among followers, love and compassion were paramount to achieving salvation: "live peacably . . . and not let one thrust another";[15] "let not contention, confusion, jarring, or wrong speaking have any place. . . . Use not whisperings . . . for whisperers separate chief friends";[16] and "Let not debate, evil surmisings, jealousies, evil speaking, or hard thinking be named among you; but be at peace among yourselves."[17]

Friend's *Advice* counseled followers on how to live pious lives, in ways both practical (such as attending meeting on the tenth hour of the day "as near as possible" and to "be punctual") and profound: "shun at all times, the company and conversation of the wicked world"; "flee from bad company as from a serpent"; and "be not weary in well-doing, for, in due season, ye shall reap if ye faint not."[18] There were some strange admonitions, particularly those aimed at controlling God-inspired speech: "when you are moved to speak . . . neither add to his words, lest . . . thou be found a liar" nor "speak nor pray any longer than the SPIRIT remaineth with you; nor linger. . . ."[19] Friend must have been worried that followers would talk too long while claiming it was God himself who directed their incontinent flow.

The list of dos and don'ts laid out in the *Advice* were not absolute rules of behavior: they were guidance on how to live a moral life. For example, although Friend counseled temperance in acts of the flesh—"keep yourselves unspotted from the world and possess your vessels in sanctification and honor"—married couples were not separated in the Society and having children was supported; the *Advice* even contained long paragraphs of advice over how to raise children (which included some very strange warnings taken from Proverbs counseling children away from those "who lay in wait for their own blood; they lurk privily for their own lives . . ."). And while the *Advice* stated, "Be not drunk with wine or any other spiritous liquors," both wine and beer were part of Society meals, and Universal Friend partook of both.[20]

Friend's tolerance was notable among Separatist sects, and was based on the minister's certainty that it was through "peace" and "bonds of love"—and not through punishment, censure, and humiliation—that redemption was achieved.[21] Instead of threatening followers with expulsion or disownment for failure to live up to its dictates, the *Advice* sternly counseled them to keep trying: "work out your salvation with fear and trembling, redeeming your time, because the days are evil."[22] Friend did warn (in a paraphrase of Christ's commandment that "Ye are my friends if ye do whatsoever I command"), "Ye cannot be my friends, except ye do whatsoever I command you."[23]

But there are no records indicating that the rules laid out in the *Advice* were ever enforced through discipline, and the *Advice* itself advises against the use of threats, because God himself "is merciful and kind to even the unthankful and the evil."[24] Nor are there records of Friend ever expelling a member from the Society, even when the minister grew angry over perceived acts of wrongdoing. After all, what purpose would expulsion serve? Sinners needed spiritual guidance—especially when they made mistakes and went off course—and the minister had been charged by God to provide it. Friend believed "Piety to God & *benevolence* to thy fellow creatures, are they not great duties?"[25] The *Advice* made clear how to fulfill those duties: "DO JUSTLY. LOVE MERCY, and WALK HUMBLY WITH THY GOD! AMEN."[26]

By mid-November of 1784 the *Advice* was published, with the help of Christopher Marshall, and advertised in the Philadelphia press at the price of six pence a copy.[27] But Friend's pamphlet never sold particularly well. Friend's appeal didn't transfer to print; it was in hearing Friend speak, and spending time with other followers that new converts were made. While still lagging in converts in Philadelphia, people were joining the sect in Worcester, and in Connecticut and Rhode Island, and from other eastern states. But it was around this time that the minister, and the flock of followers, began to think about new avenues for their mission, and a redefining of the tools for its propagation.

Friend must have been influenced by the many stories circulating through the United States about a western wilderness full of opportunities for the intrepid and the determined. Perhaps the future of the Society of Universal Friends lay elsewhere than in the comfortable environs of Little Rest, the welcoming villages of Connecticut, and the more difficult territory of Pennsylvania. The mission of salvation would never change. But the how, and the where, might have to.

11

Looking Westward

"Behold, I will do a new thing;
now it shall spring forth; shall ye not know it?
I will even make a way in the wilderness,
and rivers in the desert."

—ISAIAH 43:19

In the fall of 1785, Jeptha Wilkinson set out from Rhode Island for the western counties of New York State. Whether he was sent on his mission by Friend or made the decision by himself, he went in search of the bountiful lands rumored to be found on the state's western frontier. He left behind a pregnant wife, but perhaps he thought he could complete the entire enterprise—two weeks to get there, a few weeks to take a good look around, another two weeks to travel back—and arrive home again before the baby was born. Or maybe he was willing to go for as long as it took to find what his minister was looking for. He was young and ambitious, full of boundless energy, and curious about what he would encounter out west.

Stories about New York's western frontier had begun trickling into New England during the Revolutionary War, when soldiers who had served in the Sullivan-Clinton campaign of 1779 returned home.

The campaign, planned by General George Washington and carried out by John Sullivan (with the assistance of his second-in-command, James Clinton) had one purpose: to destroy the settlements of the Haudenosaunee Confederacy in western New York in retaliation for the Confederacy's collaboration with the British. The name "Haudenosaunee" translates to "people of the longhouse," the longhouse being the structure of their homes and meeting buildings, and the Confederacy consisted of the Seneca, Cayuga, Oneida, Onondaga, Mohawk, and Tuscarora tribes. Only the Oneida and Tuscarora had sided with the Americans in the war, while the Seneca, Cayuga, Onondaga, and Mohawk tribes had sided with the redcoats.[1] Washington was explicit in his instructions that the campaign must "chastise and intimidate the hostile nations": Sullivan was to carry out "the total destruction and devastation of their settlements, and the capture of as many prisoners of every age and sex as possible" (with the prisoners to be held as hostages).[2] Sullivan was also ordered to "ruin their crops now in the ground and prevent their planting more."[3]

In June of 1779, Sullivan and Clinton led their troops through Pennsylvania and up into western New York to carry out their campaign of destruction. The soldiers were surprised by the prosperity of the Native American villages, with their long rows of wood-framed and glass-windowed homes surrounded by large fields of all kinds of vegetables and extensive fruit orchards—but they wasted no time in setting it all on fire: the houses; the peach, cherry, and apple trees; the crops growing in the fields; "tents, rum, cheese, wine, and articles of store."[4] Washington's mandate that "the country . . . not be merely overrun, but destroyed" was fulfilled as ordered.[5]

Over five thousand Native Americans fled to British-held Fort Niagara for refuge, while of those who remained behind, at least two hundred were killed. Forty Native American villages were burned to the ground; 160,000 bushels of corn were destroyed; and, as Sullivan reported to Congress, there was "not a single settlement or field of corn [left in] the country . . . nor is there any appearance of an Indian on this side of Niagara."[6] The utter destruction of villages, crops, and hundreds of acres of fields left the Native Americans "in a miserable situation," wrote Sullivan, and they would be "unlikely to return to their homelands."[7] Washington became known among the Haudenosaunee as "Conotocaurious, or Town Destroyer" for the devastation he had wreaked upon hundreds of acres of their lands.[8]

Just as Washington had ordered, the Sullivan-Clinton campaign left "fleeing residents [with] . . . nothing to return home to."[9] For a society that was dependent on what they could produce from the land, the utter destruction of their crops was, as one historian put it, "tantamount to imposing a death sentence on all geographically proximate Indian peoples. . . ."[10] And in the brutal winter months that followed the campaign, the death sentence was carried out when over 4,500 Native Americans died of exposure, starvation, and disease brought about by their brutal displacement, equaling over 50 percent of the entire Haudenosaunee population.[11]

New England soldiers returning from the Sullivan-Clinton campaign spoke little about the annihilation they had wrought on the Native Americans. Instead, they talked about the beauty and bounty of the western lands: thickly wooded forests and flourishing meadows, hundreds of streams and lakes full of fish, and green hills and valleys under an all-encompassing blue sky. They recounted how the Native Americans living there had produced abundant harvests of corn and vegetables, even while "using the most primitive of implements, and with but indifferent cultivation."[12] Their observations of the huge crops, to which they had set fire with abandon, were accurate, but their understanding of Native American farming was without merit. The Haudenosaunee clans had been successively tilling and rotating crops with a sophisticated knowledge of plant husbandry for generations and had been generous in teaching arriving colonists how to successively cultivate the lands of the New World.[13]

The soldiers' effusive stories were seconded by Anglican missionaries to the area, who wrote of finding "a new Eden" in western New

York.[14] With the farmlands in New England overworked and largely rocky, the promise of new opportunities—of lands both rich and abundant—did seem to be a gift from God. And with the Sullivan campaign having effectively cleared the area of its Native American inhabitants, after the war white settlers from the East began trickling in to stake their claims to what Washington himself had termed "*our* frontiers."[15]

Jeptha Wilkinson arrived on the western frontier sometime in late October or early November of 1785. He spent the next few months "exploring and mapping" the lands in and around the lakes of western New York.[16] He assessed everything he saw with an eye for possible settlement: large stands of hard maple (good for syrup), white oak (for building homes and meetinghouses), and hickory and chestnut trees (nuts for sustenance). The woods were full of deer and game birds, the rivers stocked with fish, and the meadows bordered with an abundance of berry bushes and fruit trees. Everything they would need to build a new community seemed to be right there waiting for them.

Then winter arrived, suddenly and brutally, with deep snow, freezing temperatures, and icy winds. Jeptha would not have survived if not for the help of the small Native American communities he encountered. He must have been thankful that General Sullivan had been wrong in his assessment that no locals remained in the area, and just as thankful that both Sullivan and Washington had grossly distorted their supposedly warlike mentality. Jeptha experienced only kindness from the men and women he met. They provided him with shelter, a warm bed under the rafters of their wood-plank homes, and offered him sustenance, as well as helped him with his mapping, for weeks at a time. Having traded for years with both English and French traders, the local Native Americans could communicate easily with Jeptha, and he learned from them not only lessons on surviving the winter but also heard their stories about the ample summer harvests.

When Jeptha finally returned to Rhode Island in early spring of 1786, his wife met him at the door with a daughter named Nancy, born in January. Jeptha would have hugged his wife and daughter, and then quickly gone to report to Universal Friend and other members of the Society about all he had seen and experienced on the western frontier. He told them about the generosity of the Native Americans and assured them as to the beauty and fertility of the land. Encouraged by Jeptha's stories—and perhaps in response to a direct request by his minister—shortly after Jeptha's return to Rhode Island, Ezekiel Shearman, a twenty-six-year-old sect member and brother-in-law of James Parker, set out for New York to see for himself what there was to be found in the ancient homelands of the Native Americans.

Like Jeptha, Shearman traveled on his own all the way—more than three hundred miles—to the western frontier of New York State. But Shearman was less impressed with what he saw on his journey. He found the Native Americans to be hostile, and, according to him, deservedly so. He saw for himself the remains of the villages and fields destroyed by the Sullivan campaign and felt in his bones a resistance to settling under that shadow of destruction: it was just "too soon to enter the sad, dark land of the lakes."[17] Shearman suffered more than Jeptha had during his trip, fighting his way for days at a time through the deep spring snows, enduring bitter cold, and "sleeping at night on cedar boughs laid out in the snow."[18] He returned east with doubts as to how welcoming the western frontier would be to a pioneering settlement of the faithful.

And yet despite Shearman's doubts, Universal Friend and the Society began contemplating whether western New York presented an opportunity for them. During a meeting held in the New Milford meetinghouse in October of 1786, Friend and followers debated the idea of westward migration and then took a vote on whether they should purchase lands in New York. Although the number of votes made in favor of moving is not recorded, the proposal to leave the towns and villages they knew and head off into the unknown seemed to have been met with enthusiasm. Whether Universal Friend had to be persuaded to move the Society west (by followers ambitious for a new start in life) or had been the first to think of it is not known. But the records of that October meeting indicate that by the fall of 1786, the Society membership was eager to build a settlement in the wilderness. Even Ezekiel Shearman signed on to the venture, though he may still have harbored some doubts.

But how to pay for the lands upon which the western settlement would be built? The followers and their minister began considering alternatives. And again, they came to an agreement: "the land was to be purchased in one piece for the whole community . . . [but] it was not to be owned in common."[19] Suitable lands out west would be paid for through funds donated by those members of the Society who could afford to do so, and each of those purchasers would receive an allotment in proportion to the amount of money they had contributed to the fund for purchasing property. For those followers who wished to be a part of the new community but didn't have enough money to contribute to the purchasing fund, they would receive a smaller allotment in return for work performed in the settlement; as James Parker later explained, "we intended to helped them to Some Lands because they could not help themselves" and once arrived at the new community, everyone was "Expected to raise Support for them Selves and family."[20] Parker, who had recently been relieved of the duty of leading the Society's mission in Pennsylvania, was now placed in charge of collecting funds for buying property out west and issuing receipts to those members who could afford to contribute.

The land-purchase plan created by the Society of Universal Friends during the meeting in New Milford aligned with how many Quaker settlements in America had been founded (i.e., as individually owned lots creating a cohesive whole), indicating the influence that Friend's upbringing—and the upbringing of many of the Society members—had on the administrative aspects of the sect. The Society of Universal Friends didn't believe in communally held property, in contrast to outlier sects like the Shakers or the Ephrata. While followers of Friend willingly shared resources with each other as needed, their farms, properties, and profits would belong to them alone, and the choice to share would be theirs as well.

This process of decision-making, with discussion among all the members of the Society and a sharing of opinions across genders, ages, and economic backgrounds, was also similar to Quaker Society practices. As the plan for western migration developed and then the settlement itself came into being, it would become the accepted mode for reaching consensus among Society members. What is perhaps most striking about the process was that while Universal Friend may have served as the spiritual leader of the sect, when it came to administrative, financial, and practical matters, decisions were made through communal consensus. The strict hierarchy that prevailed in traditional churches, as well as sects such as the Shakers, did not exist within the Society of Universal Friends.

While the community-based and nonhierarchical decision-making process served the Society well in the years of planning and implementing a move west, did Universal Friend ever consider that the process might, in the future, be abused by members interested in goals that had little to do with faith and more to do with personal gain? Could Friend have foreseen that the lure of profit would turn the heads of certain members away from their spiritual commitments and dissolve their loyalty to Friend and the Society? Based on records of the compact made in the fall of 1786, at that time everyone in the community, including Friend, shared the same vision for their future, and there were no cracks in the walls of fellowship.[21] The land was to be purchased as a group, and then settled lot by lot, family by family, and anyone contributing to the building of the community would receive a fair share of it.

It was a utopian dream, but also a practical one: giving men and women the chance to own their own parcel of property as long as they were willing to work hard would create a stable and prosperous settlement. Each family would grow enough for themselves, for the community, and, with luck, enough to sell to outsiders as well. Given the stories they had heard about the bountiful wilderness awaiting them, the dream seemed imminently achievable.[22] In the year ahead, the plan to move west would not only seem desirable, it would become necessary. An unforeseen threat loomed on the horizon, posing danger not only to the messenger but also to members of the Society.

12

An Accusation of Murder

"As the tempest and the thunder affect not the Sun nor the Stars
but open their fury on the stones and trees below;
So injuries offend not the Souls of the greats
but waste themselves on such as are those who offer them."

—ROBERT DODSLEY

In the fall of 1786, Sarah Richards, newly widowed and living in Friend's household at Little Rest, was sent on a mission by her minister. Efforts to bolster the Society's congregation in Worcester had faltered in the past months, and Friend had summoned James Parker, who had been entrusted with sect affairs throughout Pennsylvania, back to Rhode Island. Not only had Parker failed to convert new followers in Worcester—which should have been easy with the help of the Wagener family—but he had made no headway in Philadelphia. Christopher Marshall and the Free Quakers who had been so hospitable to Universal Friend turned their backs on a man they seemed to distrust on sight, and they would not even let Parker use their meetinghouse for gatherings. Perhaps Parker was distraught over the recent death of his wife, Elizabeth, and missed his daughters back in Little Rest, but whatever the reasons for his ineptitude, Friend relieved him of his post, and asked Sarah to go in his stead.

Ever since Sarah and her seven-year-old daughter, Eliza, had moved into the Abbey, Friend had been struck by Sarah's diligence and piety. By the summer of 1786, Sarah had been entrusted with leading meetings in Rhode Island and Connecticut. Despite her frail and petite stature, Sarah showed exceptional ability as a preacher, easily commanding a room with her surprisingly strong (and at times, sharp) voice. Although infrequent, the epileptic fits that Sarah endured served as a tool in the young woman's preaching style; the trancelike states she endured inspired widely spread stories about how "she appears for some time dead" and then, "upon recovering" she talks of having "conversed with the dead [and having been] conducted by the archangel to distant parts of this world . . . sees what mankind is doing."[1] Richards herself claimed to receive "divine enlightenment" during visits she made to heaven while unconscious.[2]

Sarah dressed like Friend in long robes, and wore her hair uncovered and untethered like Friend, allowing it to hang free to her shoulders. There were those who found her appearance dismaying—"in her external appearance, and particularly in wearing her hair down like a man, she is . . . somewhat disfigured"[3]—but to members of the Society, she seemed the perfect helpmeet to carry out Universal Friend's mission. She was wholly committed, as she wrote in her journal, to fighting "amidst ten thousand dangers, Spiritual Enemys all athirst for blood," because she was certain that under the spiritual direction of Universal Friend, she would achieve an "immortal crown."[4]

When Friend asked Sarah to take over the ministry of salvation in Pennsylvania, Sarah agreed, as she did to all the requests made by her "dear friend dear indeed to my soul."[5] The travel demands of the mission would be hard on her, given her fragile health, and would also prevent her young daughter, Eliza, from coming along. But Sarah trusted in God for her health, and with so many able women living in the mansion—the Wilkinson sisters, Hitty Smith, Ruth Pritchard, Elsie Potter—she knew that Eliza would be well cared for. Universal Friend's relationship with Eliza during the months that Sarah was away is not documented, but later events indicate that the child resented both the minister who sent her mother away and the mother who had so willingly left. In the diary Sarah kept while traveling she never mentioned Eliza, except for one passing comment: "I think much of the dear ties I have Left behind."[6]

On her way south, Sarah made a stop in New Milford to pick up Abigail Dayton. Abigail was a woman of strong opinions and unyielding confidence, with a reputation for tireless devotion to whatever she set her mind to. Working side by side with her husband, Abraham, she helped to make their farm and mill operations—wood, corn, and grains—prosperous. When she joined Friend's sect in 1778 at the age of twenty-eight, Abigail became just as fervent a contributor to the cause of salvation as she had been to the tending of her family's prosperity. Together with her husband, they provided the land and money for building Friend a meetinghouse in the village, and in the years that followed, did all they could to support the congregation there. Now, approaching the age of forty, she was as confident as ever that Universal Friend was God's own messenger, a leader to be trusted and supported.

Sarah kept a detailed diary of their journey south, filling it with complaints about the weather (rain, sleet, snow), the terrible state of the roads, the large number of dangerous river crossings, and the awful lodgings they were forced to endure—"hard fare . . . [and] Savage people," and horrible hosts: "the people here are not unlike the Swine, the dirt seems to be their Element, we leave this house without Reluctance."[7] She often found herself unnerved by the lack of simple good manners in the people she encountered: "how little Affinity these people have [with] the noble race of beings they might be Expected to Imitate, we leave them without regret. . . ."[8]

Despite the hardships, Sarah and Abigail held spiritual meetings wherever they could, and Sarah duly noted both successes and failures in her diary: "We have a Comfortable meeting today Because we meet the Lord . . . the wicked come also like criminals to hear their doom yet They seem determined to go Laughing to hell."[9] Meetings concluded, Sarah and Abigail would have gotten back on their horses and continued on their way, eager to find an inn for the night and a meal before sleep. The next day, another early rising, a settling of accounts, and then they were back on the road.

But while the journey was "long and tedious," the task Sarah had undertaken—in which "I hazard my frail life" (an exaggeration of both the state of the roads and the inns) was for the glory of God and peace in the everlasting. And Sarah was confident that she was not alone on her journey: "the Arm on which I trust is strong. . . ."[10] Whether she meant the arm of God or the arm of Universal Friend is unclear, but perhaps in her mind, they were one and the same.

Parables of faith were to be found in every encounter or occurrence, from losing an oar during a remote ferry crossing—"time to sit and think of him that holds the waters in the hollow of his hand"—to waking up in the morning: "O Blessed Morning that reminds of the triumph over death." When snow fell, Sarah rejoiced over the "innocence . . . represented in the snowy mantle." After crossing the Delaware River, she wrote, "it puts me in mind of death, O if I can have the protections of holy Angels while Crossing the Cold flood and Land Safe on the immortal Shores of Bliss . . . it will be enough. . . ." Even a funeral procession was viewed with a kind of joy: "I have met with nothing So Edifying as the Sight of a funeral procession and the Passing Bell, it salutes my Ears with this Alarming warning 'be ye also ready'. . . ."[11]

In late December of 1786, the weary travelers finally arrived in Worcester, where they were welcomed into the warmth and comfort of David Wagener's stone farmhouse. Summing up the trip in her diary, Sarah compared it to the journey of life, during which one struggles onward in the hopes of finding peace in the end: "O my Soul with regard to my heavenly home the nearer my approach, the more engaged . . . we arrive Safe just in the Evening . . . am much rejoiced to meet my friends here, indeed it is a hospitable home. . . ."[12]

A few days later, on the evening of January 3, 1787, David Wagener hosted a meeting of the faithful in his farmhouse, and Sarah took charge of leading it. Among those attending were Anna Styer (a friend of the Wageners from Worcester), and Rachel Malin, Sarah Wilson, and Mary Wilson, all of whom had traveled to Worcester from Philadelphia. When Sarah and Mary had finally decided to join the Society of Universal Friends (after Friend's 1784 visit to Philadelphia), their father, George Wilson, supported their decision. But when Mary subsequently abandoned her husband, George blamed the spousal desertion on Universal Friend and tried, unsuccessfully, to convince his daughters to leave the sect. Two years later and his daughters were as committed as ever. Mary was still estranged from her husband, and the two sisters had traveled the thirty miles from Philadelphia to Worcester to attend the new year gathering.

The meeting began in silence, as was the practice for Society gatherings, and then Sarah spoke at length, possibly about her own conversion to the ministry of salvation and her devotion to Friend. Following her testimony, the guests began talking all together, sharing their experiences of faith and their hopes for the future. By Sarah Richards's account, nothing out of the ordinary happened, and later that evening she wrote in her diary, "we have a Comfortable meeting this day."[13]

But not everyone in attendance agreed with Sarah's assessment. According to a letter published in *The Freeman's Journal* (a Philadelphia newspaper) in March of 1787, the meeting had been contentious from the start. The letter contained allegations made by Sarah Wilson that Abigail Dayton had taken offense at many of Wilson's comments, especially when Wilson questioned the teachings of Universal Friend (perhaps George Wilson's arguments had been persuasive after all, planting seeds of doubt in the mind of at least one of his daughters). When Sarah Wilson argued that the "strange phenomena" that supposedly proved Universal Friend's divine powers might be "accounted for in a natural way," Abigail Dayton allegedly threatened her, warning her "to take care . . . for very strange things had happened to people who spoke against the Friend; that sudden deaths happened to some, and great misfortunes to others."[14]

After the meeting concluded, the women from Philadelphia, who had been invited by the Wageners to spend the night, went upstairs to parcel out the available beds. Sarah Wilson would share a room with Abigail Dayton and Anna Styer; her sister Mary presumably was sent to share a room with Sarah Richards. In the middle of the night, according to Sarah Wilson, Abigail Dayton had tried to strangle her bedmate Anna Styer in a mistaken attempt to attack Sarah Wilson herself; Sarah claimed to have seen Dayton "with one of her hands at the young woman's throat, and the other upon her mouth and nose, endeavoring to stop her breath."[15] Wilson alleged that when she accused Abigail Dayton of the crime, Dayton ordered Wilson to lie down and be quiet. But instead, Wilson "jumped out of the bed" and declared that she "would sooner lay with a serpent. . . ."[16] (Sarah Wilson never described Anna Styer's reaction to the alleged attempt on her life, and no record exists of anything Styer ever had to say about the incident.)

According to Sarah Wilson, Sarah Richards then came into the bedroom to see what all the yelling was about. After hearing Wilson's accusation against Dayton, Sarah Richards suggested that perhaps the devil had taken the form of Dayton's body. Wilson replied that she "had more charity for the devil than to believe any such thing."[17] In the letter written to the newspaper, Wilson alleged that Sarah Richards threatened her with bodily harm if she persisted in her claims, describing a vision she'd had in which "she saw a large field with a grave in it, and that I [Sarah Wilson] stood with one foot in it, and the other on the brink . . . she saw me suspended in the air, and a drop of water hanging over my head, which was the last drop of mercy that ever would be offered to me . . . that I had let in seven devils, and she saw an Angel with a flaming sword ready to cut me in two."[18]

Sarah Wilson would not back down from her accusation that Abigail Dayton had tried to "murder me, and then to have my sudden death represented to the world as a judgment from the Almighty. . . ."[19] Along with the allegations of attempted murder, the anonymous letter writer reporting Sarah Wilson's claims accused the entire Society of Universal Friends of deliberately creating "mischiefs" in families, separating "Men from their wives, and wives from their husbands" and sowing "confusion wherever they have been."[20] Blame for both the attempted murder and the chaos within families was laid firmly at the feet of Universal Friend as leader of the Society: for "what better can be expected where a number of people make it a point implicitly to observe the directions of a woman not in her senses."[21] The letter writer condemned those followers who "implicitly observe all her directions, and would not dare without her consent to attempt so horrid an enterprise as that of TAKING AWAY LIFE, when they are known to wait her *will* or *pleasure* in transactions of inferior consequence and the most trifling nature."[22]

In February of 1787, before the accusation of murder appeared in the press, there was an editorial piece in *The Freeman's Journal* that described Universal Friend's followers as "villainous imposters" and claimed that while the "religious imposture . . . is too ridiculous in itself . . . some virtuous people are, and some may yet be drawn into the snare and by degrees at length, involved in the most fatal of labyrinth of error."[23] Paragraphs were devoted to explaining how "her followers do not admit she is a woman, as a Female messiah appears an incongruity, and they therefore of consequence deny her name. . . ." Friend's appearance was described in great detail; both hair and dress "convey the same idea . . . of her being neither man nor woman."[24]

Male members of the Society were described as "making eunuchs of themselves" and Universal Friend as "more like a man than a woman."[25] On March 14, members of the Society were accused of being dangerous purveyors of false religion, with Friend accused of outright blasphemy and the followers of being "the prophets we are cautioned to beware of . . . that come in sheeps cloathing and are inwardly ravening wolves."[26] And on March 28, a front-page article appeared in *The Freeman's Journal* criticizing Friend for "the impropriety of her dress and appearance as a man . . . more especially so in coming to this city . . . in a religious character."[27]

Some positive press about the Society had been published in Philadelphia, with a letter in the *Journal* praising the Society for being equal to "the strictest of Quakers for decency and plainness" and referring to Sarah Richards as "a valuable and amiable woman."[28] But Universal Friend must have wondered what was causing the barrage of negative reports.

What seems never to have occurred to Friend was that disgruntled family members—like George Wilson—could stir up trouble for the Society of Universal Friends. The minister's *Advice* published in 1784 had warned followers against spreading "news, or the public reports of anyone"—and now Friend was convinced that it was the rumors and allegations spread by outsiders that were proving dangerous.[29] Writing to Sarah Richards even before Wilson's allegations appeared in *The Pennsylvania Gazette*, Friend assured her that "I have been very much troubled about thee for fear of the Treacherous Dealers. . . . I have been to Philadelphia more than once and am some acquainted with the people there. . . . And we know if it were possible, they would deceive the very Elect!" The minister warned, "be ye Wise as Serpent and harmless as Doves, that Nothing be able to harm or hurt you," and condemned the promulgators of rumors as "fearful and unbelieving & abominable Dogs & sorcerers and Whore Mungers and all Lyers."

With either wrathful glee or with somber despair—it's hard to tell from the letter itself—Friend added that the rumormongers "shall have their part in the Lake that Burnes with fire and brimstone"—for God would surely dispense justice in good time. In an effort to soothe Sarah and her fellow travelers in Pennsylvania, Friend assured them that "the wicked will find some other Business to do before it is too long besides publishing [against] me. . . . Don't be troubled, Dear Soul."[30]

But in the months following Sarah Wilson's allegations, more negative pieces were published in *The Freeman's Journal* and other Pennsylvania newspapers; some rehashed the story that Abigail had tried to strangle Sarah in her sleep, and accused Universal Friend and members of the Society of insanity, fraud, and downright evil intentions toward the innocent who fell under their sway: "What security has Mrs. Wilson, whose escape from death at that time was purely providential? . . . [What if] she should be ever so unfortunate as to fall into their hands again?"[31]

An enraged public demanded that Universal Friend and the Society be charged for the murderous assault on Sarah Wilson (although it was Anna Styer who had allegedly been attacked): "Ought not so diabolical a transaction be immediately inquired into by those who are in authority?"[32] And beyond charging them, a letter published in August proposed another punishment for members of the Society: "in this State there are gallows for rogues, and bedlams for mad folks."[33] Ann Lee had been imprisoned in Bedlam in England for preaching against the grain of tradition; would followers of Universal Friend now face the same fate?

In the fall of 1787, after months of silence, Abigail Dayton finally offered a public denial of the charges brought against her by Sarah Wilson. While she corroborated Sarah's story of having shared a bedroom in the Wagener home on the evening of January 3, Dayton said that the accusation of attempted murder was "absolutely false as ever anything was true." In fact, according to Dayton, it was Sarah who acted out "in a rage" and "very strangely" that evening. She described Wilson's allegations as typical of "the persecution" that is "always pursuing the prophets of the Lord, as it was in the days of Elijah," and declared that she (like Elijah) chose to flee "to the mountain of the Lord, or truth itself."[34]

Strangely, neither Anna Styer nor Mary Wilson nor any of the Wageners ever spoke out publicly about what had happened that night in the Wagener home. Perhaps their reticence was based on the biblical counsel to let God himself deliver justice: "Dearly beloved, avenge not yourselves, but rather give place unto wrath: for it is written, Vengeance is mine, I will repay, saith the Lord."[35] Friend's *Advice* had also directed followers to "shun . . . the company and conversation of the wicked world . . . ," which would preclude speaking out against gossipmongers and false accusers, who were sure to be very wicked indeed.[36]

No criminal or civil charges were ever brought against Abigail Dayton, but the Society of Universal Friends did lose members, including ones who had seemed so devoted. Perhaps it should have been no surprise when Sarah Wilson's sister, Elizabeth Beyerley, and her husband withdrew their support. Ever since Sarah Richards's arrival in Pennsylvania they had been kind to her, offering their home for religious meetings (which were attended by large numbers of followers); inviting Sarah to spend the night with them; and treating her to elaborate meals, including one where, with "wonderful kindness," Sarah was treated to a dinner of "oysters and . . . wine." She enjoyed that meal so much that she wrote about it in her diary: "Surely this is the Lords doings."[37]

But following her sister's accusations of attempted murder, Elizabeth broke off all contact with Sarah Richards and the Society and joined the Church of England, where, as Sarah wrote to Universal Friend, she had been "baptized and taken sacraments"; Sarah concluded that like her sister Sarah Wilson, who was "not only wicked but wickedness itself," Elizabeth was "two fold more a Child of hell than Before. . . ."[38]

Not long after Elizabeth's defection, Sarah Wilson's sister Mary also abandoned the Society. She had been living happily with Sarah Richards in Worcester for months, but now she returned to Philadelphia and to her husband. Mary's defection would have been especially painful for Sarah. She had written often about "my dear Mary" in her diary and noted how happy they were together—"I sleep with my dear Mary . . . and wake with Astonishment." (Early Americans were used to sharing beds, not only because bed space was limited, but also as a comfort and for warmth, and not necessarily for sexual fulfillment.)[39] Sarah had taken care of Mary when she was "quite sick" with "the ague" and rejoiced when she recovered: "I want to have a more grateful sense of God's mercy. . . ."[40] Having lost her husband, and with Universal Friend far away in Rhode Island (along with her daughter, Eliza), Mary Wilson's affectionate friendship had filled a need in Sarah—and now the space was empty again.

Sarah Wilson and Universal Friend met by chance on the streets of Philadelphia a few months after Mary returned home. Coming face-to-face with the minister, Sarah broke down and admitted to having made up the entire story about Abigail Dayton. She explained that she had been persuaded to fabricate the allegations of attempted murder and implied that it was her father who directed the campaign of lies.[41] But a retraction of the accusation was never printed in any paper, and although no new allegations would appear, Friend must have understood that the threat of public condemnation would always be there, and could be used as an effective tool against the Society. As long as the Society persisted in its mission, and perhaps more importantly, continued to be led by what many considered to be that most inappropriate of creatures, a woman, the sect would not be safe.

While there may have been hope that in a new nation founded on ideals of equality, the gender of a person wouldn't limit their opportunities or possibilities, things weren't exactly turning out that way—and Universal Friend quite possibly understood that the negative press about the Society was more than just the work of one man trying to get his daughters back (and return one daughter to her husband). Delegates from around the nation were gathering in Philadelphia to struggle with the growing and complicated problems of managing a nation made up of thirteen separate states. Across the nation, citizens were angry about increasingly higher taxes, the stagnant economy, and state and local government dysfunction. Could the lurid newspaper stories be understood as a signal of American anxiety in response to the problems? Was anyone who fell outside the norms of social, religious, and political discourse at risk of being attacked simply because of their differences? The backlash of conservatism seemed to grow out of the need to find order and normalcy in a world that had been turned upside down by war—and had yet to right itself.

13

Time for Change

"In God have I put my trust:
I will not be afraid what man can do unto me."

—PSALM 56:11

Universal Friend had been successful in gathering followers during the years of the American Revolution by promising to guide them toward repentance and salvation before it was too late. But the world had changed: having achieved independence, Americans weren't looking for spiritual guidance or worried about the end of times. They wanted success and security in the here and now, which they saw as the bounty they had been promised for winning freedom from England. For those men leading the new country, the biggest challenge to providing the promised benefits of independence was the fact that the economy of the new country was unstable and would remain that way until the war debts had been paid off. But how to pay off those debts without overtaxing Americans while also coaxing the listless economy back to life?

The ideals for which the Revolution had been fought, including equal opportunity, liberty in life, and freedom of religion, were placed firmly on the back burner while both state and federal officials struggled with the very basic issue of money. How to get it, how to use it, and how to make more of it so that the economy of the United States could regain the vigor and growth it had enjoyed for so many decades before the British started interfering with duties, customs, and taxes. The rest of the world was loathe to lend money to or engage in trade with the new nation until war debts had been paid, the currency stabilized, and an effective federal government established.

The Articles of Confederation, passed in 1781 by the Continental Congress, gave the states the sole authority to raise funds, and each state had gone about it in their own way. Bonds were issued, taxes levied, and paper money was churned out—or some combination of the three was implemented.[1] When the federal government demanded that states help pay off foreign debts (to countries that had helped finance the war) as well as domestic debts (such as bonds sold to Americans to fund the war or used as payment in exchange for military service or supplies), many states refused to contribute. They had their own bills to pay, as well as difficulties in collecting taxes from citizens with nothing left to give.[2]

State taxes had never been so high (with most colonists paying three or four times what they had paid under the British); property foreclosures were rampant; and only those with capital to invest in debt instruments were making any money at all. Speculators bought up bonds and other debt certificates at well below their face value from people desperate for cash (including soldiers who had been paid with certificates instead of cash during the last years of the war) and then sold them for a profit during government redemptions (Abigail Adams was one such speculator, much to the chagrin of her husband, John).[3]

The inequity of the financial burdens was felt deeply, especially among the farming class, many of whom had been the soldiers left with almost nothing by the end of the war. Without the means to pay their taxes or meet their own debts, farmers were losing their lands to foreclosures and struggling to survive; it must have especially angered them that their taxes were considerably higher than they had been under

British rule. Farmers' frustrations led to uprisings, such as the one led by Daniel Shays in Massachusetts in 1786, which ended in a bloody showdown between Governor James Bowdoin's privately funded army and the farmers. Many of the rebelling farmers fled the state, many more were arrested, and some were shot dead. By the summer of 1787, John Hancock, the newly elected governor, issued pardons for some of the rebels (including Shays himself) and the state legislature placed a moratorium on debts while also cutting taxes. While these measures may have eased the farmers' burdens, they also increased the state's own economic woes.

In May of 1787, representatives from twelve states agreed to meet in Philadelphia, in what came to be known as the Constitutional Convention, in order to "render the constitution of the United States adequate to the exigencies of the Union."[4] In other words, in order to figure out a way to raise desperately needed money and to rein in the wildly divergent economic policies of the states. The thirteenth state, Rhode Island—nicknamed "Rogue Island" in the press—refused to send delegates to the convention largely due to its concerns about granting too much power to a central government.[5] According to a letter printed in *The Freeman's Journal*, Rhode Island also objected to proposals that would have allowed the continued importation of enslaved persons in the United States when Rhode Island had already prohibited such trade within its own borders, having "outdone even the State of Pennsylvania in the glorious work of freeing the negroes in this country. . . ."[6] (If Universal Friend had been more involved in politics, surely this stance of the minister's home state would have brought a flush of pride and satisfaction.)

George Washington arrived in Philadelphia in May of 1787, traveling from Virginia and "escorted into the city by the troop of horses . . . and saluted at his entrance by the artillery . . . and the ringing of bells."[7] Given the hoopla, did the state delegates have any choice but to name him as president of the Convention? Washington was put in charge of overseeing the proceedings through the summer and into the fall.

While the initial plan may have been to revise the Articles of Confederation, it quickly became clear that an entirely new system of national governance had to be created, one which would give greater powers to the federal government and compel the thirteen former colonies to work together in governing the United States. Over the next five months, Washington presided over the fights and eventual compromises that would lead to the American Constitution.

Under the new Constitution, the representatives agreed to give Congress the authority to levy taxes and set tariffs, as well as to coin money and regulate its value, so that the looming debts of war could be paid not only to foreign nations but also to American citizens.[8] Another important matter that was resolved through a series of compromises was the issue of state representation in the federal government. The Confederation Congress (under the Articles of Confederation) had been ineffective not only because its authority was limited but also because not enough representatives actually showed up to make a quorum for decisions. Even the signing of the Treaty of Paris, which formally ended the war with Great Britain, was delayed for weeks because the required quorum of representatives from at least nine states could not be summoned to Congress.[9] The delegates meeting in Philadelphia in 1787 agreed to a two-part Congress, a House of Representatives and a Senate, with two delegates from each state serving in the Senate and representation in the House calculated according to state population (leading to the provision that enslaved persons counted as three-fifths persons for the purpose of apportioning representation in the house and electoral votes).

The issue of slavery was also hotly debated, with many of the northern delegates pushing to eradicate it; the fight for independence, after all, had been a fight for liberty. Strangely enough, even some southern slave owners urged for the prohibition of slavery under the Constitution as a matter of principle and morality. Luther Martin of Maryland, who owned six enslaved persons, declared that "it was inconsistent with the principles of the revolution and dishonorable to the American character to have such a feature in the Constitution," and George Mason of Virginia, who owned hundreds of enslaved persons, warned "Providence punishes national sins by national calamities."[10]

The final compromise reached by the delegates prohibited the foreign trade of slaves beyond 1808, but within the boundaries of the United States, the selling and transporting of slaves could continue unabated, and the practice of slavery would continue. The line between who deserved liberty and who did not had been drawn. Even Rhode Island would eventually agree to the slavery compromise when it ratified the Constitution in May of 1790 (it was the last state to do so).[11]

And what about the other ideals for which the American Revolution had been fought? Freedom of religion, freedom of conscience, security from an overreaching state? The Constitution made no mention of these promises and it was only with the addition of the Bill of Rights in 1791 (constituting the first ten amendments to the Constitution) that the rights to freedom of speech, free exercise of religion, freedom of assembly, a free press, and security in one's home and person against unwarranted search and seizure would be guaranteed (subject, of course, to legislative and judicial enforcement).[12]

Universal Friend left behind no writings—no letters or journal entries—about the doings of the Constitutional Convention. There was no mention in Friend's sermons about the aspirations of the Founding Fathers gathered in Independence Hall nor are there any written records of discussions involving Friend in any forum about the need for a Bill of Rights. Friend's goals for the ministry—and hopes for the Society itself—came not from a political ideology but from a firm faith in God; and perhaps most importantly, a faith that God had bestowed his messenger with clear guidance on what was the right thing to do in the world on earth: "DO JUSTLY, LOVE MERCY, and WALK HUMBLY. . . ."[13] And yet despite Friend's lack of political involvement, it would be the minister, in leading the Society of Universal Friends, who would go further in trying to implement the principles for which the Revolution had been fought—liberty, equality, and self-determination—than any other community of its time. But such achievements lay in the future. Now Friend had to decide how to handle the problems of the present.

As the Constitutional Convention drew to a close in the fall of 1787, its delegates scattering to their home states to rally support for ratification of the new Constitution, Universal Friend accepted that the time had come for the Society of Friends to also make a new start. The minister was weary of trying to convert "those . . . who in their hearts are turn'd and turning . . . that will not obey the truth. . . ."[14] If the people of Philadelphia so violently resisted the minister's message of repentance and redemption and sought to throw followers in an asylum or hang them from some gallows, there was little reason to pursue potential converts there. Friend warned David Wagener away from the lures of the city, pleading with him, "O do dear soul, haste, Escape!"[15] But Worcester, Wagener's hometown, could also prove dangerous for the Society: the taint of the Philadelphia press followed its members even as the congregation in Worcester grew.

From its inception, Friend's ministry had offered opportunities for all to come and be saved, man or woman, Black or white or Native American. In order to protect all those who had joined the Society, the locus of Friend's mission would have to change. Providing a spiritual sanctuary for followers was no longer enough; the time had come to find an actual physical refuge for the Society's members. A place where they could be safe from lies, accusations, and threats. Friend had never trusted governments to supply such a place: only God, "mightyer than the Noise of many waters, ye than the Mighty waves of the sea," could provide the refuge Friend's followers needed.[16]

A community established on the western frontier lands explored by Jeptha Wilkinson and Ezekiel Shearman could provide a safe refuge for followers. And it could also serve as a beacon lighting the way for all those seeking repentance and salvation, fulfilling the prophecy from Revelation: "the woman fled into the wilderness, where she hath a place prepared of God. . . ."[17] According to Abner Brownell, Friend believed "she was the woman spoken of in the revelations . . . [who] fled into the wilderness."[18] During the American Revolution, preachers in New England had begun to theorize that the exodus of the faithful to America was, in fact, the embodiment of Revelation's prophecy and Ezra Stiles "compared true believers in America with the woman who 'should flee into the wilderness, where she hath a place prepared of God.'"[19]

After the threats against the Society that occurred in Philadelphia, Friend and followers found renewed resonance in the biblical text for their own story of persecution and flight. Universal Friend, "given two wings of a great eagle, that she might fly into the wilderness," would lead them to a place of protection and peace far away from eastern cities, a refuge of hope and faith, "where [they would be] . . . nourished for a time, and times, and half a time, from the face of the serpent."[20] Universal Friend was no longer focused on the threat of an imminent Judgment Day. Instead, the minister and the mission, still centered on the goals of repentance and salvation, would create a place here on earth where all followers could come and demonstrate their commitment to God; a haven far away from negative influences, out of the public eye and removed from controversy; a light in the darkness. As the minister explained in a letter to James Parker, "I desire that there may be a town where I may dwell and no one hold a possession there any longer or upon terms than that of being true friends . . . rebels and traitors and whatsoever loveth & maketh a lie I cannot abide."[21]

Universal Friend was not the only one in America looking for a new place to build a secure home and community. Farmers from New England were looking for less expensive places to live and new lands to farm, with thousands of acres of farmland in the northeast having become spoiled through overplowing and overplanting. Despair over high taxes (the payment of which had drained savings and destroyed credit) and increasing costs of living, along with the economic uncertainty caused by the continued disruption and instability of trade (including the markets for crops and other goods) led not only farmers but also tradesmen, artisans, innkeepers, brewers, bakers, and even lawyers to look for a new life with new opportunities far away from the Eastern Seaboard.

For many people, America had always offered the promise of being able to start over. Whether fleeing religious persecution, financial or political problems, or simply the wear and tear of life, the New World promised all comers a clean slate and a future full of possibility. And for so many immigrants, the promises had been realized, the dreams of a new start had come true: refuge, along with prosperity, had been secured. The Revolution itself had been fought in part to hold on to the place where, as Samuel Sherwood, a leading Congregationalist minister put it, "liberty, peace, and tranquility" had been found by so many.[22]

But winning independence had caused a whole new set of problems for Americans, and while the provisions of the new Constitution and the Bill of Rights sought to restore economic stability and ensure liberties and opportunities, it could not solve the pressing problems of the here and now, including over-farmed lands and collapsed fortunes.

And so, Americans were on the move again, looking for another new place, another future full of possibility, another land of plenty. Even as state politicians debated ratification of the Constitution, citizens looked beyond what government could do for them (or fail to do) and took matters into their own hands. Not everyone was looking for paradise, but the Society of Universal Friends was, and Universal Friend would become the first native-born minister willing to pull up stakes and head into the wilderness in search of it.

In the fall of 1787, a group of travelers set out from Little Rest, Rhode Island. Universal Friend accompanied Abraham Dayton, Richard Smith, and Thomas Hathaway on the first leg of the journey down into Pennsylvania. When the travelers arrived in the town of Wyoming in northern Pennsylvania, Universal Friend bid the three men goodbye, and continued south to Worcester, where Sarah Richards waited for her minister in the Wagener farmhouse. Dayton, Smith, and Parker would turn to the west, heading into New York. They had been charged with the duty of finding the place where the Society of Universal Friends might build their paradise.

The three men traveled along the banks of the Susquehanna River and then turned north, following the path laid by General Sullivan in 1779 when he went to attack Native settlements in western and central New York. Crossing the border at Tioga Point, they found that the path had become a well-traveled highway (with so many people heading west looking for land) and the men's horses had no trouble with the terrain. Leaves skittered along the ground in late October and the bare trees allowed a wide view over long distances: meadows and gentle hills rising and falling along the sprawling Susquehanna. To see the encompassing blue sky, the endless spread of undulating green hills, the long and gently winding river, made the men confident in their mission: a new home for the Society of Universal Friends would be found in this wide-open land.

But they couldn't ignore that it was only wide-open because its first inhabitants had been brutally driven away; evidence of the campaign remained in the remnants of burned-out villages they passed through, and the untilled, overgrown fields. Did the eradication of Native Americans from the lands disturb them? Ezekiel Shearman had been troubled by the heavy toll exacted by Sullivan, but perhaps these men were too filled with their own purpose, too intent on seeking a new home for the Society of Universal Friends, to dwell on the past tragedies.

Along the trail heading deeper into New York, the travelers met a man camping alongside the Susquehanna. He told them he was a backwoods tracker and had traveled into the wilds of New York many times. Among all the places he had visited, he believed the best lands for settling were to be found around Seneca Lake. Seneca was the largest lake in the region, abundant with fish and with a bordering coastline of verdant fields and thickly wooded forests. All that a man needed to live well could be found along that lake, the tracker assured the three faithful followers.

Encouraged by his report, Dayton, Smith, and Hathaway followed the man's directions farther north; they followed the Susquehanna up until where the Chemung River fed into it. From there, they made their way along the Chemung farther north and west to a small settlement called Newtown, the site of one of General Sullivan's most lethal battles against the Iroquois Nation (four white American soldiers and fourteen British and Native Americans were killed, and Sullivan's troops burned to the ground dozens of homes and barns, and about 140 acres of crops). Newtown had been partially rebuilt in the years since, but little of its former vitality remained and the travelers didn't stop there. Perhaps they felt in Newtown the same haunted atmosphere experienced by Ezekiel Shearman months earlier.

After long days of riding, the three men finally arrived at the foot of Seneca Lake sometime in November. They were 200 miles west of Albany, 200 miles north of Worcester in Pennsylvania, and 150 miles south of mighty Niagara Falls: they were in a deep, overgrown wilderness. They dismounted from their horses and took a good look around. Before them, long and blue and deep, stretched Seneca Lake, bordered with pebbled beaches and long grasses, and gently sloping banks that rose up from the water into thick pine woods and rolling meadows.[23] The wilderness of the area was broken up by only a few scattered clearings—the evidence of past Native American villages indicated by lonely stands of fruit trees—and three or four cabins set back along the shoreline. The log cabins were worn down by weather and neglect, and sinking crookedly into the leave-littered soil.

French traders were camping on the shores of the lake, and Hathaway, Dayton, and Smith made camp beside them. The Frenchmen, like the backwoods tracker, spoke in glowing terms about the lands around Seneca. They had traveled through Canada and the western territories of the United States (likely the Ohio Valley), but "had seen nowhere so fine a country as the one they were in."[24] Night fell, and all was quiet under a sky studded with millions of stars. Only the murmur of lapping water and the occasional hooting of a screech owl broke the silence. The scents of lake water and shore pines mingled with wood smoke from the evening's fire. The faithful followers must have felt the same as the French traders: nothing could be as fine—so peaceful and beautiful—as this place.

When the men returned to Little Rest, they sent their scouting report about Seneca Lake and its borderlands to Universal Friend—or perhaps they brought it to their minister in Worcester, excited to share what they had found on the western frontier. Almost immediately, Universal Friend wrote to James Parker that he had a new mission to fulfill: to purchase, on behalf of the Society of Universal Friends, a large parcel of land along Seneca Lake in western New York for a good price. In 1786, after being removed from his post in Worcester, he had been placed in charge of collecting the funds for buying property out west and issuing receipts to those members who could afford to contribute. He had proved himself capable in the role of managing those funds, and Friend hoped that perhaps his background as justice of the peace and an army captain would now make him a tough and savvy land negotiator. Parker eagerly took up the charge Friend laid upon him. Escape to the western frontier was no longer just a dream. The Society of Universal Friends would make it a reality. It was time to leave.

PART
2

Flight

1788–93

"The earth is given as a common stock
for man to labour and live on."

—THOMAS JEFFERSON

14

Bargains, Deals, and Promises

"The dwelling lands of this confederacy
were admirably adapted for
convenience, for subsistence, and for conquest."

—GOVERNOR DE WITT CLINTON OF NEW YORK

James Parker set off for Hudson, New York, in the spring of 1788. Located on the Hudson River about one hundred miles north of New York City, Hudson was the epicenter of the new nation's most booming business: land speculation. The Americans' victory in the Revolution meant that property previously held by the British (or by anyone who associated themselves with the British) was now fair game, at least in the eyes of the victorious colonists. Added into the mix of available properties were the ancestral lands of Native Americans, many of whom had fought for the British and therefore their lands were viewed as war bounty. The fight for millions and millions of acres of land was on and its combatants included the most well-connected and financially cunning men in America. James Parker, wearing the brown robe and wide-brimmed hat he'd adopted since joining the Society of Universal Friends, was like a lamb among the wolves.

But Hudson must have felt safe to Parker. It had been founded in 1783 by Quaker whalers looking for a harbor away from the American coastlines, where the British navy harassed their vessels, and the town still had a strong—and peaceful—Quaker presence. Merchant vessels loaded up at the Hudson docks, carrying American harvests out after bringing in goods from all over the world: iron, salt, spices, ceramics, and textiles. Spreading out from the busy docks was a maze of streets lined with distilleries, bakeries, coopers, dry goods dealers, inns and taverns, and also factories making spermaceti candles, rope, and sails. When James Parker arrived in Hudson, the new business of land speculation was taking over. Property agents were setting up their headquarters along the main streets, eager to get down to the business of carving up western New York. The doors to the frontier were wide open and Hudson was the gateway.

The tribes of the Haudenosaunee Confederacy had long considered the lands of western New York to be their sovereign territory, having lived and farmed there for centuries (the Confederacy itself was formed in the fifteenth century and possibly earlier).[1] Even after the brutal experiences of the Sullivan campaign, the remaining Haudenosaunee claimed as theirs the lands that the American troops had done their best to destroy. After the war, when King George ceded lands held by Britain, including Native American lands, to the victorious Americans, the official policy of the new federal government was that Native American tribes were sovereign nations with rights to their territories that the British could not give away.[2] This view concurred with centuries-old international law; as stated by lawyer Francisco de Vitoria in the sixteenth century (one of the founders of international law), Indigenous Americans owned their lands in America and "discovery" by Spanish explorers could not transfer title to the land "anymore than if it had been they who had discovered us."[3] Nevertheless, the Treaties of Paris and of Versailles signed in 1783 between the United States and

Britian ending the Revolutionary War made no mention of the sovereign rights of the Native Americans.

New York governor George Clinton (brother to General James Clinton) considered the Indian lands in western New York to be the property of the state. In 1778, Clinton had been among the most vociferous advocates pushing General George Washington, John Sullivan, and his brother James to carry out the destructive—and to his mind, successful—campaign against Native Americans in New York. With the local Native tribes scattered, their lands destroyed, and the war against the British won, Clinton had no intention of respecting the so-called sovereign rights of those whom he saw as defeated enemies. As for those tribes that had assisted the colonists in battle, Governor Clinton, as well as private land speculators, used manipulation, intimidation, and bribery to gain control of their lands, or just flat-out denied that Native Americans had any property rights at all.[4] James Duane, the aide to Clinton who spearheaded the state's land grab, refused to recognize the Native tribes as "distinct nations" and argued that "if we adopt the disgraceful system of pensioning, courting, and flattering them as great and mighty nations . . . this Revolution . . . will have lost more than half its value."[5]

Governor Clinton recognized the huge economic potential not only in farming the western lands but also in using its waterways for transportation. His ambitions would be taken even further by his nephew (and secretary) De Witt Clinton, when De Witt became governor of New York in 1817 and spearheaded the campaign to build the 350-mile Erie Canal. The canal linked the Great Lakes to the Hudson River, thereby connecting the Midwest to the East Coast and ensuring the rise of New York City as the financial capital of the United States. Like his uncle, De Witt had no respect for rights of the Native Americans and gleefully (but incorrectly) predicted in 1811 that "before the passing away of the present generation, not a single Iroquois will be seen in this state."[6] And it all began with his uncle George's claim to the spoils of war: the millions of acres of fertile fields, vigorous waterways, and well-stocked forests that were the ancestral homelands of Native Americans in western New York.[7]

James Parker wanted some of those hills and valleys for the Society of Universal Friends. Did he consider from whom the properties had been taken? He never seemed to question that the land companies setting up shop in Hudson had legitimate claim to the acres they sold, and he was determined to go straight to the top, to the New York Genesee Land Company, to make a deal for the Society. The New York Genesee Land Company had been founded by a group of wealthy and influential New Yorkers who had formed good relationships with Native Americans during the American Revolution and now intended to use those connections to buy up thousands of acres from their old allies. Partners in the New York Genesee Land Company included John Livingston (to whose family King George I had granted hundreds of thousands of acres in New York in 1686) and Dr. Caleb Benton, friend and doctor to many Native Americans in western New York.

Livingston and Benton found a loophole in the law signed by Governor Clinton prohibiting sales of Native American lands to individuals. Thinking to outsmart the state, they decided to lease, rather than buy, land from tribes of the Haudenosaunee Confederacy. In the spring of 1788, they negotiated 999-year leases with Haudenosaunee representatives for millions of acres in western New York. Even before their negotiations were concluded, the New York Genesee Land Company began selling off portions of those leases to people who wanted to buy land in western New York. James Parker was one of those people.

Caleb Benton welcomed any potential settler who was interested in paying good money for the leased lands, but James Parker must have been especially appealing: How better to encourage white settlement than to show that a peace-loving and well-funded religious organization was willing to move west? Having the Society of Universal Friends invest in the New York Genesee Land Company would encourage other settlers to take the plunge, and more settlers meant more land deals and more money to be made. In addition, the more settlers that came west, the more stable and secure all the settlements along the frontier's edge would appear to be, drawing more and more people to the area. Making a deal with the Society of Universal Friends would be very good for the land company, and in the end, Benton offered Parker a sales price that he couldn't refuse.

As for Parker, he may have hoped to prove himself to Universal Friend and the other members of the Society. He had failed in his mission to bring in more followers in Pennsylvania, but now he could demonstrate his worth by securing a good land deal. Or perhaps he had caught the land speculation fever himself and wanted to secure western lands for his own future prosperity and to guarantee good prospects for his three motherless daughters, Mary, Alice, and Nancy, who were approaching marriageable age. But no matter the motivation, James Parker was as intent on reaching an agreement as Benton was, and in April of 1788, the deal was made. The two men agreed that Parker would purchase from the New York Genesee Land Company title to fourteen thousand acres on the western shores of Seneca Lake for about "£800 of New York Currancy."[8]

Taking Benton at his word that the New York Genesee Land Company had legitimate claim to the property (he was told that "it was no breach of Law their . . . taking of a lease of the Indians"), Parker purchased it on behalf of the Society of Universal Friends.[9] The Society became a shareholder in the Land Company (land title was purchased as shares), binding its future to the future of Benton and his partners (this was a typical method used for funding big land purchases throughout the states). Parker felt proud of what he'd managed to achieve. Writing to Abraham Dayton back in New Milford, Connecticut, he bragged that he had made a bargain purchase for the Society: "my ventures and labours have saved . . . near a hundred thousand dollars for [the] friends." The land was "as good title as to any land in the world and the best land I ever seen in this world."[10] Parker closed his letter by asking Dayton to organize a group of settlers "fit for Labour & three women" to travel with him to Seneca Lake to clear their promised land for the Society's settlement.[11]

Just as James Parker was packing up to leave Hudson, he received bad news. Around the same time that he had been negotiating a land deal with Caleb Benton, the governor of New York was moving forward with plans to enforce the state's prohibition of sales of Native American territories to private speculators. Although Clinton would claim his intent was to save Native Americans from fraudulent deals, his real purpose was to control all land sales within New York State and to protect private interests whose pecuniary goals aligned with his own. In other words, Governor Clinton wanted to make money for the state, for himself, and for his friends. He had fought in the French and Indian War, commanded the New York militia during the American Revolution, and served as a state representative to the Continental Congress. He wanted his reward now for all his hard service; a reward due not only to him but to all those who had fought for American independence—and American supremacy.

When Governor Clinton heard about Livingston's leasing scheme, he immediately moved to nullify any deeds acquired through it and threatened to arrest Livingston and his partners for fraud and treason and burn down any homes built on leased lands. While troops of the New York militia were put on alert by Clinton, none of these threatened actions were ever carried out. Nevertheless, Clinton made clear that he would fight the legitimacy of the leases with all the power of the state behind him.

What a terrible shock it must have been for Parker to realize the real reason why he had paid so little for so much land on the western frontier. The bargain price he had bragged about was not due to his negotiating skills. Parker understood now that the partners of the New York Genesee Land Company knew that their leases with the Native Americans were "somewhat tenuous" and therefore had offered "land in the Genesee country at bargain rates" in an effort to complete as many leases as quickly as possible, all the while hoping their legitimacy would never be questioned.[12] The company had enticed its investors, including James Parker, with promises of prosperity and ignored the legal realities of the lease transactions. The Society of Universal Friends, in other words, had been defrauded: "And we being strangers of the State they took us in. . . ."[13]

When Universal Friend received news of the fraud perpetrated by Benton and Livingston, the minister must have seen it as further proof of the need to escape from the wickedness of civilization into the wilderness. Writing to James Parker, the minister encouraged him to persevere against all "thy hardships and tryals" and assured him that "God will early destroy all the wicked and establish the just. . . ."[14] *The Kingdom is ours*, Friend seemed to say, *if only we can stay the course*. For now, the counsel offered in Universal Friend's *Advice* seemed the best course to follow: "shun . . . the company of the wicked world . . . do your business with few words and retire from them as soon as you can get your business done; remembering to keep on your watch, and pray for assistance, especially when the wicked are before you."[15]

But Parker could not retire from the business in Hudson just yet, as there was another twist in the land ownership saga raging over the lands west of Seneca Lake. Under a treaty signed by Massachusetts and New York in 1786, Massachusetts had given to New York lands that they had for decades claimed as their own (north of Albany). In return, Massachusetts was given the preemptive rights to purchase 6 million acres of Native American lands in western New York. In April of 1788, Massachusetts sold their preemptive rights to the land speculators Oliver Phelps and Nathaniel Gorham, thereby granting Phelps and Gorham the exclusive right to negotiate for 6 million acres from Native Americans, including the property for which the Society of Friends supposedly now held the rights to settle. Phelps and Gorham were willing to work with the New York Genesee Land Company and offered Benton and Livingston the right to purchase 1 million acres in western New York (which included a small portion of the lands consigned to James Parker) if they agreed to facilitate land negotiations with the

Native Americans. Livingston, Benton, and the other partners agreed to the deal, knowing that Governor Clinton would never allow their leases for those same lands to stand.

Phelps and Gorham, with the help of Livingston and possibly Benton, were able to reach a deal with a number of Native American leaders from the Seneca Nation of the Haudenosaunee Confederacy to buy the 6 million acres for the sum of 2,100 New York dollars (quite a bargain for Phelps and Gorham, given that James Parker had paid 800 New York dollars for 14,000 acres). Records of the negotiations indicate that the Native Americans were misled by the speculators: they were told that under the peace treaties signed between Britain and the United States their land claims had been extinguished and that the creation of a new federal constitution could possibly limit their rights even more (in fact, under the Constitution, the federal government would take over all land negotiation with Native Americans, whom they recognized as sovereign nations).

Desperate to make deals that might at least give them some financial security, Seneca representatives agreed to sell lands east of the Genesee River and west of Seneca Lake (while holding on to their properties on the other side of the Genesee River all the way to Lake Erie to the west and Lake Ontario to the north).[16] In the end, "of the fifty-eight chiefs and the seven chief women, who made their mark on the [purchasing] document, possibly none . . . was able to read its contents . . ." and few had understanding of what its provisions would actually mean for the Haudenosaunee Confederacy.[17]

In 1790, Seneca chief Cornplanter would complain to George Washington (now president of the United States) that "commissioners from Pennsylvania, told our chiefs, that they had come there to purchase from us, all the Lands belonging to us within the lines of their State. . . . They told us they must have the whole: That it was already ceded to them by the great King at the time of making peace with you, and was their own. . . . [Then] Our nation empowered John Livingston to let out a part of our lands on rent. He told us he was sent by

Congress to do this for us and we fear he has deceived us . . . a man of the name of Phelps has come among us, and he claimed . . . the whole country North of Pennsylvania and west of the Lands belonging to the Cayugas. He demanded it: He insisted on his demand and declared that he would have it all. . . . He then threatened us with immediate war if we did not comply. . . ."[18]

Native Americans weren't the only ones confused and dismayed by the conflicting claims of land speculators. The ever-changing tile board of who owned what and where, and how they could prove what they own, would come to define the early years of western expansion in the new country of the United States. The federal and state governments claimed authority to govern sales of both Native American lands and lands previously held by the British, while private land speculators made deals with each other and with anyone else willing to bargain with them—but many of those deals fell through and in all sorts of ways: financing collapsed, governments (state or federal) stepped in or stepped back, creditors called in their chits, and poker games went wrong.[19]

What was James Parker's reaction when he learned that under the agreement reached between Phelps and Gorham, and Livingston and Benton, the New York Genesee Land Company no longer held rights to all the lands previously promised to the Society of Universal Friends? He must have been mortified—and felt even worse when Phelps offered him settlement rights to only a small slice of the fourteen thousand acres Parker had originally been promised and had already paid for. What Parker may not have been aware of was that under the agreement Livingston and Benton had made with Gorham and Phelps, the rights of the Society to even that small slice of land was conditioned upon actions beyond the Society's control: the New York Genesee Land Company had to complete payments due to Phelps and Gorham for the one million acres (including the Society's land) over the next three years or forfeit their rights to them.

There is no record of how Parker told his fellow members in the

Society of Friends that they now held rights of settlement to only eleven hundred acres of land along the shores of Seneca Lake. Men such as Jonathan Botsford, who had given a significant amount of money to fund buying western territory for the Society and to whom Parker had promised close to one thousand acres of his own to farm, could now expect only thirteen or fourteen acres. But while the size of the settlement property was not what members of the Society had hoped for, or sacrificed their savings on, they might have consoled themselves with knowing that finally they had their place in the wilderness. Not a huge space, but nevertheless, land where they could create an isolated, protected, and fruitful community far away from those who, as Universal Friend later put it, "will not obey the truth with all their hearts."[20]

In the late spring of 1788, Parker finally left Hudson and made his way back to New Milford. A group of hearty followers were waiting for him there, waiting for him to lead them into the wilderness, where together they could begin the hard work of taming a corner of it, and making that corner a safe haven for all members of the Society of Universal Friends.

15

The Migration Begins

"Turn and be wise,
make haste, make haste, and come. . . ."

—UNIVERSAL FRIEND

In the end, the group of hearty followers willing to make the long trek to western New York numbered over twenty. On an early morning sometime in June of 1788, James Parker, John Briggs, George Sisson, Ezekiel Shearman, Abraham Dayton, and women, too, including Abigail Dayton and Bethany Sisson, made their way out of New Milford to the wide Housatonic River that ran through their valley. Riverboats waited there, their captains commissioned to carry the faithful followers down through Connecticut to Long Island Sound. From there, the boats would travel south and east to Manhattan, to curve around the island where they would then meet up with larger riverboats and join a flotilla of vessels heading north to Albany. Merchants, whalers, fishermen, hopeful settlers: all placed their faith in the Hudson River to get them north to new frontiers and new opportunities.

The pioneers carried much of what they needed in wagons pulled by oxen: fishing hooks, guns, and traps; tools for clearing the wilderness (saws and hatchets), and tools for planting crops (hoes and rakes and shovels); seeds and seedlings; clothing, blankets, tents. James Parker, walking alongside the wagons piled high, carried perhaps the most important item: a survey map of the lands purchased by the Society, and directions for how to get there.

Despite the early hour, a large and curious crowd gathered to watch the parade out of town, their leaving having "caused much talk" among the inhabitants of New Milford.[1] One observer claimed that men left behind "wives and families" and a "mother left her infant . . . several young women left their homes and kindred."[2] But no one would, in fact, be left behind: whether the wives, sisters, and other family members joined their husbands and fathers, brothers and uncles, in a few weeks or a few months, they were going west, too.

Already a second band of pioneers was preparing to leave, charged with bringing more supplies for building and feeding the new settlement, including hammers and nails, along with chickens and at least one dairy cow, and also those cherished items that couldn't be left behind: heavy family Bibles tucked in among the blankets and silver teaspoons laid in boxes of straw. The Bibles, printed on Oxford India paper and bound in stamped leather, and the spoons, betrothal gifts forged in Boston from ore mined in Mexico, might have seemed like unnecessary luxuries, but they were as necessary to survival as food and water, for they carried with them both memories and promises, and hope for the future.

Over the next ten years the sight of such a procession—wagons loaded with supplies and pulled by oxen, followed by men and women on foot and on horseback and with determination on their faces—would become commonplace across the towns and villages of New England as thousands of Americans headed west for new opportunities. But the faithful followers that left New Milford in 1788 were among the first, and not unlike their ancestors who had left the Old World for the New, these faithful pilgrims went with blind conviction as they headed into the unknown.

Once arrived at Albany, a journey of about three days, Parker, the

Daytons, Ezekiel Shearman, and the others took to the road, walking over twenty miles to the west to Schenectady (not far from the Shaker community of Niskayuna). Here they negotiated for flat-bottomed boats to travel up the Mohawk River. The pioneers paddled the boats themselves and for the next one hundred miles (and another four or five days with stops every nightfall to make camp) they rowed north and west, intent on reaching "the Oneida Carry," a winding portage path that would take them from the Mohawk River to Wood Creek, and from there to Oneida Lake.[3]

The three-mile path, used by Oneida tribe members for decades, was already well known to frontier travelers, a "dark and tortuous stream . . . fed by a decoction of forest leaves that oozed from the marshy shores, crept in shadow through depths of foliage, [and] with only a belt of illumined sky gleaming between the jagged tree-tops."[4] The lowing oxen were led carefully by Benjamin Brown Jr.; he was naturally protective of Friend's cattle, but perhaps also eager for the promised payment of $10 once the animals arrived safely on the frontier. The other travelers took charge of lugging the heavy boats through the ankle-deep marshy passage.[5] After what must have seemed like hours, they finally reached Oneida Lake. Here, they could once again launch their flat-bottomed boats and take to their oars. But first they would have made camp for the night, cooking up a meal to be shared and resting after the exertions of the day. They had been traveling for almost three weeks and the efforts of rowing, fording, portaging, making and breaking camp were beginning to take a toll, even for those among them used to the labors of working a farm or mill.

The next morning, the pioneers rose and set out again; perhaps they had slept enough to recover their energies, perhaps the fact that their long trek was reaching its final stages drove them forward. James Parker, well-versed in the Bible, might have found counsel in the words from Deuteronomy, "Arise, take thy journey before the people, that they may go and possess the land, which I sware . . . to give unto them."[6] Checking the mapped directions he carried in his pocket,

Parker guided his group of faithful followers across Oneida Lake. They then traveled southwest eight miles down the Oneida River to reach the Seneca River. Continuing west on the Seneca, they rowed on for another sixty miles, camping when needing food and rest. Mile after mile they rowed, to arrive finally at the opening onto Seneca Lake.

Seneca Lake was magnificent, a languorous blue spreading out before them as far as they could see. Sitting level with the great expanse of water in their flatboats and surrounded by vast, wild, and open lands, the pioneers would have felt as though they alone inhabited the world. Parker knew that a few white settlers lived in the area, mostly American and European traders, and also small, scattered communities of Native Americans lived here and there in the woods and alongside streams. But from where the pioneers sat in their boats, bobbing gently on the water, there was no evidence of human habitation. Just lake, forests, meadows, and a huge sky overhead.

Their journey wasn't over yet. The Seneca River had deposited them at the northeastern tip of the lake and their promised lands lay to the south and west. The pioneers once again began to paddle. Dark clouds had been gathering to the west and now a storm arrived, brought by strong, cold winds that whipped up high waves rolling thunderously over the lake; rain began to fall in torrents and the boats quickly filled with water. The oxen mooed and bayed in terror, while all hands went to bailing out the boats: buckets, hats, and even just hands—joined as if in prayer—were put to work scooping out water even as more waves rode over the bows and more rain fell. The travelers began to sing, "Show pity, Lord, O Lord, forgive; Let a repenting rebel live."[7]

While many of them continued bailing water, others began rowing, desperate to find the shoreline—and safety—through the pelting rain. When they finally reached a beach, their boats thudding up on pebbled sands, they were much farther south than they had intended, and on the eastern shore of Seneca Lake, not the western. But they had survived the perilous journey, and for that, they were thankful: "O come, let us sing unto the Lord: let us make a joyful noise to the rock of our salvation."[8]

That night the pioneers camped out on the shoreline. The skies had cleared above them as the storm moved on. The summer solstice had just passed, and the sun set late.[9] The faithful travelers might have seen the solstice as a turning point not only for the seasons but also for the Society of Universal Friends. God had brought them safely to the western frontier and here they would find their promised land, land for which they had paid—too much, as it turned out, and for too little land—but they would find their fields and meadows and woodlands, and they would build their settlement and prosper. After weeks of travel, they had reached the shores of the Seneca. Now they sat beneath a star-studded sky, warming themselves around a fire smoldering on a bed of stones in a silence broken only by the croaking of bullfrogs and the soft lapping of waves against the shore.

At daybreak, the quiet of the lake was broken by the distant but constant sound of running water. The lake itself was still, its surface like glass after the turmoil of the day before. The story passed down by Friend's followers was that the sound of the falling water called out to the travelers, rousing them once again to load up their boats and set course for the source of that sound. Crossing the lake, they found a landing spot, a flat, rocky beach at the head of a wide and strong stream leading out of Seneca Lake. The sound of rushing water they had heard came from this stream. Judging by the fury of its current, the rolling water would no doubt be strong enough to run a mill when the time came. Abraham Dayton and Richard Smith were already plotting how to get millstones to the site: they knew that every settlement needs a mill to become self-sufficient and successful, and this stream bank was the perfect place for it.

But was this their land?

James Parker would have checked the land survey of the area, looking for the notation marking the vigorous stream where they now stood. Were they in the right place? He would have told them that they were, that their future would take place here, beside this lake and roaring stream, in the expanse of verdant field and forest that surrounded them. A tremendous duty lay before them now, to tame the land, once tilled by Native Americans but now returned to wilderness. To make it once again a community would not be an easy task. But they felt certain enough and strong enough to take it on. As nineteenth-century historian Stafford Cleveland described Parker and this first wave of settlers, "they were, in truth, the pioneer party of the pioneers. They were the boldest of the bold."[10]

The men and women walked together into a lush meadow that bordered the rock-strewn beach. Birds rose from thick stands of red-berried spicebush, their sharp cries cutting through the quiet morning as they darted across the blue sky. A stream meandered through the meadow, shallow and clear, leading into the thick forests beyond. Off in the distance, the green land rose to form a plateau, flat like the palm of God's hand. They felt certain that land had been given to them by God—"Ye are the light of the world. A city that is set on a hill cannot be hid"—and they would call their settlement built on the flat green rise "City Hill."[11] The name was proof of their certainty that they could—and would—create a place of light in the world, here in the wilderness: "Beautiful for situation, the joy of the whole earth. . . ."[12]

The lands were everything they had been promised. The "small but beautiful" meadows were rich not only with wildflowers and clover but also with ryegrass and sedge.[13] Growing alongside the meadows were berms of blackberry and raspberry bushes, buzzing with bees, and stands of fruit trees, stunted from lack of care but still heavy with buds promising fruit. Long, wide streams threaded their way through forests thick with beech, sugar maple, basswood, hickory, and walnut trees, and lush with an undergrowth of ferns of all sizes. Not only was the land abundant with deer, squirrels, robins, hawks, ducks, trout, and perch, but also foxes, mink, and martins; chickadees, pheasants, turkeys, partridges, and meadow hen; and in the streams, salmon and catfish. The faithful followers had thought themselves alone in the wilderness, but now they realized that the world around them teemed with life.

Just a few weeks after the first group of settlers arrived, they were joined by the second group of pioneers. William Potter, his son Arnold, Arnold's wife, Sarah Brown, and Sarah's sister Abigail were in this second group, along with Enoch Malin of Philadelphia and Elizabeth Holmes of Stonington. Elizabeth was a young mother of at least two children: Did she make the hard journey without complaint, eager to join her husband, Jedediah, on the frontier? Along with Abigail Dayton and the two Brown sisters, and the two-dozen male faithful followers, Elizabeth's efforts had met and surpassed James Parker's request, back in April 1788, that men "fit for Labour & three women" would come west to plant not only the seeds of crops but also the seeds of community in a land long left fallow.[14]

Penelope Potter, wife of William, remained back in Little Rest with Hitty Smith, along with Universal Friend's sisters Patience and Marcy, and brothers Jeptha and Stephen; they would carry on the mission of salvation in Rhode Island. Universal Friend, meanwhile, was in Worcester, Pennsylvania, guiding the Society at large from there (using the Wagener farmhouse as headquarters) and setting in motion the plans necessary to move out west over the year ahead.

Around the same time as the second group arrived on the shores of Seneca Lake, the settlers received news of yet another complication in their ownership of land on the western frontier. Most likely brought by messenger to one of the trading posts at the foot of the lake, the letter explained that the land Oliver Phelps had turned over to the Society of Universal Friends—after they'd already leased it from the New York Genesee Land Company—might not have been his to control. Phelps had purchased the property from Massachusetts based on the assumption that under the 1786 treaty between Massachusetts and New York, it was Massachusetts's property to dispose of. Now there was a survey underway to determine the so-called preemption line that would set the boundary between which lands could be sold by Massachusetts and which could be sold by New York. If the survey showed that the land had never been Massachusetts's to sell, Phelps might not have held legal title and the deal he made with James Parker might fall apart—and the rights of occupation held by the Society of Universal Friends would again come into question.

In the wild maze of land speculating, the question of who held recognizable title to the fields and meadows and forests of western New York was as unsettled as the lands the pioneers were trying so hard to tame. Claims and counterclaims, border lines old and new, different states and entities claiming jurisdiction: it was a puzzle with no one agency in charge, leaving the land speculators to wheel and deal and outsmart and outmaneuver as many parties as they could. But at least one person was able to outsmart the speculators. Mary Jemison, known as the "White Woman of the Genesee," had been abducted as a child by an Iroquois raiding party and adopted into a Seneca Nation family. She eventually married a Seneca leader by the name of Hiakatoo, with whom she had several children. She survived the Sullivan campaign (during which her village had been burned to the ground) and resettled on the banks of the Genesee River. In 1797, representatives of the Seneca Nation granted her a deed to those lands, which were described in vague terms. Thomas Morris, an English land speculator, agreed to respect her deed while he was finalizing his own treaty with the Seneca, as he expected it to be for a few hundred acres beside the Genesee River. To his great surprise, when the land under the claim was finally surveyed, Mary's deed encompassed 17,929 acres.[15]

Did James Parker have the wit, luck, and determination necessary to fight for the lands of City Hill? Both their minister and the gospels had counseled the pioneers of faith to be like the man who "built a house, and digged deep, and laid the foundation on a rock: and when the flood arose, the stream beat vehemently upon that house, and could not shake it: for it was founded upon a rock"—and to avoid being "the foolish man, which built his house upon the sand."[16] Their narrow band of land on the western shores of Seneca Lake: Was it rock or sand? They had pooled their resources, paid their money, traveled so far—and all just to have this one small slice of Eden. But was this slice theirs?

James Parker, Abigail and Abraham Dayton, William Potter, the Benjamin Browns (senior and junior), Ezekiel Shearman, Jedidiah and Elizabeth Holmes: the pioneers of faith had a decision to make. To turn around and go back east, or to dig in deep and stand strong here in the west.

16

Trouble on the Hill

"I rejoice in hope there will be a day of Judgment!
O! The griping and grinding and worldly-mindedness. . . ."

—JAMES PARKER

The pioneers decided to stay where they were and make the best of their situation. They wouldn't wait for the results of the land survey defining which territories were Massachusetts's to buy and sell and which were New York's, and whether any of the land actually belonged to the Society. Instead, they would act as if the property they currently occupied did in fact legally belong to them; as James Parker would later explain (in a petition to New York State), "we Settled where we are now . . ." for "if we had waited to have the preemption line run before we began Improvement we Must a lost our Crops for that year which would a hurt us greatly. . . ."[1] Without crops, Parker and the other settlers knew they would not survive the winter: they would starve on the frontier. They had to clear the land, sow crops, and harvest. If they gave up and returned east, chances were slim they could find the funds and resources necessary to try settling out west all over again. Against all odds, and with no other choice available to them, they persisted in believing that this precious and beautiful spot was their promised land and that God, having gifted it to them, would move mountains to guarantee they could keep it.

Parker may have already been planning a legal strategy for holding on to the land. As a seasoned justice of the peace, he would have been familiar with the concept of adverse possession, which dictated that a claim to land can be made even when the land is owned by someone else if the inhabitants occupy the land for some time and improve its value in some way. Parker now hoped that the pioneers could, through hard work and determination, tame and settle these unoccupied lands, and thereby make the property their own no matter what the final preemption survey line showed.

Universal Friend, in a letter sent to James Parker in the fall of 1788, reassured the settlers in their work: "there is one able to deliver the righteous . . . be not weary in well doing. . . ."[2] The minister agreed that the best course was to move forward with the planned settlement, and might have relied on Psalms to prove their righteousness: "There is a river, the streams whereof shall make glad the city of God, the holy place . . . God is in the midst of her; she shall not be moved: God shall help her, just at the break of dawn."[3] Words spoken in prayer were sent on the wind to reach the faithful settlers, so far away from their minister: "Be strong and of a good courage, fear not, nor be afraid . . . for the Lord . . . doth go with thee; he will not fail thee, nor forsake thee."[4]

The pioneers on the shore of Seneca Lake were not all farming folk, and the task before them was more than just putting in a kitchen garden for a few herbs and tomatoes. Even seasoned farmers like Abigail and Abraham Dayton were daunted by the labor required to prepare a forest or an overgrown meadow for planting crops. The weather that first summer of 1788 was damp and buggy, and unusually chilly. Days went by with little sun to lighten the overhanging gloom of clouds and mist. Clinging to their rituals of fellowship as best they could (pausing on the Sabbath to meet in prayer and taking time every evening to give thanks for God's gifts), nevertheless the pioneers spent most of their days laboring to get land cleared and crops sown.

The first task was the felling of trees, burning of brush, and cutting away of undergrowth to prepare a field for sowing. It was both backbreaking and time-consuming work.[5] There were some tricks for saving time and effort; for example, girdling a tree (making a deep cut into the bark all around like an encircling belt and then cutting away the branches below the cut) set the tree up for eventual death when it could then be more easily taken down. Fallen trees could then be burned for ash, from which the settlers created potash, a fertilizer for crops. The settlers' oxen also played a role in clearing space; when set loose to graze, within a few days they could eat a substantial amount of undergrowth and low bushes, creating space large enough for a plot to be plowed and sown.

Plowing the cleared lands was also difficult and slow work, whether the soil was broken by hand or by oxen-driven plows. The settlers' muscles hardened with the daily labor and their backs ached, but they couldn't rest, not even for one day. They had to make sure there'd be enough food to carry them through the winter when meadows were barren, and fruits and berries could no longer be plucked from bushes or fish lifted from streams. And so, having plowed the fields they toiled on, hoeing rows into the broken soil, throwing seeds, raking the earth smooth. By midsummer, working thirty strong, men and women together, they managed to clear and plant close to twelve acres. And then they prayed: "speak to the earth, and it shall teach thee. . . . Who knoweth not in all these that the hand of the Lord hath wrought this?"[6] The pioneers prayed for a good harvest, for the sustenance to secure bodies and souls in the winter months to come.

Wheat was crucial for making bread. But what about other crops, the onions and squash and corn? James Parker wrote to Friend in desperation, "I wish some of the Friend's family [Society members] who are able at farming might be sent to start a garden but if nobody is sent, I mean to attempt this myself. . . ."[7] Again, the Daytons were useful and knowledgeable, as were Abel Botsford and Richard Smith. But William Potter had never planted a vegetable in his life. As Parker described him, "Potter came Tender and meaning to do well. . . ."[8] Parker also complained about John Briggs, who was "weak"; Thomas Shearman was "a poor Odd Creature" and Gideon Aldrich was "not much better off"; Stephen Card was "in open rebellion" and Sheffield Luther "was nothing [useful] and remains so."[9]

Preparing fields and sowing crops was not the only task facing the settlers. At first, they had lived in tents and then in a large, shared cabin constructed of logs and canvas. Now they had to start building individual homes for the families, "rude log houses" sturdy enough to provide shelter from winter's harsh weather—and they knew winter would come early by the lake.[10] Not only did shelter have to be built for humans but they also needed sheds for animals and chickens, and ample and secure storage for the hoped-for crops. Plans to build a gristmill were put on hold. Shelter for the winter, and food stores to carry the pioneers through until spring, were the priority.

Wild fruits and berries were gathered—plum, cherry, mulberry, grape, huckleberry, and gooseberry—and then boiled on the fire and preserved; apples from scattered apple trees (remnants of Native American settlements) were picked and then saved in barrels.[11] Venison was smoked, along with fish; large rounds of cheese were formed and laid on darkened shelves to harden and mellow; nuts were gathered, including hickory, chestnut, and hazelnut. These were God's gifts from forest, field, and stream, and from the small but complacent dairy cow, and the faithful followers were grateful for the bounty. But they were also tired with all the work they had to do: the hunting and gathering; the grinding, mashing, boiling, and preserving; the fishing and smoking; the churning and turning and settling; the packing and the storing.

As the settlers worked, dangers threatened all around them in the meadows and the forests, including bears that went on "very destructive ravages" through sown fields and wolves that made every "night hideous with frightful howls."[12] Brown wolves were deemed "more ferocious than the black ones," but the black wolves were just as scary—and to see them lurking in the corners of fields at dusk raised the hackles of not only the oxen but also of their masters.[13] Rattlesnakes lurked in the rocky outcroppings and grassy bottoms, along with milk snakes and black rat snakes (who swam along the water's edge), and "persons were frequently bitten as were cattle."[14] In time, hogs would be used to roust the snakes from the settlement—they were the only animal immune to the venom of the snakes and "old hogs would eat these snakes and track them as well as a dog would a fox"—but for now the pioneers did the best they could to avoid them.[15]

When bitten by a venomous snake, one recourse was to find the weed *Plantago major*, broadleaf plantain. The plant had been brought to America by the Puritans in the seventeenth century (for treating all sorts of injuries and bites) and spread "so rapidly in fields and roadsides that the Indians named it 'white man's foot.'"[16] Once the weed was found, it had to be chewed up, a paste created from the chewed leaves, and then the paste slathered over the bite. The paste, effectively neutralizing the venom, "could effect a cure in an hour."[17] (Modern hikers are still today advised to use such a paste when bitten by a snake: the broadleaf plantain contains "the compound aucubin, which serves as a strong anti-microbial agent.")[18] While the rattlers' bite was the most dangerous, the bites of the milk snakes and rat snakes were also very painful and caused swelling and fever. Settlers took to carrying sticks with them to fend off wild creatures and snakes, and at night, they stayed safe inside their tents and cabins.

But little could be done to protect against the swarms of mosquitoes that descended every day at dusk. These pests, thriving in the ponds and streams, wetlands and tall grasses of the western New York lakes, spread an illness that came to be called "Genesee fever" by generations of settlers arriving on the western frontier (it was malaria).[19] As some of the first white inhabitants of the area, the followers of Universal Friend found themselves vulnerable and with no place to hide: mosquitoes found their way into any tent or hut. Bites from infected mosquitoes led to itching, fever, rashes and chills and fatigue. James Parker was the first to fall ill and he soon became so weak that his companions feared for his life. A letter was sent to Universal Friend in Worcester. Lost to history, the letter must have pleaded for prayers and for advice, and most likely would have asked the minister to come help them through the darkness. But Friend couldn't leave Worcester. There were too many arrangements still being worked out for moving the ministry of salvation out to the western frontier.

The minister decided instead to send Sarah Richards to serve as nurse to the pioneers—but it was not an easy decision to make.[20] Not out of concern for Sarah's health: the slight but stubborn woman had been gaining strength ever since living in Worcester. She suffered less frequently from epileptic fits and was as robust as she had ever been. She had grown quite bold as a spiritual leader as well, willing to openly chastise those who failed to meet her own standards of piety. As one historian of the sect noted, that while there are no records of Universal Friend having "made one of her followers wear a bell as a punishment for impertinent curiosity. . . . Sarah Richards did something of that sort while she was at the head of affairs in Pennsylvania in the absence of the Friend, and that was as much a matter of hilarity as otherwise."[21]

The reluctance to send Sarah west would have stemmed from Friend's growing dependence on Sarah's companionship. The two understood each other, shared a deep faith that God had chosen them specifically to save souls, and also had a strong affection for each other. They used endearments in letters—"my dear Blessed Bosom friend"—and when Sarah was in Worcester with Friend, the two were together more often than not.[22] Whenever Friend had to send Sarah away on an errand, the minister immediately wanted the trusted ally and friend back again. Nevertheless, if Friend could not go to the City Hill settlement, Sarah was the best alternative. As the daughter of a doctor and with medical skills of her own, Sarah could nurse Parker, and any of the other pioneers who might have fallen ill, back to health.

Sarah was also an exacting and keen observer who could report back to Friend on how things were going on City Hill: Were the settlers continuing to live by the ideals of the Society? Were they dutiful in their daily work and motivated by love of God in their ambitions? Did they hold meetings and observe silence and speak the words of the Lord? Out there in the wilderness, they claimed to have found Eden. But would they keep their Eden pure and sacred?

According to a follower who still remembered the events decades later, when Sarah arrived at the settlement on City Hill, she "was not altogether pleased with the doings she saw" there.[23] What she found, to her great dismay, was that a spiritual torpor had descended over the community. Whatever Sabbath meetings they had adhered to in the summer months were now distant memories. The pioneers were simply too consumed and exhausted by the constant toll of necessary tasks and chores and worried about who owned the land they were so diligently clearing and working. While loving fellowship might have helped ease the burden and alleviate the stresses, instead the community was in danger of fragmenting. James Parker had grown so discouraged that he wrote to Friend, "ware it not for the Friends Sake and the sake of a few others, I should be willing to flee many miles into the Wilderness."[24]

Sarah Richards returned to Worcester after a few weeks with a full report of what she'd witnessed in the community by the lake. But instead of condemning the pioneers or finding Parker at fault for his role in the problems percolating there, Universal Friend sent him a very long and encouraging letter. The minister still loved and trusted Parker, assuring him of "my love to thee . . . Dear Soul" from the first sentence and filling the letter with continued declarations of esteem.[25] Friend reassured Parker that "I have not forgotten thee. . . . I have been many times seemingly present with thee into silent watches of the night," and then later again, promised him "ye need not fear, I don't forget faithful souls I bear them in my arms Continually. . . ."[26] The minster promised to be "the Comforter," sent by God, to "abide with you forever."[27] Along with the vow to always care for the followers on City Hill, Friend also offered praise for everything they had accomplished in the wilderness—"Sarah gives a good account of that new country"—and made no mention of Parker's failure to secure undisputable title of the occupied lands.[28]

Assurance was also given to Parker that his minister would soon be joining them in the wilderness, and asked him that until that time to lead by example; for him and all the settlers to "obey the truth with all their hearts," to live in "peace," and "be faithfull watch & pray."[29] Friend reminded Parker of the agreement reached by members of the Society back in 1786 that no matter the financial resources of any individual follower, they were to be given "sufficient tract of land . . . for friends and a township where none but friends hold any title of possession there . . ." and that anyone who shall "desire to live there let them abide there . . . & not be at any unnecessary trouble or expence."[30]

The only settlers who would not be welcome on City Hill were those "who in their hearts are turn'd & . . . will not obey the truth." Friend demanded that anyone refusing to live by Friend's message of repentance should leave: "let them depart . . . forever: for I don't want never to see such ones who are always shunning the Cross and opposing the proposals that I have proposed . . . make a separation between the false & the true for he that believeth hath no fellowship with an infidel. . . ."[31] As for the religious practices of the settlement, Friend warned Parker and the other pioneers against the danger of forgetting their spiritual needs while living under the hard conditions of the settlement: "fall not into temptation & whilst you are imploy'd in earthly business do not forget the food for your souls which ought to be your greatest concern. . . ." To ensure ample "food for your souls," the minister instructed Parker to organize a set schedule of spiritual meetings: "Don't let the Solemn feasts and Sabaths be forgotten in Zion."[32]

Despite the troubles reported on City Hill, Friend believed that most of the pioneers were committed to a shared mission of repentance and redemption, and asked that Parker reassure them: "fear not little flock it is the father's good pleasure to give you the kingdom . . . be not dismayed nor discouraged. . . ."[33] But the minister also understood just how desperately the community needed its leader and again told Parker to "make some provision for my coming. . . . I must come in the time when I am least expected. . . ."[34]

The promise of their minister's arrival must have bolstered spirits in the small settlement. They would no longer be alone in the wilderness, no longer rudderless on their unsteady journey to salvation. With their minister beside them, they would know "My foot standeth in an even place: in the congregations will I bless the Lord."[35] But when would Friend come? The followers wondered just how much longer they would have to wait.

In the late fall of 1788, the survey for the preemption line was finally completed. Parker had expressed their hopes that "the preemption line . . . would run across Seneca Lake somewhere, therefore we Settled where we now are Expecting it was on our own Lands which we obtained by contract. . . ."[36] But instead the new line veered to the west of the Friends Settlement and not down the middle of the lake. All the land on which the Friends lived, cleared, planted, and harvested, belonged to New York State: never to Massachusetts, and never to the New York Genesee Land Company, nor to Oliver Phelps and Nathaniel Gorham, and, by extension, not to the Society of Universal Friends. In November of 1788, yet another obstacle was added to the Society's land claim. The New York Genesee Land Company defaulted on payments they owed to Oliver Phelps for the one million acres promised to them, including the acres they had sold to the Society and which the settlers had spent the last six months clearing, plowing, sowing, and caring for.

Many of the pioneers on City Hill, exhausted and demoralized, decided to return home for the winter, back to their families and friends in Connecticut or Rhode Island. John Reynolds, his sister Hannah, and her husband, Stephen Card; Thomas Hathaway Sr.; John and Peleg Briggs; and Thomas Shearman all packed up to leave. They were not just worn out by farming and weary of the many land issues. Fear also drove them east: fear of just how difficult a winter it might be, and how inadequate were their provisions of food and fuel for the long, cold months ahead. But they promised the dozen settlers who chose to stay—including the Daytons, Elizabeth and Jedidiah Holmes and their young children, the Dains family, and the Smiths—that they would return in the spring.

William Potter and his son Arnold were among those returning to Rhode Island for the winter. Perhaps they were eager to get back to the comforts of home and rest up after the rigors of pioneering. They must also have wanted to share news with family about the private endeavors they (along with James Parker) had completed while out west. These endeavors had nothing to do with the greater good of the Society of Universal Friends. In fact, William Potter's and James Parker's private land purchases would, in the end, lead to trouble. But maybe the Potters failed to see any conflict in buying land for the Society while also making purchases for themselves. For now, all they knew for sure was that a hard winter loomed on the shores of Seneca Lake, and they wanted no part of it. They wished James Parker well and left for Little Rest.

17

The Hungry Year

"We are to be saved by our good works
which are within our power. . . ."

—THOMAS JEFFERSON

In the dark midwinter of February 1789, Elizabeth Holmes died, leaving behind her children and her husband, Jedidiah. She was buried "in a corner of the only available even partially cleared land, the wheat field. . . ."[1] Her coffin was a hollowed-out log and her grave a rough hole "hacked out of the frozen earth."[2] The hole was filled in and then broad, flat stones would have been laid on top as protection against ravening wolves. The wolf stones would be the only indication of the grave below; like the Quakers, the Society of Universal Friends didn't mark a grave with a headstone. Universal Friend preached (according to historian Stafford Cleveland) that "the living owed their best expenditure of love and labor to the living . . . the dead could be best remembered in the fragrance of lives consecrated to righteous endeavor."[3] In other words, the best way to honor the dead was to live a good life in the eyes of the Lord. No other marker was necessary.

Elizabeth died of a fever to which she had succumbed most likely due to malnourishment. Ever since the fall, supplies of food at the settlement had been dwindling and the settlers often went hungry. What they didn't yet understand was that their situation was not isolated to City Hill, but was the result of a worldwide phenomenon that would come to be known as "the Starving Year" or "the Hungry Year."[4] Throughout the world there had been profound disruptions in food supplies due to erratic and extreme weather. The strange weather was caused by volcanic eruptions in both Japan and Iceland that occurred in 1783. The eruptions released huge amounts of volcanic ash and dust into the higher atmosphere, severely limiting the amount of sunlight that could reach earth. While the effect of the reduced sunlight was not immediately felt (because the ash and dust took years to spread and then dissipate), by 1788 Great Britain and Europe were suffering catastrophic droughts that led to massive and widespread crop failures.[5]

The French government, and later the English as well, realized the political trouble that could be caused by the food shortages (and they were right: widespread famine and a faltering economy led to uprisings and revolution in France in 1789; and in England, riots took place throughout the British isles in the 1790s due to lack of food supplies).[6] Throughout the late summer and early fall of 1788, foreign governments secured trade deals for American-grown crops, setting especially high prices for wheat. Urban merchants in New England locked down lucrative contracts with northeast farmers to meet the demands overseas. Despite the wet summer, the American farmers were confident they would have enough of a harvest to both feed themselves and fulfill the contracts.

But they were wrong. The wet summer and fall, and the deep cold that settled in just at harvest time, led to crop failures throughout northeastern America, including parts of Canada, New England, New York, and Pennsylvania. The pervasively damp conditions also allowed the proliferation of a wheat parasite known as the Hessian fly, whose devastation of wheat stems further reduced crop yield. Under the terms of the contracts the New York farmers had signed with export merchants, they had to send what little wheat crops they managed to harvest to coastal ports to be carried across the ocean to Europe.[7] What was left in the farmer's own barns and silos was pitifully little.

As winter settled in, deprivations on the frontier grew only worse. Because of the extreme cold and heavy snowfall, food in the form of dairy and meat, whether venison, fish, or fowl, went lacking. Cows could not forage for feed under the snow nor was there hay adequate to sustain their milking, and many died. Herds of deer, which might have yielded a plentiful supply of meat, died off due to either starvation (what little food there was for the deer lay hidden beneath deep drifts of snow) or decimation by wolves, who could easily hunt down the weakened herds. Rivers were frozen solid, making fishing difficult, and the wildfowl seemed to have all flown away.

In coming to the frontier, settlers like the faithful followers at City Hill had expected to become self-sufficient, certain that through their own hard work and the bounty of the lands, they could grow their own ample supplies of the food they needed to survive. Now they found themselves dependent on larger farms for food—but the crops harvested by their farmer neighbors had been effectively confiscated by "the power and reach of the trans-Atlantic market."[8] The global market had depleted food supplies in western New York, and with dismal crops of their own, settlers, including Friend's followers, faced the very real possibility of starvation.

And yet the small group remaining on City Hill refused to lose hope. Abraham and Abigail Dayton; Richard Smith and his wife, Elizabeth; Jedidiah Holmes and his children; and the brothers Jonathan and Castle Dains, along with Castle's wife, Joanna: they were a hardy crew, confident of their own pioneering skills and deeply committed to both Universal Friend and the Society—and to each other. Jonathan Dains, desperate for wheat for his fellow settlers, traveled by boat and then on foot to a village fifty miles south of Seneca Lake. There he worked in a wheat field "until he obtained two bushels . . . which he had ground . . . [and then] carried on his back . . . again to his house," presumably to share with others on City Hill.[9] Abigail Dayton, who had started her own cheese-mongering enterprise (making cheese by laying "curd . . . in a hoop on a stump, and stones laid to press on it . . ."), shared with neighbors what little her poor cow could provide during this "season of great scarcity."[10]

Of all the settlers by the lake, this core group never seemed to have doubted their decision to come west over the past months of clearing, planting, and harvesting, and they wouldn't lose hope now. Somehow, they believed, all the hard work they had put into their settlement, along with all the moneys paid out to secure some kind of title to the land, must count for something. Their minister had promised them that hard work would lead to grace and eventual redemption: "I know thy works, and thy labour, and thy patience, and how thou . . . for my name's sake hast laboured, and hast not fainted."[11] Perhaps Universal Friend deliberately chose a place for followers to settle that required their hard work and dedication simply to survive, thereby guaranteeing not only a successful settlement but also their ultimate salvation.

If they could just hold on, Friend would come to them and then surely their settlement would prosper; "Have not I commanded thee? Be strong and of a good courage be not afraid, neither be thou dismayed: for the LORD thy God is with thee whithersoever thou goest."[12] The snowy and cold weather continued through the winter and didn't improve with the coming of spring. March was wet and gloomy, and by April throughout western New York, there was "a Scarcity of Provisions allmost to Famine. . . ."[13] Although settlers had been drawn to the area by its promises of bounty, "the most of them who have gone there . . . are starving to *death* and it is shocking to hear of the number of families that are dying daily for want of sustenance. . . ."[14]

In some of the western New York settlements, "there remained not one pound of salt meat nor a single biscuit . . . two hundred families about . . . and not a morsel of bread."[15] Food had grown so scarce that "armed, hungry, and penniless settlers halted and plundered" boats carrying grain up the Susquehanna River; in one instance, they surrounded the boat captain "& told him they would not starve, that they had not money to pay him but must have flour & would pay him when they were able."[16] On City Hill, the settlers resorted to "milk and boiled nettles" for sustenance.[17] Such diets were common: "wild roots and herbs . . . boiled and without salt, constitute the whole food of the most of the unhappy people. . . ."[18]

And then the news arrived. Universal Friend was not coming. Not for lack of desire or effort: the minister had almost died trying to get to City Hill in February. Traveling with Hitty Smith and Barnabas Brown, the trio had attempted, during a heavy storm, to cross a usually calm creek. But the downpour caused the creek waters to rise, turning it into a raging river. The horses pulling Universal Friend's coach abandoned it amid the surging waters, lurching through the waves to scramble up the banks of the creek and gallop away. The story told was that Barnabas jumped from his driver's bench and fought across the drag of the rising water to pull at the doors of the coach, calling to Hitty and Friend to get out, to save themselves.

Wasn't that exactly what Friend had been trying to do? Get out? The minister had pleaded with followers "to make your escape from the wrath which is to come, upon all the wicked that know not God and have not obeyed the voice of the dear Son of his Love. . . ."[19] Had the wrath now descended and would Friend die here, in a muddy creek, the dream of a "peacable habitation for me and my friends" never to be realized?[20]

Hitty and Friend pushed together to open the coach door against the rising water and finally got themselves out, fighting against the fast currents of the swollen stream to reach land. All three travelers made it safely to shore, but Friend was left "enfeebled by the shock."[21] They returned to Worcester and there they now remained, living in the Wagener farmhouse along with Sarah Richards and the two Malin sisters, Rachel and Margaret. The women had committed themselves to caring for Friend during what would be a long recuperation.

Throughout May and into early summer, the weather in the Seneca Lake settlement continued too wet and cold for planting—nor could anything have grown if planting had been attempted. Even in June, there were "frosts the three last nights—this morning ice as thick as window glass in the watering trough. . . ."[22] Chickens, and their eggs, were scarce, and the cows that had survived the winter had no spring grass to sustain them. One settler in western New York wrote of seeing women and children dining on "tadpoles boiled in water," while others resorted to eating rodents and wild plants, a dangerous practice.[23] If the wrong plants were ingested, death by poisoning could result. A common and fatal mistake was confusing water hemlock, a deadly plant, with wild leeks, a mildly nutritious one. Reports of the famine and its consequences on settler populations were published throughout the northeastern press—but such reports only led to greater "public alarm," which drove food prices even higher, encouraging speculative hoarding by merchants and making the lack of available grain and other food supplies even worse on the western frontier.[24]

It wasn't only those on the western frontier who suffered. Food shortages spread into New England all the way to Maine, and farther north into Canada, and also south through New York into the Hudson Valley and beyond. Reports were passed in letters and newspapers of "the extreme distress. . . . No bread or provision of any kind. The scene is truly painful. . . . Some have died and many are sick. . . ."[25] And what were the federal or local governments doing to alleviate the suffering? As one historian has noted, there was a "virtual absence of state action and public resources" allocated to the problem in the United States.[26] Was it a lack of coordination or an overload of issues for the new governments to deal with that led to their failure to address the famine?

The Confederation Congress had been dissolved in March of 1789, and the new Congress of the United States, convening in New York City, was too wrapped up in setting up the new government to take notice of the starving settlers to the west. One of the governmental entities they established, the Department of Foreign Affairs, was later renamed the Department of State because it took on domestic duties as well—but too late to help those suffering the deprivations of the

Hungry Year. Governor Clinton, concerned that reports of the famine would put an end to the land sales, which had so successfully been swelling state coffers, urged the New York legislature to do something to address "the distresses experienced . . . particularly in the exterior settlements, and by the poorer class of people."[27]

But the state's purchase of less than two thousand bushels of corn to alleviate the sufferings of tens of thousands of settlers and Native Americans in the western counties proved woefully inadequate, and in the end, the only useful aid they received came mostly in the form of foods distributed by speculators like Oliver Phelps and William Cooper (founder of Cooperstown, New York, and father of writer James Fenimore Cooper). Phelps helped to feed hundreds of starving Cayugas, Oneidas, and Senecas, but still "they came away hungry, notwithstanding upwards of 100 heads of Cattle was killed for them. . . ."[28] Settlements of whites and Native Americans also negotiated their own deals with private merchants; pioneers who successfully negotiated an exchange of ginseng crops for flour from a merchant named Isaac Paris were so grateful that they renamed their settlement after him (and Paris, New York, still stands).

Universal Friend, on the mend in Worcester, struggled with what to do. While anxious to provide the leadership and support so desperately needed by the settlers at City Hill, the minister must also have worried about adding to their burdens if an entourage of followers were to arrive: more mouths to feed, beds to find, futures to worry about. Did the minister wonder if God had some purpose in holding back his messenger from traveling to the western frontier? Turning to dreams for counsel and guidance, Friend told Sarah Richards about one in which a man "about 10 feet high, cloathed in a garment down to his feet . . ." presented to the minister "a large Scroll in which was written Lamentation, mourning & woe! Famine, Sword, and Pestilence For the Lord was about to put an end to the Day and time of the Wicked."[29]

"It is Sifting Time," the minister concluded, and for those "on the Lord's Side . . . [who] love Mercy, and walk humbly," there was nothing to fear.[30] Although there are no surviving letters from the minister to the settlers during this period of suffering, the words Friend penned in a journal, quoted from the German mystic Johannes Tauler, may have been shared with the pioneers: "When I am pinched with hunger, I praise God; If I suffer cold If it hail If it snow If it rain If the weather be fair or foul I praise God . . . Therefore, there never Happened Any Sad or Evil Morning to me."[31] If the small settlement at City Hill could just hold on, the morning would come when all the faithful would be reunited. But for how long could they survive?

18

Bounty Be Praised

"The nearer I get to my desired port
the more earnest I am to arrive;
May this be the Case of my Soul
with regard to my heavenly home:
the nearer my approach, the more engaged. . . ."

—SARAH RICHARDS

The weather finally turned warm in July of 1789. Rain fell on the lands of western New York, followed by days of nurturing sun. Crops and grasses grew, fruit trees and vines blossomed, and an abundant autumn harvest seemed assured. While it would be months before wheat and other fall crops could be harvested, summer vegetables were ripening on the vine, cows fed happily on meadow grasses, and deer and fowl returned to the woodlands. The Hungry Year was over. Followers that had left City Hill in late fall of 1788 now returned, including William Potter and Thomas Hathaway, who brought along his four children; Hannah Reynolds, who convinced her husband, Stephen Card, to return with her; and Hannah's sister, Mary Gardener, who traveled with her three children, leaving husband, George, behind in Rhode Island. Hannah and Mary's brother, John, having clashed with

Parker the previous fall, chose to remain in Rhode Island. He'd been an early convert to Universal Friend back in 1779, but frontier living was not for him.

The reinvigorated group cleared more land and close to forty acres of wheat were sowed. But the small square of meadow surrounding the grave of Elizabeth Holmes was left untouched, a quiet reminder of loss. Cedars would eventually be planted to create a proper cemetery (which still exists today and can be visited). But for now, the area was marked only by the grave's protective shield of wolf stones and a cluster of wildflowers left to seed: wild bergamot, chicory, Queen Anne's lace.

New life was celebrated in the community, with the birth of Lament, daughter of George and Bethany Sisson. She would be joined a few years later by a brother, Luther (in 1869, Luther would be one of the eyewitnesses who spoke in glowing terms with historian Stafford Cleveland about the Society of Universal Friends and their minister). Deaths and births were marked by the followers of Universal Friend with prayer and then life continued: "One generation passeth away, and another generation cometh: but the earth abideth for ever."[1]

There still had been no clear resolution by the summer of 1789 of who actually held title to the earth that the pioneers worked so diligently. But Parker assured his fellow settlers that the more productive they could make their claimed acres, the better it would be for them all. Their community would demonstrate to the authorities that the wilderness could be tamed, and productive and upstanding communities established. As Parker would later argue to New York State's Land Office and to Governor Clinton, "you will Judge it most for the benefit of the State to let us have these Lands . . . because our Settlement . . . has greatly Encouraged Settling that part of this State."[2] And more settlers would come, now that the Hungry Year had passed.

The fall harvest proved to be as good as the summer sun and rain had promised, and by December of 1789 ample stores of food had been laid in by Friend's followers on City Hill. They had also, over the past months, built sturdy homes with woodpiles stacked alongside to keep the wide chimneys burning throughout the cold months ahead. Well-worn paths now ran between the farmhouses and barns, and along streams and fields, which would make for easier clearing after heavy snowfalls. When the winter arrived, blowing in from the west by early December, it was as cold as it had been the year before, and the snows were as deep. But there would be no deaths this winter, and the cold and snow were endurable. And with the coming of the new year, good news arrived in the settlement. Universal Friend was finally coming west.

The minister left Worcester in February of 1790, traveling in company of a large number of followers, including Elijah Malin, Ruth Pritchard, Sarah Richards, and Sarah's ten-year-old daughter, Eliza; Silas Spink, a forty-three-year-old bachelor eager for a change; and Ezekiel Shearman, who had left the settlement in the fall of 1789 to marry Mary Supplee (the sister of the preacher who had first welcomed Friend to Worcester) and now brought her back west with him. The youngest traveler in the group was Martha Hazard, Elsie Potter Hazard's eleven-month-old baby. Elsie had reconciled with her husband, Arnold, just long enough to bring about Martha's birth, but was now once again separated from her husband and living with Friend in Worcester. Before going to City Hill, Elsie wanted to return to Rhode Island to gather supplies and so she had ridden off in the new year on her chestnut mare, leaving Martha behind. She promised to be back in time for February's planned departure. But she hadn't arrived back by early March and so Universal Friend and baby Martha left Worcester without her.

Ruth Pritchard kept a journal of the group's journey through the Wyoming Valley and into New York, demonstrating a dry sense of humor when she noted early on, "As for the pleasantness of my companions in the tedious march, I shall omit to mention at this time."[3] At every stop along the way, Universal Friend preached to the groups that gathered on the roadside or on the shores of the Susquehanna River. No matter how isolated these communities were, residents had received reports about the ministry of salvation and were curious to see the minister for themselves. While meetings held in Philadelphia in 1788 and 1789 had often been disrupted by crowds hostile to Universal Friend—"exceeding rude, Huzzahs several times"—the meetings in western Pennsylvania and into New York were peaceful affairs and may even have drawn new followers to the Society.[4]

Universal Friend and the large group of travelers finally arrived on the shores of Seneca Lake in April of 1790. A number of the pioneers, including Elizabeth and Richard Smith, and Abraham and Abigail Dayton, had not seen their minister for almost three years, and Elijah Malin was reunited with his brother Enoch, whom he had not seen since the spring of 1788. In the midst of the joyful reunions, just when one of the settlers said, "we have come to a place now where Elsie can't find us," Elsie Potter Hazard came riding out of the woods.[5] From Rhode Island to Worcester to Wyoming to City Hill, Elsie had ridden hundreds of miles through "nearly unmitigated wilderness" to arrive at Seneca Lake.[6] She would make the same journey three more times, always on horseback, and on the final return trip she carried behind her in the saddle her eight-year-old son, Brenton (another product of a brief Elsie-Arnold reconciliation).[7]

With Universal Friend now in residence, along with many women devoted to spiritual and community engagement, the bickering that had occurred under James Parker's leadership faded into a distant memory, and feelings of shared fellowship and piety soared. The heart of the Society now beat on the western frontier. Friend had no intentions to ever return east—but at the same time, the minister was not planning to conduct evangelizing missions in the west. Both the loci and the focus of Friend's God-given errand had changed. God's message of warning to a "perishing dying World, to flee from the wrath to come" had begun as a mobile movement to attract followers, but now the quest was to provide a place "for everyone that will come, may come, and partake of the waters of life freely, which is offered to sinner without money, and without price." City Hill would serve as a light in the darkness to draw "lost & perishing" souls to the settlement, where they would find the Eden they needed to heal, to repent, and to find redemption.[8]

While still in Worcester, Universal Friend had a dream in which a "large pair of Scales [were] let down to the earth, the cord held out of sight by an Invisible hand . . . to weigh all the inhabitants of the Earth, all that the Lord calls to Judgment!"[9] Settled on City Hill, did Friend interpret the dream to mean that here in the wilderness the scales would fall, here was the central gathering place where the saved came to be judged?[10]

The purpose of moving west had always been clear. Universal Friend sought a place where the minister and faithful followers—and any and all willing newcomers—could live in peace and work toward their own redemption: "a good country where [we] can live together . . . be faithful watch and pray. . . ."[11] And now it seemed as if the long-held dream was coming to life just as the minister had imagined it: "I could rest in Nothing which was less than good. . . . I have forsaken the unquiet world and . . . I have found Everlasting Peace and Rest."[12] But peace took more than a landscape. It required commitment of the individual faithful to the community as a whole. The settlers had come west to find their Eden, but Eden could not simply be found; it had to be created, one step at a time.

On the Fourth of July, 1790, Richard Smith, brother of Hitty, wrote in the family Bible, "I have this day completed my grist mill and have ground ten bushels of Rye."[13] The long-hoped-for gristmill had finally been built, constructed stone by stone on the banks of the vigorously flowing stream called "the Keuka outlet" (because it led from Keuka Lake to Seneca Lake).[14] The sound of the stream had first caught the attention of the early pioneers back in the summer of 1788, and when they found its source, they had marveled at what a good place it would be for a mill. And now it was done. Driven by the heavy current of the stream, the wooden waterwheel could revolve at a steady rate and propel the attached millstones to rotate, one above the other (the top wheel had furrows that rubbed hard against the flat lower stone, creating the grinding motion), turning corn into cornmeal and wheat into flour. The Society of Universal Friends could now mill its own grains.

Without a mill, harvested grains like wheat and corn had been ground by hand, a very difficult task involving a hollowed-out tree stump and a large wooden pestle and which resulted in a roughly ground meal known as "samp."[15] The only alternative for the pioneers had been to transport their grains long distances for grinding at an established mill, an endeavor that was both time-consuming and expensive. In a letter written by James Parker to Friend in 1788, he had complained, "our bread costs at least double what it did at Rhode Island."[16] With their own mill, the settlers could save money—and make money. Farmers from miles around—"the whole region of eastern Ontario county"—would rely on what became known as "Friend's Mill" for years to come.[17]

The millstones for the new mill, weighing up to three thousand pounds each, had been brought to New York from New Milford, Connecticut, a grueling journey likely carried out by Richard Smith and Abraham Dayton. The stones were carried by cart and by boat, landing at the dock on the southern shore of Seneca Lake just before an early snowstorm blanketed the region, and then transferred onto sleds to finally be deposited on the banks of the Keuka outlet. For the next eighteen months, Richard Smith, Abraham Dayton, James Parker, and other faithful followers put their backs into building the gristmill.

During its construction, one of the heavy millstones fell from the banks of the Keuka outlet to the water below. The men working that day, including Richard Smith, took a break. They were uncertain of how to proceed. While the others went for a meal, Richard decided to tackle the problem on his own. Using "ingenious leverage and industrious prying," he managed to raise the heavy stone back up onto the high bank. For years after, he was known as the man who "picked up a millstone and carried it in his apron."[18]

The opening of the mill was only one event in a summer full of activity. Fields of corn and rye were planted alongside the acres of wheat. Beehives (skeps made of coiled straw set on wooden platforms) popped up on hillsides. Kitchen gardens were laid out in neat rows behind the tidy log cabins of the settlers. New homes were built to provide shelter for the more than sixty families of faithful followers now living on City Hill, making it "the largest settlement by far in western New York. . . ."[19]

A home was also built for Universal Friend by Elijah and Enoch Malin and paid for by Anna Wagener. Set on a bank overlooking a meandering creek, the home was large and impressive, framed with thick beams, then vertically sided with clapboard, the "hand-sawed 1.5-inch thick planks nailed in place with hand-wrought nails," and topped with a high gambrel roof.[20] A wide-planked front door welcomed visitors, and inside, a deep central chimney fed nine fireplaces, more than enough to warm the many followers who would come to live with Friend over the next year.

Perhaps the most important structure built that summer was the new meetinghouse; for while the fields and hives, gardens and gristmill would feed the followers' bellies, the meetinghouse would feed their souls. Many hands shared in the labor of building it. First, heavy stones for the foundation were carefully laid, then logs were set one by one, overlapping and joined at the corners; windows were cut out and chinking of sand and mud was applied between the logs; and then rafters were laid and the roof raised. With a single doorway, shallow windows, and a low-pitched roof, it wasn't a large building (only thirty square feet) and recurring problems with the roof in the years to come meant that during heavy thunderstorms, "rain came down like a flood."[21] But the congregants didn't mind because now they had their minister back with them, standing tall on the preaching platform and guiding them once again to redemption. They had built an entire community by themselves—and yet they seemed grateful to Friend for having inspired them to do it.

It was most likely here at City Hill that Universal Friend first began to celebrate the Sabbath on Saturday, as practiced by the Ephrata in Pennsylvania. Raised as a Quaker, Friend understood that accepting Sunday as the day of worship was simply a matter of convenience: all other Christian religions reserved Sunday as the Sabbath and so the Quakers did, too. Now removed to the wilderness, Friend selected Saturday as "the Sabbath and primary day of worship," while Sunday would be the day of rest.[22]

But even on Sundays Friend met with individuals seeking guidance and advice. When one follower asked for advice on the opening of a distillery on the banks of the Keuka outlet, Universal Friend counseled against it, saying "it will prove a snare to thee."[23] Cider and beer could be made, but spirits would lead to intemperance and damnation. And there was no time at Friend's settlement for intemperance or any other indulgences of sloth and pleasure. Much like the Quakers, Universal Friend believed that leisure and "recreation . . . might detract from the true purpose of man," i.e., repentance and salvation.[24] The minister advised followers to "persevere in the humble service of the Lord through life and labor for a growth in grace. . . ."[25]

Not only dedicated labor was required for achieving grace (and deliverance from sins) but also sacrifice: "I beseech you therefore, brethren, by the mercies of God, that ye present your bodies a living sacrifice, holy, acceptable unto God, which is your reasonable service. . . ."[26] And the sacrifices made by the Society's pioneers at City Hill were many. They gave up the comforts of their previous established homes and the conveniences of towns and villages and moved to a place where everything had to be constructed from scratch. There were no luxuries or conveniences to offset the danger and discomforts of pioneer living. No local stores or coffeehouses, no bookshops or blacksmiths, no paved roads or stagecoach stops.

Life was just as hard for their leader. How much easier it would have been for Universal Friend to stay in Rhode Island or Pennsylvania, living in the mansion in Little Rest or in the comfortable stone house in Worcester and preaching to established congregations. As Herbert Wisbey, twentieth-century biographer of Friend, put it, by rejecting "the conveniences of settled society, and turning to the wilderness, [Universal Friend] accepted the crude life of a frontier pioneer in order to gather a community of the faithful."[27] Leading by example, the minister worked the fields, assisted in the weaving shed, helped out in the dairy, and also "hoed and weeded in her garden, picked berries, plucked grass for weaving baskets, and did other chores necessary on a frontier farm."[28]

Friend also scoured the woods for the medicinal herbs and plants needed in caring for the faithful. Lessons learned as a girl back in Cumberland were not forgotten, and now as a minister to so many, Friend was their trusted healer. A circular wooden box, always close at hand, served as a medical chest. It was filled with an assortment of remedies, salves, tonics, and bandages, because not only did Friend treat illnesses but also injuries from accidents, including broken bones.[29]

One day at City Hill, Abigail Dayton, standing on a wooden platform overlooking a wide stream, tried to knock a snake off a tree (for what purpose Abigail made such an attempt is lost to history, but she may have believed that the sooner a snake is brought to the ground, the sooner it can be killed). In the effort of swiping at the snake, Abigail lost her balance and fell from the platform, plunging thirty feet down into the stream and landing just inches from the snake, which she had successfully dislodged from the tree.

The snake began squirming its way toward her, jaws wide. Abigail screamed for help. Abraham Dayton came running to find his wife, now standing in the water, with "the bones from a broken bone protruding through the skin and stocking, while she was beating off the snake with a stick. . . ."[30] The snake finally slithered away, and Abraham carried Abigail all the way to Friend's home. The minister must have first fixed up some concoction for the pain and then, once Abigail had calmed down, set the broken bone, dressing the leg with care and skill. The leg "healed without difficulty" and Mrs. Dayton had no more problems with it, standing strong until her death at age ninety-three.[31]

To the east in New York City, while the pioneers built their settlement of faith at City Hill, the structure of a new nation was being built by men convening in Congress. Rhode Island was the last state to ratify the United States Constitution in the spring of 1790, making it the law of the land, and in the summer of 1790, Congress passed the Residence Act, directing that the capital of the United States and permanent seat of its federal government be located at a site along the Potomac River in Virginia, to be called the District of Columbia. Over the months to come, Congress would debate amendments to the Constitution, but it would not be until 1791 when the Bill of Rights, guaranteeing freedom of religion and freedom of speech, along with other specifically defined rights, was added to the document.

New traditions were also developed by the federal government to support and cement the alliance of the thirteen states into a joined nation. In January of 1790, George Washington gave the first State of the Union address and the nation's first federal budget was prepared by the nation's first secretary of the treasury, Alexander Hamilton. In August of 1790, the first census was taken of U.S. residents, with its tabulations released two years later: 3,919,023 people lived in the nation's thirteen states and four districts (Kentucky, Maine, Vermont, and Tennessee).

The settlement on City Hill was developing its own bonding traditions, such as Saturday's weekly meeting, attended by all members, and the smaller, more private sessions of family prayer held throughout the week. But while there were certainly expectations as to behavior and spiritual commitment, the community did not have laws or a delineated governing body—they accepted the government of the United States as their own—nor did the Society impose the rules dictating day-to-day activities and behaviors of its members that other religious settlements of the time enforced with rigor. For example, in the communities established by the Shakers and the Ephrata and the Moravians in Bethlehem, Pennsylvania (founded by German pietist missionaries in 1741), members were subjected to strict rules (enforced through isolation, shaming, and banishment) that regulated every aspect of their daily lives including how they dressed, how they spoke, what time they woke up and what time they went to sleep. Members of those sects also had to conform to gender-specific roles and duties and were required to contribute the fruits of their labors to the community at large.

Members of Friend's Society did not have to follow a set schedule for work (or waking or sleeping); in fact, there were no specific work requirements at all. Women were not restricted in their work choices and could take on leadership roles in the spiritual life of the community; they preached, led meetings, and counseled other members on religious questions. The Society of Universal Friends was unique in allowing women to perform such important roles; it was not until "the 1830s and 1840s . . . several decades after the Society of Universal Friends had helped to pioneer female religious leadership" that Shaker women were allowed to exercise "spiritual authority," i.e., preach and minister to their community.[32] None of Friend's followers, male or female, was prohibited from speaking at meals nor required to wear specific clothing or head covering or haircut, and there was no mandatory tithing to the sect.

Other religious sects often separated men and women for meals, work, and rest, and for the Shakers and Ephrata, celibacy was mandated. (The Shakers' prohibition of sex among its members can be traced back to founder Ann Lee's experiences with childbirth, which led her to denounce sex as the source of "human misery and sin.")[33] At City Hill, however, men and women mixed freely, and celibacy was never required. There were men and women, such as Silas Spink, William Turpin, and Hitty Smith, who chose to be celibate, but many others who did not; and there were also members who had been part of sexual unions at some point (including Friend's own sisters Patience, Deborah, and Marcy), but chose to be celibate at other points in their lives.

The acceptance of nuclear families within the community also distinguished the Society of Universal Friends from other sects of the early nineteenth century.[34] The Oneida Community, the Harmony Society, the Zoarites, and especially the Shakers, renounced the unions and obligations of family. One popular Shaker hymn even went so far as to profess hatred toward family and family ties: "Of all the relations that ever I see / My old fleshy kindred are furthest from me. / So bad and so ugly, so hateful they feel / To See them and hate them increases my zeal. . . ."[35] But within the Society of Universal Friends, nuclear families were supported and a number of followers had children (although birth rates were lower than that of neighboring communities).[36]

Children born into the community were cherished—Elizabeth Luther named her son "Beloved"—and they were nurtured and nourished by all members of the community.[37] When Elizabeth Rose died at the age of six, the child was mourned greatly, for "She was a wonderful child, whom the Friend loved."[38] Unlike many children in the western settlements, the Society's children were given an education provided by a succession of devoted schoolteachers, including Sarah Richards, Ruth Pritchard, and John Briggs (the log meetinghouse was also the Society's first schoolhouse). Universal Friend believed that "the noblest employment of the mind of Man is the study of the Works of His Creator. To him whom the science of nature delighteth, every object bringeth a proof of his God; everything that proveth it, giveth cause of adoration."[39]

While the Society of Universal Friends remained largely white, African Americans were integral and welcomed members, including Chloe Towerhill, a former enslaved person; Sarah Negus, an early follower from Rhode Island; and Jacob Weaver, recorded in the Death Book as "an Ethiopian" when he died.[40] They were treated the same as all followers were treated—equal among Society members and equal before God—and considered by Universal Friend to be family, like all members of the Society, whether or not they actually lived in Friend's household (Chloe Towerhill would live with Friend for years, and continue living in the household after Friend's death).[41]

In many ways, even while the community was deeply pious and led by a leader who relied almost entirely on biblical texts to guide it, Friend's settlement functioned more as a traditional village than as the commune implemented by the Shakers or Ephrata. Families at City Hill lived and worked in individual homes, men and women side by side, running their households and raising their families. Their faith was proven not by following rigid rules, but by working hard and sharing what could be shared; by living in peace with each other; and by coming together at weekly meeting to hear counsel of their trusted leader. One follower of the time recalled that "the Society usually gathered promptly at the proper hour and sat in silence. Friend would enter soon and sit for a few moments . . . kneel and pray aloud fervently for some time, then after remaining seated in silence for a few moments, arise and speak. . . . These discourses were always listened to with the utmost quiet . . . a more reverential body of worshippers it would be difficult to find."[42] At the end of meetings, everyone "present would make it a point to shake hands with the Friend."[43]

As 1790 drew to a close and the settlers prepared themselves for winter, they felt confident of their future. Their minister was with them for good now, and the mission of salvation would thrive. Worries over their property claims faded—after all, no one had come to drive them away from their farms and homes—and plentiful food had been stored away for the cold months ahead after a harvest season "much Better than hath been Ever Known" in the lands of western New York (claimed the founder of Cooperstown, William Cooper).[44] No one would starve on City Hill, either spiritually or physically, this winter.

Sarah Richards, who was still living in Worcester, had a dream in which she saw Universal Friend standing at the head of a gathering of followers. Voices sang out in choruses of "hallelujahs" and then Friend announced that "the time is come, the time is come." As Friend spoke, "smoke of a purple color" flowed from the minister's mouth (purple was associated with Christ and was also a favorite color of Friend). At the end of the dream, Universal Friend sat high "on an Eminence and on the Friend's Countenance a Smile."[45] To Sarah, the meaning was clear: Universal Friend's dream of creating an Eden in the wilderness had come true.

But into every Eden comes a snake.

19

A Question of Trust

"They glory in their shame and mind earthly things. . . ."

—UNIVERSAL FRIEND

By the start of the year 1791, William Potter and his sons Arnold and Thomas had amassed for themselves over fifty-five thousand acres of land west of Seneca Lake, negotiating with numerous speculators to find the best deals. Potter boasted that Oliver Phelps had become one of his great—and presumably trusted—friends, and with connections like that, there were land deals to be had.[1] And plenty of money to be made: land values continued to increase as more and more eastern "Yankees" moved west in search of fertile land and new beginnings.[2] Robert Morris, a banker from Philadelphia who had helped finance the American Revolution (and was one of only two men to sign the Articles of Confederation, the Declaration of Independence, *and* the Constitution—the other was Roger Sherman of Connecticut), almost doubled his profits on property he purchased in 1790 and sold just one year later; General Philip Schuyler, friend of both Morris and George Washington, and father-in-law to Alexander Hamilton, reaped thousands of dollars in land deals made around Albany; and William Cooper of New York amassed enough property to name an entire town after himself and still have acres left over to sell for a handsome profit.

William Potter had come west seeking a community of faith and fellowship, far from the concerns of money, status, or economic competition. But in the heady environment of vigorous land sales and always rising prices, he turned again into the man of business he had once been.[3] Perhaps he dreamed that one day there would be a town named for him on the shores of Seneca Lake (it would actually be his son Arnold who incorporated a village named "Potter's Town," later known simply as "Potter," which still exists as a tiny hamlet south of Canandaigua).

There was no attempt by either William Potter or James Parker to hide their acquisitions of large tracts of land close to the property the Society claimed for itself. But even if they wanted to keep their investments hidden, the web of family connections across the settlement (Friend's sister Patience was married to Thomas Potter; Potter's daughter Elsie was a confidante of Friend; Ezekiel Shearman, another confidant to Friend, was the brother-in-law to James Parker, and so on and so on) meant that secrets couldn't be kept among the followers.

The question for Friend was: Given their individual ambitions, were Potter and Parker still devoted to the community of faith? And was their devotion enough to keep intact their commitment to the original compact of *mutual* prosperity? While the purpose of moving west had been to find a safe place for the community to put down roots, the agreement made back in New Milford also promised self-sufficiency, implying at least moderate prosperity for everyone willing to help build a community of faith on the western frontier. As James Parker himself stated, "it was believed that land in the new country would be plentiful and cheap enough so that any member of the society who wished to participate . . . would be helped by the group to secure enough land to support himself and his family even if he could not contribute a proportionate share in the purchase fund."[4]

But the 1786 agreement to purchase western lands for the good of every member of the Society was never a signed contract. Did Friend fear that its underlying tenet of "room for all"—no matter an individual's financial situation—might be ignored now by those who wished for more room for themselves? They had the money to pay for more—but would they leave the others out in the cold?

James Parker decided in the spring of 1791 that he needed to settle the question of who owned the lands upon which the Society had built City Hill. He told Friend and the other members of the community that he would go all the way to the New York governor's office in New York City to fight for title of the lands for which he first negotiated back in 1788, and vowed to win over not only Governor Clinton but also all the influential men who sat on the State Lands Commission. Given the property ambitions of Parker, did Friend wonder if he would be arguing for the good of the community or for the good of the few? Did Parker seek to clarify the Society's ownership of land or to secure the investments that he and Potter had made on their own? Friend had reminded Parker in the fall of 1788, "I have been many times seemingly present with thee into the silent watches of the night . . ." and the minister would continue to keep an eye on him now. And not only keep an eye but remind him to stay faithful to his community and his God, and to resist the temptation of mammon: "rise and pray, lest ye enter into temptation."[5]

In the petition that James Parker delivered in person to the New York State Land Commission, he presented a persuasive history of the efforts put in by the Society of Universal Friends to make City Hill a success, highlighting the many burdens they had overcome and their hard-won successes, while leaving out the community's internal struggles. Parker began at the beginning: having scouted out "Several places" for a potential settlement, the Society "finaly gave preference to the Geneseo County. . . ." Land had then been purchased of "the Leasee Company," who "told us it would be a Great Advantage to us to be concerned with them . . . & no harm to any body. . . ."[6] Once the Society realized they had been duped by the "Leasee Company," they "agreed with Oliver Phelps for some land, and went into that Country to begin our settlement. . . ." Since that time, the followers of Universal Friend had been busy: "about sixty families are settled . . . we have a good Grist Mill and Saw mill . . . and carry on Necessary Business . . . which [has] greatly incouraged the settling of that part of the State."[7] Parker argued that the Society's justified reliance on (dubious) contracts and their subsequent hard work improving the lands that they occupied should be enough to support their claim to legal ownership of those lands.

Parker's arguments proved convincing, and on May 9, 1791, New York State agreed to convey to Parker twelve thousand acres of land (including a large portion of lands for which the Society had already paid once) for a comparatively low price (although the actual sum still had to be negotiated). When the lands given by the state were surveyed, the property would turn out to be over fourteen thousand acres. Although there were still the final negotiations to be made on price and payment terms, Parker made his way back to City Hill a happy man. Yes, the Society would have to pay again for properties they had already paid for, but this time the state was on their side, and the title presumably would not be challenged again.

Sarah Richards was also on her way to City Hill in the late spring of 1791, traveling from Worcester, Pennsylvania, with a large group of followers, including Hitty Smith, and Rachel and Margaret Malin (their brothers, Enoch and Elijah, were already on City Hill). Both Hitty and Rachel had been severely ill in the spring—Rachel, "laboring under symptoms of some terrible disorder," and Mehitable Smith "violently taken sick"—but Sarah Richards had treated the two women with bleeding and now, with their health restored, they were ready to travel.[8] Carrying wagonloads of supplies, they traveled from Worcester through the Wyoming Valley and then up the Susquehanna by boat. Sarah Richards wrote in her daybook of how they finally "safe arrived together on the west side of Seneca Lake and reach'd the Friends House which the Friend had got built for our reception. And with great joy, met the Friend once more in time, and all in walking health, and as well as usual."[9] Sarah Richards moved into Friend's home and would never leave her minister's side again.

Another traveler to the settlement in the spring of 1791 was Marcy Wilkinson Aldrich, sister to Universal Friend. Accompanied by her husband, she left Rhode Island sometime in early May. But during "His journeying to this new settlement, [William] Sicken'd and Died."[10] Marcy buried her husband in a ceremony attended by strangers and in a grave marked only by a flat stone, then continued up the Mohawk River on her own. Like Elsie Potter Hazard the year before, Marcy traveled without fear for her safety. But although she felt safe—"Be strong and of a good courage, fear not . . . for the Lord doth go with thee"—she must also have felt both very sad and very alone.[11] To find the populous household of Friend waiting for her at City Hill would have been a welcome comfort. She told fellow followers about her journey and the loss of her husband, and Sarah Richards recorded William's death in the Society Death Book: "He was aged 35. Went away . . . Spirits rejoicing . . . this he saw, the Universal Friend was a messenger sent from God."[12]

Marcy and her husband, having contributed money to the original fund to buy western lands, had been looking forward to building a home on the frontier. Marcy resolved to follow through on their dream, but for the time being she moved into Universal Friend's house. Knowing her sibling well, Marcy was not surprised to see the many books Friend had brought west. Not only religious texts but also histories and reference books, and, of course, Friend's own large and beautifully printed Bible.[13] Marcy settled easily into the home, living alongside the Malin siblings (Rachel, Margaret, and Elijah) and Hitty Smith, Eliza Richards (Sarah's daughter), Asa Richards (Sarah's brother-in-law), Ruth Pritchard, Mary Bean, and, of course, Sarah Richards.

Friend never closed a door to anyone in need, and the women and men who came to stay for a week or two often ended up becoming permanent residents. David Wagener, his wife Rebecca, and his siblings

Jacob and Anna may have stayed with Friend when they first came west, also in 1791, but they would soon build their own large homes on properties spreading across the hills from Seneca Lake toward Keuka Lake.

As a self-proclaimed messenger of God, Friend chose to not engage in worldly transactions, including financial transactions, and the minister never claimed ownership of any "earthly possession. If you talk to her of her house, she always calls it 'the house which I inhabit.'"[14] But there were debts to be paid and costs to be borne in running a household, and Sarah Richards took charge of all the necessary financial matters and concerns. On June 7, 1791, Sarah "reckoned and settled with" Thomas Orman, the boatman who had brought "up the Universal Friend's goods" the year before; on June 24, she "reckoned and settled with" Elijah Malin "for building Friend's house"; and on July 3, she "reckoned and settled with Richard Hathaway for goods which the carpenters took up at his store for building the Friend's Home." Underscoring that the debt had been fully met, Sarah added, "Settled, I say, this 3d of the 7th Month, 1791."[15]

Sarah also made down payments on properties that Friend wished to purchase for the Society; William Potter was not the only one buying up acreage in Genesee County. But were their motivations different? Potter seemed intent on enrichment, while Universal Friend purchased land in anticipation of the future needs of the growing community of faith. Just how those lands would be needed in the not-so-distant future could never have been anticipated.

But should the treachery to come have been anticipated? The temptations of envy and greed had always lurked; as Sarah Richards wrote to Friend in 1787, her fellow followers "are in such a situation as to their Earthly Concerns . . . that nothing seemingly can relieve them except the Friend."[16] In 1788, when James Parker and the first pioneers were laying the groundwork for the Society's western settlement, the minister brought up the temptations of "Earthly Concerns" and counseled him to remain vigilant in his faith: "I desire thee might wound the serpents head wherever thee finds it . . . whilst you are employed in earthly business, do not forget . . . your souls which ought to be your greatest concern."[17]

Friend must have had concerns over Society unity, because it was around this time that the minister again began to preach (as in the early 1780s when Friend sensed material ambitions growing among members) about the ways in which greed disrupted the peace of a community, because it led to treachery: "Oh, the Heart is deceitful above all things, and desperately wicked. . . ."[18] Warning that the desire for wealth posed an insurmountable obstacle on the road to redemption, the minister often referenced the biblical text "No man can serve two masters. Ye cannot serve God and Mammon."[19] Friend also reminded followers, "it is easier for a camel to go through a needle's eye, than for a rich man to enter into the kingdom of God."[20]

Despite the sermons, William Potter and James Parker made plans to build large, elegant homes (perhaps in an effort to shun forever memories of the log huts they'd suffered in during the first year of the settlement). They ordered new coaches, and horses fine enough to drive them. Parker and Potter didn't hide their wealth; they enjoyed it, and they used it, not only to build homes rich with material goods but also to be build expedient social friendships and advantageous political alliances outside of the Society of Universal Friends. By forming friendships and alliances with outsiders, Parker and Potter could increase their own wealth through all sorts of deals and connections while also broadening their own social and political influence throughout western New York. In short, they were looking beyond the community of faith in planning their futures on the frontier. They no longer looked to Friend for temporal guidance, nor did they seem constrained in their actions by the minister's spiritual teachings.

Friend didn't condemn the men for wanting to live well or owning nice things; over the years, the minister would receive many luxurious gifts that were enjoyed and the homes in which Friend lived were comfortable and spacious. But was Friend worried about the impact their activities could have on the stability and security of the Society? To say nothing of the state of their own souls.

Perhaps as a way of reminding all followers of the original mission of the Society of Universal Friends, their leader decided in the fall of 1791 to register the sect as a "religious denomination" under New York state law.[21] In 1784, New York State had codified the separation of church and state and ensured the free practice of religion as guaranteed in the state's Constitution of 1777.[22] As Rachel Malin explained, "we live in a Land of Liberty and Each one have Equal right to worship our Creator according to the Dictates of his own conscience. . . ."[23] New York was among the first states to provide legal protections for its religious societies (it was not until December 1791 that the First Amendment to the United States Constitution was finally ratified) and throughout the end of the eighteenth century and into the nineteenth, there was a burgeoning of unique religious sects in the state. On the western frontier, the Society of Universal Friends found new neighbors in denominations ranging from Baptists to Methodists to Presbyterians.[24] By registering the sect legally, Friend might have hoped to distinguish the Society as one on par with other popular, more established denominations.

Before the sect could become an officially recognized religion, New York State required it to incorporate. Incorporation required that trustees be elected, and that they take on the duties of administering so-called temporalities, i.e., properties, incomes, and other secular interests of the religious organization.[25] But the state would not allow women to serve as trustees. While it would have made sense for the Society of Universal Friends to elect Sarah Richards as trustee, given that she was in charge of Society finances, along with Hitty Smith and the Malin sisters, who had taken on many of the administrative duties, under New York's gender requirements, men had to be named as trustees. In the end, Friend chose Abel Botsford, John Briggs, Jonathan

Dains, Isaac Nichols, and Richard Smith to represent the interests of the Society of Universal Friends.

Neither William Potter nor James Parker was chosen to serve as trustees. Apparently, Friend already believed that the two men no longer held the interests of the Society paramount. In contrast to Potter and Parker, the men who had been asked to be trustees must have seemed trustworthy to the minister. They all had been among the first settlers to arrive in the wilderness in the summer of 1788 and most of them had stayed through the winter and spring of the Hungry Year. They were not known to be, nor suspected of, accumulating land or wealth for their own purposes, and seemed content with the homes they had, and the lands they farmed.

But would they change in the years to come in the same way that James Parker and William Potter had changed? Friend never outwardly displayed any doubts of their fealty to the Society—but who knew what the future would bring?

Around the same time that the process for state recognition moved forward, William Potter and Thomas Hathaway Sr. traveled to New York City to negotiate with the Land Commission over the final prices to be paid for the Society's western lands, following up on James Parker's successful petition the year before. Universal Friend and followers must have believed that Thomas Hathaway Sr. could provide the necessary check on William Potter's personal ambitions during meetings with the state, and when the two men returned with the news that City Hill now belonged to them, the faith seemed well-founded: fourteen thousand acres had been purchased at a good price (about 18.5 cents an acre in New York currency, for land worth about $6 an acre) and all necessary documents attesting to property ownership were in order.[26]

When did the Society members become aware of the fact that New York State had conveyed the lands not to the Society but to Thomas Hathaway Sr., William Potter, and James Parker as so-called tenants in common? As tenants in common, they held sole title to the entire fourteen thousand acres. Friend and followers just assumed that the territory would now be carved out to the members of the community in proportion to amounts paid into the initial fund for purchase as agreed back in 1786, or as recompense for work performed in clearing and settling the land.

Before the lands could be portioned out, the issue of the preemption line once again rose up to cast a shadow over City Hill. Under the preemption line established in 1788, New York State had the right to sell the fourteen thousand acres now held by Potter, Parker, and Hathaway. But in the fall of 1792 a new survey of the line was carried out because of doubts raised over the first line's accuracy. The new survey, completed in December 1792, showed that the work done in 1788 had been faulty, due either to inadequate equipment or to a fraud carried out to promote investments of the New York Genesee Land Company (the initial preemption line supported many of their own land claims). One of the assistants to the surveyor in 1788, a man by the name of John Jenkins, had financial ties to Livingston's company and their mutual interests may have led to a skewing of the 1788 survey results.[27]

Regardless of the cause of the incorrect survey, the results of the new survey showed that Massachusetts held original title to a portion of land for which the Society of Universal Friends had just paid New York. Title to that land, although very confused, now appeared to have passed to a consortium of British land speculators known as the Pulteney Association. Twenty-three of the original pioneers at City Hill, including Benajah Botsford, Enoch and Elijah Malin, Thomas Hathaway Sr., and Marcy Aldrich, signed onto a letter addressed to "Friend Williamson," the agent for the association. In the letter, they asked "that thee would not dispose of the land to any other person, but to us who are on the land."[28] Eventually the British group represented by Williamson would allow Friend's followers to stay on their farms—but they would have to pay one more time, for the land that they had already paid for again and again, in order to hold proper ownership.

Universal Friend had sought a wilderness in which to build a community of faith. But that wilderness was being sold away, even as global events once again played a role in the lives of western New Yorkers. In February of 1793, the new French Republic, founded after the overthrow of the French monarchy, declared war on England, Spain, and the Netherlands. King Louis XVI had been executed in January and the queen would be executed during the Reign of Terror, which began in September of that year. When the United States declared its neutrality in April of 1793, both France and England punished the States by attacking merchant trade ships carrying American goods to foreign markets (and claiming the cargoes for themselves). With lawlessness on the seas, Barbary pirates based in Algiers began to prey freely on American ships; in December of 1793, ten American vessels were captured by pirates, their cargoes seized, and their crews sold into slavery. The United States would respond by finally establishing a national navy in 1794—"adequate to the protection of the United States against the Algerine corsairs"—but in the meantime, the profits of American merchants began to sink under the pressure of the ongoing war and piracy on the high seas.[29]

The only solid ground—with profits assured—seemed to be in land, not only farmlands but lands for building American towns and villages. The property purchased from New York State by the Society now was "worth thirty-three times" more than what Potter and Hathaway had paid for it.[30] Anyone owning land in western New York was sitting on a veritable gold mine due to the constant tide of eastern migrants making their way west, and west some more.

Against this backdrop, its easy to understand why, in the spring of 1793, William Potter chose to assume sole duty of assigning which Society members owned which lands on City Hill. The question is why the rest of the members of the Society went along with it. In three meetings held between May and August of that year at the home of Universal Friend, William Potter announced his decisions as to who received land, and how much. Seventeen men who had given large amounts of money to the original fund received land, while those early settlers who had had little money to put into the fund, but who had put their lives on the line to build the settlement, received nothing. Jedidiah Holmes and Richard Smith, for example, who had been among the first settlers on the frontier and stayed through all the hard years, were not granted property under Potter's allocations.

Some of those followers who had donated funds, such as Friend's own sister Marcy, were not given any land despite their monetary contribution and no justification was offered for their exclusion. They could only look on while James Parker, who had received a large share, deeded most of his lands back over to Potter, thereby making a good profit for himself and leaving Potter with a huge sprawling tract of rolling hills and fertile fields. Thomas Hathaway Sr., disgusted with the process, submitted a written petition to the state seeking a fairer distribution of the lands, but New York turned down his plea for justice. The state held that there had never been a written contract stating that the lands were to be held on behalf of all members of the Society, and therefore Potter's allocations didn't violate any contract nor any law.[31]

William Potter's land allocations were the final step in ending his association with Universal Friend and the ministry of salvation. His wife, Penelope (still back in Rhode Island), would remain faithful to the Society for the rest of her life, and his daughter Elsie, his daughter Penelope (married to faithful follower Benjamin Brown), and daughters-in-law Sarah (married to his son Arnold) and Patience (Friend's sister and married to Potter's son Thomas) would also be lifelong devoted followers—but for William Potter and his sons, the rupture was complete. After sixteen years of devotion and commitment, they were finished with Friend.

In 1778, William Potter had been a man in crisis. After being loyal to the king his whole life, he'd started to question whether that loyalty was worth the economic and social costs exacted by his patriot neighbors and finally decided that to protect his status and prestige in the community he had better sign on with the rebels. But then family events overtook his personal ambitions. His son was mentally ill, chained to the floor of his room as if he were a wild animal. His beloved Susannah died, a daughter of grace and kindness. And what had her dying words been? To be "steadfast in the faith, that we might live in love . . . and that we might So conduct [ourselves] as to meet again in the world of peace and Joy. . . ."[32]

Potter had heeded the words of Susannah and bent himself to the teachings of Universal Friend. After all he had been through, and was going through, he wanted someone to give him not only hope but certainty. He needed clarity in the chaos. And Universal Friend gave him that clarity with simple but powerful lessons about repentance and good works, and the promise of eternal bliss. In a world that he could no longer make sense of, all Potter wanted was for someone to tell him that it could make sense. Potter needed someone to tell him that he could still control his destiny, that he still mattered; that he was of value.

Universal Friend and the Society were used by Potter to make himself feel worthy again. He chose to purge himself of enslaved people and extraneous trappings of wealth, to resign from political appointments and withdraw from social engagements. He chose to ride behind Universal Friend on their evangelical missions, bathing himself in the calming balm of righteousness and goodness. He chose to live by God's rules as translated for him through the words of a young, charismatic preacher who garnered attention everywhere they went and who brought to Potter a new certainty that he was doing well in the world.

But after a few years on the western frontier, William Potter no longer needed the minister and the community and the certainty that the Society had given him. He found a new mantra to follow, and it was as natural to him as breathing. He was a man on a mission, to build a new world of business and politics and social status on the edge of civilization. The tracts of land he claimed for himself became known as "Potter's Location" and the designation would last through generations.[33] Potter ignored—or forgot—the gifts of faith, hope, and confidence that he had found in the ministry of salvation. He now saw Friend as "a deluded woman" who no longer deserved his devotion.[34] In an explanation offered by historian Paul Moyer, William Potter and James Parker both asserted what they viewed as "their birthright" as free, white men to wield power, sway politics, and take hold of any property they deemed ripe for the taking.[35] There was no woman who could—or should—stand in their way.

While Moyer argues that "the rebellions against the Universal Friend . . . should not be understood as some sort of innate, male opposition to female power," there is no question that men like William Potter and James Parker were confounded by the way in which Friend, whom they now viewed as a woman (and maybe they always had), created and led a community that prospered no matter the obstacles thrown up before it.[36]

Whatever their motivations for the break with Universal Friend, for both Parker and Potter it was not enough to merely leave behind the minister and the Society of Universal Friends and go their own way, accumulating land and power and prestige. They wanted the Society destroyed, and its leader dethroned. "A desire to restore patriarchal order," as Moyer puts it, "likely fueled their aggression" and led them to advance a vicious, orchestrated, and long-term assault against Universal Friend.[37]

20

The Search for a New Eden

"Lord, help me to begin to begin. . . ."

—GEORGE WHITEFIELD

Universal Friend never spoke directly about the betrayals of William Potter and James Parker and never criticized either of them by name. God worked in ways that even his messenger might not understand but would accept: "Ware it sweet or bitter I gladly received It at his hands . . . and therefore I was never unfortunate."[1] But the defections of the men who had been among the Society's earliest members must have hurt and the pain was exacerbated by other losses, including the departure, six months earlier, of Abraham and Abigail Dayton.

The fiasco over land ownership, the uncertainty and stress caused by the changing claims and titles, the incorrect deeds and fraudulently surveyed property lines, had all proved too much for the Daytons. When they heard about a program begun by John Graves Simcoe, lieutenant governor of Upper Canada, inviting settlers from the United States to come north, they saw an opportunity for change. British Canada was just as interested in expanding white settlements as the United States was, and while land was first offered only to loyalists fleeing the Revolution, and then to those who had fought for the British, in time

Simcoe extended the offer to Americans willing to build settlements in remote places.[2] Believing the Daytons to be Quakers (and he trusted the Quakers), Simcoe gave the couple a land grant in lower Ontario in exchange for the promise that they would construct mills in the area and encourage settlement by desirable types. When he later found out that they were actually members of the Society of Universal Friend, he considered revoking the grant but, in the end, let it stand.

Abraham and Abigail asked Universal Friend to come to Canada with them. But the minister was not ready to give up on western New York. The Daytons, accompanied by their daughter Abiah and her husband, Benjamin Mallory, set off for Canada on their own. But their departure must have caused the minister real heartache. They had been supporters of the Society since the first meetings in New Milford in the early 1780s and had paid for the land upon which one of its first meetinghouses was built. Abigail had stood steady against the allegations of attempted murder in Philadelphia and Abraham had been one of the first scouts to look for land in western New York. Together the couple had been among the Society's first pioneers on the shores of Seneca Lake and the hardiest, staying put throughout the Hungry Year and giving whatever they could to those around them who had even less.

Now the Daytons would start all over again, settling themselves two hundred miles to the north on the outskirts of a small Canadian outpost called Burford. Under Abraham Dayton's, and then Mallory's, supervision, mills were built, farm lots were sold, and settlers came by the score. The village of Burford grew and prospered, as did the Daytons themselves. Abigail and Abraham would become well-known and well respected as the founders of their vibrant community, and even after Abraham's death in 1797, Abigail stayed in Canada, where she was wanted. On his deathbed, Abraham had told Abigail, "You have been a mother, a wife, a sister and a friend."[3]

Abigail would live until 1843, dying at the age of ninety-three. While she never saw Universal Friend again, Abigail remained both a follower and admirer until her death. Always a hardy soul, living in the wilds of Canada tested her as much as western New York had, but she persevered in Burford and then in nearby Gananoque, where she lived with her second husband, Joel Stone. In both places, she served as the local (and only) doctor, practicing skills she picked up from Friend. During the War of 1812, Abigail was shot in the hip by invading Americans, but became famous in the village for having the presence of mind to hide the family gold and silver in a flour barrel to keep it safe.[4]

After the Daytons left New York, Friend suffered yet another loss. A wave of illness had passed through City Hill during the winter of 1792–93, leaving many bedridden, including both Sarah Richards and Hitty Smith (the exact cause or nature of the illness was not recorded). Through January and into February, Friend doctored the patients with every tenderness and prayed for their recovery. By the end of February, Sarah had improved enough to rise from her bed and resume her many duties in the settlement. But on March 10, 1793, Hitty died. She was forty-six years old.

She had been Friend's trusted helper for years, spreading the word of repentance and redemption throughout Rhode Island, Connecticut, and Pennsylvania. She'd held tightly to Friend's hand when the waters overcame their carriage on Bushkill Creek in 1789 and then helped nurse Friend back to health after the near drowning. When her minister asked her to stay behind in Worcester to mind the flock there, Hitty agreed, although she was eager to go west. When Hitty finally arrived on City Hill in 1791, it was with triumphant relief: all her travels had finally come to an end.

Sarah Richards and Universal Friend were at Hitty's side when she died. Sarah wrote in her personal diary of how her beloved friend "joyfully met death."[5] She recorded in the Society's Death Book that Hitty "gladly resigned her Breath saying in her last moments O! How I love my Lord; He is all and in all to my Soul: Glory to God and the Lamb."[6]

Three days after Hitty's death, Friend preached the funeral sermon, drawing lessons on faith from a biblical text: "The righteous perisheth, and no man layeth it to heart; and merciful men are taken away from the evil to come. . . . He shall enter in peace, they shall rest in their beds, each one walking in his uprightness."[7]

Standing at the side of the grave, as "the corpse was decently buried," Friend offered a poem in lamentation: "The eyes that seldom could close, with Sorrows forbidden to sleep; sealed up in eternal repose, have strangely forgotten to weep. . . ."[8] Before turning away from the soil-laden coffin, the minister added, "Precious in the sight of the Lord is the death of his Saints."[9]

While Hitty's death was not the sole catalyst for a plan that had been percolating in Friend's mind, the loss might have hastened its implementation. The fight over land, and the greed that had inspired it, had polluted the previously peaceful atmosphere of City Hill, sullying the air and dirtying the waters. The departure of the Daytons and the death of Hitty only intensified the feeling of evil brewing, and the devil conspiring. The time had come to make a change and as was the minister's custom, inspiration was to be found in the Bible: "Let us go forth therefore unto him. . . . For here have we no continuing city, but we seek one to come."[10]

Hitty's death sounded the alarm that time was passing. How many years left did Friend—now age forty—have to carry out the God-given mission of salvation? The beacon of light in the wilderness had been lit, but was now clouded by dissension and deceit. A rekindling was needed, and for that, a separation would have to be made: "Search out them that mean to be friends and make a separation between the false and the true," the minister had written to James Parker when the first settlement at City Hill was just being laid.[11] A new and unsullied Eden had to be found for the Society of Universal Friends. The mission remained the same: to establish a shared community dedicated to fellowship, repentance, and redemption. But the location of the community would have to change.

Two years earlier, in 1791, Thomas Hathaway Sr. told Universal

Friend and Sarah Richards about lands that he and Benedict Robinson had purchased west of City Hill. The tract consisted of about twenty thousand acres of hills and valleys situated on the shores of Keuka Lake (then called Crooked Lake for its shape, two long fingers of water that joined and then continued in a single body, forming the shape of a crooked "Y"). The property included acres of timber, which Benedict described as exceeding "any I have ever seen in this or any other country. . . ."[12] He also extolled the beautiful meadows, where "tons of good hay might be made. . . ."[13] After purchasing the property, Hathaway and Robinson hired a surveyor to create out of the large tract a grid of townships. The townships were then divided up into lots that could be purchased by individual investors.

Sometime toward the end of 1791, Sarah Richards and Universal Friend were taken on a tour of the property's 7th Township, which stretched along the western shoreline of Keuka Lake. The township was divided into 72 lots of about 320 acres each. They walked through dense copses of trees and passed stands of waving grass. Turning around now and then to orient themselves, they tallied up the number of streams and clearings, contrasted the range of hills to flatland, and considered the views and the slopes, all the while trying to determine the best place for a future settlement. At that time, they had no inkling of the changes to come on City Hill with Potter's land allocations effectively taking away the farmlands of so many of Friend's followers, and they viewed the 7th Township as an extension of City Hill, not a possible replacement for it.

Sarah had preferred the more level land on the far western side of the 7th Township, but Universal Friend advocated for the northern section. The minister liked its gentle valley, its strong-flowing stream, and a rising hill that favored its southeastern slope with a gentle shelf. It would be just the place to stand in gratitude before the rising sun and give thanks to God: "I send thee to open their eyes, and turn them from darkness to light . . . that they may receive forgiveness of sins . . . [and be] sanctified by faith. . . ."[14]

In the end, Friend's choice won the day.[15] On January 5, 1792, Sarah Richards met with Benedict Robinson and gave him the first down payment toward purchasing land in the 7th Township bordering Keuka Lake, an event that Sarah recorded in her daybook: "This day I received a deed of Benedict Robinson, to hold in trust for Universal Friend, for which the Friend sent me with a hundred dollars in silver, and then sent two yoke of fat oxen . . . the deed contains five lots which makes sixteen hundred acres."[16]

Before Asa Richards died in 1792, he gave Friend two more lots in the 7th Township, in "remittance for the care of all his sickness and funeral charges. . . ."[17] In January of 1793, more acreage was purchased from Benedict Robinson, and in June of 1793, from Thomas Hathaway, with both payments again made by Sarah Richards on behalf of Universal Friend (these purchases were made before Potter announced the City Hill allocations). In 1794, Friend would arrange for an additional 400 acres to be purchased from Hathaway, and by 1795, close to 4,500 acres in the 7th Township would be held on behalf of the Society of Universal Friends.

Friend never handled any of these land transactions directly. The minister held no deeds in the name of Universal Friend (and certainly not in the name of Jemima Wilkinson) and never claimed direct ownership of the lands purchased in western New York. Followers didn't question their minister's resistance to outright ownership. They understood that any property held for the benefit of Friend and the Society would have to be held by someone else, i.e., a trustee (Sarah Richards in these early transactions), who had the interests of the Society foremost in their hearts. While the nature of the trusteeship was informal (understood as it was throughout the community), perhaps it would have been more judicious for the Society to make it clear in all its contracts in whose benefit the land was actually held. Time would tell.

All those followers who had remained faithful to the Society of Universal Friends were invited to join the new settlement in the 7th Township. The invitation was especially appealing to those who had lost both money and land under William Potter's allocations. Friend was giving them another chance—and a good opportunity—to start over, and to own their own homes and farms. As Sarah Richards described it, "The Friend has got land enough here for all that will be faithful and true . . . the Friend will have a home, and likewise for the poor friends and such as have no helper, where no intruding feet can enter."[18]

As for those who had betrayed the original intentions of the Society in coming to the wilderness in the first place, Friend regretted that they had allowed "prosperity [to] obscure the light of prudence" and become blind to faith in the pursuit of money.[19] They were sure to suffer when all the sums of good and evil were tallied, and the earth "burneth as an oven and all that are proud and all that do wickedly shall be as stubble. . . ."[20] But while Friend might have lamented their fate, and would pray for their souls, the minister was no longer responsible for their redemption.

The site for the Society's new home along Keuka Lake was not so very different from the first Friends Settlement, with similar landscapes of hills and valleys, forests and meadows, and distant glimpses of glistening lake water. And yet there were differences. The "high" of the hills and "low" of the valleys were more extreme in the 7th Township; one gully was "so steep," wrote Benedict Robinson, that "we had much to do to get the horse down, but could not drive him up. . . ." The trees—"Hard maple . . . white pine . . . black walnut and shagbark . . . elm and many other sorts of good timber"—grew in almost impenetrable walls of thick trunks and heavy canopy. There were many potential "good mill sites" in the 7th Township, and smaller "very pretty streams" ran everywhere, providing abundant fresh water.[21]

The lands were certainly as overtaken by wilderness as City Hill had been when Parker first arrived there in 1788, although remains of Native American habitations survived: one "tolerable good Indian house" and an "old palace" (as Benedict Robinson described it; most likely it had served as the main meetinghouse for the Native Americans living there).[22] Along with the long-deserted dwelling, a few worn paths still wound through scattered stands of fruit trees. Without such totems, the 7th Township would have appeared as land untouched since Creation. To celebrate the new beginnings offered by the site, Universal Friend chose to give the settlement on Keuka Lake a special name: Jerusalem. Friend must have hoped to re-create the place celebrated in the Bible: "Be ye glad and rejoice forever in that which I create: for, behold, I create Jerusalem a rejoicing, and her people a joy."[23]

During the weeks of clearing and preparing the lands for settling the 7th Township, Sarah Richards once again became stricken with an unidentified illness. Already in the summer of 1793, she suffered through cycles of debilitating fevers and fatigue, followed by days of recovered strength, and then once again, the tolls of illness. Whether this was the same sickness that had taken Hitty in the winter but spared Sarah, or a new sickness, no one knew. Universal Friend "tarried" at Sarah's bedside when Sarah felt "very low," and on those days when Sarah woke feeling stronger, the two went out together, traveling as far as the dozen miles to Keuka Lake in order to see the new hamlet of faith rising amid the slowly cleared forests.[24] There were even a few days when Sarah had enough energy to swing up on her horse and help carry supplies to the rising settlement, including the carefully swaddled panes of glass destined for the home being built for Universal Friend.

The new house was going up beside a brook that had been dubbed "Brook Kedron," named after the stream that King David crossed when fleeing the wrath of his rebellious son Absalom; and that Jesus would later cross with his disciples on his way to the garden of Gethsemane, where he was betrayed.[25] Brook Kidron in the Bible was a site of treachery, but it was also a symbol of strength and faith in the face of adversity: *Kidron* in Hebrew meant "darkness," and to pass over it was to pass over the darkness. In the 7th Township, the Brook Kedron symbolized the journey of Friend's true followers. They had come so far through betrayal and disappointment and now had found their place of peace. From Friend's home beside the Brook Kedron, the minister would provide the necessary beacon to guide the faithful onward to salvation; “a beacon upon the top of a mountain, and . . . an ensign on a hill.”[26]

The house in Jerusalem would not be built of clapboard like the one in the first Friends Settlement. Instead, it was constructed “only of the trunks of trees,” in what was described as “a triple log house.”[27] The two outer sections provided a kitchen on one side and lodgings on the other (with room enough for all the current inhabitants of Friend’s home on City Hill as well as any newcomers), while the largest section in the center of the house was used to host meetings of the entire community (and most likely housed Friend’s library as well). Described by contemporaries as both “extremely pretty and commodious,” the house would serve as the anchor of the community for many years.[28]

As the fall deepened, making its way toward winter, Sarah grew increasingly weak and was confined to her bed for days at a time. Friend stayed by her side as much as possible, offering both medical ministrations and heartfelt prayers. Not only household members but followers from all around came by daily to help in Sarah’s care, doing what they could to ease her mind and her body. Did Sarah’s child Eliza, a slip of a girl at just thirty years old, stay close to her mother’s bed? The two had often been separated, but the separation that loomed over mother and daughter now would be a lasting one.

Dr. Moses Atwater of Canandaigua was summoned in mid-November. Atwater was a friend to the Society, providing not only medical services but also supplies when needed; he bartered with the faithful followers, swapping “peafowl for beer” and one time asking “for black turkeys and a setting of their eggs.”[29] When a follower fell ill or injured beyond what Friend could relieve, the doctor had always been willing to come and offer his assistance. But there was nothing Dr. Atwater could do now for Sarah. He informed his patient that only a matter of days remained to her time here on earth.

If he could not cure her, Sarah asked, could he help her write a will?

Dr. Atwater agreed to try. On November 16, 1793, following Sarah’s instructions, he wrote out her last will and testament. David

Wagener, Abel Botsford, and John Briggs served as witnesses. Due to the minister's refusal to participate in earthly concerns of law or finance, Friend couldn't serve as witness or executor of the will; instead, Sarah appointed Rachel Malin to be the executor (Rachel would also take over as trustee of Universal Friend's property). No one present in the room that day could have foreseen the world of trouble that would flow from that one document. But the trouble would come.

Sarah died on November 30, 1793. She was thirty-six years old. The Society Death Book that Sarah had maintained for so long now became the responsibility of Ruth Pritchard. Like it had been for Sarah, the keeping of the Death Book was a duty that Ruth held sacred, and she willingly took on the mantle of serving as "an Eye and Ear witness of the departures of my Friends." She knew that by being such a "living witness of the deceased," she ensured that every member's life would be remembered, and their faith and commitment honored.[30]

The first death Ruth recorded in the Book was Sarah's: "At Eve 7 on the clock She Expired! . . . Seventeen weeks she patiently endured one fever after another, till at last . . . Did waft her soul to everlasting rest."[31] At the funeral held on December 4, Universal Friend preached a "very great Sermon," in which all those gathered were reminded that "It was better to go to the house of mourning than to the house of feasting, for that is the end of all men. . . ."[32] As God's own messenger on earth, Friend preached that death was not to be lamented but to be celebrated. And yet the death of Sarah left "weeping friends to mourn for themselves" for all they had lost.[33] Eliza had lost her mother; Ruth Pritchard, her friend and fellow teacher; Rachel Malin, to whom she owed her life when Sarah saved her from a terrible illness and then guided her through the wilderness to reach the Friends Settlement.

Universal Friend had lost the closest of confidantes, most steadfast of helpmates, and most beloved of friends. Even after Sarah died, Friend insisted that Sarah "yet speakest"—and Friend would continue to hear the voice in the years to come.[34] But Sarah herself was absent from the everyday routines, the weekend meetings, and the nightly conversations. Within the span of eleven months, three women had left Friend behind, two by death and one by emigration: Sarah Richards, Hitty Smith, and Abigail Dayton. Women who had supported Friend through setbacks and triumphs and never doubted that the minister was a messenger sent from God to guide sinners to repentance and redemption.

Friend would try to not give in to the grief; had the minister not written in a journal that sadness was but "a feebleness of the soul. What giveth it power but the want of spirit?"[35] When the minister counseled followers to resist the lures of melancholy and sorrow, the imagery used was bold—"Rouse thyself to the Combat. . . . She [sadness] is an enemy to thy race [to redemption], therefore drive her from thy heart . . ." —and now the minister, too, would have to be bold.[36]

Was the sorrow caused by death harder to overcome than that caused by the treachery and deceit of James Parker and William Potter? Losing the companionship of a good woman might have brought greater heartache, but the balm offered was great, too, because Friend was certain that Sarah, and Hitty before her, had met "death with joy and went down to the grave in Peace."[37] Sarah and Hitty would be greeted in heaven by "the innumerable host of angels" waiting there.[38] At Sarah's funeral, Friend promised "the time is coming when it will be like a Jubilee Trumpet to have it said, There is Mercy for the Soul."[39]

For men like William Potter and James Parker, however, there would be no jubilee trumpets at the time of their deaths, no angels waiting to greet them. Punishment would be levied by God against those who engaged in betrayal and deceit, the "unbelieving and whore mongers and all Lyers. . . ." Traitors had nothing to look forward to but "their part in the Lake that burns with fire and brimstone."[40] God took care of all wrongs at the final judgment; for "if you write nothing . . . but black Lines of Sin, you will find nothing in God's Book but the red Lines of damnation. . . ."[41] But their fate was no longer in the minister's hands, while the future of the Society of Universal Friends was.

For years, Friend had preached about the message that God had charged his chosen messenger to deliver, that "everyone that will come, may come, and partake of the waters of life freely. . . ."[42] It wasn't the message, or even the messenger, that mattered as much as the acts of the messenger. How Friend met obstacles and disappointments and tragedies had to serve as an example for others; as the minister wrote to Christopher Marshall in 1795, "it is written him that Overcometh shall inherit all things & because . . . Iniquity Hath abounded in the world . . . he that Endureth Until the end . . . shall be saved. . . ."[43]

For the sake of the faithful followers, it was important to endure but also to overcome, and to serve the community as a leader in words and in deed; to be a role model for goodness, for caring, and also for commitment to the community—and always, always to God: "the Lord is the same and the way too remains the same. . . ."[44] Friend would march onward and not look back. The move to Keuka Lake might be delayed by the death of Sarah Richards, but it would happen.

After persecution by the press and the public in 1787, Universal Friend had directed followers to take flight; had begged them to "make your escape from the wrath which is to come, upon all the wicked, that know not God; and have not obeyed the voice of the dear Son of his Love. . . ."[45] Now once again, the faithful would have to flee. This time, the escape was not from civilization, as the journey west had been in 1788, but instead it was escape from a broken community; escape from the greed of certain former members who had thought nothing of destroying what had been built on City Hill. Those "who wished to make a better order" of their lives would build a new community and leave "these speculators to their own ends."[46]

When the first settlement had been built, Friend watched from afar, directing as best could be done over the miles between the pioneers and their minister. This time, Friend was present from its very beginning: from the first tree girdled, the first logs laid, the first roof framed, and the first meeting held. Under Friend's guidance, would any evil dare enter this Eden? Would any despoiler be able to break through the defenses of faith and fealty? Friend and followers hoped that Jerusalem would become the new light that "shineth in darkness, and the darkness comprehended it not."[47]

Jerusalem as a community would be built, stone by stone, home by home, farm by farm, and the Society of Universal Friends would again create a place founded on ideals of loving fellowship and shared faith and fueled by dreams of eternal bliss. But this time, even while Friend would continue to guide faithful followers to their place in heaven, Friend would also show each and every one of them how to fight for their place on earth. They would never flee again.

PART
3

Fight

1794–1819

"If Men will not fight and defend
their own particular spot,
if they will not drive the
Enemy from their Doors,
they deserve the slavery and
subjection which awaits them."

—ABIGAIL ADAMS

21

Building Jerusalem

"While thou are most happy . . .
Thou dost him most honor."

—UNIVERSAL FRIEND

On February 20, 1794, Ruth Pritchard wrote in her diary, "the Dear Universal Friend Moves from this Settlement. . . ."[1] Jerusalem might have been "but 12 miles further into the Wilderness," but it was still hard to get to.[2] Towering trees grew thick on the slopes and valleys of the 7th Township, and the paths through the trees and dense undergrowth were narrow and winding. Friend and followers would have heard the lapping water of Keuka before they saw it, and then suddenly, they found themselves there, on the shores of a lake. It was smaller than Seneca Lake, but still impressive, because although it was narrow, it was very long, almost twenty miles, and very deep. For the tribes of the Haudenosaunee the lake's abundance of trout, salmon, and bass had been vital to their survival through centuries. Now Friend's faithful followers would also turn to fishing to carry them through while they started all over with the process of planting crops, building dairies, and making fenced enclosures for their livestock.[3]

In building the new settlement, the pioneers did not force onto the naturally undulating landscape the rigid grid so typical of late nineteenth-century villages; instead, they recognized the flow of paths and trails left by the Seneca Nation, which followed the hills and dips of the land. Rather than creating a central "town square" so crucial to most white villages, the community created several focal points of activity, including Friend's own home and a working mill, again in a layout similar to traditional Seneca settlements.[4] As the community grew, it would spread out in an ovular form, creating an ever-widening grid of the faithful. In both activity and appearance, Jerusalem from its start was unlike any other white settlement in western New York: a religious community that depended not on the usual framework of rules and rituals, and square and centers, to survive, but instead on a strong bond of shared purpose and deep faith, which was fostered and led by a charismatic minister claiming to be God's chosen messenger.

It was a brave group, these men and women who had pulled up stakes already once to come west and now did it again. Not all the faithful left City Hill; there were those, like Anna Wagener, who had set down roots in what they considered to be "a region of rare beauty and natural wealth, where they had already made a goodly beginning," and they didn't wish to start all over.[5] But many families and single people, especially those with no property to call their own anymore on City Hill, followed Friend to Jerusalem. Daniel and Anna Brown, originally from Stonington, Connecticut, came with their three boys. They built their new farmhouse close to a deep spring and felled the bordering stands of hard maple and shagbark to create rolling fields for plowing and planting. For years, well into the twentieth century, their solid farmhouse stood by the cold spring, even as the fields yielded again to trees and the family itself faded into memory.

Ezekiel Shearman and his wife, Mary, were among those who had lost everything when Potter claimed their lands on City Hill. To compensate their losses and reward their fealty and faith, Universal Friend and David Wagener together gifted the couple over three hundred acres in Jerusalem. The Shearmans set to work and, from seeds alone, they created a vast apple orchard where a towering forest had stood. Generations of New Yorkers would benefit from their orchard, spring through the winter: fragrant blossoms in May, sweet fruit in September, and provisions of apples and cider to carry families through many long winters.

David and Rebecca Wagener, and David's brother Jacob, also chose to follow Friend to Jerusalem in 1790. David built his new home on the banks of the Keuka outlet, taking over the mill that Abraham Dayton had built. Not only locals but also outsiders from miles away came to get their grains milled at the Wageners'. David and his son Abraham also planted an apple orchard on the western edge of their land; they grew what came to be known as "the Wagener apple," favored for its "very crisp" flesh and "sweet flavor."[6] The legend was passed down among faithful followers that David Wagener, while traveling to the new settlement, broke off a branch from an apple tree "to use as a whip in driving his horses. When he arrived . . . he planted the whip in the ground; it grew into an apple tree, from which was developed the famous Wagener apple."[7]

Chloe Towerhill and Mary Bean followed Friend to Jerusalem, with Chloe taking command of the kitchen and kitchen garden (which was "kept in good order"), while Mary became mistress of the dairy.[8] All told, up to a dozen women would come to live in the household, and a dozen more would live close by. Stafford Cleveland called these women, bound so closely to their minister by faith and friendship, "the faithful sisterhood" and "the jewels of the Friend's coronet," and they were entrusted by Friend in "all social and domestic concerns" of the community.[9]

Ruth Pritchard had been with Friend since the early days of the Society—"I would follow no other voice than Thine," she wrote in an early letter to Friend—and would live with the minister in Jerusalem until her marriage to Justus Spencer either in the late 1790s or early 1800s (Ruth's marriage to a man thirteen years her junior was "very unhappy" and it seems that Ruth often returned to stay with Friend).[10] Elizabeth Kinney, a widow and mother of five, who had been one of the first settlers on City Hill, chose to live with Friend rather than with her grown children. Rachel and Margaret Malin also lived with Friend. Rachel loved to walk out from the house into the surrounding countryside: "I feel myself happy in exploring these shady groves, for wherever I turn my eyes I find something to invite my curiosity and engage my attention . . . the woods offer their shades, and the fields their harvests and the hills flatter with an extensive view and the valley invites with shelter, fragrance, and flowers."[11]

Lucy Brown, a hardy soul who never married, lived on a corner of Friend's property in a house she built by herself (according to Stafford Cleveland) and made her living "making butter and cheese and other little industries."[12] Lucina Goodspeed also lived on Friend's property, just past the barns and not far from from the springhouse built over a stream to keep fresh the fruits of the women's labor: "milk, cheese, butter, butcher's meat and game."[13] Anna Styer, the one whom Sarah Wilson involved in her attempted murder allegations against Abigail Dayton back in Philadelphia, lived with Lucina for a time; she was prone to depression and needed to be kept close to a warm soul like Lucina (described by Stafford Cleveland as "an excellent woman and a zealous Friend").[14] Elizabeth Kenyon lived in a small house not far from the Society's weaving shed. Known as "Mother Kenyon," she was an avid weaver, having brought her own loom with her when she moved to Jerusalem and leaving her husband, Remington, behind in Rhode Island.[15] When Remington finally joined her in 1806, she welcomed him, as did Friend, into the community of faith.

Of the thirteen households in close proximity to the home of Universal Friend, at least eight were led by women, most of them widows, and a number of these included "an unusual proportion of adult men who lived under the domestic authority of women."[16] Men also lived in

Friend's household, including for a time Elijah Malin (he would move out in 1803 when he married Friend's sister Deborah after her first husband, Benajah Botsford, died). Abiding in the home under the leadership of their minister, these men did their part in household chores and farming duties. Many children also lived in Friend's household: the land surveyor Amos Guernsey "left his six motherless children" in the house to be watched over by Friend, and when follower Anna Brown died, she "gave her Children to the Friend, desiring them to mind the Friend. . . ."[17] Asa Ingraham, the orphaned teenage son of early settlers Elisha and Jerusha, lived with Friend for years before taking up the trade of shoemaking and moving to Canada.

For the women of Jerusalem, Friend's settlement offered freedoms and opportunities that had been promised by the American Revolution but not realized. Ignoring the roles that women had played in the fight for independence—managing farms and businesses, organizing boycotts, raising money for the troops, running political groups, and even joining in battle themselves—after the war many men chose to see women as "permanent dependents in a society that valued independence above all; women were viewed as weaklings, incapable of taking part in civic life.[18] Traits that had been touted as "American" in the rhetoric of revolution—independence, self-reliance, strength, and bravery—were now claimed to be "exclusively masculine" qualities that justified men taking on all leadership roles in the new country, while women were viewed as "essentially selfish and frivolous creatures" who were "naturally" unfit for and could not be trusted with public civic duties or responsibilities.[19]

Only in the state of New Jersey did women have the right to vote—and that right would be stripped away in 1807, when white men used claims of voter fraud to pass a sweeping voting reform bill that led to the disenfranchisement not only of women but also of Blacks and immigrants.[20] Women were viewed as second-class "domestic citizens" confined to the home, while men belonged in the larger world, where they could be masters of "business, religion, politics, and government."[21]

But in the community built by Universal Friend, over 150 women (mostly white, but there were Black women as well) managed their own households and properties, engaged in farming and in trade, and "preached and prophesized . . . and . . . they did all of these things as *women*."[22] Ranging in age from their twenties to their sixties, as many as half of them were single women: they had either never married or were widowed (the percentage of single women in Jerusalem—14 percent—was much higher than the norm of 5 to 8 percent in other American communities).[23]

The high number of single or widowed women in Jerusalem who held property and chose not to marry or remarry can in part be explained by the law of coverture.[24] The concept of coverture, adopted by the Americans from English common law, held that "The very being or legal existence of the woman is suspended during marriage, or at least is incorporated into that of the husband, under whose wing, protection, and cover, she performs everything."[25] But in Jerusalem, women could avoid the status of "femme couvert" because they did not have to marry for status or security; under Friend's leadership they could count on having both a place to live and a place to work, while also holding on to and managing their own property without any interference from a man.

Those women in Jerusalem who were married, while still subject to the law of coverture, were nevertheless never expected to be subservient to, nor dependent upon, their husbands. Nowhere in the dogma of the Society of Universal Friends, nor in the spiritual or economic practices exercised in Jerusalem, was there a requirement of subservience by women to men; Friend instead preached that "women obey . . . God rather than men."[26] Single women who remained celibate enjoyed a complete break from the roles of mother or wife, and even those with husbands and children moved beyond traditional boundaries of the home in managing their own lives.[27]

The prevailing economic and social system in post-Revolutionary America that defined the roles of men and women—"the binary that associates women with the household and men with the state"—was never allowed to take hold in Jerusalem.[28] There was no binary in Universal Friend nor in Friend's community. The minister provided a strong role model for female followers by normalizing behavior deemed "masculine" by the outside world; in Jerusalem, taking action was not "masculine" but an exercise in faith. Universal Friend encouraged women, as an act of faith and religious duty, to take on roles traditionally ascribed to men: for example, Marcy Aldrich, Experience Ingraham, Lucy Botsford, and Lucina Goodspeed presided over weekly religious meetings and preached to the faithful; and Ruth Pritchard and Rachel Malin managed business and administrative affairs for the Society, carrying out necessary purchases and sales, and keeping records of deaths and dreams. (It's important to note that when Stafford Cleveland wrote his biography of Universal Friend, Experience Ingraham was still alive and provided firsthand testimony to Cleveland about life with Friend.)

Women played traditional roles in Jerusalem as well—but with a twist. Sarah Clark "shared a roof with and kept house for Thomas Hathaway [Senior]."[29] Although they were never formally linked, Hathaway left his three-hundred-acre farm to Sarah in his will when he died. When Alice Parker moved into the home of Thomas Prentiss to work as his housekeeper, her parents worried about the propriety of a young woman living with a single man. They eventually convinced their daughter to marry faithful follower Perley Gates, but the union was never consummated, and when a child was born to Alice, she admitted the baby was the son of Prentiss (who in fact was *not* single, but had a wife and children whom he had left behind in New Jersey when he came west).[30] Eventually Alice and Thomas left with their boy to live in Canada, where they had more children together, but they would return to Jerusalem sometime around 1810 to live out their days there.

Subscribing to no one's expectations, and appearing neither male nor female, Universal Friend acted as conscience alone dictated—and the minister's followers were encouraged to do the same: "Establish unto thyself principles of Action, and see that thou ever act according to them."[31] Rachel Malin echoed those ideas years later, writing in her journal, "all . . . are equal before God: wisdom, talents, virtues, make all the difference between them."[32] Not gender, not race, but one's own actions defined one's self in the world. Friend told followers, as in a letter the minister wrote to Anna Wagener in 1787, "be a Dooer of the Word and Not a hearer only. . . ." Go out, and find happiness in this world, and "Do well as to Meet me again, whither it be in time or Eternity."[33]

In Jerusalem, Friend created a community where for both men and women self-reliance and deep personal faith existed side by side with the sharing of heavy burdens and everyday joys, and where the goal of repentance and redemption was tempered by living fully in the here and now. Just as Lucy Brown measured out and built the exact house she wanted, Rachel Malin treasured her walks in the fields, Elizabeth Kenyon wove her dreams of wool, and even Universal Friend enjoyed the touch of silk underneath the dark ministerial robe and a glass of wine or beer at dinner, life on earth was to be treasured. A young Universal Friend had focused primarily on the hereafter; the mature minister understood the importance of appreciating life on earth.

Every season offered its joys: the fields of endless snow under moonlight in the winter; the brilliant yellow of marsh marigold popping up across the meadows in the spring; the scent of lilac in May; endless blue skies over rolling green hills in the summer; the apple orchards, heavy with fruit in the fall; and then, before winter came again, the layering of all the fallen leaves across the dirt paths, making every step a riot of crackling noise and floating color. Rachel Malin described the western settlement as a place that "abounds with almost everything we could wish for."[34] Harvests were good; the mills, dairies, coopers, and blacksmith shops flourished; the population of the settlement grew with new births and new arrivals from the east.

Jerusalem wasn't the only community growing along the shores of Keuka, Seneca, and the other Finger Lakes. Throughout the 1790s, more and more outsiders continued to settle the lands of "Genesee country . . . principally immigrants from the New England states."[35] In early February 1795, over twelve hundred sleighs carrying New

Englanders and all their worldly possessions passed through Albany on their way west to new settlements.[36] Most of those arriving on the frontier were farmers, but there were also pioneers setting up stores and trading posts, establishing blacksmith shops and working as coopers. Roads were built to connect the settlements, some of which followed old Native American paths through the wilderness and some newly blazed by the settlers.[37]

For the most part, interactions between the newly arrived settlers and the followers of Universal Friend were cordial and mutually beneficial. Trade went on between outsiders and the Society (made easier by the new roadways) and relationships were created. Friend was asked to perform funerals outside the community, which the minister did, and Ruth Pritchard taught school in Penn Yan, not far from Jerusalem (the village derived its name from the fact that most of its inhabitants came from either Pennsylvania or Yankee New England). The men and women who lived close by seemed to approve of the Society and its precepts, and they accepted Universal Friend without question as a religious leader. Historian Herbert Wisbey, in researching "reminiscences of her neighbors," found that they usually described the minister as a "sincere, kindly, benevolent woman who taught basic religious and moral principles. . . ."[38]

Those neighbors whose claims to the land dated much further back than Friend's also seemed to have accepted the Society of Universal Friends. In the years after the Revolution, a number of Native Americans whose families had come from the Genesee Valley returned to resettle the small villages that the forces of Sullivan and Clinton had done their best to destroy. When the Society of Universal Friends arrived on the shores of Seneca Lake, interactions between the two groups grew slowly, but seemed to have consistently been both "cordial and sincerely friendly."[39] In Jerusalem, Friend invited members of local clans to hunt where they wished, and in return, they kept "Friend's larder well supplied with venison. . . ."[40] Goods were bartered and exchanged and Native Americans were invited both to Society meetings and to shared meals; according to Wisbey, "at her [Friend's] home and at those of the members of her society, the Indian visitor was treated with the same respect shown any other guest."[41] When a child was born to John and Achsa Supplee in 1793, a party was held with "the Indians taking part and making presents in honor of the occasion."[42]

When Eliphalet Norris, a shopkeeper with a store on the shores of Seneca Lake, began trading "fire water" to Native Americans in exchange for furs in the early 1790s, Friend sent messages to the shopkeeper asking him to stop.[43] The minister must have witnessed what others acknowledged but few worked to eradicate; that alcohol shattered Native communities, with its abuse leading to violence, poverty, and a breakdown in clan relationships. Alcohol was shamelessly used by white outsiders to manipulate and control them, furthering its damaging effects. The shopkeeper Norris was married to Thomas Hathaway Sr.'s daughter Mary—but proved to be more of a friend to her brother Thomas (who had broken away from the Society) because Norris continued to trade whiskey to Native Americans. (His business ultimately failed, and he and Mary moved to Maryland, but when he died in 1821, Mary would return with her four sons to live on the lands left to her by her father.)

Universal Friend was not the only religious figure to visit with the Native Americans. Missionaries had been active in the area since the mid-eighteenth century, intent on converting members of the Haudenosaunee clans to Christianity. Presbyterian minister Samuel Kirkland lived for years among the Seneca, Oneida, and Tuscarora, and converted a number of Oneida to Christianity. With their help, in 1793 he founded the Hamilton-Oneida Academy, a school for Native Americans that became Hamilton College. Quakers also sent missions to the area, spreading the word and also teaching farming and housekeeping skills (which the Native Americans already possessed); while these missions resulted in no conversions, there was a trust built up between Quakers and Native Americans, in large part due to the long Quaker tradition, established by William Penn already in the seventeenth century, of respecting Native Americans' rights to the lands that they had occupied for centuries.

Even before coming to America, Quaker William Penn had written a letter to "Kings of the Indians in Pennsylvania" explaining his wish to settle on their land, "but I desire to enjoy it with your Love and Consent, that we may always live together as Neighbors and Friends."[44] He promised to pay them fairly for land, even though he had been granted ownership of the colony of Pennsylvania by King Charles II in repayment of a debt owed to his father. Once arrived in America in 1682, Penn largely lived up to his promises and paid the Delaware (Lenape) and Susquehannock tribes of Pennsylvania for the lands that the king of England had granted him.

Friend's relationship with local Native Americans was different from that of the evangelizing missionaries. While the minister did occasionally ask to preach to their clans, there was no push for conversions nor for the Native communities to change the ways in which they lived. Friend believed, according to followers, that "kind treatment and upright dealing" with the Native neighbors would ensure the peaceful and beneficial coexistence of the Society and the clans, and eyewitnesses to the relationship noted that Friend and the Society did succeed "in making a favorable impression" on their Native American neighbors.[45]

That favorable impression would deepen when Friend took the unusual step of becoming involved in the welfare of the Native Americans who had lived for centuries in western New York. The first battle Friend would fight from Jerusalem was not on behalf of the Society, although that battle would come. For now, Friend fought for Native neighbors. As Friend penned in a journal, "Nobility resideth in the Soul; nor is there true honor except in Virtue."[46] To be a good friend and neighbor was a virtue, but to stand with those oppressed was true nobility.

22

Friends, Neighbors, and Enemies

"Follow peace with all men, and holiness, without which no man shall see the Lord. . . ."

—HEBREWS 12:14

On October 21, 1794, Universal Friend was invited to dine with Timothy Pickering, George Washington's designated "Indian commissioner," who had been charged by the president to implement the Indian Trade and Commerce Act. The Act, passed by Congress in 1790, prohibited negotiations (and manipulations) of Native American lands by the states and put the federal government in control: "no purchase of Indian Land would be valid unless it was conducted in a public treaty under authority of the United States."[1] The luncheon with Pickering was in Canandaigua, New York, where three weeks earlier Pickering had convened a treaty conference with the Haudenosaunee tribes of New York.

From Pickering's point of view, the purpose of the conference was to head off potential alliances between the Haudenosaunee and the tribes of the Northwest Indian Confederacy in the Ohio Valley (including the Miami, the Delaware, the Shawnee, the Potawatomi, the Ottawa, and the Ojibwa clans). White settlers moving west into the Ohio Valley had been met with violent resistance by the Native tribes, and the American government worried that if the Haudenosaunee joined the Northwest Indians in their land battles, war could break out, the British would come to the aid of the Native Americans, and the United States could lose large swaths of territory (the British had refused to cede control of territory they had claimed along the border with Canada, which included their forts at Niagara, Detroit, and Mackinac, and they had shown they were willing to make concessions to Native tribes to secure their support against the United States).

The goals of the Haudenosaunee clans in attending the conference at Canandaigua was the return of the 6 million acres that had been lost to them over a century of whites taking their lands by force or by trickery. Governor Clinton's aggressively devious land policies implemented after the Revolution had led to such a reduction in Haudenosaunee lands that they were confined now to living within "three small reservations, totaling a mere 4 percent of their prewar territory."[2] The Society of Universal Friends was only one community among hundreds that lived and flourished on lands that had belonged for generations to the Seneca tribe. Would Friend assist the Haudenosaunee in getting some of their land back? Or would the minister side with the United States?

While Timothy Pickering was ostensibly in charge of responding to the claims of the Haudenosaunee, the United States' new policy toward such claims was largely shaped by Henry Knox, Washington's secretary of war. Knox became an early hero of the American Revolution when he stole 120,000 pounds of cannon and mortar from the British at Ticonderoga, New York, in the winter of 1775–76 and carried it three hundred miles through snow and ice to army headquarters in Cambridge, Massachusetts, where it was used to oust the British from their occupation of Boston. Then, in December of 1776, Knox planned out Washington's famous crossing of the Delaware, and for the rest of the war, he played an instrumental role in keeping the army supplied with necessary artillery, not an easy task.

As secretary of war in the new United States, Knox repudiated the concept of "right of conquest," which had led to so much Indian territory being confiscated following independence from England. Knox did not view the Native tribes as equals—he called them "savages" and "ignorant"—but he did believe that "as prior occupants," Native Americans had "a right of property" in the lands they had held previous to the war and he would do what he could to see those rights restored.[3] With Washington's support, Knox ensured that the Northwest Ordinance, a document that guided settlement (and eventual statehood) of the northwest territory (including present-day Ohio, Michigan, Indiana, Illinois, and Wisconsin) explicitly promised that "the utmost good faith shall always be observed towards the Indians; their land and property shall never be taken from them without their consent."[4] As Knox advised Washington, it was more "cost-effective" to secure land "through purchase at treaty conferences" than going to war and fighting for it.[5] Knox also believed that "the blood and injustice" of any military efforts to wrest Native Lands from their rightful owners "would stain the character of the nation . . . beyond all pecuniary calculation."[6]

In New York State, attempts had been made already in 1791 to address the Haudenosaunee claims, when Timothy Pickering organized a treaty conference at Newtown Point, which was attended by one thousand hopeful members of the Haudenosaunee Confederacy. About five hundred Seneca, including prominent leaders Red Jacket and Cornplanter, had camped close to City Hill on their way to the conference. Universal Friend met with them, offering refreshments and supplies and enjoying "an interchange of civilities." Friend also preached to the large gathering and throughout the sermon was reportedly treated with "attention and respect."[7] But the conference itself achieved little between the United States and the Haudenosaunee, and so in 1794 the second conference was convened at Canandaigua.

This time over fifteen hundred members of the Six Nations of the

Haudenosaunee Confederacy, led by fifty-nine tribal chiefs, traveled from near and far to attend. The Oneidas were the first to arrive; the Senecas, led by Chief Cornplanter, were among the last. They arrived on foot and on horseback, many of them "in full Indian dress, and painted in an extraordinary manner."[8] They brought food and supplies to carry them through the weeks of the conference, along with gifts, ornamental regalia, weaponry, and also large bundles of sticks, meant to represent all the "persons, men, women and children" for whom the chiefs would speak, which were laid before Colonel Pickering upon their arrival.[9]

Pickering knew that trust was an issue for the Native Americans coming to Canandaigua. He wrote to George Washington, "Indians have been so often deceived by white people that *White Man* is, among many of them, but another name for *Liar*. . . . I am unwilling to be subjected to this infamy. I confess I am not indifferent to a good name even among Indians."[10] Washington was himself viewed with hostility and suspicion by many of the Haudenosaunee due to his role in ordering the devastations of the Sullivan campaign.[11] In 1792, Mohawk chief Joseph Brant described Washington as "very cunning, he will try to fool us if he can. He speaks very smooth, will tell you fair stories, and at the same time want to ruin us."[12] Captain John, an Oneida chief, believed that "however good and honest white men might be in other matters, they were all deceivers when they wanted to buy Indian Lands."[13]

Pickering asked for advice about running the treaty conference from Red Jacket, a Seneca leader who had been born on the shores of Keuka Lake. Red Jacket took seriously his role as Pickering's guide and instructed him in great detail on the negotiating practices, protocols, and rituals that Native Americans had been using for generations among themselves. These practices included lengthy discussions of any proposed actions, with both men and women taking part; the ceremonial exchange of gifts; and the sharing of gratitude and condolence rituals in order to demonstrate shared respect and esteem between groups.

These practices were both spiritual (invoking a higher power to oversee the proceedings) and social (acknowledging the connections between clans) and were very "effective at creating consensus without resorting to coercion."[14]

Following Red Jacket's advice, Pickering instructed his representatives to participate with the Native Americans in their rites of shared meals and exuberant dances, the exchanging of gifts, and their many gratitude and condolence rituals. Colonel Pickering himself took part in a ritual "to wipe away the tears from the eyes of the Delawares who had lost a young brother murdered by a white man."[15] Pickering acted out the taking of the "hatchet [from] the head of the deceased" and burying it in the ground "so that it should never more be taken up."[16] He then spoke about opening "the path to peace, which the Indians were requested to keep open at one end, and the United States at the other, as long as the sun shone," and passed out "many strings of wampum," in the stated hope "that all might be cleared out of the way before the business of the treaty commenced."[17]

Another tool Pickering used to prove his trustworthiness to the Haudenosaunee was allowing the attendance of Quakers at the conference. Native Americans seemed to trust the Quakers: while other white Americans "are friendly to us till they get our lands and trees . . . the Quakers are good people, and do not serve us so. . . ."[18] William Penn's "reputation for fair dealing, a standard to which the natives hoped [all] whites would again aspire" seemed to inspire Pickering, and he agreed to invite the Haudenosaunee's "old Friends, the Quakers" to participate in the negotiations at Canandaigua.[19] James Emlen and William Savery came from Philadelphia to represent the Society of Friends, along with two other Quakers.[20]

Savery and Emlen threw themselves into the activities of the conference. Savery wrote in his journal of participating in a large celebration where he was seated for a long time "in company with an Indian queen, who had a small child in one of their kind of cradles, hung about with about one hundred small brass bells, intended to soothe the child to rest."[21] James Emlen wrote about attending a religious meeting where the Native Americans sang hymns; "the Indian language being one of the softest in the World, their singing exceeded anything of the kind that I have remember to have heard, the voices of the squaws were truly melodious. . . ."[22]

Did Pickering's invitation to the Quakers also inform his decision to invite Universal Friend to attend a luncheon meeting of the treaty conference? Others had mistaken the Society of Universal Friends to be an offshoot of Quakers, and maybe he made the same assumption. He had heard numerous stories about Universal Friend, and perhaps he was merely curious about the controversial minister who had founded two settlements in the wilderness, both prosperous. Or maybe he had heard of Friend's reputation for fair treatment of Native neighbors. He asked Thomas Morris, a Canandaigua lawyer and land speculator (and son of the wealthy banker and speculator Robert Morris) to arrange a meeting with the minister, and just as the treaty conference was getting into the meat of its work (negotiations over land for the Haudenosaunee in exchange for fealty to the United States), the luncheon was arranged.

Friend arrived in Canandaigua accompanied by David Wagener, Rachel Malin, and one of the Malin brothers (William Savery wrote in his journal that it was Enoch who attended the lunch, while James Emlen recorded the presence of Elijah). The meal, attended not only by the Society members but also by Thomas Morris, William Savery, and James Emlen, was cordial and lively; Savery noted in his journal, "The Colonel paid great attention to Jemima. . . . She was placed at the head of the table, and the conversation being on a variety of subjects, she bore a considerable part therein."[23]

James Emlen and William Savery were not fans of Universal Friend. Perhaps their opinions had been soured by what they'd heard from William Potter, in whose house they had been guests. Potter told both of them about his experiences of having "some years back been induced to entertain a favourable opinion of Jemima Wilkinson and her doctrines." But as Savery relates the story, Potter's "good understanding" allowed him to finally see that Friend was "an assuming, presumptuous woman." He subsequently threw off "the shackles" entwining him to Friend and "her fraternity." Telling the story of his City Hill land grab, Potter explained that "her whole scheme was for self-interest and aggrandizement; he himself having suffered by her pecuniary point of view but now had asserted his right to a part of the land occupied by these people and forbade their making use of it."[24]

The two Quakers took a tour of Jerusalem to see Friend for themselves, after which Savery wrote about the settlement's "hovels . . . which are the residences of women who have forsaken their husbands and children; and . . . men who have left their families" all for the sake of "an artful and designing woman."[25] He described how insulted he'd felt when the minister called him "by name" and complained that "[s]o great was her volubility . . . we were obliged to interrupt her, in order to express our disapprobation of the exalted character she gave to her own mission and that is savored strongly of pride and ambition to distinguish herself from the rest of mankind by the appellation of the Universal Friend."[26]

James Emlen also described the minister as both strange and disturbing, including how the minister appeared: "her deportment, dress, features . . . are so very masculine that I think no one would suppose her to be a Woman."[27] Like Savery, Emlen thought Universal Friend talked way too much; he wrote that the manner in which the minister continually chattered on had the effect of "keeping the waters in a state of continual perturbation—it seem'd silence would be Death to her."[28] (Given the minister's propensity to speak enthusiastically about the duty God had given his chosen messenger, both Savery and Emlen might have been accurate in their assessment of Friend's volubility.)

Emlen wrote in his journal that Friend told him the story about being rebuked, as a young minister, by the Smithfield Society of Friends and told to be quiet, but Friend had refused, thinking "it not her duty to be a Man pleaser." The Smithfield Quakers then, and Emlen and Savery now, seemed to see Friend as a member of their faith who had broken with important practices of humility and community. And even worse, as a woman who grasped for power far beyond what gender dictated. And perhaps worst of all, a woman who had the appearance of a man and tried to act like one as well—and who just would not stop talking! In his journal, a disturbed Savery predicted that Friend's community was "declining fast . . . their fall is at no great distance . . . the last days of this deluded woman may be spent in contempt, unless her heart becomes humbled and contrite, and the mercy of the Lord be eminently manifest to pity, and spare her."[29]

Throughout the luncheon at Canandaigua, however, Timothy Pickering seemed charmed by Universal Friend and also impressed by the Society's accomplishments in their settlements. Following the meal, he invited Friend, Wagener, and the Malins to join him and the Quakers at that afternoon's Treaty meetings. A very large group had gathered, with hundreds of Native Americans in attendance. Friend and followers stood at the back, listening as several people spoke. First Pickering gave a long speech and then he introduced the Quakers, who came forward to offer their prepared "certificate" in which they called for peace and fair dealing; according to the journal kept by James Emlen, the Native Americans received their certificate with "satisfaction."[30]

After the Quakers finished their presentation, Universal Friend suddenly rose up and, followed by David Wagener and the Malins, walked to the front of the room, then turned to face the large assembly. Hesitating only for a moment, "Jemima and all her company kneeled down, and she uttered [as described by William Savery] something in the form of a prayer."[31] When the prayer concluded (and was "explain'd to the Indians by one of the Interpreters"), Friend asked permission to deliver a sermon.[32] According to Emlen's account, Timothy Pickering was dismayed that Friend "had intruded herself not only without his knowledge, but contrary to his inclination & request. . . ."[33]

Pickering would later describe Universal Friend's "conduct [as] altogether impertinent" (the charms Friend had exerted at lunch apparently wearing off), but he had little choice in the moment but to allow the minister to preach to the crowd.[34] Not only because Friend "prayed for peace" but also, as Emlen explained in his journal, because of "the deference" that Native Americans "were used to pay to the fair sex."[35] Pickering knew that Native Americans involved women in their political and administrative affairs (and the Native Americans who interacted with Universal Friend viewed the minister as a female). To listen to what a woman had to say about an issue affecting the larger community was a common practice among the Six Nations and Pickering must have believed they wanted to hear what Friend had to say.

With all eyes on the minister, Friend began to preach, David Wagener and the Malins standing a short distance behind. They must have been as surprised as Pickering and the Quakers by their minister's request to speak at the conference meeting; after all, diplomacy in the affairs of outsiders was beyond anything Friend had ever tried to do before. But as witness to the deprivations suffered by neighboring Native Americans, it seemed Friend had become convinced that caring for their welfare was integral to God's mandate that there was "Room, Room, Room, in the Many mansions of eternal glory for Thee and for everyone. . . ."[36] The opportunity to offer a sermon advising how God would view the ongoing negotiations was just too good to pass up.

With the large audience at attention, and using "many texts of scripture," Friend spoke on the usual themes of repentance, fellowship, and love, but composed them around the issues being debated at the conference.[37] According to the accounts provided later by Friend's followers, the minister quoted from the Bible—"Blessed are the Peace makers for they shall be Called the Children of God"—and then Friend spoke at length of the importance of "Peace and Love among the Indians and all men."[38] The minister also admonished the crowd to acknowledge equality between all men and women: "Hath we not all one father? Hath not one God created us?"[39] Friend would have continued preaching even longer, but with "Night coming on . . . was obliged to cut short" the sermon.[40] The gathered Haudenosaunee subsequently bestowed upon the minister the name "Shinnewawna gis tau, ge," meaning "A Great Woman Preacher."[41]

But the next day, a group of Native American women, addressing the crowd, scolded Friend for telling "the Indians to repent." The women proclaimed that the time had come for all "the white people to repent, for they had as much need as the Indians, and . . . they should wrong the Indians no more."[42] The women asked that the United States government ensure that all lands and privileges taken from the Haudenosaunee be restored, so that "they should feel themselves much relieved and more at liberty. . . ."[43]

The deceits and losses suffered by Friend and the Society on City Hill were minuscule compared to those imposed on the Native Americans throughout western New York, but Friend's own experiences of betrayal and fraud would have made the minister especially sympathetic to the cause of the Haudenosaunee. Friend's sermon advocating equal and beneficent treatment at the conference was not only in support of Native Americans' position in the treaty negotiations but was also likely a venting of the minister's own frustrations with fraudulent dealing and untrustworthy negotiators.

But Friend's sympathy only went so far. For centuries, the Seneca had lived on the shores of Keuka, and while Friend always welcomed Native Americans to hunt on properties belonging to the Society, an offer was never made—nor contemplated—to return to them the lands on which Jerusalem had been built.[44] Friend's position seemed to be woefully in line with the policy of the United States, which would only return lands in exchange for something given by the Native Americans, whether it be loyalty or passive acceptance. If the Native Americans had expressed an interest in joining the Society, would they have been given property in Jerusalem? Which raises the question: Did Friend's revolutionary ideals of self-determination, liberty, equality, freedoms only extend to those who accepted Friend as God's own messenger?

Heavy snows came on that year at the end of October—"it snowed very fast and was a stormy time"—and Friend traveled back to Jerusalem to check on the community and make sure the households and farms were prepared for an early winter.[45] Such work was typical for farmers everywhere, and just as necessary as it was time-consuming: "All was bustle . . . in preparing for winter, by gathering in the corn, digging potatoes, fattening hogs, preparing cabins."[46] As the settlement battened itself down for months of cold, snow, and isolation, they waited for news from Canandaigua. Would there be peace between nations, would there be a place for Native Americans to live and build, to farm and grow, to remain as neighbors to Friend even amid a steady onslaught of eastern settlers?

The news arrived in mid-November. A treaty had been reached, and all the parties had agreed to its terms regarding the return of taken lands and the setting of new property lines, and also its vows of lasting friendship.[47] It was, as historians, and later courts, would describe it, "a treaty between sovereigns," in which all signatories were recognized as representing independent and autonomous nations.[48] The treaty set the boundaries of territory belonging to "the Oneidas, Onondagas, Cayugas, and Senekas" and confirmed that Native American reservations in New York State were the sovereign property of the Six Nations. The United States agreed "never to claim the same [lands] nor to disturb them, or any of the Six Nations, or their Indian friends . . . in the free use and enjoyment thereof. . . ."[49]

The property returned to the Haudenosaunee Confederacy under the treaty constituted over 1 million acres, contained more or less within an area bound to the north by Lake Ontario, to the west by the Niagara River and Lake Erie, to the south by the New York State line, and to the east by the property line of land sold by the Seneca to Oliver Phelps in 1788 (the lands upon which Friend's first settlement and Jerusalem were located were not part of the territories that now belonged to the Haudenosaunee Confederacy).

Pickering may have been sincere in the promises made in the treaty, including the tribes' sovereignty over their lands, the establishment of "a firm and permanent friendship with" the members of the Haudenosaunee Confederacy, and that "Peace and friendship . . . shall be perpetual between the United States and the Six Nations."[50] But over the following two centuries, the promises made to the Haudenosaunee would be broken many times over, and they would lose hundreds of thousands of acres of land without compensation or even consultation for projects such as the construction of the Erie Canal in the nineteenth century, and the St. Lawrence Seaway in the twentieth; the building of dams, which required flooding thousands of acres of Native lands; the construction of power lines, highways, and vast public parklands throughout western New York; and the unchallenged homesteading of whites on Native lands. Andrew Jackson in the 1830s ordered the removal of entire clans to be relocated west (many Native Americans fled to Canada to escape the forced move), and the Haudenosaunee lands were confiscated, while their communities were decimated.

Nevertheless, the terms of the 1794 treaty have given the Native Americans of western New York legal firepower to fight back for their taken lands and to demand protection and preservation of their rights in the region.[51] In 1974, the Supreme Court ruled that "title of an Indian tribe guaranteed by treaty and protected by statute has never been extinguished," and "federal law now protects, and has continuously protected from the time of the formation of the United States, possessory rights to tribal lands."[52] This case, *Oneida Indian Nation v. County of Oneida*, paved the way for hundreds of cases, some successful, some not, brought by Native American tribes to retrieve their lands or receive compensation for taken lands.[53]

The role played by the Quakers in the outcome of the 1794 Canandaigua treaty is hard to gauge. Although their presence had been insisted upon by the Native Americans, tribal leaders were disappointed when Emlen and Savery refused to sign the final document. As James Emlen tried to explain to them, "we do not interfere with Government as we can take no part in war; neither do we apprehend ourselves competent judges as the transactions of the Treaties . . . have not been fully made public."[54]

Nor is there any way to measure what impact, if any, Friend's sermon had on the overall treaty negotiations. But it would have made an impact on Friend's own community. The outreach demonstrated by Friend in going to Canandaigua and speaking on behalf of outsiders was something new. Friend welcomed all races and genders to the Society, and condemned slave ownership by anyone wanting to join the Society, but had never started or joined or supported manumission campaigns. And while Friend might have remonstrated with an individual shop owner for trading alcohol to Native Americans, the minister had never involved the Society in promoting widespread prohibition of such practices. Would Friend now continue to involve the Society of Universal Friends in matters outside of their own settlement? Would that involvement evolve into something more, a national presence on issues involving equality and liberty?

Which leads back to the question of how far Friend was willing to go to fight for those outside the circle of the Society of Universal Friends. Friend's attendance at the treaty conference would prove, in the end, to be an anomaly. Perhaps the minister would have continued to involve the Society in issues affecting the larger community outside of Jerusalem, and maybe even become a leader tackling inequality outside the confines of the sect—but problems within the Society would pull Friend's attention back to the 7th Township. In the years ahead, reaching outside the settlement to promote peace and battle injustice would take a back seat to matters occurring in Jerusalem. The minister would still be fighting for peace, and against treachery. But this time, the battle would take place closer to home.

23

Sowing of Greed

"When I reflect upon Human Nature,
the various passions and appetites to which it is subject,
I am ready to cry out with the Psalmist, Lord what is Man?"

—ABIGAIL ADAMS

Friend might have predicted that trouble would follow the Society of Universal Friends from Seneca Lake west to Keuka Lake—as one follower would later describe it, City Hill's "bad odor has reached Jerusalem, and will poison its air"—but no one could have known in whose rucksack the stink would be carried.[1] Enoch Malin was the carrier and the men who fanned the stench were those who filled Enoch's mind with dreams of gold. Enoch was described by one observer as "a rolicking fellow, somewhat addicted to drink, but not naturally a bad man."[2] He'd been among the first settlers to arrive on the shores of Seneca Lake in 1788 and stayed through the Hungry Year. In 1790, he welcomed Friend to City Hill, and along with his brother Elijah built the minister's home there. Despite having since abandoned membership in the Society, Enoch remained "the pet of the Malin family" and was still well-liked throughout the community of faithful followers.[3]

The trouble didn't start with Enoch, but can be traced back to Sarah

Richards's last days on earth, when the dying woman asked Dr. Atwater to help her write out her last will and testament. Under the terms of the will, Richards left to her daughter Eliza "all my property." Sarah would have understood that to mean lands held in her name in Connecticut, along with "one sorrel Mare & colt, one pide [pied] Cow and four sheep."[4] The lands that she held in trust for Friend, including the thousands of acres of the 7th Township, were not "my property," but belonged to Universal Friend (on behalf of the Society), having been bought on Friend's behalf for the good of the Society as a whole: "all income or proceeds of the land, were expended in the society for the common benefit of all, and for the improvement and cultivation of the land."[5] After Sarah died, Rachel Malin was designated trustee and charged with holding the lands of Jerusalem for Universal Friend the same way that Sarah Richards had.

Dr. Atwater was a good man, but he had trained in medicine not the law, and the will that he wrote up for Sarah Richards was ambiguous. Under the language that he used, the trustee ownership by which Sarah Richards held lands for Universal Friend was not clearly defined (lacking details about the land in trust, including how much and on whose behalf it was held). Taking the will on its face, the argument could be made that Eliza now held title to all the properties purchased by Sarah Richards, including those lands on which Friend and followers had resettled following their flight from City Hill.

As long as young Eliza remained single, no one gave much thought to the terms of her mother's will. But Enoch Malin must have understood—or someone must have told him—that under the law of coverture, any lands that arguably belonged to Eliza would ultimately belong to any man who married her. Enoch had likely paid little attention to Eliza in the years they had lived together in the settlement, as she was ten years younger than him. But after her mother died, circumstances changed: in Enoch's eyes, the thirteen-year-old girl had become an heiress.[6]

When did he make the actual plan to seduce young Eliza? And how long was he prepared to wait until making his final intentions clear?

Maybe he really did fall in love with her and courted her not out of covetousness of her property but out of covetousness of her very being. She was described as "golden-haired, blue-eyed," "giddy," and high-spirited—and she would have likely welcomed Enoch's amorous attentions.[7] She had lived with Universal Friend since earliest childhood, watched over by the many women populating the household. Barely a teenager, had she grown weary of living under Friend's watchful eye, and longed for something new? Maybe she even wanted a home of her own.

Enoch could give her a way to escape the constraints of Friend's household and Eliza could give him, if they married, all the lands in Jerusalem that had been held in her mother's name. He must have known that going against both his natural family—his sisters Rachel and Margaret and his brother Elijah—and his adopted family headed by Universal Friend, would have shattering consequences. He surely knew what the fallout would be if he stole Eliza away from Friend's household: disbelief, anger, and sorrow. For now, he would simply court young Eliza and bide his time before making a move.

Already in the fall of 1794, a spat over ownership of a horse had marred the peace of Jerusalem. After lending a mare to Patience Wilkinson Potter, Universal Friend asked for its return. Patience lived with her husband, Thomas Potter, in a large house close to the first Friends Settlement. Patience offered instead to send the minister a colt that had just been born of the mare. But then Patience found out that her husband had already sold the colt and so she returned the mare as requested.

But Thomas wanted to keep the mare for himself. He had made a pretty profit on the colt and hoped for more offspring to sell. Caring little about his wife's interest in keeping peace with Friend, he asked James Parker for help in getting the horse back. Parker had been appointed the first justice of the peace for Ontario County in 1793. His duties included performing marriages (one of his first acts had been to marry three couples who rowed themselves across Seneca Lake for the joined ceremony), but he was eager to flex his judicial muscles over more meaty issues. Attacking his old mentor proved particularly appealing, and Parker wasted no time in sending a sheriff to serve a writ upon Friend demanding that the horse be returned to Potter's stable.

When Sheriff Norton attempted to serve the "Writ on Jemima Wilkinson at the suit of Judge Potter's son Thomas," Friend refused to acknowledge the name "Jemima Wilkinson" and wouldn't accept delivery of the writ.[8] Only after it was redrafted to address "Universal Friend commonly called Jemima Wilkinson," did the minister accept the writ—and then only to deny its accuracy or relevance. No record exists as to the final disposition of the case, but the incident seems to have further worsened already poisoned relations between Patience and Thomas (following his break with the Society), and rumors abounded that "her and her husband are unhappily Connected."[9] Although Patience continued to live in Thomas's house, everyone knew that her allegiance was to the minister who had been born her sister.

Thomas Potter's "opening shot" against Friend set off a series of property actions intended to harass the minister and the Society of Universal Friends.[10] Over the next few years, complaints and ejectment suits were brought against Friend and members of the Society for all sorts of reasons, but most based on the premise that the lands upon which the Society had settled did not, in fact, belong to them. In some cases, the sued members responded with counterclaims or suits of their own.[11] How many of the faithful were actually evicted from their lands is not known, but there is no question that they were bullied, threatened, and that lies were spread about them and the Society. The home of at least one follower, Susannah Spencer, was seized through ejectment and then "her house was burned."[12]

William Potter brought the most ejectment suits, targeting those Society members who, despite not having received land under Potter's 1793 allocations, had refused to leave their farms and homes.[13] George Sisson and John Briggs were among those served with ejectment notices by Potter. They had been among the first pioneers on City Hill, staying through the first lonely winter (along with George's wife, Bethany) and then persevering through the terrible year of hunger. George and Bethany's children, Lament and Luther, were the first babies born on the frontier, and somehow, they had all survived.

Determined to fight for their land on City Hill, Briggs and Sisson hired a lawyer to represent them against Potter. But the lawyer ran off with Sisson and Briggs's money, leaving both men destitute: "all their property [was] sold by the Sheriff to the last and least of their household goods," and George Sisson even ended up in debtor prison (Bethany traveled to and from Canandaigua for weeks bringing him food and news from Friend).[14] Friend would try to make up for the Sissons' losses and hardships by giving them a sizable property in Jerusalem, but securing that piece of land proved unexpectedly difficult—and led members of the Society to allegedly engage in their own strong-arm tactics. Jesse Dains had built himself a farmhouse on the property designated for the Sisssons and refused to leave. Dains would later testify that one of Friend's followers threatened to "cut the spring house all to peaces and take his house all to peaces" if he did not agree to share the land with the Sissons.[15] George and Bethany were finally given access to a portion of the property. They built themselves a new home and began farming—but soon their claims to those lands would be challenged, and from an unexpected claimant.

At the same time as William Potter was bringing his ejectment suits against former followers, he was doing all he could to keep the rumor mill against Friend going. Duke de La Rochefoucauld-Liancourt was a French nobleman who traveled through the United States in the early 1790s while in exile from France and its ongoing revolution. He stayed with Thomas Jefferson at Monticello (having met Jefferson in France in the 1780s) and when he traveled in western New York, he was likely hosted by both Benedict Robinson and William Potter in their grand homes overlooking the first Friend Settlement. In the diary that the duke kept while traveling, he recorded numerous slanderous stories he heard about Universal Friend and the Society, including one alleging that Chloe Towerhill had murdered an unwanted infant by "smothering . . . [the baby] between two mattresses. . . ."[16] Another story implied that Friend had enjoyed sexual relations, possibly with both men and women, and that after hearing Universal Friend speak about seeing the Messiah in her bed, "a young girl of only fourteen" had been enticed into that same bed only to encounter then-follower James Parker.[17] As a self-proclaimed critic of "dervishes, pontiffs, and priests of most religious persuasions throughout the world," the duke recorded all the stories in his travel diary.[18]

Curious to see this "imposter" minister for himself, Liancourt arranged a visit to Friend's home in Jerusalem.[19] The minister, who was either unaware of the poison that had been poured into the nobleman's ear or disdainful of it, treated Liancourt with generosity and courtesy, and Liancourt wrote in his diary that the dinner that Friend had provided him was "better in quality than any, of which we had partaken, since our departure from Philadelphia"; they had enjoyed "good fresh meat, with pudding, an excellent salad, and a beverage of a peculiar yet charming flavor."[20] In return for Friend's generous reception, Liancourt gave the minister an opulent velvet satchel stitched in gold thread and silver thread (and much less graciously, in 1799 he published his travel diary with the defamatory stories about Friend for all the world to read).[21]

If Friend heard about the "malicious tales" told about the Society and its minister, the chosen response would have been to pay no attention at all to the falsehoods; according to one of Friend's favored aphorisms, "injuries offend not the Souls of the Greats."[22] And in the *Advice* that the minister wrote in 1784, followers were counseled to "shun . . . the conversation of the wicked world as much as possible."[23] Assuring followers that "the Lord on high is mightyer than the Noise of many waters," the minister knew there was little to be gained by worrying about what outsiders said or did.[24] Friend believed that adversity, whether in human form or in forces of nature, was to be faced with "the same countenance" as prosperity, that is, an attitude of stoicism and acceptance: "the wise maketh every thing the means of advantage."[25]

There was still a sizable community of the faithful at City Hill as the turn of the century approached and Friend made a practice of traveling back and forth between Seneca Lake and Keuka Lake to hold religious meetings in the old log meetinghouse. Meetings were also held in Anna Wagener's farmhouse or in other "commodious framed dwellings" large enough to hold a large group of the faithful. During these weekends away, Friend would stay with Anna Wagener, in a room kept ready just for the minister; no one else was ever allowed to sleep in the room until 1812, when, due to ill health, the minister's visits to the old settlement grew less frequent. The other travelers from Jerusalem, including Margaret and the Malin sisters, were put up at the homes of other faithful followers. There was no rancor between the followers in one place and the other, only deep friendships and shared commitment to the original precepts of repentance and salvation. The concept of community wasn't defined by physical space, but was instead an ideal: "if we walk in the Light, as he is in the Light, we have fellowship with another. . . ."[26]

Perhaps in an effort to protect the community from the barrage of legal actions against its members, it was around this time that Universal Friend sought to clarify the sect's property holdings by asking William Carter, a local lawyer and faithful follower, to put together a legal document listing all the lots held on behalf of the Society of Universal Friends in Jerusalem. The various properties had come to Friend through a variety of conveyances beginning in the year 1792 (when Sarah Richards purchased on Friend's behalf the first fourteen hundred acres in Jerusalem), continuing with grants of land given to Friend through wills and gifts, and then in 1795, the purchase of hundreds more acres from Thomas Hathaway through Rachel Malin.

The document created by William Carter, dated August 14, 1795, listed a total of fourteen lots held by Friend in Jerusalem, equaling about 4,480 acres.[27] While Friend would never claim direct ownership of these properties (and relied on the validity of first Sarah Richards's, and then Rachel Malin's trusteeship of those lands), did the minister hope that Carter's documentation would be enough to prove ownership of those lands in case of a challenge? Friend must have already suspected that new attacks were being planned to hurt the Society and its minister. But what Universal Friend never saw coming was the betrayal that would once again shake the trees of Eden and spread a dusting of venom over a community of the faithful.

In the summer of 1796, Enoch Malin convinced Eliza Richards to climb out of her bedroom window and meet him at a house nearby, where they were married by James Parker, acting in his role as justice of the peace. Friend returned home from the Sabbath-day meeting to find, as the minister described it, that "Enoch stole Eliza away."[28] Friend had cared for Eliza since childhood and Enoch ever since he joined the community on City Hill in 1788 at the age of eighteen; the minister had written to James Parker then, alerting him to look out for the somewhat lost young son of "a large and devoted family," and asking Parker to "Be a father to" Enoch.[29] Friend had no idea that Parker would turn against the community of faith and take Enoch with him. And now Eliza was lost as well. The "entire flock" of followers were as shocked as their minister; how could the two young people they had doted on as their "pet lambs" reject the community that had cared for them?[30]

It didn't take long for the married Enoch to begin selling off lots in Jerusalem that had been purchased by Sarah Richards on Friend's behalf. He considered all the lands that Sarah Richards held in trusteeship for Friend to be the lawfully inherited property of Eliza—and now his property to be sold as he wished. When chided by his brother Elijah for selling off Society land, Enoch replied that because he could claim title through his wife, no one could blame him for trying to make money. In addition, he argued, "Friend had got a great deal of property together and . . . he [Enoch] might just as well have it as anybody else."[31] There is no record of what Eliza thought of her husband's machinations, but she did stay with him as he began to tear the community apart.

In 1797, Enoch sold four hundred acres in Jerusalem to two sons of Elnathan Botsford, Elnathan Jr. and Benajah. He then sold fifty acres to Asahel Stone and sixty-two to Asa Ingraham. Benajah Botsford was married to Friend's sister Deborah, and his sister Lucy was married to Friend's brother Stephen. The Botsfords had been among the earliest pioneers on City Hill and were all devoted followers of Friend, as were both Asahel Stone and Asa Ingraham. Before the sale to the Botsford brothers went through, Elnathan Botsford came to Universal Friend asking for the minister's approval, which was granted. Perhaps Friend acquiesced in the sales of these properties because the lands were staying within the "family" of the Society of Universal Friends. The low prices for which Enoch sold the property might also have assured Friend that his intent was to help members of the Society, not to make a profit for himself.

But the low prices demanded by Enoch, along with the rapid turnover of deeds, should have raised a red flag. Enoch was desperate for cash and most likely hoped to get as many deals done, with anyone he could find, before Universal Friend started raising any objections. Why was Enoch so eager for money? He was skilled as a carpenter and millwright, but he could not make enough money plying his skills, and it was hard work as well. He tried his hand at running his own tavern in a log cabin not far from City Hill. But that enterprise failed, and Enoch found himself increasingly strapped for funds. In June of 1799, Enoch's obligations would only increase when an Ontario court found that he had fathered "a female bastard . . . on the body of Mary Kinney" (the unmarried daughter of Elizabeth Kinney, a faithful follower of Universal Friend) and had to pay a settlement to Mary of $30.[32] He was also made liable for weekly payments to cover the child's care.

Court-ordered child support payments were common and derived from colonial-era practices that in turn were based on early Congregationalist mandates (and English "poor Laws") that every person in a community be cared for. In order to save church and state from having to bear the costs of such care, fathers were held responsible for their children, no matter the marital status. A midwife called in to the birth of an illegitimate child was often required to confirm the name of the father before being allowed to assist in the birth.[33]

In the fall of 1798, Enoch filed a lawsuit in Ontario County seeking the legal ejectment of all settlers currently living on lands held by Sarah Richards before she died, including Universal Friend. Friend could no longer avoid the obvious: Enoch Malin wanted Jerusalem for himself, to sell off as he wished. The ejectment suit was brought by a lawyer named Elisha Williams, an inveterate land speculator from Hudson, New York. He'd been part of the New York Genesee Land Company that had sold land to James Parker on behalf of the Society in 1788—and Universal Friend knew all too well how that had turned out. To see his name on the legal papers filed against members of the Society would have stirred up bitter memories. Williams soon brought even more lawyers into the fight against the settlers in Jerusalem: Robert Stoddard of Geneva, New York, and Stoddard's law partner David Hudson. All three lawyers encouraged Enoch's dreams of easy wealth. They had land speculations of their own and wanted a piece of the pie, any pie, in western New York.

Even with such motivated and ambitious legal firepower behind him, in June of 1799 the trial jury hearing Enoch Malin's ejectment case ruled against him. They found that the land purchases made by Sarah Richards in Jerusalem had been carried out on behalf of Universal Friend and the Society, and therefore Friend and followers lawfully resided on those lands; they were "not Guilty of Trespass" and could not be evicted.[34] Enoch had lost and the question of who owned the lands in Jerusalem should have been settled once and for all. But Enoch and his lawyers would not give up. Another judge or another jury, if the case was framed a different way, might rule against Universal Friend and the Society—and Enoch's lawyers would do their best to make that happen.

The lawsuits brought against Universal Friend and the Society by Enoch Malin, William Potter, and later Benedict Robinson were largely motivated by their desire for more and more profit in the form of valuable meadows and forests and fields. Potter and Robinson had gained property and status through the 1793 allocations on City Hill, and the idea of having even more property appealed to them greatly. But alongside their avarice—they "had gained much from their move to New York and hoped to gain more"—a desire for revenge seemed to be motivating them.[35] While they had accepted Friend's non-gendered claims when they were faithful followers of the Society, now they only saw their former minister as "an assuming, presumptuous woman"—and they fiercely regretted ever having bowed down to a woman.[36]

Going after the properties of the Society and its followers was not enough for these men, and in September of 1799 Parker, using his authority as justice of the peace, issued a warrant for the arrest of Universal Friend on the criminal charge of blasphemy, claiming that the minister purported to be an incarnation of Jesus Christ. Historian Paul Moyer notes that "the sect's collective pronouncements never identified Universal Friend as the Messiah" and Moyer and other historians have concluded that Friend, while portraying "Messianic tendencies, ultimately did not pose as Christ returned."[37] Contemporaries of the minister, like Reverend Eeles of Stonington, Connecticut, also understood that even when the minister "called herself the Comforter . . . she did not mean she was the holy ghost but [instead was] raised up by God to give comfort to his people."[38]

For those interested in destroying Friend's ministry, the accusation that Friend "pretended to be Jesus Christ in the form of a Woman" was a powerful weapon.[39] Blasphemy was punishable by both imprisonment and fines and had been widely prosecuted in the colonies before the Revolution.[40] If Universal Friend were found guilty and sent to prison, and Society money was spent paying off fines and legal fees, the Society of Universal Friends might very well falter, then fail. Having hatched their plan, Potter and Parker dispatched Thomas Hathaway Jr., son of one of Friend's most devoted followers, to deliver the arrest warrant to Friend and bring the minister in to face the charge of blasphemy.

But Universal Friend would not go quietly.

24

Invoking Law and God

"Can God judge through the thick and the dark cloud?
O yes he can and there is no place
where the workers of iniquity can hide themselves. . . ."

—UNIVERSAL FRIEND

Universal Friend and Rachel Malin, after making their rounds visiting sick members of the Society, had just left their last patient. Bethany Sisson was feeling better, and the two felt confident leaving her in the care of her husband, George. As Rachel and Friend rode their horses toward home, the minister spotted movement among a scattering of trees to the east. Thomas Hathaway Jr., riding hard on his horse, was breaking through the tree line and galloping toward them.[1] Had young Hathaway hoped to surprise the two tired travelers? Come upon them so suddenly that they would stop in their tracks and surrender themselves?

According to the story passed down through the Society, Friend and Rachel stopped their horses and turned to face the oncoming rider. As soon as Hathaway drew near, Friend cracked a riding whip through the air, spooking Hathaway's horse. The horse reared up and while Hathaway struggled to bring his mount back under control, Friend took off at a gallop. The goal was to find shelter in the home of Richard Smith, just down the hill on the banks of the Keuka outlet. An enraged Hathaway lashed at the rump of his horse; leaving Rachel Malin behind (there was no warrant for her arrest), he went in hot pursuit of Friend, desperate to catch up with the fleeing horse before the minister arrived at Smith's homestead. But he was too late. By the time he cantered up to the cabin, Smith had brought Friend inside and then shut tight the doors and windows, pushing benches and a table into place to secure his home against intrusion. Smith had been as skilled in building his log cabin as he had been in building the Society's first mill, and it was impenetrable against Hathaway's efforts. In the end, Hathaway had no choice but to ride away.[2]

The arrest warrant that Hathaway carried was based on a complaint signed by Chloe Dains. Chloe's husband, Jesse, along with his siblings, Jonathan, Castle, and Abigail, had come to Seneca Lake in 1788 with James Parker. Jesse had not been happy when his minister pressured him into sharing his farmlands with George Sisson, and now had likely influenced his wife to swear in an affidavit that Friend claimed to be "the Son of God" and that she had heard Friend say, "I am the son of God as true as the breath in thy nostrils."[3] William Potter and James Parker also secured sworn affidavits from Thomas Judd (another early follower), Eliza Malin, and Jesse Dains stating that Friend "held herself to be the Son of God."[4] With such ammunition, Universal Friend's criminal conviction for blasphemy must have seemed certain.

But first Friend had to be served with an arrest warrant.

After Friend's successful dodge of Thomas Hathaway Jr., Parker and Potter made a second attempt to serve the warrant, this time enlisting the help of Enoch Malin and Eliphalet Norris. Norris, the whiskey-selling shopkeeper, was also a constable; he was charged with delivering the warrant, while Enoch came along as muscle man and backup. This second arrest attempt was made while Friend was working in the weaving shed in Jerusalem alongside several women from the community. As soon as the weavers saw Norris enter, they laid aside their work and created a wall of protection around their minister. Led by Lavina Dains (Chloe's niece by marriage), the angry women rushed toward Norris and, using all their strength, successfully "pitched the constable out doors."[5] (There was nothing in Universal Friend's *Advice* against physical defense of oneself or one's minister.)

According to stories passed down by the weavers, they "handled him with so little care, that some of his garments were badly torn, and a renewal of the onslaught was impossible without a repair of his breeches."[6] Eliphalet Norris and Enoch Malin beat a hasty retreat from Friend's property, intent on repairing both their clothes and their pride before confronting Friend and the faithful women again.

For their third attempt to serve a warrant on Friend, Potter and Parker enlisted at least thirty men to help in capturing their prey, including Enoch Malin, Eliphalet Norris, Benedict Robinson, and Griffin Hazard (who, like Norris, served as a constable in the county). This time they decided to try and catch the minister at home. The posse of angry men surrounded the log house and demanded to be let in. When the front door remained closed to them, one of the men attacked it with an axe, broke it wide open, and the vigilantes stormed inside.

Thundering upstairs, they found Friend sick in bed, pale and shivering. The "one-armed Dr. Calvin Fargo," who had been brought along by the men to make sure Friend could be safely transported away, examined the minister and determined the illness was so severe that any attempt to move the patient would be dangerous.[7] From outside the house, Benedict Robinson, who had brought with him oxen and cart to transport Friend to jail, was heard to yell, "throw her in the cart and carry her off!"[8] (The oxen he brought might have been the same oxen he'd received from Friend in exchange for five lots in Jerusalem in 1793.) But calmer heads prevailed, and the men retreated, warrant in hand and unexecuted.

The continuing failure to serve the warrant that ordered "Jemima Wilkinson" to appear in his court enraged James Parker. He wanted Friend placed under his jurisdiction as magistrate of Ontario County so that he alone could determine the outcome of the charge of blasphemy. Fines, imprisonment, censure: Parker wanted to wield the axe that would finally bring down Universal Friend. His determination to hurt his former minister seemed to come from many sources, including his own confusion over faith and God. Despite his apparent ambitions for wealth and status, he was still a man in search of a religion. He tried various sects, perhaps looking for one that would not challenge his desire for earthly goods and wealth but could also ensure him some degree of spiritual certainty and assurances that he wasn't going to hell. He attended meetings of the Free Will Baptists (even becoming an ordained minister of the sect) and also tried out the Universalists; both groups had congregations east of Keuka Lake. (The Free Will Baptists would eventually throw him out for refusing to preach about the certainty of hell, and in the late 1820s, he would finally join a congregation of Methodists.)

Maybe Parker's anger with Friend was fueled by the fact that the ministry of salvation had continued on without him; that Friend had not just given up and returned east to Rhode Island when he quit the sect. Or perhaps he was shamed—and that shame turned to anger—by Friend's disappointment in his failure to protect those members who had given so much to the first settlement and then lost everything. He might have been confounded by the Society's prosperity in Jerusalem despite the many obstacles placed in their way. No matter the reasons, despite having loved Friend for years, and given up so much to follow the ways of the Society, now he seemed to have nothing but contempt for the minister.

Parker tried every sort of abuse to bring Friend down. He, along with William Potter, had tried to evict the minister and followers from City Hill; he had tried to impoverish them through denying their land claims; he had tried slander; he had tried ridicule. Now he would try to use the legal system to silence Friend. He was certain of victory this time. Parker and his friends William Potter and Eliphalet Norris held "key positions of power and prestige" in the "backcountry regions" of Ontario County, and they would be unstoppable in their plan of revenge.[9] Once the warrant was served—and he would make sure it was—he would act as Friend's prosecutor and judge, no matter the ethical violations involved.

Although Universal Friend condemned Parker's arrest warrant as "malicious," the minister finally agreed to a "parley" (a meeting to discuss it), during which the arrest warrant was accepted.[10] But Friend refused to accept the jurisdiction of Justice Parker, knowing that appearing in his courtroom would result in a guilty verdict. Not only had Parker made his intentions toward Friend clear, but in other situations involving members of the Society, Parker had so openly mistreated them that he had been sanctioned and fined by the overseeing Ontario County District Court "for misconduct in the office of the justice of the peace." (In one case, Parker failed to administer the necessary oath of office to Asahel Stone so that he could perform assessor duties for Jerusalem.)[11] It was finally agreed that the charges against Universal Friend would be heard in the Court of Oyer and Terminer, a criminal court charged with hearing felony cases and presided over by a Supreme Court justice and two or more judges of the state court system.[12]

Before the charge against Universal Friend could move forward in the Court of Oyer and Terminer, however, the judges overseeing the case had to decide whether in the new country of the United States of America the act of blasphemy could be considered a crime. Under laws that prevailed throughout the colonies before the American Revolution, blasphemy was considered an indictable criminal offense, defined as statements "against the Almighty, by denying his being or providence; or by contumelious reproaches of our Saviour Jesus Christ . . . profane scoffing at the Holy Scripture, or exposing it to contempt or ridicule."[13] The charge was widely used to punish those who fell outside the religious mainstream, especially in religiously heterogeneous colonies such as Massachusetts. Even in the colony of New York, which had been historically hospitable to a wide range of religions, blasphemy was a recognized and prosecuted crime.[14] But under the first amendment of the United States Constitution, and provisions of New York State's constitution, both freedom of religion and freedom of speech were protected. How would this court, sitting out on the western frontier, rule?

The court hearing Friend's case met in June of 1800 in the Ontario County Courthouse, newly built in 1794. The large courtroom was packed with former followers, faithful followers, and curious spectators. James Parker would have been there and most likely William Potter as well, with Rachel and Margaret Malin sitting across the aisle from them and behind their minister. Decided by a vote of two to one, the judges declared that under both the New York and federal constitutions, blasphemy was no longer an indictable offense in America. The charge of blasphemy against Universal Friend was dismissed.

Judge Morgan Lewis asked if the minister had anything to say. Friend would not let such an opportunity pass and eagerly rose to deliver an impromptu but persuasive sermon about repentance and redemption. Perhaps the minister relied upon a favorite biblical quote, "And as Moses lifted up the serpent in the wilderness, even so must the Son of man be lifted up: That whosoever believeth in him should not perish but have eternal life."[15] Friend would have explained that sins, prowling like serpents in the grass, would be judged on earth and by God. But "the rod of the wicked shall not rest upon the lot of the righteous. . . . Do good, O LORD, unto those that be good, and to them that are upright in their hearts."[16]

After Universal Friend had finished speaking, Judge Lewis recommended to everyone gathered in the courtroom, "We have heard good counsel, and if we live in harmony with what that woman has told us, we shall be sure to be good people and reach a final rest in heaven."[17] Court was then adjourned. By insisting that the case be heard before a higher county court and not by James Parker, Universal Friend had avoided fines and imprisonment, and successfully thwarted plans to destroy the Society of Universal Friends.

Were the judges who ruled for Universal Friend so taken by the ideals embraced in the recently enacted Bill of Rights, and so eager to stake their claim on the frontier as leading the way for those ideals, that they boldly ruled for freedom of speech and religion? What is certain is that they went against English common law—which had largely been adopted "lock, stock, and barrel" by the fledgling courts of the new United States—in denying the blasphemy charges. It was a truly remarkable outcome for Universal Friend, given that for the next 152 years, in cases from Arkansas to Maine, blasphemy charges would be upheld by U.S. state and federal courts, including the United States Supreme Court.[18]

The most famous case was decided in New York State in 1811. John Ruggles had been found guilty of blasphemy after being overheard saying, "Jesus Christ was a bastard, and his mother must be a whore."[19] The Supreme Court of New York upheld his conviction, stating that "Though the Constitution has discarded religious establishments, it does not forbid judicial cognizance of those offences against religion and morality which . . . are punishable because they strike at the root of moral obligation, and weaken the security of the social ties . . . [and are] a gross violation of decency and good order."[20] It was not until 1952 that the United States Supreme Court held that "It is not the business of government in our nation to suppress real or imagined attacks upon particular religious doctrine."[21]

There were further attempts by former followers to ensnare the minister in criminal proceedings, including another complaint issued in Chloe Dains's name. Dains claimed that Universal Friend had threatened her and her family, and that she was "afraid our lives and property will be destroyed by the said Jemima. . . ." Dains included in the complaint allegations of intruders "lying round our House in the night a number of times," implying that such intruders had been sent by the minister to intimidate Chloe and her family.[22] But the complaints of Dains and other disgruntled followers never resulted in charges brought against Universal Friend or the Society, and when the minister later encountered Chloe at the house of a sick neighbor and asked, "Did thee think I would kill thee?" Chloe shook her head and replied that she did not. "Then why did thee swear so wickedly?" Friend asked. Chloe claimed she had been "put up to it," that she'd been bullied into giving evidence against Friend by enemies of the Society.[23]

With the harassment of both the minister and the Society continuing, Universal Friend was faced with a decision. Something had to be done that would make their enemies think twice before launching legal missiles or spreading rumors or taking the law into their own hands and selling off properties they deemed theirs. It was not enough to successfully defend against lawsuits and criminal indictments; not enough to ignore rumors and under-the-table land deals. Could the legal system that enemies had tried to manipulate for themselves now be used against them?

Universal Friend must have thought long and hard about seeking justice in the earthly courts of man. After all, God was the ultimate judge of traitors "for their evil, and the wicked for their iniquity" and would "cause the arrogancy of the proud to cease, and will lay low the haughtiness of the terrible."[24] But Friend had a responsibility to members of the Society of Universal Friends. Invoking both law and God, Friend would do what had to be done.

In late 1801 or early 1802, four lawsuits were brought by the Society against those who had used violence in attempting to serve the blasphemy arrest on Universal Friend. The suits were brought by Rachel Malin on behalf of the Society, but everyone involved, from the judges to the accused and their lawyers, knew that the lawsuits had been brought by Universal Friend. The "exact nature" of the lawsuits is not recorded nor are the specific injuries for which damages were demanded.[25] But every one of those suits resulted in successful verdicts, and the defendants had to dig deep in their pockets to compensate Friend for the injuries they had inflicted. Eliphalet Norris and Thomas

Hathaway each were punished with $39.09 in damages (about $1,150 in today's dollars); Daniel Brown and Isaac Kinney had to pay $103 each (over $3,000); and Griffin Hazard had to pay the very large sum of $551 (over $16,000).[26]

The legal actions brought against enemies of the sect had been successful. But the trials of Universal Friend and the Society were not yet over. What could Friend do to finally calm the troubled waters at Keuka and bring peace to Eden?

25

The Courage of Faith

"Let Righteousness be the girdle of your Loins . . .
Faithfulness the Girdle of your Reins, and fear not. . . ."

—UNIVERSAL FRIEND

As the year 1804 gave way to 1805, Universal Friend called for a counting to be made: a counting of the faithful. The minister asked every man and woman of the Society who still believed Universal Friend to be a messenger sent by God to come forward and attest to their faith. Each was asked to sign a document of faith and Friend asked for nothing more—no gift, no fee, no dropping to a knee or taking up a collection. Just "the simple act of coming and signing your name, or by staying away . . ." in order to demonstrate commitment to the community—or not.[1]

It was a "roll call" of the faithful and the faithful came, in "heavy enrollment" and with deeply felt assurances of loyalty. Friend "took that signing on faith, she did not denounce or renounce anybody . . ." who did not come forward, but instead took comfort in the large numbers of followers who had signed their names. The ministry of salvation would have continued regardless—as the minister explained, "I am the same, the way is the same even if all men forsake it, the way remains."[2]

But how much better it was for Friend to know that so many of the faithful had not forsaken their community.

Of course, there were those who did not come to be counted. Enoch and Eliza, still living in Jerusalem, would not come, but Enoch's sisters Rachel and Margaret did, and so did his brother Elijah. The Dains family, living side by side with the Sissons, stayed away, but Bethany and George, as devoted as ever, came to be counted. Ruth Pritchard would be counted, but not her husband, who never joined the Society. The five men who served as trustees to the corporation of the Society, having been named back in 1791 and reappointed year after year, remained faithful, and they, too, came forward: Abel Botsford, John Briggs, Jonathan Dains, Isaac Nichols, and Richard Smith.

To protect the faithful, Universal Friend knew that more than spiritual energies would have to be expended, and in 1811 the minister once again made the bold decision to employ the earthly courts of justice in pursuit of temporal stability for the Society of Universal Friends. The question of who owned the hills and valleys, fields and orchards of Jerusalem, had to be settled once and for all. Although a jury had decided against Enoch Malin's ejectment suits in 1799, Enoch and Eliza Malin continued to live on the lands they claimed had been left to Eliza by her mother, and so did the farmers to whom they had sold deeds. Friend could have let matters rest, but must have been wary of what the future might bring. And so, Thomas R. Gold, a prominent Yale-trained lawyer, was hired to bring an ejectment suit in New York's chancery court. The lawsuit was brought on behalf of Rachel Malin representing the Society of Universal Friends, against Enoch and Eliza Malin, and all those who had purchased lots from Enoch; the suit sought the ejectment of the named defendants from all lands that had been bought and held on behalf of Universal Friend by Sarah Richards in the 1790s.

Gold would be joined a few years later in his fight on behalf of the Society of Universal Friends by Abraham Van Vechten and John C. Spencer. The three lawyers were among the most renowned—and expensive—in New York State. Gold would go on to become a member of Congress. Van Vechten, known as "Father of the New York Bar" for having been the first member ever admitted to the state association of lawyers, served as attorney general for New York. And Spencer, still a young man, was the son of New York Chief Justice Ambrose Spencer and connected by family to the Clintons and other New York political families, and would later be appointed secretary of war and then secretary of the treasury under President John Tyler in the 1840s. Why these men agreed to help Universal Friend had nothing to do with their spiritual interests or religious backgrounds (the Van Vechten family were members of the Dutch Reformed Church, and Gold was likely mainstream Protestant, as was Spencer); they were in it for the glory of the fight and for the money they were being paid by the Society.

The ejectment suit brought by Thomas Gold on behalf of the Society was the final straw for Enoch and Eliza Malin. They had grown weary of the battle over Jerusalem, and Enoch just wanted hard cash and the chance to leave behind the troubles he'd had in western New York. In 1812, the Malins sold their claims in Jerusalem for the sum of $1,000 to Elisha Williams, the land speculator and lawyer who had represented Enoch in the unsuccessful ejectment case. Having been paid off by Williams, Enoch and Eliza left western New York and headed into Canada.

It was a strange course for them to take. War between the United States and Britain had just erupted with both sides fighting for territory in America (and the United States fighting in protest of British impressment of Americans into their navy as well against British interference with U.S. shipping). Native Americans found themselves once again caught between the U.S. and Britain, and again calculating which party best protected their own territorial interests. Battles among all the interested parties were being fought along the border between the United States and Canada, with the U.S. intent on invading Canada to secure more lands for its ever-hungry white pioneers, the

British desperate to stave off invasion, and Native American tribes like the Shawnee (led by brothers Tecumseh and Tenskwatawa), the Peoria, and the Ottawa, fighting to secure their land rights in Canada and the Ohio Valley.

And yet the Malins crisscrossed the border lines, wandering from town to town as Enoch looked for work. When he died in 1813 or 1814, Eliza was left alone with two young boys to care for. In November of 1815, living in Ohio on the edge of poverty with a man named either "Jabe or Jabez Brunson," Eliza would fall ill and die at the age of thirty-five.[3] Did Universal Friend learn of her death at the time? If the minister felt any responsibility for the young woman's fate, no record exists of such regrets, but it was a sad ending for Eliza, who effectively lost both of her parents at a young age and perhaps never found her bearings again. For some reason, Eliza never found security or happiness in the life of faith offered by Friend and the Society. Maybe she could never accept the terms of that life, believing that her mother had given up too much—including her own daughter—in order to dedicate her life to Universal Friend.

Elisha Williams, after purchasing the interests of Enoch and Eliza, took over the job of defending against Rachel Malin's ejectment suit with venomous zeal. Not only did he represent the interests of Enoch and Eliza but also of several of the other defendants who were living on land sold to them by Enoch Malin, including Elnathan Botsford and Asahel Stone. In a larger sense, Elisha Williams represented all the powerful men of Ontario County eager for more land of their own, including men such as former follower William Carter, who sold land in Jerusalem to Universal Friend in the 1790s, but now threatened the Society of Universal Friend with "further troubles and disputes" and potential lawsuits in an effort to take those lands away (the basis for his threatened suit was unclear).[4] If Elisha Williams could win a judgment against the Society, Universal Friend's hold on Jerusalem would be placed into doubt and the floodgates would open for anyone hungry for a piece of Jerusalem pie.

In court papers submitted by Williams in response to the Society's ejectment suit, he once again argued that Sarah Richards had owned the property in Jerusalem on her own and not as a trustee for Universal Friend and the Society. But he also made a new counterclaim against the Society contending that the will of Sarah Richards had been altered after her death (with little evidence to prove such a claim) and because it was altered, it was null and void, and therefore inheritance would revert solely to the legal heirs of Sarah Richards, i.e., Eliza Richards and her husband, and their children. Because Williams had purchased these rights and interests, now Williams himself was entitled to Eliza Richards's inheritance.

With the opposing sides awaiting a hearing and then a ruling from the Court of Chancery on the ejectment suit, Elisha Williams poured resources and time into mounting a countywide campaign of slander against Friend and the community of faithful followers, alleging the former was a pompous, narcissistic, and delusional tyrant and the latter were fanatics who would do whatever their domineering minister instructed them to do, including forge documents and lie under oath.[5] Williams had one goal in mind: to prejudice the judges and potential juries in Ontario County against the minister in order to undermine any chance for Friend or the Society to have their fair day in court.

Perhaps in an effort to portray the stability and piety of their minister, the Society contracted for a portrait to be painted of Universal Friend in late 1815 or early 1816. It would hang in Friend's new house, which had taken five years to build, but had finally been completed in the spring of 1814. Designed by Thomas Clark, a Free Will Baptist and architect from Philadelphia and husband of Elizabeth Malin (oldest sister of Rachel and Margaret), the house with its tall windows provided "vast views of other hills" and the "blue of the lakes" off in the distance.[6] A visitor to the community described the house as "most spacious and elegant. It is three stories high and has six rooms on the floor . . . the whole scenery of the neighborhood are uncommonly beautiful, and fit to nourish the enthusiasm of its inhabitants. . . ."[7] The house still stands today on the hills overlooking Keuka Lake, marked by tall stands of pine trees on both sides.

Sheds and barns were constructed nearby to house the weavers, the dairy cows, and other farm animals (including more than "seventy head of cattle meat stock"), and a brick cavern was built into the hillside to provide eventual resting places for those followers who had gone out of time.[8] Peacocks were set free to wander among the wide border of pine trees, and on the surrounding hills, "2,000 maple trees could be counted," which, in the years to come, would produce sap "in wonderful abundance."[9] One year, followers Henry Barnes and Rachel Ingraham produced a harvest of over 1,500 pounds of maple sugar, which they boiled down to 220 gallons of syrup, plenty of sweetness to reward them—and benefit so many others—for their hard labor.

Universal Friend traveled to Canandaigua to have the portrait painted by John Lee Douglas Mathies, a well-known artist who four years later would paint a portrait of the Seneca chief Red Jacket that became famous throughout the United States. In Mathies's portrait of Universal Friend, the minister sits upright, eyes penetrating, and eyebrows drawn together. Dressed in the usual costume of dark gown with a shining white cravat at the neck, Friend's head is uncovered, dark hair drawn back behind the ears and falling in loose curls to full and broad shoulders. A sharp widow's peak at the temple with a slightly receding hairline underscores the androgyny of Friend, while the relaxed mouth gives both serenity and strength to the image. The minister displays no arrogance, no rigidity, no pretense; one hand extends slightly forward, as if welcoming the viewer into a conversation or maybe gently inviting a sinner to repentance and salvation.

While the portrait would have originally hung in the front hall of Friend's new home, where all visitors could see it and be impressed, after a time it was moved to the privacy of the room where Friend slept and meditated, wrote and prayed. Perhaps the minister felt public display of the portrait gave an impression of arrogance or vanity, and that could not be tolerated: "for the LORD seeth not as man seeth; for man looketh on the outward appearance, but the LORD looketh on the heart."[10] At some point, the portrait was put in a heavy frame that had been carved with elaborate beaded ornamentation. Artfully camouflaged within the raised beads were the initials "U + F," which only the sharpest eye could discern.[11]

What the portrait does not show is the inner turmoil Friend seems to have been suffering from at this time.[12] Perhaps it was age creeping up on Friend, who would turn sixty-four in November, along with the onset of symptoms of an illness that included swollen limbs, fatigue, and pain, and then the endless threat of lawsuits and harassment by former followers—but whatever the reason, Friend felt, for a brief time, a faltering of courage, writing in a journal, "O! may the sins of omission and commission be forgiven, and my back sliding healed, and I be restored into the favor of the Lord, where my conversation may be in Heaven, that I might know the Lord's will. . . ."[13]

Friend had chosen to take on temporal issues—the legal questions and financial decisions that would either guarantee the future of Jerusalem and the Society, or mire both in controversy and debt for decades to come—and the stress must have been tremendous. Which was the right way to go? All Friend could do was prepare for the worst and then trust in God: "The horse is prepared against the day of battle: but safety is of the Lord."[14]

The war with Britain continued, and while most of the northern battles were fought hundreds of miles away from Jerusalem, men from the Finger Lakes were conscripted by the New York militia and they also volunteered. Jonathan Sisson, son of George and Bethany, served as a calvary officer during the war and received 160 acres of "bounty land" for his service.[15] Although there was little chance of a British invasion from Canada, there were fears that Native Americans, supported by the British, would come south to reclaim more of the lands that had been taken from them, and never returned. There were bloody skirmishes involving Native American forces along the Canadian border (mostly to the west of New York), with several border towns destroyed and white settlers driven away.

But the region surrounding Jerusalem remained peaceful. Nevertheless, farmers and merchants did suffer in the war years, with the British navy blockading ports and impeding trade both in and out of the United States. Any "orderly marketing" of goods (and relying on trade) was turned on its head and farmers and traders alike saw their revenues from selling crops and goods both at home and abroad plummet. And this time, as "prices fell, land values plummeted."[16]

Uncertain markets weren't the only reason for falling land values in New York State. Even before the war with the British ended in 1815 with the signing of the Treaty of Ghent (restoring boundaries between the U.S. and Canada to what they had been before the war), American pioneers had been going farther west, and south, in search of new lands and new opportunities. Ohio, admitted as a state in 1803, and the Territories of Indiana and Illinois (which became states in 1816 and 1818), welcomed thousands of settlers from New England, New York, and Pennsylvania in the first decades of the nineteenth century, and thousands more went to the lands of the Louisiana Purchase (made in 1803), which included the Missouri Territory. With the Missouri River winding its way north and west all the way to present-day Montana, Missouri became known as the "Gateway to the West" and served as the launching point for expeditions of explorers like Lewis and Clark (in 1804) and for settlers looking for new lands and new opportunities farther west in America.

Even if land values were falling, those on either side of the ejectment case brought by the Society in 1811 were anxious to know to whom the lands of Jerusalem belonged. Throughout the war years they waited for a ruling from Chancellor James Kent, the head of the Court of Chancery, New York State's highest court. Finally, in November 1816, the Society's case was heard, but the court's findings were not what either side had been hoping for. Chancellor Kent refused to rule on the validity of either side's arguments and put off a decision on the ejectments that the Society had asked for. He stated that certain issues of fact had to be heard in front of a lower court, including the question of whether Universal Friend had given payment to Benedict Robinson for lands in Jerusalem and if Sarah Richards's will had been altered after her death. More depositions would have to be taken, more evidence gathered, and more testimony presented from all key witnesses and players.

Off the record, Chancellor Kent also advised Thomas Gold to convince Universal Friend to formally sign onto Rachel Malin's lawsuit, and under the name given by the minister's parents. Gold appealed to Rachel Malin in desperation: "Does she [Universal Friend] not sense that everything is at stake, the roof over her head. . . ."[17] He wrote that in the hearing held before Chancellor Kent, it became clear that "Your cause . . . assumes a formidable aspect & you will have to contend for the whole property . . . the Chancellor [further] determined that the *Friends name must be used, to wit Jemima Wilkinson*, as Complainant with you."[18]

To lay claim to a name long rejected was a momentous step for Friend to take. But the needs of the community demanded a new posture of conciliation, and Friend might have reasoned that sticking to rules that did nothing to help others actually undercut the duty owed to God: Friend had preached before that all the gifts of life—including the gift of choice—should be cherished not for personal enrichment "but for the good it may be of to others."[19] Or perhaps, having become resigned to playing a role in temporal (and financial) affairs, Friend now accepted what that role required. In the end, the minister agreed to have the complaint amended to include the minister as a party to the suit, under the name "Jemima Wilkinson."[20]

If Friend had made such a decision in the 1790s and agreed then to purchase the lands in Jerusalem in the name of Jemima Wilkinson on behalf of the Society, would all the legal troubles of the past twenty years have been avoided? Perhaps—but the faithful followers never chided their minister for trying to stay above temporal and financial affairs for so long; nor did they call out Friend for a stubbornness that might have been better to subdue. Maybe they preferred to see Friend's decision to finally let the name "Jemima Wilkinson" be used on a legal document as a demonstration of their minister's flexibility (which underscored the strength of Friend's piety—the signing of a mere document would not alter spiritual conviction or commitment) and also Friend's courage: the courage to do what had to be done in order to protect the Society and the courage to believe that, in the end, the faithful would be victorious against those who sought to destroy their community and bring down their minister.

A larger question now loomed for the Society of Universal Friends. Would their minister be with them at the end of the battle? Would Universal Friend share with them the final victory and savor the peace such victory would bring? Because while Friend's mind remained strong, the minister's body was failing. Even as the hope of triumph and courage of belief spurred them on, the faithful followers feared that their messenger's time on earth was running out.

26

Out of Time

"The Counsel, if obeyed, Brings Peace to my Soul. . . .
I have Obeyed the words that are Spoken,
They are Spirit and they are Life. . . ."

—UNIVERSAL FRIEND

Already back in July of 1816, a healer by the name of Elizabeth Walker had traveled to Jerusalem to diagnose the illness that relentlessly plagued Universal Friend. A persistent and painful swelling of the legs and feet, accompanied by bulbous blisters, made walking difficult and riding on horseback impossible; while going by coach allowed the minister some mobility, the jolting of the wheels over even smooth paths was uncomfortable, and over rough paths, the journey became torturous. Friend spent more and more time at home, confined to a chair or, more frequently, lying down in an effort to reduce the swelling. At times the pustules on Friend's swollen feet erupted, discharging a fetid liquid that, though abhorrent to observers, did bring a measure of relief to the suffering minister.[1]

Walker diagnosed Universal Friend as suffering from dropsy, or in modern terms, edema. Edema is a swelling of the soft tissues (such as muscles, tendons, and ligaments) caused by an accumulation of excess fluid due either to a weakening of the heart's ability to pump or to failure of the kidneys. Knowledge of the causes of the illness was limited in the early nineteenth century and Walker's only recourse at the time was to treat the symptoms suffered by Friend to relieve the worst of the pain, and to hope for the best.

The minister was advised to follow "an abstemious Diet and [take] as much exercise as can possibly be taken." In addition, "the inflamed parts of feet and Legs [should] be folded round with raw cotton made very soft." Walker told Friend to wear flannel undergarments to promote perspiration and to drink three or four times a day a double dose of diuretic: first, "a strong solution of salt petre . . . in a wine glass," and then, a dose of "old strong cider with scraped horseradish & rolled mustard seed." The drinks taken in succession would "carry off the dropsical humors" and over time reduce the swelling in Friend's legs and feet.[2] Drinking the tonics could not have been pleasant: saltpeter (a key ingredient of gunpowder) was a by-product of bird droppings (or dirt soaked with human or animal urine), boiled down to form crystals.[3] Old cider with horseradish and mustard wouldn't have tasted much better.

There is no record of what Walker recommended for the pain suffered by Friend. What kind of concoction could ease the torment of skin stretched tight like a drum, feet swollen beyond the fit of any shoe, painful blisters that erupted without warning? A poultice recipe found in Friend's papers might have been used to offer some pain relief, although its ingredients seem strange: "a spoon full of glass and a spoon full of salt and a spoon full of leaven and spoon full of vinegar all to mixt to gather . . ."[4]

While the advice offered by Walker could possibly relieve some of the symptoms Friend suffered, she could give no cure for what ailed the minister. After returning home, Walker wrote a letter to Rachel Malin: "the sympathetic impressions thy trying situation produced on my mind . . . are not easily eradicated" and expressed regret at "Thy Friend declining. . . ."[5] And yet Friend's grip on life was still strong. As much as heaven was a gift from God, so too was life on earth: "O

LORD, how manifold are thy works! in wisdom hast thou made them all: the earth is full of thy riches."[6] Sermons would continue, along with personal meetings with members of the community, as well as visits at deathbeds and to the ill, for as long as Friend could manage.

In the summer of 1816, Anna Styer, a devoted follower who joined the Society in the 1780s, committed suicide. Going out to the woods behind the home she shared with Lucina Goodspeed, she "hung herself by means of her apron."[7] While always a quiet and gentle woman, in the past years Anna had suffered "an occasional alienation of mind, and fits of melancholy and self-reproach."[8] How sharply Friend must have felt the loss, not only of an old friend but of a soul who had fallen victim to overwhelming—and fatal—despair. Anna had been with the Society for a long time. She was present in the home of David Wagener all those years ago when Sarah Wilson claimed that Abigail Dayton had tried to kill her; Anna had disavowed the story and devoted herself as a faithful follower. She came west with Friend in 1790 to City Hill, and then west again to Jerusalem a few years later. Now she would be laid to rest on one of Jerusalem's green hills, in the Society's burial ground not far from Friend's home. Many of the faithful had already been buried there and in the years to come many more would be, including, thirty years later, Anna's housemate, Lucina Goodspeed.[9]

Universal Friend believed that melancholy drained its sufferer—"he who despaireth of the end shall never attain it"—and encouraged followers to persevere in the face of misery and sorrow.[10] God had promised that the bliss of salvation would be eternal while "pain that endureth long is moderate; blush therefore to complain of it . . . behold thou seest the end of it."[11] But for Anna Styer, the pain of living had become too much and she could not see an end to it. Did Friend now pray for God to have mercy on Anna's tormented soul?

Friend began to have dreams about death and transformation,

including one in which the head of a "great woman . . . talked with the Friend and said that is was going to have its body again."[12] A few months later, the minister "dreamed that there was a fine frost appeared in the north skies then the tops of the trees . . . letters were written [and] on the lower part appeared a wreathe of green laurel. . . ."[13] Laurel was viewed as a symbol of achievement, and for Friend, death was the ultimate achievement, because it meant entrance into the presence of God: "Precious in the Sight of the Lord is the Death of his Saints."[14]

In October of 1816, "Friend dreamed that everything was cut short, that the hair was cut short, and that the time for sinners to Repent was cut short . . . no longer than from midnight to midday."[15] The dream seemed to portend the end of times for everyone on earth. But perhaps the end of Friend's time was even closer—and Friend was ready. As a young minister, Friend "was as much prepared for the moment she enter'd the world to leave it again and go to the immeasurable host of angels. . . ."[16] Now in the sixth decade of life, Friend's attitude had not changed. The minister would welcome "the will of God" to call his messenger "out of the world before the light of another day."[17] To rise to heaven was a gift, a gift that Friend believed had long been promised: "So, while I Dwell in bonds of Clay / Methinks My Soul Should Groan / When shall I wing my Heavenly way / And stand before thy throne?"[18]

Almost every letter Friend signed included the ending salutation "The Friend is yet in time."[19] While this was meant as a reassurance that the minister was still alive, Friend also preached that death was nothing to be frightened of. The end of life on earth led to resurrection of the spirit and commencement of eternal bliss, when all earthly concerns, worries, and griefs would be finished: "all that thou certainly knowest is that it [death] putteth an end to thy Sorrows."[20] To be out of time was to be on the way to heaven.

Ruth Pritchard and Rachel Malin both noted in their journals that October 13, 1817, was an important anniversary for their minister: it had been "41 years since the Friend first spake." In 1776, Friend, only twenty-three years old and standing tall underneath an old oak tree, had preached with "great assurance and conviction" about repentance and God's promise of salvation.[21] The gathered crowd might have been less interested in the sermon than the preacher, having been drawn in by the rumors of rebirth and transformation, but they had listened with attention and the ministry of salvation was born.

Now the minister was the leader of a large community of the faithful and the founder of a place known for its fellowship, piety, and prosperity: "the people who allied themselves to the Friend were earnest, honest, upright men and women . . . no intelligent speaker has given voice to sentiments other than praise for the Society and its most zealous founder and head."[22] The Society had survived and even thrived through difficult times, persevered against hardships and celebrated their faith in seasons of bounty as well as seasons of loss: under the guidance of their minister, they were resilient. As Friend had preached, drawing from intimate knowledge of the Bible, so Friend had lived: "And he shall be like a tree planted by the rivers of water, that bringeth forth his fruit in his season; his leaf also shall not wither; and whatsoever he doeth shall prosper."[23] The community of Jerusalem had not withered, it had prospered against all odds, all threats, all assaults.

But there was a new threat on the horizon. In June of 1817, Elisha Williams sought to wrest the case out of the hands of Chancellor Kent by filing an ejectment suit in a lower court and asking the judge there to order the eviction of Universal Friend and twelve of the faithful followers from the lands they occupied based on the grounds that Sarah Richards's will had been altered and was invalid. Williams felt confident of success in the circuit court. For the past five years, he had busied himself convincing the influential men of Ontario County (including those in the judicial and legal networks) of Friend's dangerous tendencies and urging them toward "deep prejudice" against the minister and the Society.[24] He had worked to circulate long-standing rumors about Universal Friend, alleging sexual deviancies and blatant acts of blasphemy, and doing everything he could to undermine the standing of the Society in the larger community of western New York. Using both money and time to swell the tide of resentment and distrust against the Society of Universal Friends, Williams was sure that his ejectment suit against Friend and followers would be successful.

And he was right: in the summer of 1817, the local circuit court ruled in Williams's favor in finding that Sarah Richards's will had been altered and was invalid and the disputed lands in Jerusalem therefore should have passed to Eliza Richards Malin. The court then ordered the ejectments of Universal Friend and followers from the properties where they had settled and lived for decades. It appeared that with his slippery machinations, Williams had won the battle and finally secured the long-sought banishment of Friend and the faithful from Jerusalem.

Thomas Gold quickly took action to undermine the circuit court ruling. He filed for an injunction in the Court of Chancery against the ejectments, alerting Chancellor Kent to Williams's efforts to undermine Kent's jurisdiction over the Jerusalem land controversy. Kent granted Gold's request for injunction and quashed the ejectment orders, nullifying Elisha Williams's short-lived victory. Kent also declared that he alone would decide whether Sarah Richards's will had been altered, taking it out of the hands of any other judge or jury. Thomas Gold reported to Rachel Malin with glee: "I have at length got the better of your enemies. . . ."[25]

But for how long? And how much longer would Friend and the Society have to wait before Chancellor Kent ruled on their case? Time was passing by and Universal Friend, along with so many household family members and trusted followers, was growing old. Patience and Marcy were seventy and sixty-seven, respectively; Anna Wagener was in her sixties (her brother Jacob had died that year, brother David died in 1799, and his wife, Rebecca, died in 1813). Lucy Wilkinson, wife of Jeptha, came back to Jerusalem after Jeptha died of yellow fever in New Jersey in 1803 and set up life anew as a farmer along with six of her children; she was now in her sixties (and would live as a faithful follower until the age of one hundred). Ruth Pritchard was fifty-nine. Chloe Towerhill was in her early fifties, and Mary Bean was in her late forties; Rachel and Margaret Malin among the youngest (in their early forties). There were young followers, such as Rachel Ingraham and Henry Barnes, but when Friend was gone, who would lead the faithful? Friend, "knowing that shortly I must put off this my tabernacle," had to make plans for when that tabernacle would finally be laid aside.[26]

In February of 1818, Friend met with lawyers to write up a final will and testament. There was still no decision from the Court of Chancery about who owned the lands of Jerusalem, but Friend was confident that Chancellor Kent would rule in favor of the Society and the will was written to reflect that certainty. In order to forestall any future problems with Universal Friend's own will, the final document unambiguously states that it was created in the name of the person "who in the year one thousand seven hundred seventy-six was called Jemima Wilkinson" and was now known as "Universal Friend," the "new name which the mouth of the Lord hath named." A signed provision was later added in which Friend once again made clear, "Be it remembered, That in order to remove all doubts of the due execution of the foregoing Last will and Testament I being the person who before the year one thousand seven hundred & seventy seven was known & called by the name Jemima Wilkinson but since that time as the Universal Friend."[27] The will itself was signed by Friend with an "X": the name of a person whom Friend considered dead and gone would not be used in a signature.

Under the provisions of Friend's will, Rachel and Margaret were named executors of Friend's estate and all the minister's personal property was bequeathed to them ("all my wearing apparel all my household furniture and all my horses cattle sheep & swine . . . and also all my carriages wagons and Carts . . ."). James Brown Jr., who lived in Friend's household, had been managing the farming operations since 1810 and he would continue to do so, but the Malin sisters were charged with holding "all my Land" in trust to be used for the care of all members of the Society of Universal Friends. The will explicitly stated: "all the present members of my family . . . be employed . . . and if employed supported during natural life . . . and when any of them become unable to help themselves they are . . . Kindly to be taken care of . . . and my Will also is that all poor persons belonging to the Society of Universal Friends shall receive . . . such assistance comfort & support during natural life as they need. . . ."[28]

However, if "any either of my family or else where in the society shall turn a way, such shall forfeit the provision made herein for them."[29] In other words, those not loyal to the ideals of the Society would be cast off under the terms of Friend's will. For the past forty plus years, there had been "no expulsions" from the Society, although "the offender went down a step or two" in the minister's esteem.[30] But the mercy of Universal Friend, exhibited throughout the minister's life, would not extend past death. God would judge them as he would judge Friend, and the minister had no doubt that God would punish or reward fairly: "For we must all appear before the judgment seat of Christ; that every one may receive the things done in his body, according to that he hath done, whether it be good or bad."[31]

Not long after the will was completed, Thomas Gold wrote to Rachel Malin that Elisha Williams had approached him with a settlement offer to end the pending court case. Williams offered to renounce claims to all but four hundred acres in Jerusalem, leaving the remaining contested acres to the Society, and asking that his court costs be paid. If Universal Friend agreed to such terms, Gold wrote, the long legal battles over land would be over. While Gold admitted that he could not see "the justice of any such terms" as offered by the settlement, he believed there were nevertheless "reasons in favour of a compromise. The increasing costs in court . . . [versus] the benefit of . . . peace and quietness in advanced life are worth considering." He encouraged the minister to take the offer, arguing that it was reasonable: "Were the case my own, I would give up the 400 acres."[32]

Universal Friend would not. As Rachel Malin quickly informed Gold, "Friend has no idea of compromising with Williams. . . ."[33] For one last time, the minister would exhibit a stubbornness that perhaps should have been restrained. But Friend was determined to see the case through, if not to its end, to the end of the minister's time on earth, which—it was becoming increasingly clear—was not too long off.

The minister now suffered from almost constant pain, no matter how diligently the advice of healer Elizabeth Walker was followed. Diuretics and poultices could only do so much, and the illness was winning. For over sixty years, first as a girl and then a young woman, and then after 1776 as Universal Friend, the minister had been strong, active, resilient. But now Friend could barely walk from chair to bed, much less work beside the women in the weaving shed or dig in the garden or ride out to the fields "with Rachel or Margaret . . . to look over the crops or cattle stock," calling out to Henry Barnes "to let down the fence bars" so they could pass through.[34] Friend couldn't even stand up long enough to give a sermon to faithful followers and was "borne to the room where meetings were held . . . and would address her flock while keeping her seat in a chair."[35]

Nevertheless, Friend continued "day in and day out" to preach and advise the flock of followers, acting with "unbounded faith and trust" to fulfill the God-given mission of salvation.[36] Persevering through the pain, Friend sought to deliver by example the message that, since the very earliest days of the ministry, had been preached to all who came to listen: "As in War an Error is death, so in death an Error is damnation. Therefore, live as you intend to die and die as you intend to live."[37] Friend had tried to live in full harmony with the message of God's love and mercy, and the minister's firm belief in salvation can be found in an undated poem: "Salvation was as plentiful / As water in the sea, / And every drop keeps whispering / Redeeming love is free."[38]

As October passed into November, Friend rarely left the bedroom of the house on the hill, even for matters of fellowship and faith. As noted in a follower's diary, November 21, 1818, was "the last time Friend attended meeting."[39] Rachel Malin and Marcy Wilkinson Aldrich took over the meetings with the help of other members of the Faithful Sisterhood. But the minister continued to welcome followers who came by to visit. God had sent the world a messenger—"the Spirit of Life"—and that messenger was still hard at work, demonstrating by example that there was no reason to fear death: "Blessed are they that do his Commandments . . . they have a right to the tree of [eternal] Life and may Enter in through the Gates into the Holy City."[40]

In the fall, Universal Friend received a letter from Ruth Pritchard, who lived in Milo on the northeastern shore of Keuka Lake. Although the village was only a short distance from Jerusalem, Ruth was suffering from bad health and couldn't travel to see Friend or attend a meeting. Yet she continued in her faith and was as confident now as she had been in 1785 when she first heard Friend speak that the words spoken had been sent directly by God through his messenger: "O may the Friend be with us & Live, while the wicked are no more. Yes, live in every heart, that may become a temple for the living God." In the letter, Ruth wrote of how much she missed Friend, lamenting "the painful distance" between them, and how she longed "to see [Friend's] Majestick countenance once more. . . ." Calling on God's "Mercy and Boundless Grace," she felt certain that they would meet again: "I desire to be very thankful that my health is returning, thus far, And that the Friend's Health is better, Let us all rejoice!"[41]

But the rejoicing was only wishful thinking, and all hopes of recovered strength faded. In February of 1819, Ruth wrote another letter to Friend, explaining that her health had worsened further. She feared the two might never meet again: "When shall I see the Friend?" She could only hope they would pass together from this world to the next, where the follower and her minister might be joined forever together: "Let me be fastened to thy cross; rather than lose thy love."[42] For thirty-four years, Ruth had loved Universal Friend; from their first meeting, she had expressed her "desire with all the remainder of my Days, to devote to thee. . . ."[43] As certain as she was of salvation, she worried that death would separate her—even if only for a little while—from her beloved friend. It was not the fact of living that was so hard to let go off; it was the gifts of living—the friendship of her minister, the beauty of the rolling hills, the meetings of shared faith—that Ruth wanted to hold on to for just a bit longer.

Ruth died in March: "suddenly snatched out of Time she was seized with a fit of the Palsy and Expired in less than one Minute." Having been charged with keeping the Death Book of the Society after the death of Sarah Richards in 1793, the duty would now pass on to someone else, but for now, her daughter, also named Ruth, wrote the record of her mother's passing out of time: "Ruth Spencer dyed . . . in the full belief of the Public Universal Friend."[44] Two weeks later, the daughter delivered the Death Book to Margaret Malin, handing over the role of scribe to yet another faithful follower.

One month after Ruth's death, Friend's sister Patience died. From the very first days of Friend's ministry, Patience had been a loving and devoted follower, and her loyalty had lasted even through her marriage to Thomas Potter.[45] When news of Patience's death arrived on the hill, Friend insisted on being the one to preach the funeral sermon and was carried in a chair to speak before the waiting congregation. There is no record of the sermon Friend gave, but the death of Patience would have been both mourned and celebrated. Mourned because she would be missed, a woman of such fierce love and devotion. And celebrated because the death of one so pious meant the fulfillment of promised salvation: "Blessed is the people that know the joyful sound. . . ." The sound of salvation that will ring forever for the faithful, even when "the Corpse" is laid "in the silent earth."[46]

For the next two months Universal Friend labored on, confined to bed, but still warming to visitors and dispensing words of faith and promise. Death was nothing to be feared, nor to be fixated upon: "Nothing is so sure as death and nothing so uncertain as the time when we may be too old to Live. . . . I will therefore live every hour as if I were to die the next."[47] No word came from the Chancery Court and Friend must have anticipated that its resolution would occur after the minister was gone.

Friend would have been confident of its resolution, but also must have hoped that the faithful followers had been shown how to fight for what they knew they deserved, during life and after death. God himself promised, through the words of the Psalms, to "cover thee with his feathers, and under his wings shalt thou trust: his truth shall be thy shield and buckler."[48] The feathers of love, faith, and hope covered them all, this Friend knew with certainty, just as the minister had known forty-three years earlier that God had sent the "Spirit of Life" to take "full possession of the Body" of a dying Jemima Wilkinson, transforming her into a messenger charged with bringing light to lost souls and faith to a "dying World."[49]

Early in the dark hours before dawn on July 1, 1819, Rachel and Margaret Malin, along with Lucy Brown, witnessed the death of Universal Friend, which was duly recorded in the Society's Death Book: "25 minutes past 2 on the Clock, the Friend went from here. . . ."[50] For forty years, Friend had been vigilant at the bedsides of the dying. When Lucy Holmes died in August of 1790, her final words, delivered while "looking at the Friend . . . [were] My dear Redeemer, I love; I love; I love. . . ." When Candace Kenny died in March of 1791, age fifteen, her last words were "My Friend! My Friend!" With Friend at her side, "She departed."[51] And many other such vigils were described by Sarah Richards: "The Friend was with her at the last"; "She died in the arms of the Friend. . . ." When necessary, Friend wrote to relatives far away: in one letter she described for a young man's mother: "I closed his Eyes—he appeared to have his senses to the last; and repeated these words over three times saying, 'I have got ready to die . . . I feel a perfect tranquil mind. . . .'"[52]

And what were Friend's last words? According to Society lore, the minister calmly bid farewell: "my friends I must soon depart—I am going—this night I leave you."[53] The news passed quickly through Jerusalem and then to the greater world beyond: Universal Friend had "met death with the calmness of a saint and the fullness of hope."[54]

The next day, a Saturday, Friend's sister Marcy gave a sermon at the regular meeting of the Society. A large crowd gathered outside the house where the minister's body lay, made up not only of members of the community but also people from all around the western New York county. Upstairs, the Malin sisters took care of Friend's body, which was "wrapped in a winding sheet" and laid out on a fine board planed from the trunk of a sturdy cherry. On the following day, another meeting was held for Society members, which was unusual for a Sunday, but it was not, as Friend had requested, "a regular funeral."[55] Nor would there be a graveside ceremony, again in accordance with Friend's own wishes.

Instead, the body of Universal Friend was placed in a stone vault in the cellar of the house on the hill, which was then walled up with brick and plaster. There had been rumors that "some of the physicians" wanted to "secure the body for dissection."[56] Did the doctors want to verify the gender of Universal Friend or was there some other reason for their deranged desire? The more likely explanation is that the supposed dissection was a rumor started by outsiders to stir up emotions among the members of the Society of Universal Friends. Whatever the cause for the internment in the cellar, Friend was eventually buried on a hillside somewhere in the township in an unmarked grave, as was the custom of the Society. What was not customary was that the location of the grave was kept a secret from both followers and outsiders, its exact placement known only to the two men who had carried the body there and buried it. The secret was allegedly passed down through the families of the two men and the location of the grave has been lost to history.[57]

On July 12, almost two weeks after Friend died, the northwestern skies over Jerusalem presented an unusual and marvelous display: "A Comet of Considerable magnitude and brilliancy . . . with its tail pointing to the pole star" passed overhead.[58] Much as the Dark Day of 1780 had proven the prophetic powers of Universal Friend to faithful followers, now the celestial messaging across the evening sky reassured those remaining behind that Universal Friend had been called to heaven: "And the stars of heaven shall fall . . . then shall he send his angels, and . . . gather together his elect from the four winds, from the uttermost part of the earth to the uttermost part of heaven."[59]

On the rolling green hills of Jerusalem, beside the shimmering waters of Keuka Lake, a community founded and led by a nonbinary minister flourished for a brief time. Against tides of greed and duplicity, against constricting definitions and pervasive discriminations, Universal Friend brought to life the ideals of freedom, equality, and self-determination that had been promised to all Americans in the fight for independence. Friend most likely never intended to create a community that empowered women and the disenfranchised, and that lived up in so many ways to the spirit and ideals of the American Revolution—Friend was more interested in saving souls than in breaking barriers—but there were those among the followers who did recognize what had been achieved in Jerusalem and described their minister as "a saint in homespun whose hands rocked the cradle of the republic."[60]

For almost half a century Universal Friend provided a light of hope when many found themselves in darkness and reassured them not only of the possibility of eternal salvation but also of happiness now, here on earth. The message, which Friend believed came directly from God to be conveyed to a lost and dying world, had been delivered. A message of repentance and salvation for the times in which Friend lived; but even more, a message of resilience and courage, and of resistance and perseverance, for all times.

The messenger had been called back. But the message would live on.

Epilogue

"As We are in Life, for the most part
We are in Death"

—UNIVERSAL FRIEND

Two years after Universal Friend died, a biography of the minister was published, written by David Hudson, a friend of Elisha Williams who had worked with him on the lawsuits over Jerusalem. Hudson's biography was filled with many of the salacious stories that had circulated about Universal Friend and the Society for years (insanity, infanticide, and fraud), and also included some new ones, including the accusation that Friend had been impregnated by a British officer during the Revolution and allusions to lesbianism among members of the Society. As historian Frances Dumas has described it, the book contained "nothing but scurrilous gossip, unrelieved by fact"—a sentiment shared by every serious biographer of Universal Friend, from Stafford Cleveland to Paul Moyer.[1] But Hudson, Williams, and their collaborators didn't concern themselves with the truth of the slanderous tales they spread. Their goal was to influence the ongoing court proceedings concerning the contested lands of Jerusalem.

Hudson's biography made no difference in the end on the legal resolution of the dispute over Jerusalem. On July 11, 1823, Chancellor James Kent finally ruled on the case that Universal Friend and Rachel Malin had brought twenty-two years earlier, and after years of delay and uncertainty, Kent held for the Society of Universal Friends, declaring that Jerusalem belonged to those men and women who had settled the land, cleared the overgrown meadows and thick forest, sowed and harvested crops, built homes and farms, and founded a community of faith, fellowship, and opportunity.

The decision was appealed by Elisha Williams in 1828 to the New York Court of Errors (the only court that had jurisdiction to reconsider decisions made by the Court of Chancery). But after hearing arguments from Abraham Van Vechten on behalf of the Society and from Elisha Williams, the court ruled definitively in favor of Universal Friend and Rachel Malin, basically holding that through hard work and determination, the Society of Universal Friends had led the way in settling the western frontier in New York State and not only their deeds to land but also their efforts in taming the land should be celebrated and supported, with all claims to the contrary rejected.

As for claims that the will had been altered, the court found that Moses Atwater, the doctor who had written out Sarah Richards's will for her, "swears that it is now in the same state as when it was executed by her. . . ." And even if the will had been altered, the court went on to say, the alteration would have made little difference: "the alteration did not change the effect or construction of the will, and an immaterial alteration in a deed, if made by a stranger, will not destroy it. . . ."[2]

The legal victory over Elisha Williams and all those who sought to steal Jerusalem from the Society was duly celebrated. But the celebration was somewhat muted because so many of the original combatants were gone. Enoch and Eliza were both dead; and at least one of the others, Asahel Stone Jr., had already moved away. William Potter had died in 1814 (his granddaughter Susan claimed that, in the end, he "reconciled to the Friend, spoke of her kindly, and even visited her");

Arnold Potter, in 1810; and Thomas Potter, in 1807.[3] James Parker died soon after the final ruling in the case, in 1829 at the age of eighty-six.[4] Under the court's ruling, Elnathan Botsford Jr. was allowed to hold on to the four hundred acres he had purchased from Enoch because he'd had no notice that Friend owned the property and had paid well for it; these were the same four hundred acres that Elisha Williams had asked for from Friend in order to settle the case ten years earlier (Thomas Gold had been right after all, that court costs could have been avoided and peace of mind achieved if Friend had just agree to settle the case in 1818).

Rachel Malin was still alive, but the long court battle had imposed an emotional toll on her and a financial one on the Society of Universal Friends, which she now led along with her sister Margaret. The considerable legal bills paid to keep the litigation going over so many decades had emptied Society coffers. Plans to build a new meetinghouse in Jerusalem had to be put on hold. The land for the building had been donated by David Wagener before he died (in 1799) and the first logs had been cut, but there were no longer savings enough to keep the project going. In the years that followed, the Malin sisters proved to be terrible stewards of the Society's finances and of Friend's estate, selling off Society lands at below-market prices, including sales made by Rachel to family members at ridiculously low prices.

When Margaret died in 1842, she left her estate to James Brown to be managed for the interests of the Society, but when Rachel died in 1847, she left all the properties she held on behalf of the Society to her own relatives. She even bequeathed Friend's three-story house on the hill to her niece Mary Ann without any provisions made for the benefit of Society members. Without Friend's guidance at hand, the very human traits of covetousness and selfishness displayed by William Potter, Benedict Robinson, and James Parker now appeared again, and the actions of the Malin sisters would achieve what those men had longed for: the end of the Society of Universal Friends as it had existed under its charismatic and formidable leader.

Perhaps there was no one who could have held the community of faith together, given that it was the magnetic personality and penetrating presence of Universal Friend that had for decades supplied the glue. Historian Stafford Cleveland explained in his biography of Friend that the doctrinal message of salvation and repentance mattered less, in the end, than the minister's actual presence in leading the community: "The secret of her power rested in her sterling humanity, far more than any peculiarity of doctrinal teaching."[5] (Marcy Aldrich, who along with Rachel had taken over preaching to the Society during Friend's final illness, might have had the gumption to carry on, but she, too, suffered the ills of old age and she died in 1830.)

The void left by Friend's death created an opening for various potential candidates—all men—to try and argue their way into the positions of power in the Society. In the early 1830s, Michael Barton insinuated himself into the fellowship of the faithful by claiming to have seen visions of Universal Friend, which led him to travel from Maine to New York to join—and lead—the Society.[6] He was eventually driven away by Margaret Malin, who never trusted him. Following on his heels, George Clark attempted to "give a fresh inspiration of the Friend's doctrine" to the Society, but "the strictness of the Friend's faith and discipline was not maintained by the new discipline."[7] Clark eventually married Mary Ann Hopkins, the niece of Rachel and Margaret who inherited Friend's house. After marrying Mary Ann, Clark no longer pursued any kind of leadership role in the Society, making "little if any pretence to religious character, and his career was not favorable to the interests of the establishment. . . ."[8]

The Society of Universal Friends was also weakened by the diminishing number of its members. Followers near and far were growing old and dying. Bethany Sisson had died already in 1811, and George died in 1831, as did Anna Wagener. Friend's brother Stephen Wilkinson died in 1821, and Alice (Alcy) Potter Hazard died in 1822. William Turpin, one of Friend's earliest followers who had lived for years in South Carolina managing a plantation (and enslaving Black workers), died in 1833. He wrote out a long will before he died, in which he finally abided by Friend's ideals of liberty and opportunity by freeing all his enslaved workers and giving the bulk of his estate (including his home and properties in Charleston) to those people whom he had formerly held as enslaved (the will provided that white people were only permitted on the properties if they agreed to protect the rights of the newly freed Black Americans). Turpin also left a generous bequest to the Society of Universal Friends in the amount of $6,000, and spoke of Friend in his will: "I now resign my soul to rest in the divine love of God, and Christ my Savior and Universal Friend. . . ."[9]

Chloe Towerhill, another early follower who had lived with Friend since the early 1790s, continued to live in the house on the hill after Friend's death; she died in 1835 around the age of seventy. Mary Bean, also a member of Friend's household, died in 1840; she was in her sixties. Rachel Ingraham died in 1873, the same year as her cousin, Experience Ingraham (Barnes); and in 1874, Henry Barnes, who had come to Jerusalem as a child and remained a devoted follower his entire life, died at the age of eighty-five. He was the last remaining member of the Society of Universal Friends.[10]

After David Hudson published his scurrilous biography of Universal Friend, Rachel Malin composed a rebuttal, which she titled "The Love of Money Is the Root of All Evil." In the rebuttal, she stated that "living with Friend for more than thirty years," she knew for certain that the minister had cared only for "the glory of God, and the perfection of mankind, and is innocent of all these slanders and lies that are now circulating in the world."[11] But Malin's piece was never published or circulated, and unfortunately, as Paul Moyer points out, "Hudson's book became a frequent stop among early historians who wrote about the Universal Friend, and thus the fabrications and half truths that fill it became lodged in the historical record," influencing decades of histories published about or mentioning Universal Friend and the Society.[12]

Nevertheless, even many detractors admitted that Friend, whom they described as "an imposter," was also "celebrated and successful";

had "a kindly spirit," and sincerely wished "to promote the temporal welfare of her followers," with a "perseverance [that] was most extraordinary"; and that Friend "drew to her faith many good and honest people."[13] In 1873, Stafford Cleveland published his biography of Friend and the Society after interviewing a number of living members of the community along with neighbors and other eyewitnesses. In the book, he concludes that "this courageous and large-hearted woman, in her remarkable force of character, in her benevolence and generosity, in her power to rule, her wealth of affectionate feeling, in her love of justice, in her persevering fidelity to her convictions" demonstrated "genius and originality, and . . . sincerity of heart and greatness of mind. . . ."[14]

Over the next few decades, the lands all around Jerusalem and Friend's first settlement at City Hill would become known as the "Burned-over District" due to the large number of religious sects founded in the area. The name came from the spiritual fires started by these new and impassioned religious communities, such as the Church of Latter-Day Saints (established by Joseph Smith in 1828 after he claimed to have found the Book of Mormon buried in the dirt of Hill Cumorah in Palmyra, New York); the Millerites (who believed the Second Coming would arrive sometime in 1843 or '44); the Oneida Society (who believed the Second Coming had already occurred and a perfect world could now be created on earth); and also Spiritualists such as the Fox sisters (who claimed to communicate with the dead).[15] The building of the 363-mile Erie Canal connecting Albany and the Hudson River (and New York City) to Buffalo and the Great Lakes played a big role in bringing a wide variety of religious seekers and utopian sects into western New York; its completion by 1825 allowed for the easy movement of hundreds of people into its wide-open hills and valleys.

But the legacy of Universal Friend's Jerusalem community was also an important factor in drawing dozens of outlier sects to the region through its example of sincere piety and economic success. As the first sect founded and led by an American in the United States, and one of the most prosperous in New York, the Society of Universal Friends, according to historians, "helped to light the spiritual fires of western New York" and continued over the following decades to exert "a demonstrable influence upon the Burned-over District."[16]

By establishing a place where women were empowered to exert control over their own lives and hold positions of leadership and authority in the larger community (and be respected for taking on such roles), Universal Friend also set the stage for generations of women to claim for themselves the rights of property ownership, enfranchisement, and self-determination, and perhaps inspired to some degree the abolitionist, suffragist, and prohibition movements that proliferated in western New York in the nineteenth century.

It may be a mere coincidence that the Woman's Rights Convention of 1848, the first national conference focused on promoting equal rights for American women, including suffrage and property rights, was held at Seneca Falls, New York. But maybe not. The water from Keuka Lake drains into Seneca Lake, into which fall the waters of Seneca Falls. Perhaps it would be more fitting if the water flowed against gravity; after all, Friend had worked against the presiding religious, social, and political currents of the time. Surely it was the spirit of Universal Friend that flowed upstream into the crowds gathered at Seneca Falls in 1848 and animated their proclamation "that all men and women are created equal; that they are endowed by their Creator with certain inalienable rights; that among these are life, liberty, and the pursuit of happiness. . . ."[17] Message received, and delivered.

Acknowledgments

Esther Newberg has given me unwavering support through many years of being my agent, my guardian, my friend. Dorothy Ko and Michael Flamini offered me enthusiastic encouragement, assuring me (and anyone that would listen) that I had the ability to tell the story of Universal Friend. My editor Megan Hogan's kind and wise guidance helped me every step of the way (and there were many, many steps along the way), and Jennie Miller prodded me to tighten the storyline through her astute comments and suggestions. Shannon Hennessy, Elizabeth Venere, Laura Wise, Lewelin Polanco, Jackie Seow, Beth Maglione, and Jay Schweitzer were also instrumental in bringing this book vividly to life in both its prose and its presentation.

Much of the research for this book was carried out during the COVID years and could not have been accomplished without the assistance of the librarians and archivists of Cornell University, Brown University, the American Antiquarian Society, the Historical Society of Pennsylvania, and the Yates County History Center. They helped me access the primary documents I needed, and they also pointed me toward documents I didn't know I was looking for but which ended up proving invaluable to my research. I depended more than ever on the help of Christine LaRusso of Westport Library in hunting down many secondary sources. Charlotte Rogan offered me perceptive insights into my work as it progressed and provided the steady companionship and commiserations of a fellow writer.

My large and wonderful family has helped me in so many ways through all the years of research and writing. Their confidence in me and their abiding love underscores everything I do. My sister Natasha stepped in at just the right moment to save me from errors, and her sharp eye, critical observations, and constructive comments forced me to a higher rigor in my arguments.

My mother, Tilde Sankovitch, and my husband, Jack Menz, contributed enormously to the writing of this book, engaging in long conversations with me about Friend and the years of the American Revolution and its aftermath. Very sadly, my mother died in 2021 and my husband in 2024. They were both true innovators, charting their own ways through life but always with our families front and center. They were the epitome of generosity and kindness, and they were also intelligent, funny, broad-minded, curious, and wildly enthusiastic about new adventures, ideas, places, books, people, food, films. I will always love and admire my mother so much. Jack is the love of my life, my best friend, my all-time favorite companion in everything, and he was also my most stalwart critic and staunch cheerleader. He was a brilliant and loving man, who showed me how to embrace every moment of every day.

Readers may have recognized my homage to Leonard Cohen in the first chapter. His wonderful line—"that's how the light gets in"— just seemed so appropriate for that point in the life of Jemima Wilkinson. But perhaps it also applies to me now and in a different way. This book is dedicated to Jack, nestled forever in my broken heart. May the light of love and remembrance always shine on him.

Notes

AAS—American Antiquarian Society
JWP—Jemima Wilkinson Papers, Cornell University, Division of Rare and Manuscript Collections
KJV—King James Version Bible
MHS—Massachusetts Historical Society
YCHP—Public Universal Friend Collection, Yates County History Center

INTRODUCTION

1. Abigail Adams to John Adams, March 31, 1776, Adams Papers, MHS.
2. John Adams to Abigail Adams, April 14, 1776, Adams Papers, MHS.
3. Friend's statement in response to a question about whether the minister was the messiah, quoted in *The Freeman's Journal, or, The North-American Intelligencer (Philadelphia, [Pa.]) 1781–1792*, March 28, 1787.
4. In Congress, July 5, 1776, "The unanimous Declaration of the thirteen United States of America," National Archives, https://www.archives.gov/founding-docs/declaration-transcript.
5. Paul Moyer, *The Public Universal Friend: Jemima Wilkinson and Religious Enthusiasm in Revolutionary America* (Cornell University Press, 2015), 203 (hereafter cited as "Moyer").
6. *Freeman's Journal,* February 14, 1787, 3; Moyer, 8–9; Herbert A. Wisbey, Jr., *Pioneer Prophetess: Jemima Wilkinson, the Publick Universal Friend* (Cornell University Press, 1964), 25 (hereafter cited as "Wisbey"); Catherine A. Brekus, *Strangers and Pilgrims: Female Preaching in America, 1740–1845* (University of North Carolina Press, 1998), 83; Scott Larson, "'Indescribable Being': Theological Performances of Genderlessness in the Society of the Publick Universal Friend, 1776–1819," *Early American Studies* 12, no. 3 (Fall 2014): 579; Susan Juster, "To Slay the Beast: Visionary Women in the Early Republic," in *A Mighty Baptism: Race, Gender, and the Creation of American Protestantism*, ed. Susan Juster and Lisa MacFarlane (Cornell University Press, 1996), 29; Thomas S. Kidd, *The Great Awakening: The Roots of Evangelical Christianity in Colonial America* (Yale University Press, 2008), 319;

Karen-Edis Barzman, "The Subject of 'Woman' and the Discipline of Early Modern Studies: Jemima Wilkinson and the Publick Universal Friend," in *Culture and Change: Attending to Early Modern Women*, ed. Margaret Mikesell and Adele Seeff (University of Delaware Press, 2003), 347.

7. See https://lgbt.foundation/who-we-help/trans-people/non-binary.
8. Other scholars seem to agree that Friend wanted no gendered pronouns to be used. See Sharon V. Betcher, "'The Second Descent of the Spirit of Life from God': The Assumption of Jemima Wilkinson," in *Gender and Apocalyptic Desire*, ed. Brenda E. Brasher and Lee Quinby (Equinox, 2006), 78–79; and Larson, "Indescribable Being," 578: "The society of followers . . . marked themselves as believers by refusing to use gendered pronouns. . . ." Because followers adhered to practices as set forth by their minister, I conclude that Friend asked that no pronoun be used, as any pronoun would be inaccurate in describing the self-proclaimed genderless minister. Paul Moyer writes that "Friend's disciples . . . consistently used the male pronoun 'he' and 'him,'" but I did not find evidence of this beyond the few instances provided by Moyer, 9, 100.

1: DEATH AT THE DOOR

1. Universal Friend, "A Memorandum of the Introduction of the Fatal Fever Call'd in the Year 1776, the Columbus Typhus Fever," n.d., YCHC. See also JWP. Wisbey notes that the memorandum "was found tucked into her [Universal Friend's] Bible and was preserved with her papers. . . ." Wisbey, 11.
2. See P. H. Hardacre, "The Royalists in Exile during the Puritan Revolution, 1642–1660," *Huntington Library Quarterly* 16, no. 4 (August 1953): 353–70.
3. In 1646, Roger Williams wrote, "Having made covenant of peaceable neighborhood with all the sachems and natives round about us . . . I, in grateful remembrance of God's merciful providence unto me in my distresse, called the place PROVIDENCE: I desired it might be a shelter for persons distressed of conscience." *Congressional Record* 157, no. 99 (July 6, 2011): S4391–S4392.
4. Israel Wilkinson, *Memoirs of the Wilkinson Family in America* (Davis & Penniman, 1869): i, 35–37.
5. Israel Wilkinson, *Memoirs*, 44.
6. This widely accepted figure comes from historian Steven Mintz, but as Kim Hensley Owens points out in her book *Writing Childbirth*, Mintz overstated his conclusion, and using the same figures as Mintz, Owens comes up with "a ratio closer to one in twenty . . . still an unpalatable figure. . . ." Kim Hensley Owens, *Writing Childbirth: Women's Rhetorical Agency in Labor and Online* (Southern Illinois Press, 2015), 173–74 n7.
7. Quoting from 1738 and 1729 Quaker epistles, found in *Epistles from the Yearly Meeting of Friends held in London, etc., from 1681 to 1857* (Edward Marsh, 1858).

8. Universal Friend's extracts are taken from Robert Dodsley's *The Oeconomy of Human Life: An "Ancient Bramin" in Eighteenth-Century Tibet* (1750), JWP (hereafter cited as "Universal Friend, extracts, *Oeconomy of Human Life*").
9. Original Deed of the Newport (R.I.) Liberty Tree, copied in *The Historical Magazine, and Notes and Queries Concerning the Antiquities, History, and Biography of America*, vol. IV, 2nd series (Henry B. Dawson, 1868), 91. And see Alfred E. Young, *Liberty Tree: Ordinary People and the American Revolution* (New York University Press, 2006), 7.
10. Stephen Hopkins, Rhode Island representative to the Continental Congress, in a speech given in 1774 recorded by Paul Revere and quoted in William E. Foster, *Stephen Hopkins: A Rhode Island Statesman* (Sidney S. Rider, 1884), 131. Stephen Hopkins was related to Jemima Wilkinson and her brothers through his mother, Ruth Wilkinson, whose father, Samuel, was Lawrence Wilkinson's oldest son.
11. Stephen Hopkins, *The Rights of Colonies Examined* (Printed by William Goddard, 1764), Brown University Digital Repository, 6.
12. Wisbey, 8.
13. Thomas Paine, *Common Sense* (Printed and sold by R. Bell, in Third Street, 1776), 30.
14. "Thomas Paine: The Original Publishing Viral Superstar," *Constitution Daily Blog*, National Constitution Center, January 10, 2023, https://constitutioncenter.org/blog/thomas-paine-the-original-publishing-viral-superstar-2. As of 2005, Thomas Paine's *Common Sense* remained the all-time bestselling book in America according to historian Harvey J. Kaye in *Thomas Paine and the Promise of America* (Hill and Wang, 2005), 43.
15. Abigail Adams to John Adams, February 21, 1776, Adams Papers, MHS; and see "Thomas Paine: The Original Publishing Viral Superstar." "*Common Sense* sold 120,000 copies in its first three months [in 1776], and by the end of the Revolution, 500,000 copies were sold."
16. Jonathan Edwards, "The Eternity of Hell Torment," April 1739, in *The Works of Jonathan Edwards, A.M.*, vol. 2 (Ball, Arnold, 1840), 88.
17. Reverend Charles Chauncy, quoting two female visionaries he met in 1742, in Charles Chauncy, *Seasonable Thoughts on Religion in New England* (1743), 129.
18. Brekus, *Strangers and Pilgrims*, 49.
19. "The Colonies: 1690–1715," National Humanities Center, https://nationalhumanitiescenter.org/pds/becomingamer/growth/text1/text1read.htm.
20. George Whitefield, "The Righteousness of Christ, an Everlasting Righteousness," cited at https://reformedsermonarchives.com/whitefieldtitle.htm.
21. George Leon Walker, *Some Aspects of Religious Life in New England* (Silver Burnett, 1897), 89–92, quoted at http://www.christianity.com/church/church-history/timeline/1701-1800/controversial-george-whitefield-11630198.html.
22. *The Works of the Reverend George Whitefield*, vol. 1 (Edward and Charles Dilly, 1771), 67.

23. *The Autobiography of Benjamin Franklin with Illustrations* (Houghton Mifflin, 1906), 94.
24. 1 Timothy 1:18–19, KJV, used in a sermon titled "The Care of the Soul as the One Thing Needful," https://www.ccel.org/ccel/whitefield/sermons.
25. Frances Dumas, *The Unquiet World: The Public Universal Friend and America's First Frontier* (Yates Heritage Tours Project, 2010), 17, citing Smithfield Meeting Minutes, as quoted by Austin Meredith in "Jemimah Wilkinson, Rhode Island's Publik Universal Friend," 2013, http://www.kouroo.info/kouroo/places/towns/CumberlandRI.pdf.
26. Dumas, *The Unquiet World*, 17.
27. Samuel Fothergill, *Memoirs of the Life and Gospel Labours of Samuel Fothergill*, ed. George Crosfield (Collins, Brother, 1844), 281.
28. Oscar Lugusa Malande, "The Concept of Hierarchy and Doing Ministry in the Church: Evaluating the Roles of Leaders and the Use of Authority in Quakerism," *Quaker Religious Thought* 133, article 5 (2019): 32–41.
29. Moyer, 44 (emphasis mine). And see Thomas D. Hamm, *The Quakers in America* (Columbia University Press, 2003), 32–33, on the Quaker Reformation and disownments/dismissals.
30. Dumas, *The Unquiet World*, 17.
31. "The Publick Universal Friend," in *Rhode Island History*, vols. 24–27 (Rhode Island History Society, 1965), 105.
32. Universal Friend, "A Memorandum of the Introduction of the Fatal Fever."

2: NEW LIFE

1. Recollection of a Wilkinson brother, described as "her brother" (no name) and quoted in Wisbey, 12. I believe it must have been Jeptha who was with her at the time. Jeptha was an ardent support of Friend's ministry, which could be explained by his being present at the first revelations of Friend's transformation on the morning of October 10, 1776. Wisbey cites "her brother, more than forty years later," as being present. Jeptha, Stephen, and Benjamin were all in the Cumberland militia, but all could have been staying at home at the time. Jeremiah Jr. lived close by and could have been called home specifically to care for Jemima. See Wisbey, 12, 206.
2. Universal Friend, "A Memorandum of the Introduction of the Fatal Fever."
3. Universal Friend, "A Memorandum of the Introduction of the Fatal Fever."
4. George Fox, *The Journal of George Fox* (Cambridge University Press, 1952), 27; and see Larson, "Indescribable Being," 598, in which Larson argues persuasively that innocence meant a form of genderlessness.
5. Testimony of Margaret Brewster, *Records of the Governor and Company of the Massachusetts Bay in New England, 1674–1686*, ed. Nathaniel B. Shurtleff (W. White, 1853–1854), quoted in Robert R. Mathisen, *Critical Issues in American Religious History* (Baylor University Press, 2006), 47.

6. Whitefield quoted in Stephen A. Marini, *Radical Sects of Revolutionary New England* (Harvard University Press, 1982), 1.
7. Joseph Gurney, ed., *Eighteen Sermons Preached by the Late Rev. George Whitefield, A.M.* (Joseph Gurney, 1771), 308; and see Fox, *Journal*, 27: "I come up in Spirit through the flaming sword. . . . All things were new; and all the creation gave another smell unto me than before. . . ."
8. Merrill D. Smith, ed., *The World of the American Revolution: A Daily Life Encyclopedia*, vol. 1 (Greenwood, 2015), 177–78.
9. Galatians 3:28, KJV.
10. David Hackett Fischer, *Albion's Seed: Four British Folkways in America* (Oxford University Press, 1989), 490.
11. Fischer, *Albion's Seed*, 491.
12. Fox, *Journal*, 520.
13. Brekus, *Strangers and Pilgrims*, 75–76.
14. George Whitefield, Letter to Mr. J.D., July 12, 1749, in *The Works of Reverend George Whitefield*, vol. 2 (Edward and Charles Dilly, 1771), 268.
15. John 15:14, KJV; and see Fox, *Journal*, 16: "And they that walk in this light come to the mountain of the house of God established above all mountains, and to God's teaching, who will teach them his ways. These things were opened to me in the light."
16. Wisbey, 35.
17. Reverend Eeles of Stonington, Connecticut, quoted in Ezra Stiles, *Literary Diary of Ezra Stiles*, vol. 2, ed. Franklin Bowditch Dexter (Scribner and Sons, 1901), 382.
18. I scoured records looking for the name of Patience's illegitimate child. The practice at the time would have been for the child to be enveloped into the mother's family, but there is no mention of a child living in the farmhouse at the time, nor is there any reference to Patience's first child when she later travels with Friend or moves to the western settlement and marries and has two more children.
19. Stafford C. Cleveland, *History and Directory of Yates County . . .* , vol. 1 (S. C. Cleveland, Chronicle Office, 1873), 39 (hereafter cited as "*History and Directory of Yates County*").
20. Marcy was disowned in December 1778, and Deborah and Elizabeth in May 1779. Moyer, 26, citing records of the Smithfield Local Meeting.
21. Wisbey, 14–15.
22. Wisbey, 15.
23. Universal Friend, June 1780 Sermon, quoted in Abner Brownell, *Diary of Abner Brownell, 1779–87*, vol. 2, AAS, 10 (hereafter cited as "Brownell Diaries").
24. Universal Friend, "A Memorandum of the Introduction of the Fatal Fever."
25. Brownell Diaries, vol. 2, 5.
26. Observer quoted in Wisbey, 24; Wisbey also quotes an observer who wrote under the name "Lang Syne," p. 24; and see *Freeman's Journal*, February 14,

1787: "her features [were] regular and the whole of her face thought by many to be beautiful."

27. *Freeman's Journal*, March 14, 1787.
28. Ezra Stiles, *Literary Diary*, 381.
29. Statement of observer, *Freeman's Journal*, March 29, 1787.
30. Journal of William Savery, October 22, 1794. William Savery Papers, 1750–1804, Haverford College Quaker Collections (hereafter cited as "William Savery").
31. Juster, "To Slay the Beast," 29.
32. Brekus, *Strangers and Pilgrims*, 53; and see Moyer, 206–7, fn 15.
33. Statement of observer, *Freeman's Journal*, February 14, 1787.
34. Friend's statement in response to question about whether the minister was the messiah, quoted in *Freeman's Journal*, March 28, 1787.
35. Exodus 3:14, KJV.
36. Rachel Malin, follower of Universal Friend, explained to William Savery, a Quaker, in 1794 that Universal Friend found "that [type of] Dress the most convenient" for traveling around. As recorded by William Savery in his journal on October 22, 1794, 46.
37. Abner Brownell, *Enthusiastical Errors Transpired and Detected in a Letter to His Father, Benjamin Brownell* (Printed for the Author, 1783), 4.
38. Universal Friend, "A Memorandum on the Introduction of the Fatal Fever" (emphasis mine).
39. Testimony of Moses Brown, quoted in Moyer, 22–23; John Lincklaen, *Travels in the Years 1791 and 1792 in Pennsylvania, New York and Vermont: Journals of John Lincklaen* (G. P. Putnam's Sons, 1897), 762.
40. Universal Friend, sermon titled "An Answer to Roxbury People," n.d., in Wisbey, 58.
41. Universal Friend, "A Memorandum on the Introduction of the Fatal Fever."
42. All quotes in this paragraph are from the story as told by Universal Friend and recorded by James Emlen in his journal. William N. Fenton, ed., "The Journal of James Emlen Kept on a Trip to Canandaigua, New York," *Ethnohistory* 12, no. 4 (Autumn 1965): 295 (hereafter cited as "James Emlen").
43. James Emlen, 295.
44. John 15:15, KJV.

3: THE MESSAGE

1. Brownell, *Enthusiastical Errors*, 7. Even when critiquing Friend's ministry for the slavish devotion of its followers, Brownell acknowledged Universal Friend was a great and persuasive speaker. François Barbé-Marbois, *Our Revolutionary Forefathers: The Letters of François, Marquis de Barbé-Marbois during His Residence in the United States as Secretary of the French Legation* (Duffield, 1929), 165; Christopher Marshall Diaries, May 20, 1788, Christopher Marshall Papers, Historical Society of Pennsylvania (hereafter cited as "Marshall Diaries");

Moses Brown, n.d., quoted in Wisbey, 26; observer quoted in *Freeman's Journal*, March 28, 1787.

2. *Freeman's Journal*, March 28, 1787.
3. Ruth Pritchard, quoted in Wisbey, 80; and see Ruth Spencer (Pritchard)'s journal describing Friend's early activities and giving the texts of her sermons 1793–1798, JWP (hereafter cited as "Ruth Pritchard's Journal").
4. Jeremiah 7:28, KJV, sermon of Universal Friend recorded in Ruth Pritchard's Journal; Abner Brownell would also note in his diary that Friend had used this text from Jeremiah. Brownell Diaries, vol. 2, 3.
5. Wisbey, 16.
6. Moyer, 25.
7. See Brownell Diaries, vols. 1 and 2; Ruth Pritchard's Journal; Sarah Richards's Daybook, 1789–1803, JWP.
8. Universal Friend, quoted in Brownell Diaries, vol. 1, 3–4.
9. Revelation 20:6, KJV; Brownell Diaries, vol. 2, 10.
10. Carla Gerona, *Night Journeys: The Power of Dreams in Transatlantic Quaker Culture* (University of Virginia Press, 2004), 13.
11. Dream recorded by Sarah Richards, April 14, 1789, Sarah Richards's Daybook, 1789–1803, JWP. Sarah Richards died in 1793, and the entries dated after her death most likely were written by Ruth Pritchard, just as Ruth had taken over maintenance of the Death Book of the Society of Universal Friends after Sarah's death. Not all the entries in this daybook are dated; footnotes will only list dates when written in the daybook itself.
12. See, for example, Notes Taken of Susannah Potter's Dreams; Journal of James Hathaway, April 1779–March 1780; and Sarah Richards's Daybook, all found in JWP.
13. Sarah Richards's Daybook, JWP.
14. Jeremiah 26:13 , KJV; Brownell Diaries, vol. 2, 3.
15. George Fox, "SOME PRINCIPLES OF THE Elect People of God Who in Scorn are called QUAKERS, For all People throughout all Christendome to Read over, and thereby their own States to Consider" (Printed for Robert Wilson, 1661), Introduction.
16. Sermon of Universal Friend, quoted in Ruth Pritchard's Journal.
17. Universal Friend to Sarah Richards, March 11, 1787, JWP; Universal Friend quoting Isaiah 13:9, KJV, as recorded in Ruth Pritchard's Journal.
18. Abner Brownell made this complaint after breaking with Universal Friend, not during the period when he was a devoted follower. See Brownell, *Enthusiastical Errors*, 8–9.
19. Sermon, undated, Universal Friend, Ruth Pritchard's Journal.
20. Sermon of Universal Friend, quoted in Brownell Diaries, vol. 1, 6. See also James Parker to Universal Friend, September 17, 1788, YCHC; Ruth Pritchard to Universal Friend, September 23, 1818, YCHC.
21. Universal Friend, "An Answer to Roxbury People," undated sermon, quoted in Wisbey, 58; follower quoted in *History and Directory of Yates County*, 79.

See also Ruth Pritchard's Journal; Sarah Richards's Daybook, November–December 1786.

22. See Moyer, 59–60, quoting both Abner Brownell and Ruth Pritchard on Friend's sermons; and see Universal Friend, *The Universal Friend's Advice: To Those of the Same Religious Society Recommended to Be Read in Their Public Meetings for Divine Worship* (Francis Bailey, at Yorick's Head, Market Street, 1784), reprinted in Wisbey, 197–204 (hereafter cited as "*The Universal Friend's Advice*, quoted in Wisbey"), 201.
23. Rev. L. Tyerman, *The Life of Reverend George Whitefield*, vol. 1 (Anson D. F. Randolph, 1877), 113.
24. Sermon of Universal Friend, combining texts from Job 28:28 and Proverbs 9:10, KJV, as recorded in Ruth Pritchard's Journal.
25. Brownell Diaries, vol. 2, 10.
26. Universal Friend, undated "Meditation," JWP.
27. Universal Friend, "A Memorandum of the Introduction of the Fatal Fever."
28. Isaiah 13:9, KJV, and see Ruth Pritchard's Journal, in which Pritchard writes that Universal Friend often used Isaiah 13:9, KJV, in sermons.
29. Sermon of Universal Friend, Brownell Diaries, vol. 2, 2–3.
30. Sermon of Universal Friend, Brownell Diaries, vol. 2, 2–3.
31. Juster, "To Slay the Beast," 28; Brekus, *Strangers and Pilgrims*, 90.
32. Galatians 3:28, KJV.
33. Juster, "To Slay the Beast," 29. To prove her point, Juster uses a quotation from a pamphlet that Friend plagiarized in 1779 (see chapter 4), but that Friend never again referred to nor is there any recorded sermon in which Friend utilized such language.
34. Universal Friend to Sarah Richards, March 11, 1787, YCHC, JWP. In Juster, "To Slay the Beast," 29, Juster lists words such "witches, whores, fornicators, 'painted Jezebels'" as those used by Friend in sermons; all such imagery can be found in Revelation 2:20, 19:2, 21:8, and 22:15, KJV.
35. As former president and devout Christian, Jimmy Carter so aptly put it in 2009, following the requirement adopted by the Southern Baptist Convention, that women must be "subservient" to their husbands and prohibiting them from serving as deacons, pastors, or chaplains in the military service (prompting him to sever ties with the Convention): "This view that women are somehow inferior to men is not restricted to one religion or belief. It is widespread. Women are prevented from playing a full and equal role in many faiths. Nor, tragically, does its influence stop at the walls of the church, mosque, synagogue, or temple. This discrimination, unjustifiably attributed to a higher authority, has provided a reason or excuse for the deprivation of women's equal rights across the world for centuries. The male interpretations of religious texts and the way they interact with and reinforce traditional practices justify some of the most pervasive, persistent, flagrant, and damaging examples of human-rights abuses." Jimmy Carter, "The Words of God Do Not Justify Cruelty to Women," *Observer*, July 12, 2009.

36. Universal Friend to James Parker, September 27, 1788, JWP, in which Friend used text from Malachi 4:1, KJV.
37. See Universal Friend, "A Memorandum of the Introduction of the Fatal Fever."

4: THE DEVIL IN NEWPORT

1. *The Norwich Packet*, July 8, 1776.
2. Ruth Pritchard's Journal; Wisbey, 18–19.
3. Abigail Adams to John Adams, February 8, 1777; April 7, 1777; May 6, 1777, Adams Papers, MHS.
4. John Adams to Abigail Adams, January 19, 1777, Adams Papers, MHS.
5. John Adams to Abigail Adams, January 14, 1777, Adams Papers, MHS.
6. Christopher Hawkins, *The Adventures of Christopher Hawkins* (Privately printed, 1864), 11.
7. Joseph Plumb Martin, *A Narrative of Some of the Adventures, Dangers and Sufferings of a Revolutionary Soldier* (Glazier, Masters, 1830), 208.
8. Thomas Paine, *The American Crisis*, pamphlet published in December 1776, Library of Congress, https://www.loc.gov/resource/cph.3b06889/.
9. As John Adams described it, the Boston Massacre of 1770, in which five colonists were killed by British soldiers, was caused by the inevitable tensions created when "soldiers are quartered in a populous town." "Adams' Argument for the Defense, 3–4 December 1770," *Legal Papers of John Adams*, vol. 3, Adams Papers, MHS.
10. Governor Cooke to Nathaniel Greene, April 19, 1778, quoted in Alan Gilbert, *Black Patriots and Loyalists: Fighting for Emancipation in the War for Independence* (University of Chicago Press, 2012), 100.
11. Brownell Diaries, vol. 1.
12. Abigail Adams to John Adams, September 29, 1775, Adams Papers, MHS.
13. Revelation 16:2–4, KJV.
14. Psalm 96:13, KJV.
15. Joseph Bellamy, "Jeremiah 18.6," May 17, 1776, Joseph Bellamy Sermons, Connecticut Historical Society.
16. "Religion and the Founding of the American Republic," Library of Congress exhibition, https://www.loc.gov/exhibits/religion/rel03.html.
17. Abraham Keteltas, *Arising and Pleading His People's Cause; Or the American War . . . Shewn to Be the Cause of God* (John Mycall for Edmund Sawyer, 1777), Rare Book and Special Collections Division, Library of Congress.
18. Jack Darrell Crowder, *Chaplains of the Revolutionary War: Black-Robed Warriors* (McFarland, 2017), 4.
19. Sermon of Jonathan Edwards, "Judges, 12.5,6," December 22, 1775, J. Edwards Jr. Papers, H. 166.2735.7516, Hartford Seminary. For more on this fascinating topic, see Mark Valeri, "The New Divinity and the American Revolution," *William and Mary Quarterly* 46, no. 4 (October 1989): 741–69.

20. This story was widely passed around at the time, but most likely is derived from the statement of Horace Walpole, English politician, at the start of the Revolution, that "Cousin America had run off with the Presbyterian parson, and that is the end of it." Alexander Leslie Klieforth and Robert John Munro, *The Scottish Invention of America, Democracy, and Human Rights: A History of Liberty* (University Press of America, 2004), 360.
21. Sermon of Universal Friend, Brownell Diaries, vol. 1, 6.
22. Hebrews 12:14, KJV.
23. Philosophy of Universal Friend, as recorded by follower Henry Barnes in the early nineteenth century, in *History and Directory of Yates County*, 99.
24. Observer of Universal Friend's mission to Newport, Wisbey, 41. There is no record of any British soldiers deserting their post to join the ministry of Universal Friend.
25. Ezra Stiles, *Literary Diary*, 380–81.
26. John Sullivan to John Hancock, August 25, 1777, in *Letters and Papers of Major-John Sullivan, Continental Army*, vol. 1, 443–44, ed. Otis G. Hammond (Concord, NH: New Hampshire Historical Society, 1930–39); Norman E. Donoghue II, *Prisoners of Congress: Philadelphia's Quakers in Exile, 1777–1778* (Pennsylvania State University Press, 2023), 66–78.
27. William Vernon Senior to John Adams, May 26, 1778, Adams Papers, MHS.
28. John Adams to Thomas Cushing, July 25, 1778, Adams Papers, MHS.
29. Matthew 19:26, KJV.

5: GATHERING THE FLOCK

1. Rhode Island Military Units: Kingston Reds, https://portsmouthhistorynotes.com/2022/10/22/rhode-island-military-units-kingston-reds/.
2. Wisbey, 51.
3. Brownell, *Enthusiastical Errors*, 7.
4. For further insights into Rhode Island slavery and its role in wealth in the colony, see Christy Clark-Pujara, *Dark Work: The Business of Slavery in Rhode Island* (New York University Press, 2016).
5. Caroline, E. Robinson, *The Hazard Family of Rhode Island, 1635–1894* (Printed for the Author, 1896), 60.
6. Letter to General Public, signed by William Potter, Joseph Wanton, Darius Sessions, and Thomas Wickes, dated April 25, 1775, reprinted in Robinson, *The Hazard Family of Rhode Island*, 57–58.
7. Robinson, *The Hazard Family of Rhode Island*, 58.
8. Letter to General Assembly of Rhode Island from William Potter, June 12, 1775, reprinted in Robinson, *The Hazard Family of Rhode Island*, 58.
9. Robinson, *The Hazard Family of Rhode Island*, 58–59.
10. Robinson, *The Hazard Family of Rhode Island*, 59.
11. Brownell Diaries, vol. 2, 3.
12. Brownell Diaries, vol. 2, 3.

13. All quotes in this paragraph are in Brownell Diaries, vol. 2, 3–4.
14. Brownell Diaries, vol. 2, 5.
15. Brownell Diaries, vol. 2, 5.
16. Brownell, *Enthusiastical Errors*, 14. Brownell regretted his captivation at the time he wrote *Errors*, but never denied the power of Friend's message.
17. Brownell Diaries, vol. 2, 5.
18. Brownell Diaries, vol. 1, 3–10.
19. Brownell Diaries, vol. 1, 3–10.
20. Brownell Diaries, vol. 2, 4.
21. William Cothren, *History of Ancient Woodbury, Connecticut: From the First Indian Deed in 1659 to 1854* (Bronson Brothers, 1854), 396; John Davis Skilton, *Doctor Henry Skilton and His Descendants* (Press of S. Z. Field, 1921), 17.
22. Horseback travel at a rate of fifty miles per day was considered fast, with thirty-five miles a day being the norm. Traveling by foot for long distances was common; an extreme example would be the four-hundred-mile trek undertaken by Moravians in 1766, who traveled from Bethlehem, Pennsylvania, to Wachovia, North Carolina, in thirty days. William S. Powell, *North Carolina through Four Centuries* (University of North Carolina Press, 1989), 141.
23. Brownell, *Enthusiastical Errors*, 6.
24. Brownell Diaries, vol. 2, 5.
25. See Rebecca Tannenbaum, *Health and Wellness in Colonial America* (Greenwood, 2012), 49.
26. See Wisbey, 63; Moyer, 72–73.
27. Psalms 139:14, KJV.
28. Moyer, 25, quoting Elijah Brown to the Smithfield Monthly Meeting, January 4, 1779, in which Brown recalls the early ministry of Universal Friend. Moses Brown Papers, Papers of the American Slave Trade, Brown University.
29. Moyer, 25, quoting Elijah Brown to the Smithfield Monthly Meeting, January 4, 1779, in which Brown recalls the early ministry of Universal Friend. Moses Brown Papers, Papers of the American Slave Trade, Brown University.
30. Elisha Brown to Moses Brown, January 4, 1779, quoted in Mark Thompson, *Moses Brown: Reluctant Reformer* (University of North Carolina Press, 1962), 148.
31. The "Quakers fully recognized women's right to speak in public." Brekus, *Strangers and Pilgrims*, 75.
32. Rebecca Larson, *Daughters of Light: Quaker Women Preaching and Prophesying in the Colonies and Abroad, 1700–1775* (University of North Carolina Press, 1999), 110–11.
33. Moses Brown to Elisha Brown, February 12, 1779, quoted in Thompson, *Moses Brown*, 148.
34. Moyer, 66; and see Brekus, *Strangers and Pilgrims*, 29.
35. Sermon of Universal Friend, Brownell Diaries, vol. 2, 3.

36. Brownell, *Enthusiastical Errors*, 18–19.
37. Brownell Diaries, vol. 2, 27; Moyer, 28; Wisbey, 61.
38. Brownell Diaries, vol. 2, undated entry for 1781, 27.
39. Moyer, 28.
40. Ezra Stiles, *Literary Diary*, 381.

6: MIRACLES AND PROPHECIES

1. *New England Magazine, New Series, Vol. 28, March 1903–August 1903* (America Company, 1903), 140; *The Book of Rural Life, Knowledge and Inspiration: A Guide to the Best in Modern Living*, vol. 4 (Bellows-Durham, 1925), 2338.
2. The village was renamed "Kingston" in 1825. See "Historical and Architectural Resources of South Kingstown, Rhode Island: A Preliminary Report," https://preservation.ri.gov/sites/g/files/xkgbur406/files/pdfs_zips_down-loads/survey_pdfs/south_kingstown.pdf.
3. Willian Davis Miller, "The Removal of the County Seat from Tower Hill to Little Rest, 1752," *Rhode Island Historical Society Collections* 19, no. 1 (January 1, 1926): 13.
4. Universal Friend, undated "Meditation," JWP.
5. See Last Will and Testament of Universal Friend, February 25, 1818, JWP; and Letter from "A Neighbor," Wisbey, 166.
6. Ezra Stiles, *Literary Diary*, vol. 2, 381.
7. See Patricia Ann Watson, *The Angelical Conjunction: Preacher-Physicians of Colonial New England* (University of Tennessee Press, 1991), 32.
8. Lynn Gamwell and Nancy Tomes, *Madness in America: Cultural and Medical Perceptions of Mental Illness before 1914* (Cornell University Press, 1995), 9.
9. For more information on treatment of mental illness during the colonial period, see Mary Ann Jimenez, *Changing Faces of Madness: Early American Attitudes and Treatments of the Insane* (Brandeis University Press, 1987), 43; and also Watson, *The Angelical Conjunction*, ch. 1.
10. Albert Deutsch, "Public Provision for the Mentally Ill in Colonial America," *Social Service Review* 10, no. 4 (December 1936): 607.
11. Ezra Stiles, *Literary Diary*, 381.
12. Universal Friend, undated "Meditation," JWP.
13. Brownell, *Enthusiastical Errors*, 9–10. Brownell seemed to believe that Friend had successfully treated William, even while writing a document that criticized other aspects of Friend's ministry.
14. Brownell, *Enthusiastical Errors*, 10.
15. Brownell, *Enthusiastical Errors*, 10. Brownell was very involved in trying to help the young man and never seems to question either Friend's sincerity in treating William or the minister's best efforts at helping the troubled young man.
16. Brownell Diaries, vol. 2, 12.
17. Entry dated October 20, 1779, Ezra Stiles, *Literary Diary*, 382.

18. Entry Dated October 20, 1779, Ezra Stiles, *Literary Diary*, 383.
19. Letter to the Editor, *Boston Evening-Post*, quoted in https://christianhistory institute.org/magazine/article/miracles-of-power-and-grace.
20. George Whitefield, "Sermon 1: Soul Prosperity," reprinted in John Gillies, *Memoirs of the Life of the Reverend George Whitefield* (Printed by Joseph Barber, 1812), 279.
21. Universal Friend, "Some considerations, propounded to the several sorts and sects of professors of this age. On the following important subjects. I. The Jew outward, being a glass for the professors of this age; with a postscript to the same subject. II. A warning, in the bonds of love, to the rulers, teachers, and people of this nation, concerning their church and ministry. III. An advertisement to the powers and people of this nation. IV. An answer to that common objection against the united Friends, that they condemn all but themselves. To which is added, an exhortation to the united Friends, everywhere scattered abroad" (Bennett Wheeler, 1779).
22. Brownell, *Enthusiastical Errors*, 39–40 (italics mine).
23. John Wesley, "A Calm Address to Our American Colonies" (Bristol, 1775), quoted in Henry Abelove, "John Wesley's Plagiarism of Samuel Johnson and Its Contemporary Reception," *Huntington Library Quarterly* 59, no. 1 (1996): 73.
24. Americanus (Caleb Evans), "A Letter to the Rev. John Wesley, Occassioned by His Calm Address to the American Colonies" (London 1775), quoted in Abelove, *John Wesley's Plagiarism*, 74.
25. John Wesley corrected and enlarged version of "A Calm Address to Our American Colonies," quoted in Abelove, *John Wesley's Plagiarism*, 75.
26. As reported in a letter from Moses Brown to Thomas Eddy, July 5, 1822, quoted in Moyer, 29.
27. Abelove, *John Wesley's Plagiarism*, 79.
28. *History and Directory of Yates County*, 82.
29. Samuel Adams, *An Oration Delivered at the State House in Philadelphia* (Philadelphia, 1776), 2.
30. Amos 5:20, KJV.
31. Revelation 11:2, KJV, states that "the holy city shall they tread under foot forty and two months." This text was the basis of the prediction. See Moyer, 64.
32. Entry dated October 30, 1779, Ezra Stiles, *Literary Diary*, 381; Brownell, *Enthusiastical Errors*, 13; Moyer, 64; Wisbey, 47.

7: A DARK DAY

1. Abigail Adams to James Lovell, May 24, 1780, Adams Papers, MHS.
2. Samuel Phillips Savage Diaries, 1770–1795, May 1780, MHS.
3. Abigail Adams to James Lovell, May 24, 1780, Adams Papers, MHS.
4. Abigail Adams to James Lovell, May 24, 1780, Adams Papers, MHS.

5. Frank Moore, *Diary of the American Revolution*, vol. 2 (Charles Scribner, 1859), 280; Joseph Plumb Martin, *Private Yankee Doodle: Being a Narrative of Some of the Adventures, Dangers and Sufferings of a Revolutionary Soldier*, George Scheer, ed. (Eastern Acorn Press, 1962), 181.
6. "A few lines composed on the dark day, May 19, 1780" (New Hampshire, 1780), Library of Congress, Ephemera Collection, Portfolio 88, Folder 25.
7. Donald Jackson and Dorothy Twohig, ed., *The Diaries of George Washington*, vol. 3 (University of Virginia Press, 1978), 353.
8. Moore, *Diary of the American Revolution*, vol. 2, 280.
9. Thomas J. Campanella, "'Mark Well the Gloom': Shedding Light on the Dark Day of 1789," *Environmental History* 12, no. 1 (January 2007): 48–49, quoting from John Kennedy, "Some Remarks on the Great and Unusual Darkness . . . " (Printed and sold by E. Russell, next the Bell-Tavern, 1780); Moore, *Diary of the American Revolution*, vol. 2, 281.
10. Moore, *Diary of the American Revolution*, vol. 2, 281.
11. Reverend Timothy Dwight, quoted in Dumas, *The Unquiet World*, 51.
12. Brownell, *Enthusiastical Errors*, 8.
13. The Shakers, still a small sect at the time, "gained a substantial number of converts" following the Dark Day. Stephen J. Stein, *The Shaker Experience in America* (Yale University Press, 1992), 12.
14. Enclosure No. 2, "Account of the Dark Day on May 19, 1780," in letter written by Cotton Tufts to John Adams, July 25, 1780, Adams Papers, MHS.
15. See "Mystery of Infamous 'New England Dark Day' Solved by Tree Rings," Science Daily, June 8, 2008, https://www.sciencedaily.com/releases/2008/06/080606145620.htm.
16. Death Book of the Society of Universal Friends, YCHC, JWP, and quoted in Wisbey, 188.
17. Brownell Diaries, vol. 1, 14.
18. Wilkins Updike, *History of the Episcopal Church in Narragansett, Rhode Island* (Henry M. Onderdonk, 1847), 233.
19. Diary of Jefferey Watson, quoted in Wisbey, 48.
20. Universal Friend, extracts, *Oeconomy of Human Life*.
21. Jonathan Sewall to Samuel Curwen, August 24, 1780, reprinted in George A. Ward, *The Journal and Letters of Samuel Curwen: An American in England, from 1775–1783* (Little, Brown, 1864), 289. Sewall was likely making fun of fearful colonists and didn't really believe the devil had caused the Dark Day.

8: FAITH IN A NEW COUNTRY

1. Valentine Rathbun, "An Account of the matter, form, and manner of a new and strange religion, taught and propagated by a number of Europeans, living in a place called Nisquenia, in the state of New York" (Bennett Wheeler, 1781), 20 (hereafter cited as "Rathbun"). For more about Valentine Rathbun, see Stephen J. Paterwic, "The Tyringham Shakers," from a talk given on July

21, 2012, on the Tyringham Shakers, at Union Church, Tyringham, sponsored by Bidwell House Museum, *American Communal Societies Quarterly*: https://digitalcommons.hamilton.edu/acsq/vol7/iss2/5.

2. Rathbun, 22.
3. All quotes in this paragraph are from Rathbun, 20, 22, 23, 25.
4. For more on the Shakers and the life of Ann Lee, see Richard Francis, *Ann the Word: The Story of Ann Lee, Female Messiah, Mother of the Shakers, the Woman Clothed with the Sun* (Arcade, 2001).
5. Edward Deming Andrews, *The People Called Shakers: A Search for the Perfect Society* (Oxford University Press, 1953), 7–8; Priscilla J. Brewer, "'Tho' of the Weaker Sex': A Reassessment of Gender Equality among the Shakers," *Signs* 17, no. 3 (Spring 1992): 611.
6. Ann Lee quoted in Andrews, *The People Called Shakers*, 11, relying on *Testimonies of the Life, Character, Revelations, and Doctrines of Our Ever Blessed Mother Ann Lee* (Hancock, 1816).
7. Andrews, *The People Called Shakers*, 12.
8. Wisbey, 70–71.
9. Rathbun, 20.
10. Ezra Stiles, *Literary Diary*, 382, 510–11.
11. Reverend John Pittman Diaries, entry dated September 22, 1780, Rhode Island Historical Society; and William Bentley, D.D., characterized Friend's ministry as "the most wretched fanaticism . . . ," Wisbey, 156.
12. Wisbey, 55.
13. See *Testimonies of the life, character, revelations and doctrines of our ever blessed Mother Ann Lee, and the elders with her: through whom the word of eternal life was opened in this day of Christ's second coming / collected from living witnesses, by order of the ministry, in union with the church* (Printed by J. Tallcott & J. Deming, Junrs., 1816), 195–96.
14. See *Testimonies of the life*, 92–98.
15. Brownell, *Enthusiastical Errors*, 9–10.
16. Brownell, *Enthusiastical Errors*, 27.
17. Mark J. Adair, "Plato's View of the 'Wandering Uterus,'" *Classical Journal* 91, no. 2 (December 1995–January 1996): 163.
18. Brownell, *Enthusiastical Errors*, 27.
19. Brownell Diaries, vol. 1, 7; Moyer, 50.
20. Brownell, *Enthusiastical Errors*, 32.
21. Brownell, *Enthusiastical Errors*, 33.
22. Brownell, *Enthusiastical Errors*, 33.
23. Brownell, *Enthusiastical Errors*, 34.
24. Brownell, *Enthusiastical Errors*, 4.
25. Brownell, *Enthusiastical Errors*, 7.
26. Brownell, *Enthusiastical Errors*, 37.
27. Abner Brownell, Letter to a Friend, "Beloved and Respected Cousin," March 16, 1780, Brownell Papers, AAS.

9: THE MISSION SOUTH

1. See https://founders.archives.gov/documents/Franklin/01-07-02-0136.
2. "The Streets of Philadelphia," https://www.encyclopedia.com/history/news-wires-white-papers-and-books/streets-philadelphia.
3. Report dated February 23, 1787, published in *The American Museum*, vol. 1 (Philadelphia, 1787), quoted in Wisbey, 79.
4. See observations of Marquis de Chastellux, François Jean, in his *Travels in North America in the Years 1780, 1781, and 1782*, vol. 1 (G. G. J. and J. Robinson, 1787), 288–89 (hereafter cited as "Marquis de Chastellux, *Travels*").
5. Psalm 71:20, KJV.
6. Dumas, *The Unquiet World*, 203, quoting Leonard Bolles Ellis, *History of New Bedford and Its Vicinity* (D. Mason, 1892), 124.
7. Proverbs 22:2, KJV; Universal Friend's translation of Proverbs 28:6, found in undated handwritten notes, loose papers, JWP.
8. *The American Museum*, vol. 1, and see Wisbey, 79.
9. *The American Museum*, vol. 1, and see Wisbey, 79.
10. *The American Museum*, vol. 1, and see Wisbey, 79.
11. Chris Coehlo, *Timothy Matlack: Scribe of the Declaration of Independence* (McFarland, 2013), 60–61.
12. S. Spencer Wells, "'That Everyone Should Enjoy His Sentiments': Samuel Wetherhill and the Renovation of Quaker Speech, 1780–1793," *Quaker History* 108, no. 2 (Fall 2019): 23, quoting Samuel Wetherhill, "Samuel Wetherhill's Defense of Himself against the Charges of the People Called Quakers," Box 41, Folder 9, Marian S. Carson Collection of Manuscripts, 1656–1995, Library of Congress.
13. Elaine Forman Crane, ed., *The Diary of Elizabeth Drinker: The Life Cycle of an Eighteenth-Century Woman* (Northeastern University Press, 1991), 404.
14. Marquis de Chastellux, *Travels*, 288. François-Jean de Chastellux was a French military officer who led French forces during the American Revolution, as well as a writer and philosopher and lifelong friend of George Washington.
15. Diary of Marquis de Barbé-Marbois, quoted in Robert St. John, "Jemima Wilkinson," *Quarterly Journal of the New York State Historical Association* 11, no. 2 (April 1830): 165–66.
16. All quotes in this paragraph are from the Diary of Marquis de Barbé-Marbois, as quoted in St. John, "Jemima Wilkinson," 166.
17. All quotes in this paragraph are from the Diary of Marquis de Barbé-Marbois, quoted in Wisbey, 81.
18. Diary of Marquis de Barbé-Marbois, quoted in St. John, "Jemima Wilkinson," 166.
19. *American Journal of Pharmacy*, vol. 93 (Philadelphia, 1921): 87–89; William C. Kashatus, *Conflict of Conviction: A Reappraisal of Quaker Involvement in the American Revolution* (University Press of America, 1990), 109; "Marshall Collection Sold," *New York Times*, February 20, 1910. Marshall's sons carried

on the apothecary business after he retired, followed by his granddaughter Elizabeth Marshall, one of the first female pharmacists in America.

20. Marshall Diaries, May 20, 1788.
21. Marshall Diaries, May 19–20, 1788, November 16, 1788.
22. All quotes in this paragraph are from Lloyd G. Blakely, "Johann Conrad Beissel and Music of the Ephrata Cloister," *Journal of Research in Music Education* 15, no. 2 (Summer 1967): 121–22; Julius Friedrich Sacshe, *The Music of the Ephrata Cloister and Conrad Beissel's Treatise on Music* (Press of the New Era, 1903), 11.
23. For more on this very interesting sect, see Jeff Bach, *Voices of the Turtle Doves: The Mystical Language of the Ephrata Cloister* (Penn State University Press, 2003).
24. Arnold James Potter, "Manuscript of the Life of Universal Friend" (unpublished, written in 1941), YCHC (hereafter cited as Potter, "Life of Universal Friend"), quoting from an unpublished autobiography of David Wagener; and Wisbey, 80, quoting from *The American Museum*, vol. 1.
25. Psalm 119:105, KJV.
26. All quotes in this paragraph are from an excerpt from David Wagener's unpublished autobiography, quoted in Moyer, 85.
27. David Wagener quoted in St. John, "Jemima Wilkinson," 167.
28. All quotes in this paragraph are from an excerpt from David Wagener's unpublished autobiography, quoted in Wisbey, 83, and Moyer, 48.
29. Marshall Diaries, quoted in Wisbey, 82.
30. Diary of Marquis de Barbé-Marbois, quoted in Wisbey, 81.

10: MESSAGE IN RETURN

1. Samuel Orcutt, *History of the Towns of New Milford and Bridgewater, Connecticut* (Case, Lockwood, and Brainard, 1882), 239.
2. Orcutt, *History of the Towns*, 325; and on 183: The meetinghouse was built in "the north end of town."
3. Brownell, *Enthusiastical Errors*, 15.
4. All quotes in this paragraph are from the "Public Statement of the Trustees of the Society of Universal Friends at East Greenwich, September 18, 1873," extracted in Wisbey, 52.
5. All quotes in this paragraph are from the "Public Statement of the Trustees of the Society of Universal Friends at East Greenwich, September 18, 1873," extracted in Wisbey, 52.
6. "Public Statement of the Trustees of the Society of Universal Friends at East Greenwich, September 18, 1873," extracted in Wisbey, 52.
7. Manumission papers signed by Benjamin and Sarah Brown found in Charles Rathbone Stark, *Groton, Connecticut, 1705–1905* (Palmer Press, 1922), 423–24; and see quoted in Moyer, 35.
8. Universal Friend, "A Memorandum of the Introduction of the Fatal Fever."

9. Ruth Pritchard, quoted in Wisbey, 30.
10. As mid-twentieth-century biographer Herbert A. Wisbey Jr. put it, "Eventually all the leading families in the Society of Universal Friends were linked by ties of marriage." Wisbey, 68.
11. As a girl, Universal Friend had ridden sidesaddle, and as a minister, the practice continued: the sidesaddle form accommodated Friend's long robes as well as it had accommodated dresses. The blue velvet saddle can be viewed in the Scherer Carriage House Museum of the Yates County History Center, Penn Yan, New York.
12. *The Universal Friend's Advice*, quoted in Wisbey, 197–204.
13. *The Universal Friend's Advice*, quoted in Wisbey, 199.
14. *The Universal Friend's Advice*, quoted in Wisbey, 198, 204.
15. *The Universal Friend's Advice*, quoted in Wisbey, 198.
16. *The Universal Friend's Advice*, quoted in Wisbey, 201.
17. *The Universal Friend's Advice*, quoted in Wisbey, 198.
18. All quotes in this paragraph are from *The Universal Friend's Advice*, quoted in Wisbey, 197, 198, 201.
19. *The Universal Friend's Advice*, quoted in Wisbey, 201, 203.
20. All quotes in this paragraph are from *The Universal Friend's Advice*, quoted in Wisbey, 199, 202.
21. *The Universal Friend's Advice*, quoted in Wisbey, 198, 199, 203.
22. *The Universal Friend's Advice*, quoted in Wisbey, 201. Historian Paul Moyer refers to "elaborate rules for behavior—injunctions against drunkenness, lewdness, profanity, and dishonesty" (Moyer, 71), but I couldn't find any record of specific rules written down or elaborated for the members of the Society of Universal Friends, nor is there any record of disciplinary protocols or measures for the breaking of rules. While lack of proof doesn't mean there were no disciplinary measures taken against followers, I understand Friend's *Advice* as counsel given followers to speak in ways that "becometh the gospel of Christ" and against "foolish talking," "vain jesting," and being "drunk with wine"; counsel meant to advise them (hence *Advice*) and not as elaborate rules subject to discipline. See Wisbey, 198–99. Furthermore, for an organization that kept elaborate records of dreams, deaths, and financial transactions, I find it hard to believe there would be no record book of disciplinary actions.
23. John 15:14, KJV; *The Universal Friend's Advice*, quoted in Wisbey, 200–201.
24. *The Universal Friend's Advice*, quoted in Wisbey, 203.
25. Universal Friend, extracts, *Oeconomy of Human Life* (emphasis mine). All Christian denominations incorporate the lessons of Jesus Christ to "love the Lord thy God with all of thy heart, and with all thy soul, and with all thy strength, and with all thy mind; and thy neighbor as thyself" (Luke 10:27, KJV). The Old Testament also requires the people of Israel to be a benevolent people. Leviticus 19:10; Leviticus 23:22, KJV.
26. *The Universal Friend's Advice*, quoted in Wisbey, 204.
27. Wisbey, 85.

11: LOOKING WESTWARD

1. When the Tuscarora joined the confederacy in the eighteenth century, the confederacy became known as the Six Nations. For a full exploration of the role of the Haudenosaunee Confederacy in the American Revolution, see Barbara Graymont, *The Iroquois in the American Revolution* (Syracuse University Press, 1972). "Nation" was a designation used by colonists to group Native Americans "who shared the same language, cultural, practices and territory." Timothy Shannon, *Iroquois Diplomacy on the Early American Frontier* (Viking Penguin, 2008), 20–21 (hereafter cited as "Shannon"). The term is still used today.
2. George Washington to General Gates, forwarded to Major General Sullivan, March 6, 1779, Founders Online, National Archives, https://founders.archives.gov/documents/Washington/03-19-02-0391. Philander D. Chase and William M. Ferraro, ed., *The Papers of George Washington, Revolutionary War Series*, vol. 19, January 15–April 7, 1779 (University of Virginia Press, 2009), 377–79; George Washington to Major General John Sullivan, May 31, 1779, Founders Online, National Archives, https://founders.archives.gov/documents/Washington/03-20-02-0661; Edward G. Lengel, ed., *The Papers of George Washington, Revolutionary War Series*, vol. 20, January 15–April 7, 1779 (University of Virginia Press, 2010), 716–19.
3. George Washington to Major General John Sullivan, May 31, 1779.
4. Rhiannon Koehler, "Hostile Nations: Quantifying the Destruction of the Sullivan-Clinton Genocide of 1779," *American Indian Quarterly* 42, no. 4 (Fall 2018): 442, Table I.
5. George Washington to Major General John Sullivan, May 31, 1779.
6. William Wait, "Sullivan's Campaign," *Proceedings of the New York State Historical Association* 6 (1906): 86.
7. Koehler, "Hostile Nations," 434.
8. George Washington to Captain Montour, October 10, 1755, in *Old and New, Volume 5: January 1872–July 1872*, ed. Edward Everett Hale (Roberts Brothers, 1872), 145.
9. Koehler, "Hostile Nations," 442.
10. Koehler, "Hostile Nations," 433.
11. Koehler, "Hostile Nations," 446.
12. George Engs Slocum, *Wheatland: Monroe Country, New York* (I. Van Hooser, 1908), 13.
13. In fact, studies have shown that "the absence of plows [in North America] allowed Iroquois farmers to maintain high levels of soil organic matter, critical for grain yields" and when displaced from their lands by white farmers who began using plows, the yield of tilled land plummeted. Yields rebounded only when "US farmers adopted practices [similar to Native American practices] that countered the harmful effects of plowing." Jane Mt. Pleasant, "The Paradox of Plows and Productivity: An Agronomic Comparison of Cereal Grain

Production Under Iroquois Hoe Culture and European Plow Culture in the Seventeenth and Eighteenth Centuries," *Agricultural History* 85, no. 4 (Fall 2011): 460.

14. Missionaries quoted in David Maldwyn Ellis, "The Yankee Invasion of New York, 1783–1850," *New York History* 32, no. 1 (January 1951): 6.
15. George Washington to General John Sullivan, March 6, 1779, Founders Online, National Archives, https://founders.archives.gov/documents/Washington/03-19-02-0401; Philander D. Chase and William M. Ferraro, ed., *The Papers of George Washington, Revolutionary War Series*, vol. 19, January 15–April 7, 1779 (University of Virginia Press, 2009), 388–89.
16. See Wisbey, 100.
17. Ezekiel Shearman, quoted in Wisbey, 100.
18. *History and Directory of Yates County*, 43.
19. Petition of James Parker to Governor George Clinton and Commissioners of New York Land Office, April 1791, quoted in Wisbey, 102.
20. Petition of James Parker to Governor George Clinton and Commissioners of New York Land Office, April 1791, quoted in Wisbey, 102.
21. The most compelling proof of the plans made by the Society for their foray into the western wilderness and settlement in New York State is in the Petition of James Parker to Governor George Clinton and Commissioners of New York Land Office, April 1791, quoted in Wisbey, 102–3.
22. In 1784, Hugh White, who claimed to be the first white farmer in Genesee County, sent proof of the land's fertility to his friends in Connecticut. The baskets that he sent contained produce the likes of which had never been seen in New England: White's friends were amazed by the "tallest stacks of Indian corn, his largest potatoes, and onions." Pomroy Jones, *Annals and Recollections of Oneida County* (Rome, 1851), 790.

12: AN ACCUSATION OF MURDER

1. *Freeman's Journal*, February 14, 1787.
2. "Views" and claims of Sarah Richards, as reported in St. John, "Jemima Wilkinson," 165; and see Wisbey, 63.
3. *The American Museum*, vol. 1, 153, quoted in Wisbey, 63.
4. All quotes in this paragraph are from Sarah Richards's Daybook, 1786–1787, November 27, 1786.
5. Sarah Richards to Universal Friend, October 21, 1787, JWP.
6. Sarah Richards's Daybook, 1786–1787, November 1786.
7. Sarah Richards's Daybook, 1786–1787, November 22, 1786, November 20, 1786.
8. Sarah Richards's Daybook, 1786–1787, December 4, 1786.
9. Sarah Richards's Daybook, 1786–1787, November 26, 1786, JWP.
10. All quotes in this paragraph are from Sarah Richards's Daybook, 1786–1787, November 1786.

11. All quotes in this paragraph are from Sarah Richards's Daybook, 1786–1787, November–December 1786, January 1787.
12. Sarah Richards's Daybook, 1786–1787, December 1786.
13. Sarah Richards's Daybook, 1786–1787, January 1787.
14. *Freeman's Journal*, March 28, 1787.
15. *Freeman's Journal*, March 28, 1787.
16. *Freeman's Journal*, March 28, 1787.
17. *Freeman's Journal*, March 28, 1787.
18. *Freeman's Journal*, March 28, 1787.
19. *Freeman's Journal*, March 28, 1787.
20. *Freeman's Journal*, March 28, 1787.
21. *Freeman's Journal*, March 28, 1787.
22. *Freeman's Journal*, March 28, 1787.
23. *Freeman's Journal*, February 14, 1787.
24. *Freeman's Journal*, February 14, 1787.
25. Marquis de Chastellux, *Travels*, 228; Jacob Cox Parsons, ed., *Extracts from the Diary of Jacob Hiltzheimer of Philadelphia, 1765–1798* (Wm. F. Fell & Co., 1893), 66.
26. *Freeman's Journal*, March 14, 1787.
27. *Freeman's Journal*, March 28, 1787.
28. *Freeman's Journal*, March 14, 1787.
29. *The Universal Friend's Advice*, quoted in Wisbey, 198.
30. All quotes in this paragraph are from Universal Friend to Sarah Richards, March 11, 1787, JWP.
31. Articles alluding to the allegations and/or about Universal Friend and the Society appeared in *The Freeman's Journal* on February 14, March 14, March 28, of 1787; and more would be published on August 22 and August 29, 1787; articles also were published in *The Pennsylvania Gazette* on March 28 and April 4, 1787; and reprints of articles published in *The Freeman's Journal* would appear in the *American Museum* in February, March, April, and May of 1787; quote is from *Pennsylvania Gazette*, April 4, 1787.
32. *Pennsylvania Gazette*, April 4, 1787.
33. *Freeman's Journal*, August 29, 1787.
34. All quotes in this paragraph are from *Freeman's Journal*, August 22, 1787.
35. Romans 12:19, KJV.
36. *The Universal Friend's Advice* quoted in Wisbey, 198.
37. Sarah Richards's Daybook, 1786–1787, December 12, 1786.
38. Sarah Richards to Universal Friend, October 21, 1787, JWP.
39. Sarah Richards's Daybook, 1786–1787, January 6, 1787.
40. Sarah Richards's Daybook, 1786–1787, January 9–10, 1787.
41. See Marshall Diaries, May 20, 1788.

13: TIME FOR CHANGE

1. Most states that produced their own paper money based its value off the Spanish dollar, which had been the currency of choice in the colonies for decades; for example, the value of a one-pound unit of New York currency was roughly equivalent to two-and-a-half Spanish milled dollars in 1787. Donald W. Marshall, "100 Pence to the Dollar," *New York Times*, February 15, 1971, 23. And see Lawrence H. Officer, "Dollar-Sterling Mint Parity and Exchange Rates, 1791–1834," *Journal of Economic History* 43, no. 3 (September 1983): 579–616.
2. For a comprehensive study of the complicated and chaotic economic problems in post-Revolution America, see Woody Holton, *Unruly Americans and the Origins of the Constitution* (Hill and Wang, 2007).
3. See Woody Holton, "Abigail Adams, Bond Speculator," *William and Mary Quarterly*, 3rd series, vol. 64, no. 4 (October 2007): 821–38.
4. Report of the Annapolis Convention of 1786, quoted in John Vile, *The Constitutional Convention of 1787*, vol. 1 (ABC CLIO, 2005), 20.
5. See Pauline Maier, *Ratification: The People Debate the Constitution, 1787–1788* (Simon & Schuster, 2011), 52, 225.
6. *Freeman's Journal*, November 21, 1787.
7. *Freeman's Journal*, May 16, 1787.
8. The delegates at the Constitutional convention rejected a clause that would have given Congress the authority to issue paper money but also rejected a measure that would have *denied* that power to the federal government and in 1819, the Supreme Court ruled that banknotes issued by the Bank of America on behalf of the federal government were constitutional.
9. The Congress of the Confederation met in Philadelphia until mid-1783. Congress then moved its meeting site to Princeton, New Jersey; followed by Annapolis, Maryland; then to Trenton, New Jersey; and in January 1785 to New York City.
10. Albert Bushnell Hart, ed., *American History Told by Contemporaries*, vol. III (Macmillan, 1901), 216–17.
11. In September of 1787, the United States Constitution was adopted by the Constitutional Convention and in December, Delaware was the first state to ratify it; when New Hampshire became the ninth state to ratify in June of 1788, the United States Constitution became legal, and the Articles of Confederation were rendered invalid.
12. As Woody Holton writes in *Unruly Americans*, "it became clear that roughly half the electorate would refuse to accept the Constitution until it contained a Bill of Rights" providing a bulwark against an overreaching Federal Government, and James Madison was charged with writing up the necessary amendments.
13. *The Universal Friend's Advice*, quoted in Wisbey, 204.
14. Universal Friend to James Parker, September 2, 1788, JPW.

15. All quotes in this paragraph are from Universal Friend to David Wagener, September 17, 1787, Sidney Ayers Papers, Cornell University, quoted in Moyer, 118.
16. Universal Friend to Sarah Richards, March 11, 1787, JWP.
17. Revelation 12:6, KJV.
18. Brownell, *Enthusiastical Errors*, 12–13. The followers of Ann Lee associated Lee "with the figure in the Book of Revelation, equating her flight to America with the biblical flight into the wilderness." Stein, *The Shaker Experience in America*, 29.
19. See James West Davidson, *The Logic of Millennial Thought: Eighteenth-Century New England* (Yale University Press, 1977), 250–52. Davidson quotes Ezra Stiles on 251.
20. Revelation 12:14, KJV.
21. Universal Friend to James Parker, September 27, 1788, JWP.
22. Samuel Sherwood, minister in Fairfield, Connecticut, Sermon titled "The Church's Flight into Wilderness" (1776), quoted in Davidson, *The Logic of Millennial Thought*, 251.
23. Seneca Lake is the largest of eleven long and narrow lakes in western New York; because the lakes are shaped like fingers, they are called "the Finger Lakes."
24. Orasmus Turner, *History of the Pioneer Settlement of Phelps & Gorham's Purchase, and Morris' Reserve* (William Alling, 1851), 155.

14: BARGAINS, DEALS, AND PROMISES

1. Graymont, *The Iroquois in the American Revolution*, 14.
2. Article 1, Section 8, of the new Constitution would make explicit that "Congress shall have Power . . . To regulate Commerce . . . with the Indian Tribes" and there was general agreement among Secretary of War John Knox, Secretary of the Treasury Alexander Hamilton, and President Washington that Native Americans owned their lands, and the policy of the new government should be to purchase their lands from Tribal Governments as sovereign nations.
3. Francisco de Vitoria, *De Indis et de Ivre Belli Reflectiones* (Jaques Boyer, ed., 1557, Alonso Munoz, ed., 1565, & Johann G. Simon, ed., 1696), quoted by Anthony Peirson Xavier Bothwell, "We Live on Their Land: Implications of Long-Ago Takings of Native American Indian Property," *Annual Survey of International & Comparative Law* 6, no. 1 (2000): 3.
4. See Shannon, 197–202, for a comprehensive rendering of the "factors contributing to the speed with which [Governor] Clinton [of New York] and other public and private interests dispossessed the Iroquois."
5. Shannon, 195–96.
6. Dewitt Clinton, *Discourse Delivered before the New York Historical Society, at Their Anniversary Meeting, 6th December 1811* (James Eastburn, 1812), Israel

Thorndike Pamphlet Collection (Library of Congress), Miscellaneous Pamphlet Collection (Library of Congress), New York Historical Society.

7. Shannon, 197. And also see Barbara Graymont, "New York State Indian Policy after the Revolution," *New York History* 57, no. 4 (October 1976): 438–74.
8. Wisbey, 103; Dumas, *The Unquiet World*, 126.
9. Petition of James Parker to Governor George Clinton and Commissioners of New York Land Office, April 1791, quoted in Wisbey, 103.
10. James Parker to Abraham Dayton, April 14, 1788, JWP.
11. James Parker to Abraham Dayton, April 14, 1788, JWP.
12. Petition of James Parker to Governor George Clinton and Commissioners of New York Land Office, April 1791, quoted in Wisbey, 103–4.
13. Petition of James Parker to Governor George Clinton and Commissioners of New York Land Office, April 1791, quoted in Wisbey, 103.
14. Universal Friend to James Parker, September 27, 1788, JWP.
15. *The Universal Friend's Advice*, quoted in Wisbey, 198.
16. For more on the history of the negotiations surrounding these leases and their terms, see Blake McKelvey, "Historic Aspects of the Phelps and Gorham Treaty of July 4–8, 1788," *Rochester History* 1, no. 1 (January 1939): 1–24, and Esther V. Hill, "The Iroquois and their Lands Since 1783," *Quarterly Journal of the New York State Historical Association* 11, no. 4 (October 1930): 335–53.
17. McKelvey, "Historic Aspects of the Phelps and Gorham Treaty of July 4–8, 1788," 7.
18. "To George Washington from the Seneca Chiefs, 1 December 1790," Founders Online, National Archives, https://founders.archives.gov/documents/Washington/05-07-02-0005; Jack D. Warren Jr., ed., *The Papers of George Washington, Presidential Series*, vol. 7, December 1, 1790–March 21, 1791 (University of Virginia Press, 1998), 7–16. In late December, George Washington replied with a promise, "Here then is the security for the remainder of your lands—No state nor person can purchase your lands, unless at some public treaty held under the Authority of the United States. The general Government will never consent to your being defrauded—But it will protect you in all your just rights." From "George Washington to the Seneca Chiefs, 29 December 1790," Founders Online, National Archives, https://founders.archives.gov/documents/Washington/05-07-02-0080. Jack D. Warren Jr., ed., *The Papers of George Washington, Presidential Series*, vol. 7, December 1, 1790–March 21, 1791 (University of Virginia Press, 1998), 146–50.
19. For a fascinating study of land speculation and the taking of Iroquois lands in central New York, see Alan Taylor's *William Cooper's Town: Power and Persuasion on the Frontier of the Early American Republic* (Alfred A. Knopf, 1995); for an exploration of land speculation and the taking of Iroquois lands in western New York, see Shannon, ch. 6. For a review of New York State's

land policy toward Native Americans following the Revolution, see Graymont, "New York State Indian Policy After the Revolution," 438–74.

20. Universal Friend to James Parker, September 27, 1788, JWP.

15: THE MIGRATION BEGINS

1. Orcutt, *History of the Towns*, 326; Dumas, *The Unquiet World*, 135.
2. Orcutt, *History of the Towns*, 326; Dumas, *The Unquiet World*, 135.
3. For more information on the Oneida Carry, called "Deo-wain-sta" by the Oneidas, see https://www.oneidaindiannation.com/the-oneida-carry-an-important-link-in-haudenosaunee-travels/.
4. Frances Parkman, *Montcalm and Wolfe*, vol. 1, 6th ed. (Macmillan, 1885), 321.
5. Benjamin Brown would be eventually paid $10 for the service of "driving the Friend's cattle from New England." Sarah Richards's Daybook, 1789–1803, July 7, 1792, JWP, and excerpted in *History and Directory of Yates County*, 53. Although Sarah Richards died in 1793, her daybook is dated through 1803, and it is presumed that Ruth Pritchard maintained the daybook after Richards's death, just as she had taken over the keeping of the Death Book of the Society of Universal Friends.
6. Deuteronomy 10:11, KJV.
7. As related by the grandson of one of the pioneers, quoted in Dumas, *The Unquiet World*, 1.
8. Psalm 95:1, KJV.
9. The date of the party's actual arrival in western New York is unclear. According to nineteenth-century historian Stafford Cleveland, the group arrived in August (*History and Directory of Yates County*, 43); however, according to twentieth-century historian Herbert Wisbey, the group "reached the Genesee country in the spring of 1788" (Wisbey, 105), and according to twenty-first-century historian Paul Moyer, the group arrived in early summer (Moyer, 128–29). What is clear from documentary records in the form of letters sent back and forth between James Parker and Universal Friend is that by September of 1788 fields had been cleared, some crops planted, and a few crude buildings put up for shelter (Universal Friend to James Parker, September 27, 1788, James Parker to Universal Friend, September 17, 1788, JWP). For all that work to have been achieved, the latest date by when the pioneers could have arrived at Seneca Lake is around the summer solstice of 1788.
10. *History and Directory of Yates County*, 22.
11. The stony beach where they had landed would come to called Friend's Landing. Another name for this first area of settlement was "the Gore": see "Abstract of the Case of the Settlers Commonly Called the Gore," JWP.
12. Psalm 48:2, KJV; and description from Benedict Robinson, Notes from 1789 Survey, quoted in Dumas, *The Unquiet World*, 168.
13. Benedict Robinson, Notes from 1789 Survey, quoted in Dumas, *The Unquiet World*, 168.

14. James Parker to Abraham Dayton, April 14, 1788, JWP.
15. For a fascinating history of the life of Mary Jemison, see James Seaver, *A Narrative of the Life of Mary Jemison: The White Woman of the Genesee* (J. D. Bemis, 1824); and for more about her land claims, see Cindy Amrhein, *A History of Native American Land Rights in Upstate New York* (History Press, 2016), 88–102.
16. Luke 6:48, KJV; Matthew 7:26, KJV.

16: TROUBLE ON THE HILL

1. Petition of James Parker, to Governor George Clinton and Commissioners of New York Land Office, April 1791, quoted in Wisbey, 106.
2. Universal Friend to James Parker, September 27, 1788, JWP.
3. Psalm 46:4–5, KJV.
4. Deuteronomy 31:6, KJV.
5. Between "1790 and 1825 . . . they enlarged the amount of improved land more than six times." David Maldwyn Ellis, *New York: State and City* (Cornell University Press, 1979), 104.
6. Job 12:819, KJV.
7. James Parker to Universal Friend, October 9, 1788, JWP.
8. James Parker to Universal Friend, September 17, 1788, JWP.
9. James Parker to Universal Friend, September 17, 1788, JWP; quoted in Wisbey, 108.
10. Wisbey, 107.
11. Benedict Robinson's survey, 1789, Dumas, *The Unquiet World*, 168; *History and Directory of Yates County*, 34.
12. *History and Directory of Yates County*, 456, 457.
13. *History and Directory of Yates County*, 456.
14. *History and Directory of Yates County*, 459.
15. *History and Directory of Yates County*, 459.
16. *Weed Technology: A Journal of the Weed Society of America*, vol. 1 (1987): 250.
17. *History and Directory of Yates County*, 459.
18. https://www.countrywalkers.com/blog/4-surprising-plants-to-use-for-wilderness-first-aid/.
19. Wisbey, 107.
20. Wisbey asserts Sarah Richards was sent to the settlement in June to tend to Parker, which is possible, but it's more likely that Sarah went later in the summer based on Friend's letter to James Parker in early September in which the minister mentions Sarah Richards's recent report of her visit to the camp. See Universal Friend to James Parker, September 27, 1788, JWP.
21. *History and Directory of Yates County*, 81.
22. Universal Friend to Sarah Richards, March 11, 1787, JWP.
23. *History and Directory of Yates County*, 45. How Sarah Richards arrived there is unfortunately not recorded: By horse? By boat? Although the journey could

be made entirely on horseback, it was not an easy journey, and we have no idea whether Sarah was an able horsewoman.

24. James Parker to Universal Friend, September 17, 1788, JWP; quoted in Wisbey, 108.
25. Universal Friend to James Parker, September 27, 1788, JWP.
26. Universal Friend to James Parker, September 27, 1788, JWP.
27. Friend often quoted from John 15:26, KJV.
28. Universal Friend to James Parker, September 27, 1788, JWP.
29. All quotes in this paragraph are from Universal Friend to James Parker, September 27, 1788, JWP.
30. All quotes in this paragraph are from Universal Friend to James Parker, September 27, 1788, JWP.
31. All quotes in this paragraph are from Universal Friend to James Parker, September 27, 1788, JWP.
32. All quotes in this paragraph are from Universal Friend to James Parker, September 27, 1788, JWP.
33. Universal Friend to James Parker, September 27, 1788, JWP.
34. Universal Friend to James Parker, September 27, 1788, JWP.
35. Psalm 26:12, KJV.
36. Petition of James Parker to Governor George Clinton and Commissioners of New York Land Office, April 1791, quoted in Wisbey, 6.

17: THE HUNGRY YEAR

1. Dumas, *The Unquiet World*, 142.
2. Wisbey, 109.
3. *History and Directory of Yates County*, xv.
4. David McCullough, *The Pioneers: The Heroic Story of the Settlers Who Brought the American Ideal West* (Simon & Schuster, 2020), 79. And see Alan Taylor, "The Hungry Year: 1789 on the Northern Border of Revolutionary America," in *Dreadful Visitations: Confronting Natural Catastrophe in the Age of Enlightenment*, ed. Alessa Johns (Routledge, 1999), 145–81.
5. Taylor, "The Hungry Year," 155.
6. In both France and England, women played a large role in leading the protests against their governments and demanding more food supplies for their families; they were "central actors in grain and bread riots in town and country. . . ." Natalie Zemon Davis, *Society and Culture in Early Modern France: Eight Essays* (Stanford University Press, 1975), 146; and see R. B. Rose, "Feminism, Women, and the French Revolution," *Historical Reflections/Reflexions Historiques* 21, no. 1 (Winter 1995): 187–205; and John Bohstedt, "Gender, Household and Community Politics: Women in English Riots, 1790–1810," *Past & Present*, no. 120 (August 1988): 88–122.
7. "New York farmers were more market-oriented than farmers in many other parts of the Northeast. The Hudson River made it easy . . . to send their

products to market. Farmers living at a distance from the river drove to river landings or sleighed. . . ." "One man remembered how they carried wheat by sleigh to Albany in the 1790s: 'It was a curious sight to observe the immense number of sleighs . . . a string a mile long, was not uncommon occurrence in those days. . . .'" Ellis, *New York*, 107.

8. Taylor, "The Hungry Year," 157.
9. *History and Directory of Yates County*, 45.
10. *History and Directory of Yates County*, 60.
11. Revelation 2:2–3, KJV.
12. Joshua 1:19, KJV.
13. John Tunnecliff to William Cooper, April 14, 1789, quoted in Taylor, "The Hungry Year," 158.
14. Benjamin Young to Benjamin Rush, June 2, 1789, quoted in Taylor, "The Hungry Year," 149.
15. Taylor, "The Hungry Year," 148.
16. Taylor, "The Hungry Year," 148.
17. *History and Directory of Yates County*, 45.
18. Benjamin Young to Benjamin Rush, June 2, 1789, quoted in Taylor, "The Hungry Year," 149.
19. Universal Friend to John and Orpha Rose, 1789, quoted in Wisbey, 29.
20. Universal Friend to James Parker, September 27, 1788, JWP.
21. All quotes in this paragraph are from *History and Directory of Yates County*, 44.
22. "A correspondent from the Susquehanna valley of northern Pennsylvania," quoted in Taylor, "The Hungry Year," 159.
23. Taylor, "The Hungry Year," 161–62.
24. Taylor, "The Hungry Year," 52.
25. "Extract of a Letter from a Gentleman Living on Lake Champlain . . . May 9, 1789," quoted in Taylor, "The Hungry Year," 151.
26. Taylor, "The Hungry Year," 148.
27. Clinton speech, New York (State) Journal of the Assembly . . . Thirteenth Session (New York, 1790: State of New York, Evans #22009), quoted in Taylor, "The Hungry Year," 167.
28. Oliver Phelps to Nathaniel Gorham, July 14, 1789, quoted in Taylor, "The Hungry Year," 175.
29. Undated Dream of Friend, quoted in Moyer, 75.
30. Universal Friend to John and Orpha Rose, 1789, quoted in Wisbey, 29.
31. These lines come from a work written by Johannes Tauler (German mystical writer of the fourteenth century) titled "A Short Dialogue between a Learned Divine and a Beggar." Friend might have seen it in a variety of printed forms, including the one printed in 1795 by John Trumbull of Norwich, Connecticut; the entire dialogue is found copied out in the personal papers of Universal Friend, JWP.

18: BOUNTY BE PRAISED

1. Ecclesiastes 1:4, KJV.
2. Petition of James Parker to Governor George Clinton and Commissioners of New York Land Office, April 1791, quoted in Wisbey, 114.
3. Diary of Ruth Pritchard's Journey to the Friend's Settlement, 1790, YCHC.
4. Marshall Diaries, May 19, 1788.
5. *History and Directory of Yates County*, 12, 89.
6. Dumas, *The Unquiet World*, 201.
7. *History and Directory of Yates County*, 89; Brenton was born in May 1792. There would be no further reconciliations and Arnold Hazard died in 1802 in Rhode Island.
8. All quotes in this paragraph are from Universal Friend, "A Memorandum of the Introduction of the Fatal Fever."
9. Record of Dream, April 14, 1789, Sarah Richards's Daybook, 1789–1803, JWP.
10. Record of dream, April 14, 1789, Sarah Richards's Daybook, 1789–1803.
11. Universal Friend to James Parker, September 27, 1788, JWP.
12. Tauler, "A Short Dialogue." Samuel Fothergill, a Quaker missionary from England whose work Universal Friend would have known, believed that "retreat" from civil and political life allowed one "to live in peace and quietness, minding their own business. . . ." See Daniel J. Boorstin, *The Americans: The Colonial Experience* (Random House, 1958), 67.
13. Lewis Cass Aldrich, *History of Ontario County New York*, George S. Conover, ed. (D. Mason, 1893), 106.
14. *History and Directory of Yates County*, 46.
15. *History and Directory of Yates County*, 185.
16. James Parker to Universal Friend, September 17, 1788, JWP.
17. *History of Ontario County*, 106.
18. *History and Directory of Yates County*, 47.
19. Wisbey, 111.
20. Wisbey, 112. And see *History and Directory of Yates County*, iii–iv.
21. Recollection of Henry Barnes, quoted in *History and Directory of Yates County*, 66.
22. Moyer, 65.
23. As quoted in *History and Directory of Yates County*, 79.
24. J. W. Frost, *The Quaker Family in Colonial America* (St. Martin's Press, 1975), 207.
25. Recollections of follower Henry Barnes, in *History and Directory of Yates County*, 100.
26. Romans 12:1, KJV.
27. Wisbey, 97.
28. See Rosabeth Moss Kanter, *Commitment and Community: Communes and Utopias in Sociological Perspectives* (Harvard University Press, 1972), 119; Wisbey, 127.

29. The medicine chest can be seen in the Scherer Carriage House of the Yates County History Center in Penn Yan, New York, which houses a permanent exhibit on Friend and displays a collection of fascinating artefacts.
30. *History and Directory of Yates County*, 60.
31. Wisbey, 128.
32. Moyer, 237, fn 50; and see Priscilla J. Brewer, "'Tho' of the Weaker Sex': A Reassessment of Gender Equality among the Shakers," *Signs* 17, no. 3 (Spring 1992): 611: "In daily practice, female leaders dealt with affairs affecting the sisters while their male counterparts handled matters involving the brethren. Economic management and relations with the outside world were the charge of male trustees." And on 612, "Mother Ann envisioned a social structure in which both men and women would participate, but with unequal authority . . . the man is first and the woman . . . second . . . After Lee's death in 1784, the sect's theology and government were restructured along [even] more rigidly patriarchal lines." And finally, on 635, "The feminization of the Society's leadership beginning in the last half of the nineteenth century came about only because of a worsening gender imbalance."
33. Lee endured painful childbirths and then all four of her children died in their infancy. Andrews, *The People Called Shakers*, 7–8. In 1770, Lee claimed to have received a message from Christ "that the root of human sin and misery was the illicit sexual intercourse 'committed by the first man and woman in the Garden of Eden.'" Brewer, "'Tho' of the Weaker Sex,'" 611.
34. While there are no records of Universal Friend conducting a wedding service, families and couples were supported in the community of faithful. The many marriages between followers (and involving Friend's own siblings) testify to Friend's tolerance of marriage and sexual activity. Although stories have circulated of Friend punishing certain adherents for wanting to get married (see Moyer, 245, fn 4, and 152), the fact is there are no records of Universal Friend prohibiting anyone from getting married, nor of disowning them from the Society for doing so.
35. Quoted in Kanter, *Commitment and Community*, 90.
36. Moyer, 151.
37. *History and Directory of Yates County*, 95; and see Potter, "Life of Universal Friend."
38. Death Book of the Society of Universal Friends, quoted in Wisbey, 188.
39. Universal Friend, extracts, *Oeconomy of Human Life.*
40. Death Book of the Society of Universal Friends, quoted in Wisbey, 189.
41. The will of Universal Friend specifically and repeatedly defined the people with whom the minister lived as "my family" and the inhabitants of the households through the years also saw themselves that way. Last Will and Testament of Universal Friend, February 25, 1818, JWP; and see Letter from "A Neighbor," Wisbey, 166.

42. *History and Directory of Yates County*, 69.
43. *History and Directory of Yates County*, 69.
44. William Cooper to Henry Drinker, July 21, 1790, quoted in Taylor, "The Hungry Year," 164.
45. Undated Dream, Sarah Richards's Daybook, undated manuscripts, JWP (hereafter cited as "Sarah Richards's Daybook").

19: A QUESTION OF TRUST

1. See Moyer, 126–27; see Universal Friend to Sarah Richards, December 17, 1788, JWP.
2. Taylor, *William Cooper's Town*, 91–92.
3. Potter, in particular, "had the money to purchase large tracts of land in New York after he followed the Friend there." Moyer, 37.
4. James Parker's Petition to Governor Clinton and Commissioners of the Land Office, 1791, quoted in Wisbey, 102.
5. Luke 22:46, KJV.
6. All quotes in this paragraph are from the Petition of James Parker to Governor George Clinton and Commissioners of New York Land Office, April 1791, quoted in Wisbey, 102–3.
7. All quotes in this paragraph are from the Petition of James Parker to Governor George Clinton and Commissioners of New York Land Office, April 1791, quoted in Wisbey, 104, 114.
8. Sarah Richards to Universal Friend, May 23, 1790, JWP.
9. Sarah Richards's Daybook Recording, 1791, Journey to Friend's Settlement, June 1, 1791, JWP.
10. Death Book of the Society of Universal Friends, quoted in Wisbey, 189.
11. Deuteronomy 31:6, KJV.
12. Death Book of the Society of Universal Friends, quoted in Wisbey, 189.
13. Universal Friend's Bible can be seen in the Scherer Carriage House of the Yates County History Center in Penn Yan, New York, which houses a permanent exhibit on Friend and displays a collection of artefacts which belonged to the minister.
14. Duke de La Rochefoucault Liancourt, *Travels through the United States of North America: The Country of the Iroquois & Upper Canada in the Years 1795, 1796, and 1797* (T. Giller, 1897), 206.
15. Sarah Richards's Daybook, 1789–1793; *History and Directory of Yates County*, 51.
16. Sarah Richards to Universal Friend, October 24, 1787, JWP.
17. Universal Friend to James Parker, September 27, 1788, JWP.
18. Ruth Pritchard's Journal; text is from Jeremiah 17:9, KJV.
19. Ruth Pritchard's Journal; text is from Matthew 6:24, KJV.
20. Notes of gospel text, Luke 18:25, KJV, presumed to be written by Universal Friend, Loose papers, JWP.

21. Moyer, 157; and see "Minutes of Meetings to Elect Trustees for the Society of the Universal Friend, November 17, 1791–November 17, 1792", JWP.
22. John Webb Pratt, *Religion, Politics, and Diversity: The Church-State Theme in New York History* (Cornell University Press, 1967), 100.
23. Rachel Malin, unpublished rebuttal to David Hudson book on Universal Friend (see footnote 433), extracted in Dumas, *The Unquiet World*, 223, and found in documents of YCHC.
24. See Curtis D. Johnson, *Islands of Holiness: Rural Religion in Upstate New York, 1790–1860* (Cornell University Press, 1989), 6, 17–21.
25. Pratt, *Religion, Politics, and Diversity*, 101; and see New York Religious Corporation Law, Section 5: "The trustees of every religious corporation shall have the custody and control of all the temporalities and property, real and personal, belonging to the corporation and of the revenues therefrom, and shall administer the same in accordance with the discipline, rules and usages of the corporation and of the ecclesiastical governing body, if any, to which the corporation is subject, and with the provisions of law relating thereto, for the support and maintenance of the corporation. . . ."
26. Wisbey, 117, although Moyer, 125–26, states the amount paid was about 12.5 cents per acre.
27. See *History of Yates County*, 23–24; Wisbey, 106–7; Dumas, *The Unquiet World*, 105–6.
28. Letter described and quoted in Potter, "Life of Universal Friend"; and see *History of Yates County*, with text of letter, 55.
29. Report of the Third Congress of the United States, in United States Congress, American State Papers, Documents, Legislative and Executive, of the Congress of the United States, 38 vols. (Gales and Seaton, 1832–1861), Class VI, Naval Affairs, 1:5.
30. Moyer, 126.
31. See Moyer, 127, fn 25.
32. Brownell Diaries, vol. 1, 14.
33. Moyer, 126; Potter, "Life of Universal Friend": "William Potter gathered up the loose ends of Parker and Hathaway and that first settlement of Friend's on the west side of Seneca Lake became known as . . . 'the Potter Location.'"
34. According to William Savery, as recorded in his diary, 59.
35. See Moyer, 185.
36. Quote is from Moyer, 176, who argues that greed was the underlining motivation for former followers William Potter and James Parker's break with Friend: "In short, the rebels were men who had gained much from their move to New York and hoped to gain more."
37. Moyer, 178–79.

20: THE SEARCH FOR A NEW EDEN

1. Tauler, "A Short Dialogue."
2. See L. H. Tasker, *The United Empire Loyalist Settlement at Long Point, Lake Erie* (William Briggs, 1900), 25–27.
3. Mel Robertson, "Burford's First Family," *The Burford* (Ontario) *Advance*, November 28, 1979.
4. See *Ontario Historical Society, Papers and Records*, vol. XVI (Ontario Historical Society, 1918), 78–90, for a full account of Abigail's second marriage to Joel Stone, whom she married in 1799.
5. Sarah Richards's Daybook, 1789–1803.
6. Death Book of the Society of Universal Friends, quoted in Wisbey, 190.
7. Death Book of the Society of Universal Friends, quoted in Wisbey, 190.
8. Death Book of the Society of Universal Friends, quoted in Wisbey, 190.
9. Death Book of the Society of Universal Friends, quoted in Wisbey, 190.
10. Hebrews 13:4, KJV.
11. Universal Friend to James Parker, September 27, 1788, JWP.
12. Benedict Robinson to Sarah Richards, December 1789, JWP.
13. Benedict Robinson to Sarah Richards, December 1789, JWP.
14. Acts 26:17–18, KJV.
15. Wisbey, 121.
16. Sarah Richards's Daybook, 1789–1803.
17. Sarah Richards's Daybook, 1789–1803, JWP; *History and Directory of Yates County*, 52.
18. Sarah Richards to Ruth Pritchard, March 12, 1793, JWP.
19. Universal Friend, extracts, *Oeconomy of Human Life*.
20. Universal Friend to James Parker, September 27, 1788, JWP.
21. All quotes in this paragraph are from the Diary of Benedict Robinson, cited in Potter, "Life of Universal Friend," and extracted in Dumas, *The Unquiet World*, 167–68.
22. Benedict Robinson to Sarah Richards, December 1789, JWP, quoted in Dumas, *The Unquiet World*, 168.
23. Isaiah 65:18, KJV.
24. Ruth Pritchard Spencer, Notes taken, 6th day of 10th Month, 1793, YCHC.
25. John 18:1, KJV.
26. Isaiah 30:17, KJV.
27. Liancourt, *Travels*, 236; *History and Directory of Yates County*, 67.
28. Liancourt, *Travels*, 236.
29. Dumas, *The Unquiet World*, 177.
30. All quotes in this paragraph are from the Death Book of the Society of Universal Friends, notation of Ruth Pritchard, October 28, 1794, JWP, quoted in Wisbey, 187.
31. Death Book of the Society of Universal Friends, quoted in Wisbey, 191.

32. Death Book of the Society of Universal Friends, quoted in Wisbey, 191; Universal Friend was quoting Ecclesiastes 7:2, KJV.
33. Death Book of the Society of Universal Friends, quoted in Wisbey, 191.
34. Universal Friend to Christopher Marshall, June 1795, JWP.
35. Universal Friend, extracts, *Oeconomy of Human Life.*
36. Universal Friend, extracts, *Oeconomy of Human Life.*
37. Death Book of the Society of Universal Friends, notation of death of Margaret Briggs, July 6, 1800, JWP, quoted in Wisbey, 193.
38. Brownell's recollection of Universal Friend, quoted in Wisbey, 50: "she was as much prepared the moment she entered the world to leave it again, and go to the innumerable hosts of angels."
39. Universal Friend's Funeral Sermon for Sarah Richards, quoted in Wisbey, 123.
40. Universal Friend to Sarah Richards, March 11, 1787, JWP.
41. Universal Friend, "An Answer to Roxbury People," undated sermon, quoted in Wisbey, 58.
42. Universal Friend, "A Memorandum of the Introduction of the Fatal Fever."
43. Universal Friend to Christopher Marshall, June 1795, JWP.
44. Universal Friend to Christopher Marshall, June 1795, JWP.
45. Universal Friend to John and Orpha Rose, 1789, quoted in Wisbey, 29.
46. Potter, "Life of Universal Friend."
47. John 1:5, KJV.

21: BUILDING JERUSALEM

1. Ruth Pritchard's Notebook, 1793–1797, JWP/YCHC.
2. *Malin v. Malin*, 656.
3. "During a period when other sources of subsistence became increasingly unreliable, fishing helped sustain the Iroquois through their worst periods. . . . The continued availability and abundance of fish in the eighteenth century remained an important force that ran counter to the Iroquois' increasing dependence on unreliable Euro-American food supply." Michael Recht, "The Role of Fishing in the Iroquois Economy, 1600–1792," *New York History* 78, no. 4 (October 1997): 454.
4. Anne Schaper Englot, "Situating Jerusalem: Poiesis and Techne in the American Urbanism of Jemima Wilkinson and Thomas Jefferson," in *Modern Architecture and Religious Communities, 1850–1970* (Routledge, 2018), 166–68; and John L. Creese, "Rethinking Early Village Development in Southern Ontario: Toward a History of Place-Making," *Canadian Journal of Archaeology/Journal Canadien d'Archéologie* 37, no. 2 (2013): 190–91, 197–99 (site maps), 200, 205–6.
5. *History of Yates County*, 65.
6. See Tom Burford, *Apples of North America* (Timber Press, 2013), 198.
7. Potter, "Life of Universal Friend."
8. Potter, "Life of Universal Friend."

9. *History and Directory of Yates County*, 86.
10. Ruth Pritchard to Universal Friend, in Wisbey, 31–32; Wisbey and Dumas think they married around 1803, Wisbey, 69, Dumas, *The Unquiet World*, 263; Cleveland thinks they married in 1797, *History and Directory of Yates County*, 260. Wisbey says it was not a happy marriage, and Spencer never became a member of the Society of Universal friends, Wisbey, 69.
11. Rachel Malin, undated letter from Jerusalem to a friend, quoted in Wisbey, 128.
12. *History and Directory of Yates County*, 88.
13. Liancourt, *Travels*, 206.
14. *History and Directory of Yates County*, 89.
15. *History and Directory of Yates County*, 95.
16. Moyer, 145.
17. Dumas, *The Unquiet World*, 187; Death Book of the Society of Universal Friends, quoted in Wisbey, 189.
18. Juster, "To Slay the Beast," 24.
19. Paula Baker, "The Domestication of Politics: Women and American Political Society, 1780–1920," *American Historical Review* 89, no. 3 (June 1984): 624; and see Sheila L. Skemp, "Women and Politics in the Era of the American Revolution," in *Oxford Research Encyclopedia* (Oxford University Press, 2022).
20. Campbell Curry-Ledbetter, "Women's Suffrage in New Jersey 1776–1807: A Political Weapon," *Georgetown Journal of Gender and the Law* 21 (2020): 718.
21. Teresa Anne Murphy, *Citizenship and the Origins of Women's History in the United States* (University of Pennsylvania Press, 2013), 16, 61–68.
22. Moyer, 8 (emphasis his).
23. "[T]he proportion of Friend's followers who never married was significantly greater than the national norm" (Moyer, 35); and "four-fifths (86 percent) [of converts] married . . . The rest (14 percent) remained single . . ." (Moyer, 35); and in Moyer, 214, fn 12, an "estimate of between 5 and 8 percent" of Americans remained single at the time.
24. Dumas made this assessment relying on her review of primary sources relating to Friend's communities in western New York. Dumas, *The Unquiet World*, 181. And see Moyer, 184–86; Dorothy A. Mays, *Women in Early America* (ABC-CLIO, 2004), 91–92.
25. William Blackstone, *Commentaries on English Law*, Book I (Clarendon Press, 1765), 430.
26. Quoting Universal Friend, Sharon V. Betcher, "The Second Descent of the Spirit of Life from God: The Assumption of Jemima Wilkinson," in *Gender and Apocalyptic Desire*, ed. Brenda E. Brasher and Lee Quinby (Equinox Publishing, 2006), 77.
27. Moyer, 163; and see Moyer, 7–8: "[The female followers] preached and prophesized, owned property, came to dominate spiritual life within the sect, and . . . eschewed the traditional roles of wife and mother. Importantly, they did all of these things as *women*."

28. Murphy, *Citizenship*, 8.
29. Englot, "Situating Jerusalem," 166; and see Moyer, 156.
30. See Dumas, *The Unquiet World*, 207.
31. Universal Friend, extracts, *Oeconomy of Human Life.*
32. Rachel Malin's Book, 1816–1818, 1, JWP.
33. Universal Friend to Anna Wagener, March 6, 1787, YCHC.
34. Rachel Malin, quoted in Wisbey, 128.
35. "Diary of Rev. William Colbert," in *Early Methodism within the Bounds of the Old Genesee*, ed., George Peck (Carlton and Porter, 1860), 134.
36. Moyer, 119.
37. See Johnson, *Islands of Holiness*, 13–14.
38. Wisbey, 173.
39. *History and Directory of Yates County*, 49, 50. And see St. John, "Jemima Wilkinson," 169.
40. History and Directory of Yates County, 50.
41. Wisbey, 134.
42. *History and Directory of Yates County*, 663.
43. *History and Directory of Yates County*, 666.
44. William Penn, "Letter from William Penn to the Kings of the Indians in Pennsylvania," Penn Family Papers, Historical Society of Pennsylvania.
45. *History and Directory of Yates County*, 49.
46. Universal Friend, extracts, *Oeconomy of Human Life.*

22: FRIENDS, NEIGHBORS, AND ENEMIES

1. Shannon, 203.
2. Shannon, 197.
3. "Report of Henry Knox on the Northwestern Indians," *American State Papers: Indian Affairs* 1 (June 15, 1789): 13–14; Shannon, 203.
4. Ordinance for the Government of the Territory of the United States North-West of the River Ohio; 7/13/1787, Article 3; Miscellaneous Papers of the Continental Congress, 1774–1789; Records of the Continental and Confederation Congresses and the Constitutional Convention, Record Group 360; National Archives Building, Washington, DC.
5. Shannon, 203; and see Paul Frymer, "'A Rush and a Push and the Land Is Ours': Territorial Expansion, Land Policy, and U.S. State Formation," *Perspectives on Politics* 12, no. 1 (March 2014): 123.
6. In "Relative to the Northwestern Indians," (June 15, 1789), in "Wabash, Creeks, Cherokees, Chickasaws, and Choctaws," *American State Papers: Indian Affairs* 7, no. 2 (August 7, 1789): 13.
7. All quotes in this paragraph are from *History and Directory of Yates County*, 49–50.
8. William Savery, 64.
9. William Savery, 64.

10. Jack Campisi and William A. Starna, "On the Road to Canandaigua: The Treaty of 1794," *American Indian Quarterly* 19, no. 4 (Autumn 1995): 474.
11. In his book *George Washington and Native Americans*, Richard Harless argues convincingly that Washington tried—but failed—throughout his administration to implement a just and fair policy toward Native Americans. See Richard G. Harless, *George Washington and Native Americans: Learn Our Arts and Ways of Life* (George Mason University Press, 2018).
12. Colin Gordon Calloway, *The Victory with No Name: The Native American Defeat of the First American Army* (Oxford University Press, 2015), 146.
13. John Brant, as quoted in William Savery, 69.
14. See Shannon, 22. As James Emlen would later note in his journal, during the conference at Canandaigua the Native Americans were "remarkably deliberate on all their proceedings" and that this deliberation led to more successful negotiations. James Emlen, 291.
15. William Savery, 66.
16. William Savery, 66–67.
17. William Savery, 67.
18. For more on Native Americans and Quakers, see Karim M. Tiro, "We Wish to Do You Good: The Quaker Mission to the Oneida Nation, 1780–1790," *Journal of the Early Republic* 26, no. 3 (Fall 2006): 353–76, 373.
19. Tiro, "We Wish to Do You Good," 357–58.
20. James Emlen, 291; and on 285, Emlen identifies the four Quakers as David Bacon, John Parrish, William Savery, and James Emlen.
21. William Savery, 65.
22. James Emlen, 299–300.
23. William Savery, 68.
24. All quotes in this paragraph are from William Savery, 58.
25. William Savery, 58.
26. All quotes in this paragraph are from William Savery, 59.
27. James Emlen, 294.
28. James Emlen, 295.
29. William Savery, 59.
30. James Emlen, 304.
31. William Savery, 68, and see James Emlen, 305.
32. James Emlen, 305.
33. James Emlen, 323.
34. James Emlen, 323.
35. James Emlen, 323.
36. Universal Friend, "A Memorandum of the Introduction of the Fatal Fever."
37. William Savery, 68.
38. Matthew 5:9, KJV; Wisbey, 136, citing "the account of her followers." Friend often used this text from Matthew in sermons, with heavy reliance on the word "peacemaker." See, for example, Universal Friend's Sermon dated 1793, notetaker unknown, YCHC.

39. Wisbey, 136.
40. James Emlen, 105.
41. Wisbey, 136.
42. William Savery, 70.
43. James Emlen, 306.
44. The Owasco, ancestors of the Seneca, began farming the lands around Keuka in the year 1000. See James Wesley Bradley, *Evolution of the Onondaga Iroquois: Accommodating Change, 1500–1655* (University of Nebraska Press, 1987), 9–11.
45. William Savery, 67, describing weather on October 21, 1794; and on October 25, he wrote, "snow was seven or eight inches deep."
46. Typical preparations for winters as described in Boorstin, *The Americans*, 349.
47. The final treaty was signed by all parties to the conference on November 11, 1794, and then signed by George Washington and ratified by Congress in January of 1795. See Campisi and Storna, "On the Road to Canandaigua," 484–87.
48. Campisi and Storna, "On the Road to Canandaigua," 487; and see *Oneida Indian Nation v. County of Oneida*, 414 U.S. (1974) at 676–79.
49. Treaty of Articles II–IV, https://americanindian.si.edu/static/nationtonation/pdf/Treaty-of-Canandaigua-1794.pdf.
50. Preamble and Article I of the Final Treaty, https://americanindian.si.edu/static/nationtonation/pdf/Treaty-of-Canandaigua-1794.pdf.
51. "Modern Iroquois living on reservations in New York trace their claims to political and legal sovereignty to the Canandaigua treaty, although the exact nature of their relationship to the state government of New York remains hotly contested to this day." Shannon, 208. And see Lee M. Hanover, "New York Oneida: Land Claims, Federal Policies, State Intervention and Casino Development" (2015), 28–31, https://digitalscholarship.unlv.edu/cgi/viewcontent.cgi?article=1113&context=award.
52. *Oneida Indian Nation v. County of Oneida*, 414 U.S. (1974) at 676–79. For a fascinating history of the 1974 landmark case, see George C. Shattuck, *The Oneida Land Claims: A Legal History* (Syracuse University Press, 1991).
53. Insofar as other provisions of the treaty, as a sovereign nation the Haudenosaunee issue their own valid passports to their citizens and still receive the yearly gift, provided for in the treaty, of goods including a square yard of cloth per tribal citizen (paltry compensation but symbolically important). And for more about how the treaty is being used today to protect land rights, see https://www.climaterealityproject.org/story/canandaigua-treaty-acknowledging-past-will-shape-our-future.
54. James Emlen, 329.

23: SOWING OF GREED

1. Potter, "Life of Universal Friend."
2. Quoted in Wisbey, 143.
3. Dumas, *The Unquiet World*, 180.

4. Final Will and Testament of Sarah Richards, November 16, 1793, JWP, YCHC. An inventory taken of her goods and chattel at the time of her death included an old wagon, harness, teapot and tea "ware," looking glass, plough, six swine, three Bibles, "one old gun," and "one Log house." Inventory of Sarah Richards's goods and chattel, YCHC.
5. *Malin v. Malin*, 629.
6. Final Will and Testament of Sarah Richards, November 16, 1793, JWP, YCHC.
7. Potter, "Life of Universal Friend."
8. William Savery, November 5, 1794.
9. William Savery, November 5, 1794. Resolution of the dispute over the horse is not recorded.
10. Moyer, 168: William Potter and James Parker's efforts to "transform opposition against the prophet into legal action" began with "the opening shot . . . from Judge Potter's eldest son Thomas."
11. Records of Ontario County's Court of Common Pleas, Moyer, 238, fn 6.
12. *History and Directory of Yates County*, 89.
13. Moyer, 177.
14. *History and Directory of Yates County*, 59.
15. Deposition of Jesse and Frances Dains, September 26, 1799, quoted in Moyer, 177.
16. Liancourt, *Travels*, 214.
17. Liancourt, *Travels*, 213–14.
18. Liancourt, *Travels*, 215.
19. Liancourt, *Travels*, 215.
20. Liancourt, *Travels*, 209.
21. The satchel is just one of the many artefacts of Universal Friend that can be viewed at the Scherer Carriage House of the Yates County History Center in Penn Yan, New York.
22. Universal Friend, extracts, *Oeconomy of Human Life*.
23. *The Universal Friend's Advice*, quoted in Wisbey, 198.
24. Universal Friend to Sarah Richards, March 11, 1787, JWP.
25. Universal Friend, extracts, *Oeconomy of Human Life*.
26. John 1:7, KJV.
27. See Moyer, 135, 232, fn 41: "All told, the Universal Friend ended up owning the following lots in Jerusalem: 21 through 28, 45 through 47, and 50 through 52." The area totaled 4,480 acres according to Cleveland, 63.
28. Quote ascribed to Universal Friend, in Potter, "Life of Universal Friend." And see Wisbey, 142–43.
29. Universal Friend to James Parker, September 27, 1788, JWP; and see Potter, "Life of Universal Friend."
30. Potter, "Life of Universal Friend." And see Wisbey, 142–43.
31. Sworn testimony of Elijah Malin in court proceedings as recorded by Arnold James Potter and quoted in Dumas, *The Unquiet World*, 182.

32. Ontario County Court of General Sessions Minute Books, June 6, 1799, November 1800, June 1800, quoted in Moyer, 180.
33. See Douglas Lamar Jones, "The Transformation of the Law of Poverty in Eighteenth-Century Massachusetts," *Volume 62: Law in Colonial Massachusetts, 1630–1800*, Colonial Society of Massachusetts, 153–59; Alyssa Kirkman, "The Meeting of Mothers, Midwives, and Men," *Tenor of Our Times* 2, article 4 (Spring 2013), https://scholarworks.harding.edu/tenor/vol2/iss1/4, 12.
34. Moyer, 182, citing Ontario County Circuit Court Minutes, June 1799, Ontario County Archives. Moyer also points out that "the ejectment case heard in 1799 may not have been the first attempt that Enoch and Eliza Malin made to gain possession of the Friend's estate. In 1797 and 1798 the Ontario County Court of Common Pleas minute books record suits and countersuits concerning . . . efforts to have . . . a tenant of Rachel Malin, ejected from the disputed tract." Moyer, 241, fn 38. In researching his book, *The Public Universal Friend*, Moyer made an exhaustive search of court records of the Ontario County (New York) Archives, including examinations and depositions of Universal Friend, Jesse Dains, Frances Dains, Thomas Judd, and Eliza Malin, providing important details for how the legal actions brought by and against Universal Friend and the Society proceeded.
35. Moyer, 176. In 1805, Benedict Robinson would threaten Universal Friend with an ejectment suit—and violence: "If you will consent to lease the [land I desire] . . . I will withdraw the suit . . . but if not, perhaps a man may come there which you may not think neighborly," but Robinson seemed to have no valid claim given that in 1792 Sarah Richards paid for and received from him the deed for land in Jerusalem and his threats went nowhere. See Benedict Robinson to Universal Friend, July 7, 1805, YCHC.
36. The men described their former minister this way, according to William Savery. William Savery, 58.
37. Moyer, 23; and see footnote 26 in Moyer, 210–11, for a thorough review of the historians' explorations and conclusions on the question of Friend's views on whether the 1776 rebirth meant rebirth as Christ.
38. Ezra Stiles, *Literary Diary*, 382.
39. Undated quote of James Manning, President of Rhode Island College (later Brown University), Wisbey, 20.
40. *People v. Ruggles*, 8 Johns. 290 (1811); the case will be discussed further in chapter 24.

24: INVOKING LAW AND GOD

1. Details of this encounter are found in Potter, "Life of Universal Friend"; Dumas, *The Unquiet World*, 159.
2. Potter, "Life of Universal Friend"; Dumas, *The Unquiet World*, 159; Wisbey, 151.

3. Deposition of Chloe Dains, *Chloe Dains v. Jemima Wilkinson*, Court of Oyer and Terminer, 1799, Ontario County Archives, quoted in Moyer, 172.
4. Depositions of Thomas Judd, Jesse Dains, and Eliza Malin, September 26, 1799, quoted in Moyer, 172.
5. Story as related in Potter, "Life of Universal Friend," and in *History and Directory of Yates County*, 92. Jonathan Dains and Jesse Dains were brothers, and Jesse was husband to Chloe. Having come to the first settlement in 1788 with his siblings, Castle, Jesse, and Abigail, Jonathan Dains (along with Castle and Abigail) remained faithful to the minister his whole life. Jesse and his wife, Chloe, however, broke with the Society over land issues.
6. *History and Directory of Yates County*, 70.
7. Potter, "Life of Universal Friend"; Dumas, *The Unquiet World*, 160.
8. *History and Directory of Yates County*, 71; and see Dumas, *The Unquiet World*, 160.
9. Moyer, 175.
10. *History and Directory of Yates County*, 71.
11. Indictment of James Parker, Indictments (1793–1818), Ontario County of Oyer and Terminer, 1801, cited and quoted in Moyer, 175.
12. While both Cleveland in *History and Directory of Yates County* and Dumas in *Unquiet World* assert that the case was heard in Ontario's Circuit Court, Paul Moyer in *Public Universal Friend* makes a convincing argument for the case having been heard in the Court of Oyer and Terminer, including the fact that one of the depositions in the case specifically refers to Oyer and Terminer Court. Moyer, 239, fn 18. At the time, New York State law provided that the Court of Oyer and Terminer hear all felony cases including those punishable by life imprisonment or death. The Court of Oyer and Terminer was abolished by the Constitution of 1895 and its jurisdiction was transferred to the New York Supreme Court. See https://history.nycourts.gov/court/court-oyer-terminer/.
13. William Blackstone, *Commentaries on the Laws of England*, Book the Fourth, Chapter 4, Avalon Project, Yale Law School, Lillian Goldman Law Library, https://avalon.law.yale.edu/18th_century/blackstone_bk4ch4.asp.
14. See David H. E. Becker, "Free Exercise of Religion Under the New York Constitution," *Cornell Law Review* 84, no. 4 (May 1999): 1088–1132.
15. John 3:14–15, KJV.
16. Psalms 125:3–4, KJV.
17. Cleveland quoting Justice Ambrose Spencer, whom he mistakenly identified as the presiding judge in the case. *History and Directory of Yates County*, 71. And see Dumas, *The Unquiet World*, 162; Wisbey, 152; Moyer, 174. It is interesting to note that Judge Ambrose's son, John Spencer, would become a lawyer for the Society of Universal Friends sometime around 1813 or '14. See *History and Directory of Yates County*, 74.
18. Philip I. Blumberg, *Repressive Jurisprudence in the Early American Republic* (Cambridge University Press, 2010), 2; and see "Blasphemy and the Original

Meaning of the First Amendment," *Harvard Law Review* 135, no. 689 (December 10, 2021): 689–710.

19. *People v. Ruggles,* 8 Johns. 290 (1811), 290.
20. *People v. Ruggles,* 8 Johns. 290 (1811), 295–96.
21. In *Burstyn v. Wilson*, the Court ruled that the New York State Film Censorship Board had violated the United States Constitution when it banned the film *The Miracle* about a pregnant girl who believed she was the Virgin Mary about to give birth to Jesus, as sacrilegious. The state court had agreed with the board, stating that the film treated Christianity with "contempt, mockery, scorn, and ridicule." The Supreme Court, however, unanimously decided that sacrilege could not be used as a basis for film censorship. See *Burstyn v. Wilson*, 342 U.S. 495 (1952). The last blasphemy case heard in the United States was in 1971, when two Pittsburgh shopkeepers were charged for having displayed a poster with the image of Jesus Christ as a wanted man. The prosecutors themselves asked that the charges be dropped.
22. Deposition of Chloe Dains, September 26, 1799, Ontario County Archives, cited and quoted in Moyer, 173.
23. All quotes in this paragraph are from *History and Directory of Yates County*, 72.
24. According to Ruth Pritchard, Friend often relied on Isaiah 13:9–11, KJV, in preaching sermons. See Ruth Pritchard's Journal.
25. Moyer, 239, fn 20.
26. Moyer, 239, fn 20, citing Ontario County Circuit Court minute books, June 17, 1802, 180, Ontario County Archives, and Ontario County Court of Common Pleas Vol. 1, 1794–1803, June 3, 1801, Ontario County Archives, and William Stuart to Rachel Malin, October 2, 1802, JWP.

25: THE COURAGE OF FAITH

1. Potter, "Life of Universal Friend."
2. All quotes in this paragraph are from Potter, "Life of Universal Friend."
3. Wisbey, 146; Moyer, 183; *History and Directory of Yates County*, 74.
4. William Carter to Rachel Malin, October 1808, JWP.
5. Wisbey, 149.
6. Potter, "Life of Universal Friend."
7. *Miscellaneous Writings of Charles Eliot, to Which Are Prefixed Some Notices of His Character* (Hillard and Metcalf, 1814), 181.
8. Potter, "Life of Universal Friend."
9. *History and Directory of Yates County*, v.
10. 1 Samuel 16:7, KJV.
11. According to Cleveland, John Malin (younger brother of Margaret, Rachel, Enoch, and Elijah) had the portrait framed, perhaps as late as the 1870s. *History and Directory of Yates County*, 110. The frame and portrait have been beautifully restored and can be seen in the exhibited collection devoted to Universal Friend at the Yates County History Center, Penn Yan, New York.

12. According to a follower in Potter, "Life of Universal Friend."
13. Potter, "Life of Universal Friend."
14. Proverbs 21:31, KJV.
15. Dumas, *The Unquiet World*, 215.
16. Ellis, *New York*, 110.
17. Potter, "Life of Universal Friend."
18. Thomas R. Gold to Rachel Malin, November 19, 1816, JWP.
19. Universal Friend, extracts, *Oeconomy of Human Life*.
20. See *Malin v. Malin*, 664.

26: OUT OF TIME

1. See letter of Elizabeth Walker to Rachel Malin, July 17, 1816, quoted in Wisbey, 162.
2. All quotes in this paragraph are from Elizabeth Walker to Rachel Malin, July 17, 1816, quoted in Wisbey, 162–63.
3. John Adams shared his recipe for saltpeter in a 1775 letter: "Earth dug up from under a Stable [so as to be full of horse urine and feces], put into a Tub. . . . Filled with Water. Stand 24 Hours. Then leaked off Slowly. Then boil'd for one Hour. Then run thro another Tub full of ashes. . . . Then put into a Kettle and boiled, until it grows yellow. Then drop it on a cold stone or cold Iron, and it will christallise for a Proof. Then set it by in Trays in cool Places. . . . And the Salt Petre is formed." John Adams to Joseph Palmer, June 19, 1775, Adams Papers, MHS.
4. "Probably used as a poultice" recipe (note of transcriber) found in loose papers of Universal Friend, JWP.
5. Elizabeth Walker to Rachel Malin, July 17, 1816, quoted in Wisbey, 162.
6. Psalms 104:24, KJV.
7. *Geneva Gazette*, August 21, 1816.
8. *History and Directory of Yates County*, 92–93.
9. For a list of followers buried in the Jerusalem burial ground, see Dumas, *The Unquiet World*, 240–42.
10. Universal Friend, extracts, *Oeconomy of Human Life*.
11. Universal Friend, extracts, *Oeconomy of Human Life*.
12. Dream dated September 10, 1815, recorded in Rachel Malin's Dream and Date Book, JWP.
13. Dream dated December 29, 1815, recorded in Rachel Malin's Dream and Date Book, JWP.
14. Universal Friend, sermon spoken at funeral for Mehitable Smith, quoted in Wisbey, 157.
15. Dream dated October 26, 1816, recorded in Rachel Malin's Dream and Date Book, JWP.
16. Abner Brownell, quoted in Wisbey, 50.
17. Abner Brownell, quoted in Wisbey, 50.

18. Isaac Watts Hymn, copy found in papers of Universal Friend, JWP.
19. Wisbey, 50.
20. Universal Friend, extracts, *Oeconomy of Human Life*.
21. Wisbey, 15.
22. Aldrich, *History of Ontario County*, 104.
23. Psalms 1:3, KJV.
24. Moyer, 183.
25. Thomas R. Gold to Rachel Malin, May 25, 1818, JWP.
26. 2 Peter 1:14, KJV.
27. Last Will and Testiment of Universal Friend, February 25, 1818, JWP.
28. All quotes in this paragraph are from Last Will and Testiment of Universal Friend, February 25, 1818, JWP.
29. Last Will and Testiment of Universal Friend, February 25, 1818, JWP.
30. Potter, "Life of Universal Friend."
31. 2 Corinthians 5:10, KJV.
32. Thomas R. Gold to Universal Friend and Rachel Malin, December 14, 1818, JWP.
33. Rachel Malin to Thomas R. Gold, January 12, 1819, JWP.
34. Potter, "Life of Universal Friend."
35. *History and Directory of Yates County*, 78.
36. Potter, "Life of Universal Friend."
37. Universal Friend, "An Answer to Roxbury People," undated sermon, quoted in Wisbey, 59.
38. Universal Friend, undated poem titled "Redeeming Love," quoted in Potter, "Life of Universal Friend."
39. Record of final appearance, author unknown, quoted in Wisbey, 163.
40. Universal Friend, "A Memorandum on the Introduction of the Fatal Fever"; Universal Friend to Sarah Richards, March 11, 1787, JWP.
41. All quotes in this paragraph are from Ruth Pritchard Spencer to Universal Friend, September 23, 1818, YCHC.
42. All quotes in this paragraph are from Ruth Pritchard Spencer to Universal Friend, February 1819, YCHC.
43. Wisbey, 31.
44. All quotes in this paragraph are from the Death Book of the Society of Universal Friends, noting the death of Ruth Pritchard, March 21, 1819, and quoted in Wisbey, 188.
45. While Thomas Potter never reconciled with Universal Friend, his father Judge William Potter is alleged to have made his peace with Friend before his death in 1814; former follower Benedict Robinson also "mended fences" with Friend at some point according to Moyer, 188.
46. Sermon given by Friend for Eunice Kenny, died April 1794, recorded in Death Book of the Society of Universal Friends, JWP; and quoted in Wisbey, 192. The text "Blessed is the people . . ." comes from Psalms 89:15, KJV: "Blessed is the people that know the joyful sound: they shall walk, O LORD, in the light of thy countenance." After the funeral, Patience's body was interred in a

burial ground overlooking Keuka Lake, close to the grave of her husband, Arnold, who had died in 1807. At some point, a stone marker bearing the initials "P. P." was added to the burial site.

47. Universal Friend, "An Answer to Roxbury People," undated sermon, quoted in Wisbey, 59.
48. Psalm 91:4, KJV.
49. Universal Friend, "A Memorandum of the Introduction of the Fatal Fever."
50. Death Book Society of Universal Friends, and quoted in Wisbey, 195.
51. All quotes in this paragraph are from the Death Book of Universal Friend, and quoted in Wisbey, 189.
52. See Death Book of the Society of Universal Friends, JWP, and quoted in Wisbey, 187–95; Universal Friend to Hannah Wall, August 2, 1803, YCHC.
53. Family genealogy quoted in Wisbey, 163 (Wisbey doesn't say which family).
54. Reverend Willian Bentley, Diary entry, July 25, 1819, in which Bentley also wrote, "This extraordinary woman had been the minister of a most wretched fanaticism. . . ." Wisbey, 164–65.
55. All quotes in this paragraph are from the eyewitness account of follower Huldah Davis, quoted in Dumas, *The Unquiet World*, 197–98.
56. *History and Directory of Yates County*, 78.
57. According to Society legend, the families of the two men passed down the secret of the location of Friend's grave to the first-born child of each generation. Wisbey, 171.
58. *Otsego Herald*, July 12, 1819, https://www.coopercrier.com/opinion/the-otsego-herald-a-great-comet-was-seen-in-the-night-sky-in-1819/article_c28ff257-2f7a-567b-a9c4-92ec2bf6a29d.html.
59. Mark 13:25–27, KJV.
60. Potter, "Life of Universal Friend."

EPILOGUE

1. David Hudson's biography, *The History of Jemima Wilkinson: A Preacheress of the Eighteenth Century*, was published in 1821; see Dumas, 271; Moyer, 202; and Wisbey, 180–81.
2. *Malin v. Malin*, 659.
3. Dumas, *The Unquiet World*, 203.
4. *History and Directory of Yates County*, 119.
5. *History and Directory of Yates County*, 68.
6. See Moyer, 196–97.
7. *History and Directory of Yates County*, 110.
8. *History and Directory of Yates County*, 110.
9. St. John, "Jemima Wilkinson," 167.
10. Abigail Adams, who had asked her husband to remember the ladies in creating a new government for a new country, died on October 28, 1818, of typhoid fever. She was seventy-three years old.

11. Rachel Malin, "The Love of Money is the Root of All Evil," YCHC.
12. Moyer, 202.
13. *Freeman's Journal*, December 6, 1819; Turner, *History of the Pioneer Settlement*, 161; *History of the State of Rhode Island with Illustrations* (Hoag, Wade, 1878), https://usgenwebsites.org/RIProvidence/histories/hist2.html.
14. *History and Directory of Yates County*, 82.
15. For more on the history of the Burned-Over District, see Whitney R. Cross, *The Burned-Over District: The Social and Intellectual History of Enthusiastic Religion in Western New York, 1800–1850* (Cornell University Press, 1982).
16. Moyer, 198; Cross, *The Burned-Over District*, 34; and see Barbara Weisberg, *Talking to the Dead: Kate and Maggie Fox and the Rise of Spiritualism* (HarperCollins, 2009), 36 (although Weisberg insists Joseph Smith played a more significant role).
17. Elizabeth Cady Stanton, *Declaration of Sentiments*, Seneca Falls Convention, 1848, https://www.nps.gov/wori/learn/historyculture/declaration-of-sentiments.htm.

Selected Bibliography

"It would be very gratifying . . . to see a correct history
of her life, ministry, and doctrines,
written with intelligence and candor.
But the idle and malicious tales in circulation,
respecting her, are utterly unworthy of belief."

—A NEIGHBOR OF UNIVERSAL FRIEND IN ONTARIO COUNTY

A limited number of Universal Friend's writings survive, including letters, personal journal entries and texts that the minister copied into journals, and notes scribbled on pieces of paper. These documents, along with diaries and journals, letters and memorandum authored by a number of the followers of Friend (including both the most trusted members of the sect and disenchanted followers), are largely found within the collection of Jemima Wilkinson Papers at Cornell University, as well as in the Public Universal Friend collection held at the Yates County History Center in Penn Yann, New York.

In 1941, Arnold James Potter completed his opus, *Manuscript of the Life and Times of Universal Friend*, a nine-hundred-page-plus biography (never published) of Universal Friend. Potter was a descendant of Thomas Hazard Potter and Patience Wilkinson, and in writing his biography, Potter relied on a trove of documents that had been passed down to him by his family, and that included numerous documents written by Universal Friend, such as poems, letters, and journal entries. After Arnold Potter's death, the documents were to be gifted to Cornell University, but his niece Mary Leah Potter contested the terms of Arnold Potter's will and for years refused to turn over the documents. Even when directed by a judge to do so, the niece apparently didn't fully comply with the order: certain documents that Potter owned and which he referred to in his biography were not included in the materials turned over to Cornell. I encourage all those interested in the history of Universal Friend to visit the Yates County History Center and see for themselves Potter's complete original manuscript, including scratch-outs and addendums. I also highly recommend visiting their Scherer Carriage House Museum, which houses fascinating personal belongings of Universal Friend, including a carriage, a lap desk, a medicine bag, the famous portrait of Friend, and many, many other items.

Throughout the book, I've made ample use of quotations from letters, journal entries, and other written documents (with citations provided in the endnotes). In the text, I've edited the quoted documents to correct spelling and grammar errors only when absolutely necessary to ensure readers understand the chosen quotations. I also quote frequently from the King James Bible, the Bible used by Universal Friend, and most of the quotes I use are documented favorite texts of Universal Friend based on records kept of the minister's sermons and conversations. Because Universal Friend took inspiration from a variety of sources, copying out and memorizing numerous poems, hymns, and even entire pages from admired texts, I use recorded extracts (fully footnoted) to illustrate the thought processes of the minister. And finally, in order to re-create what life was like in eighteenth-century Rhode Island and Pennsylvania, and then on the western frontier of New York, I relied on diaries and letters of Sarah Richards, Ruth Pritchard, Universal Friend, and Arnold James Potter, all found in the Jemima Wilkinson Papers held at Cornell University; the diaries of

Christopher Marshall held at the Historical Society of Pennsylvania; the journals of Abner Brownell, held at the American Antiquarian Society; the published memoirs of François Jean de Beauvoir, Marquis de Chastellux, and François-Alexandre-Frederic, Duke de La Rochefoucault Liancourt; the published memoirs of Quakers James Emlen and William Savery; and numerous travel journals and memoirs of eighteenth- and early-nineteenth-century explorers, pioneers, ministers, society figures, and politicians.

I am indebted to Paul Moyer not only for his wonderful book *The Public Universal Friend: Jemima Wilkinson and Religious Enthusiasm in Revolutionary America* (2015) but also for the ample notes and bibliography provided therein. In particular, his detailed history of the many trial documents resulting from the numerous court cases involving Universal Friend and followers proved an invaluable resource in my efforts to untangle the legal battles waged by and against Friend and the Society over properties in western New York.

Herbert A. Wisbey Jr.'s *Pioneer Prophetess: Jemima Wilkinson, the Publick Universal Friend* (1964) was my first introduction to Friend. Wisbey is thorough in his details of Friend's life, and completely engaging in his storytelling. He had access to the documents held by Cornell University in its collection of Jemima Wilkinson Papers, and was able to integrate ample information into his biography. Unfortunately, he didn't footnote his research (although he did provide endnotes that helped somewhat in tracking down relied-upon documents within the Cornell collection).

Stafford Cleveland's *History and Directory of Yates County*, vol. 1 (1873) provides a history of Jemima Wilkinson and the Society of Universal Friends based on his interviews with surviving members of the sect, as well as access to documents which have since been lost to history. As one of Friend's biographers, Frances Dumas, has pointed out, Cleveland "interviewed a number of people who had known Universal Friend, including Henry Barnes . . . Barnes was the last surviving member of the Society, and thankfully remembered the Friend very well."

Cleveland's account is accepted as verified and accurate, and is relied upon by all historians of Universal Friend.

Frances Dumas's book *The Unquiet World: The Public Universal Friend and America's First Frontier* (2010) provides a history of Friend based on the many documents found in the Yates County History Center, and includes maps, photographed documents, and thorough genealogies of the followers of Universal Friend.

PRIMARY SOURCES

Archival/Manuscripts

Abner Brownell Diary, 1779–87, 2 vols., American Antiquarian Society, Worcester, Massachusetts.

Brownell, Abner, *Enthusiastical Errors Transpired and Detected in a Letter to His Father, Benjamin Brownell* (New London, CT: Printed for the Author 1783), American Antiquarian Society, Worcester, Massachusetts.

Christopher Marshall Papers, Historical Society of Pennsylvania, Philadelphia, Pennsylvania.

Jemima Wilkinson Papers, Division of Rare and Manuscript Collections, Cornell University Library, Ithaca, New York.

Macdonald, A. J., Notes on American Utopian Communities, 1843–1865, Beinecke Library, Yale University, New Haven, Connecticut.

Moses Brown Papers, UMass Amherst Libraries, Amherst, Massachusetts.

New England Yearly Meeting of Friends, UMass Amherst Libraries, Amherst, Massachusetts.

Potter, Arnold James, "Manuscript of the Life of Universal Friend" (unpublished, written in 1941), Yates County History Center.

The Public Universal Friend Collection, Yates County History Center, Penn Yan, New York.

William Savery Diaries, 1794–1798, Haverford College Quaker and Special Collections, Haverford, Pennsylvania.

Published

Adams, Hannah, *An Alphabetical Compendium of the Various Sects Which Have Appeared in the World.* Boston: B. Edes & Son, 1784.

Bacon, Margaret Hope, ed., *Wilt Thou Go On My Errand? Journals of Three 18th Century Quaker Ministers.* Wallingford, PA: Pendle Hill Publications, 1994.

Brekus, Catherine A., ed., *Sarah Osborn's Collected Writings.* New Haven: Yale University Press, 2017.

Marquis de Chastellux, François Jean. *Travels in North America in the Years 1780, 1781, and 1782*, vol. 1. London: G.G. J. and J. Robinson, 1787.

Crane, Elaine Forman, ed., *The Diary of Elizabeth Drinker: The Life Cycle of an Eighteenth-Century Woman*. Boston: Northeastern University Press, 1991.

Dexter, Franklin Bowditch, ed., *The Literary Diary of Ezra Stiles, D.D., LL.D.*, vol. 2. New York: Scribner and Sons, 1901.

Fenton, William N., ed., "The Journal of James Emlen Kept on a Trip to Canandaigua, New York," *Ethnohistory* 12, no. 4 (Autumn 1965): 279–342.

Fox, George, *Journal of George Fox, Vol. 1: Being an Historical Account*. London: W. and F. G. Cash, 1852.

Liancourt, Duke de La Rochefoucault, *Travels through the United States of North America: The Country of the Iroquois, & Upper Canada in the Years 1795, 1796, and 1797*. London: T. Giller, 1800.

Lincklaen, John, *Travels in the Years 1791 and 1792 in Pennsylvania, New York, and Vermont*. New York: G. P. Putnam's Sons, 1897.

Parsons, Jacob Cox, ed., *Extracts from the Diary of Jacob Hiltzheimer of Philadelphia, 1765–1798*. Philadelphia: Wm. F. Fell & Co., 1893.

Savery, William, *A Journal of Life, Travels, and Religious Labors of William Savery*. Compiled by Jonathan Evans. London: Charles Gilpin, 1844.

Turner, Orasmus, *History of the Pioneer Settlement of Phelps & Gorham's Purchase, and Morris' Reserve*. Rochester: William Alling, 1852 ("Memoir of Thomas Morris," 477–78).

Eighteen Sermons Preached by the late Rev. George Whitefield, A.M. London: Joseph Gurney, 1771.

Newspapers

The American Museum
The Freeman's Journal
Philadelphia Gazette
Potter's American Monthly

SECONDARY SOURCES

Books

Alderfer, E. G., *The Ephrata Commune: An Early American Counterculture*. Pittsburgh: University of Pittsburgh Press, 1985.

Aldrich, Lewis Cass, *History of Ontario County New York*. Edited by George S. Conover. Syracuse, NY: D. Mason, 1893.

Amrhein, Cindy, *A History of Native American Land Rights in Upstate New York*. Charleston, SC: History Press, 2016.

Andrews, Edward Deming, *The People Called Shakers: A Search for the Perfect Society*. New York: Oxford University Press, 1953.

Angell, Stephen Ward, *Early Quakers and Their Theological Thought, 1647–1723.* New York: Cambridge University Press, 2015.

Bach, Jeff, *Voices of the Turtle Doves: The Mystical Language of the Ephrata Cloister.* University Park: Penn State University Press, 2003.

Bacon, Margaret Hope, *Mothers of Feminism: The Story of Quaker Women in America.* San Francisco: Harper and Row, 1986.

Berkin, Carol, *Revolutionary Mothers: Women in the Struggle for America's Independence.* New York: Alfred A. Knopf, 2005.

Bestor, Arthur Eugene, Jr., *Backwoods Utopias: The Sectarian and Owenite Phases of Communitarian Socialism in America, 1663–1829.* Philadelphia: University of Pennsylvania Press, 1950.

Blumberg, Philip I., *Repressive Jurisprudence in the Early American Republic.* New York: Cambridge University Press, 2010.

Boorstin, Daniel J., *The Americans: The Colonial Experience.* New York: Random House, 1958.

Brekus, Catherine A., *Strangers and Pilgrims: Female Preaching in America, 1740–1845.* Chapel Hill: University of North Carolina Press, 1998.

Brekus, Catherine A., ed., *The Religious History of American Women: Reimagining the Past.* Chapel Hill: University of North Carolina Press, 2007.

Brewer, Priscilla, *Shaker Communities, Shaker Lives.* Hanover, NH: University Press of New England, 1986.

Brown, Thomas, *An Account of the People Called Shakers.* Troy, NY: Bliss, 1812.

Buel, Joy Day, and Richard Buel Jr., *The Way of Duty: A Woman and Her Family in Revolutionary America.* New York: W. W. Norton, 1984.

Butler, Jon, *Awash in a Sea of Faith: Christianizing the American People.* Cambridge, MA: Harvard University Press, 1990.

Calloway, Colin Gordon, *The Victory with No Name: The Native American Defeat of the First American Army.* New York: Oxford University Press, 2015.

Clark-Pugara, Christy, *Dark Work: The Business of Slavery in Rhode Island.* New York: New York University Press, 2016.

Cleveland, Stafford C., *History and Directory of Yates County, Containing a Sketch of Its Original Settlement by the Universal Friends, the Lessee Company and Others, with an Account of Their Individual Pioneers and Their Families: Also of Other Leading Citizens. Including Church, School and Civil History and a Narrative of the Universal Friend, Her Society and Doctrine*, vol. 1. Penn Yann, NY: S. C. Cleveland, Chronicle Office, 1873.

Cott, Nancy F., *The Bonds of Womanhood: "Woman's Sphere" in New England.* New Haven, CT: Yale University Press, 1977.

Cross, Whitney R., *The Burned-Over District: The Social and Intellectual History of Enthusiastic Religion in Western New York, 1800–1850.* Ithaca, NY: Cornell University Press, 1982.

Dallimore, Arnold. *George Whitefield: God's Annointed Servant in the Great Revival of the Eighteenth Century.* Wheaton, IL: Crossway Books, 1990.

Davidson, James West, *The Logic of Millennial Thought: Eighteenth Century New England*. New Haven, CT: Yale University Press, 1977.

Desrosiers, Marian Mathison, *The Banisters of Rhode Island in the American Revolution, Liberty and the Costs of Loyalties.* Jefferson, NC: McFarland, 2020.

Dishman, Christopher, *Warfare and Logistics along the US-Canadian Border during the War of 1812.* Lawrence: University of Kansas Press, 2021.

Dumas, Frances, *The Unquiet World: The Public Universal Friend and America's First Frontier.* Dundee, NY: Yates Heritage Tours Project, 2010.

Earle, Alice Morse, *Customs and Fashions in Old New England*. New York: Charles Scribner's Sons, 1893.

Ellis, David Maldwyn, *New York: State and City*. Ithaca, NY: Cornell University Press, 1979.

Epstein, Barbara Leslie, *The Politics of Domesticity.* Middletown, CT: Wesleyan University Press, 1981.

Francis, Richard, *Ann the Word: The Story of Ann Lee, Female Messiah, Mother of the Shakers, the Woman Clothed with the Sun*. New York: Arcade Press, 2001.

Frost, J. W., *The Quaker Family in Colonial America.* New York: St. Martin's Press, 1975.

Garrett, Clarke, *Origins of the Shakers: From the Old World to the New*. Baltimore, MD: John Hopkins University Press, 1998.

Gerona, Carla, *Night Journeys: The Power of Dreams in Transatlantic Quaker Culture.* Richmond: University of Virginia Press, 2004.

Graymont, Barbara, *The Iroquois in the American Revolution*. Syracuse, NY: Syracuse University Press, 1972.

Hallowell, Richard P., *The Quakers in New England.* Philadelphia: Merrihew & Son, 1870.

Hamm, Thomas D., *The Quakers in America.* New York: Columbia University Press, 2003.

Harless, Richard G., *George Washington and Native Americans: Learn Our Arts and Ways of Life*, Fairfax, VA: George Mason University Press, 2018.

Hathaway, Mrs. William, Jr., *A Narrative of Thomas Hathaway and His Family, Formerly of New Bedford, Massachusetts: With Incidents in the Life of Jemima Wilkinson*. New Bedford, MA: E. Anthony and Sons, 1869.

Hawkesworth, Mary, *Gender and Political Theory.* Cambridge, UK and Medford, MA: Polity Press, 2019.

Hazard, Caroline, *The Narragansett Friends' Meeting in the 18th Century.* Boston: Houghton, Mifflin, 1900.

Holton, Woody, *Unruly Americans and the Origins of the Constitution*. New York: Hill and Wang, 2007.

Jimenez, Mary Ann, *Changing Faces of Madness: Early American Attitudes and Treatments of the Insane.* Waltham, MA: Brandeis University Press, 1987.

Johnson, Curtis D., *Islands of Holiness: Rural Religion in Upstate New York, 1790–1860.* Ithaca, NY: Cornell University Press, 1989.

Juster, Susan, *Doomsayers: Anglo-American Prophecy in the Age of Revolution*. Philadelphia: University of Pennsylvania Press, 2003.

Juster, Susan, and Lisa MacFarlane, ed., *A Mighty Baptism: Race, Gender, and the Creation of American Protestantism*. Ithaca, NY: Cornell University Press, 1996.

Kanter, Rosabeth Moss, *Commitment and Community: Communes and Utopias in Sociological Perspective*. Cambridge, MA: Harvard University Press, 1972.

Kashatus, William C., *Conflict of Conviction: A Reappraisal of Quaker Involvement in the American Revolution*. New York: University Press of America, 1990.

Kaye, Harvey J., *Thomas Paine and the Promise of America*. New York: Hill and Wang, 2005.

Kerber, Linda L., *Women of the Republic: Intellect and Ideology in Revolutionary America*. Chapel Hill: University of North Carolina Press, 2000.

Ketcham, Ralph, *From Colony to Country: The Revolution in American Thought, 1750–1820*. New York: Macmillan, 1974.

Kidd, Thomas S., *The Great Awakening: The Roots of Evangelical Christianity in Colonial America*. New Haven, CT: Yale University Press, 2008.

Kittelstrom, Amy, *The Religion of Democracy: Seven Liberals and the American Moral Tradition*. New York: Penguin Press, 2015.

Klein, Laura F., and Lillian A. Ackerman, ed., *Women and Power in Native North America*. Norman: University of Oklahoma Press, 1995.

Laing, Olivia, *Everybody: A Book About Freedom*. New York: W. W. Norton, 2021.

Larson, Rebecca, *Daughters of Light: Quaker Women Preaching and Prophesying in the Colonies and Abroad, 1700–1775*. Chapel Hill: University of North Carolina Press, 1999.

Mahood, Wayne, *General Wadsworth: The Life and Wars of Brevet General James S. Wadsworth*. New York: Da Capo Press, 2003.

Marini, Stephen A., *Radical Sects of Revolutionary New England*. Cambridge, MA: Harvard University Press, 1982.

Marini, Stephen A., *Sacred Song in America: Religion, Music, and Popular Culture*. Champaign: University of Illinois Press, 2003.

Mathisen, Robert R., *Critical Issues in American Religious History*. Waco, TX: Baylor University Press, 2006.

Mays, Dorothy A., *Women in Early America*. Santa Barbara, CA: ABC-CLIO, 2004.

McCullough, David, *The Pioneers: The Heroic Story of the Settlers Who Brought the American Ideal West*. New York: Simon & Schuster, 2020.

Mead, Sidney E., *The Lively Experiment: The Shaping of Christianity in America*. New York: Harper & Row, 1963.

Morris, Adam, *American Messiahs: False Prophets of a Damned Nation*. New York: W. W. Norton, 2019.

Moyer, Paul, *The Public Universal Friend: Jemima Wilkinson and Religious Enthusiasm in Revolutionary America*. Ithaca, NY: Cornell University Press, 2015.

Murphy, Teresa Anne, *Citizenship and the Origins of Women's History in the United States*. Philadelphia: University of Pennsylvania Press, 2013.

Murtagh, William J., *Moravian Architecture and Town Planning: Bethlehem, Pennsylvania and Other Eighteenth-Century American Settlements*. Philadelphia: University of Pennsylvania Press, 1967.

Norton, Mary Beth, *Founding Mothers and Fathers: Gendered Power and the Forming of American Society*. New York: Vintage Books, 1996.

Orcutt, Samuel, *History of the Towns of New Milford and Bridgewater, Connecticut*. Hartford, CT: Case, Lockwood, and Brainard, 1882.

Pencak, William A., and Daniel K. Richter, ed., *Friends and Enemies in Penn's Woods: Indians, Colonists, and the Racial Construction of Pennsylvania*. University Park: Pennsylvania State University Press, 2004.

Pratt, John Webb, *Religion, Politics, and Diversity: The Church-State Theme in New York History*. Ithaca, NY: Cornell University Press, 1967.

Puls, Mark, *Henry Knox: Visionary General of the American Revolution*. New York: Palgrave Macmillan, 2008.

Salmon, Marylynn, *Women and the Law of Property in Early America*. Chapel Hill: University of North Carolina Press, 1986.

Sankovitch, Tilde A., *French Women Writers and the Book: Myths of Access and Desire*. Syracuse, NY: Syracuse University Press, 1988.

Schiller, Lee Chambers, *Liberty, a Better Husband: Single Women in America, the Generations of 1780–1840*. New Haven, CT: Yale University Press, 1984.

Schneiderman, Howard G., *Engagement and Disengagement: Class, Authority, Politics, and Intellectuals*. New York: Routledge, 2018.

Shannon, Timothy, *Iroquois Diplomacy on the Early American Frontier*. New York: Viking Penguin, 2008.

Shattuck, George C., *The Oneida Land Claims*. Syracuse, NY: Syracuse University Press, 1991.

Shipton, Clifford K., *New England Life in the Eighteenth Century*. Cambridge, MA: Harvard University Press, 1963.

Skilton, John Davis, *Doctor Henry Skilton and His Descendants*. New Haven, CT: Press of S. Z. Field, 1921.

Smith, John Howard, *The First Great Awakening: Redefining Religion in British America, 1725–1775*. Madison, NJ: Fairleigh Dickinson University Press, 2015.

Stein, Stephen J., *The Shaker Experience in America*. New Haven, CT: Yale University Press, 1992.

Taylor, Alan, *The Divided Ground: Indians, Settlers, and the Northern Borderland of the American Revolution*. New York: Alfred A. Knopf, 2006.

Taylor, Alan, *William Cooper's Town: Power and Persuasion on the Frontier of the Early American Republic*. New York: Alfred A. Knopf, 1995.

Thompson, Mark, *Moses Brown: Reluctant Reformer*. Chapel Hill: University of North Carolina Press, 1962.

Turner, Frederick Jackson, *The Frontier in American History*. New York: Henry Holt, 1921.

Turner, Orasmus, *History of the Pioneer Settlement of Phelps and Gorham's Purchase.* Rochester, NY: William Alling, 1851.

Ulrich, Laurel Thatcher, *A Midwife's Tale: The Life of Martha Ballard, Based on Her Diary, 1785–1812.* New York: Random House, 1991.

Watson, Patricia Ann, *The Angelical Conjunction: Preacher-Physicians of Colonial New England.* Knoxville: University of Tennessee Press, 1991.

Weidensaul, Scott, *The First Frontier: The Forgotten History of Struggle, Savagery, and Endurance in Early America.* New York: Houghton Mifflin Harcourt, 2012.

Wilkinson, Israel, *Memoirs of the Wilkinson Family in America.* Jacksonville, IL: Davis & Penniman, 1869.

Williams, Walter L. L., *Spirit and the Flesh: Sexual Diversity in American Indian Culture.* Boston: Beacon Press, 1986.

Wisbey Jr., Herbert A., *Pioneer Prophetess: Jemima Wilkinson, the Publick Universal Friend.* Ithaca, NY: Cornell University Press, 1964.

Young, Alfred E., *Liberty Tree: Ordinary People and the American Revolution.* New York: New York University Press, 2006.

Zagarri, Rosemarie, *Revolutionary Backlash: Women and Politics in the Early American Republic.* Philadelphia: University of Pennsylvania Press, 2007.

Essays, Research Papers, and Articles

Abelove, Henry, "John Wesley's Plagiarism of Samuel Johnson and Its Contemporary Reception," *Huntington Library Quarterly* 59, no. 1 (1996): 73–79.

Adams, Arlan M., and Charles J. Emmerich, "William Penn and the American Heritage of Religious Liberty," *Journal of Law and Religion* 8, no. 1/2 (1990), 57–70.

Baker, Paula, "The Domestication of Politics: Women and American Political Society, 1780–1920," *American Historical Review* 89, no. 3 (June 1984): 620–47.

Banner, Stuart, "When Christianity Was Part of the Common Law," *Law and History Review*, 16, no. 1 (Spring 1988): 27–62.

Barzman, Karen-Edis, "The Subject of 'Woman' and the Discipline of Early Modern Studies: Jemima Wilkinson and the Publick Universal Friend," in *Culture and Change: Attending to Early Modern Women*, Margaret Mikesell and Adele Seeff, ed. (Newark: University of Delaware Press, 2003).

Becker, David H. E., "Free Exercise of Religion Under the New York Constitution," *Cornell Law Review* 84, no. 4 (May 1999): 1088–32.

Betcher, Sharon V., "The Second Descent of the Spirit of Life from God: The Assumption of Jemima Wilkinson," in *Gender and Apocalyptic Desire*, Brenda E. Brasher and Lee Quinby, ed. (London: Equinox Publishing, 2006), 76–89.

Bilharz, Joy, "First Among Equals? The Changing Status of Seneca Women," in *Women and Power in Native North America*, Laura F. Klein and Lillian A. Ackerman, ed. (Norman: University of Oklahoma Press), 1995, 101–12.

Blakely, Lloyd G., "Johann Conrad Beissel and Music of the Ephrata Cloister," *Journal of Research in Music Education* 15, no. 2 (Summer 1967): 120–38.

Bloch, Ruth H., "The Gendered Meanings of Virtue in Revolutionary America," *Signs* 13, no. 1 (Autumn 1987): 37–58.

Braisted, Todd W., "The Black Pioneers and Others: The Military Role of Black Loyalists in the American War for Independence," in *Moving On: Black Loyalists in the Afro-Atlantic World*, John W. Polis, ed. (New York and London: Garland Publishing, 1999), 3–37.

Brekus, Catherine, "The Revolution in Churches: Women's Religious Activism in the Early American Republic," in *Religion and the New Republic: Faith in the Founding of America*, James H. Hutson, ed. (Lanham, MD: Rowman & Littlefield Publishers, 1999), 115–30.

Brekus, Catherine A., "Sarah Osborn's Enlightenment: Reimagining Eighteenth-Century Intellectual History," in *The Religious History of American Women: Reimagining the Past*, Catherine A. Brekus, ed. (Chapel Hill: University of North Carolina Press, 2007), 108–41.

Brewer, Priscilla J., "'Tho' of the Weaker Sex': A Reassessment of Gender Equality among the Shakers," *Signs* 17, no. 3 (Spring 1992): 609–35.

Bronner, Edwin B., "Quakers Labor with Jemima Wilkinson, 1794," *Quaker History* 58 (1969): 41–47.

Campanella, Thomas J., "'Mark Well the Gloom': Shedding Light on the Dark Day of 1789," *Environmental History* 12, no. 1 (January 2007): 35–58.

Campbell, D'Ann, "Women's Life in Utopia: The Shaker Experiment in Sexual Equality Reappraised—1810 to 1860," *New England Quarterly* 51, no. 1 (March 1978): 23–38.

Campisi, Jack, and William A. Starna, "On the Road to Canandaigua: The Treaty of 1794," *American Indian Quarterly* 19, no. 4 (Autumn 1995): 467–90.

Cott, Nancy F., "Divorce and the Changing Status of Women in Eighteenth-Century Massachusetts," *William and Mary Quarterly* 33, no. 4 (October 1976): 586–614.

Creese, John L., "Rethinking Early Village Development in Southern Ontario: Toward a History of Place-Making," *Canadian Journal of Archaeology/Journal Canadien d'Archéologie* 37, no. 2 (2013): 185–218.

Curry-Ledbetter, Campbell, "Women's Suffrage in New Jersey 1776–1807: A Political Weapon," *Georgetown Journal of Gender and the Law* 21 (2020): 705–23.

Deutsch, Albert, "Public Provision for the Mentally Ill in Colonial America," *Social Service Review* 10, no. 4 (December 1936): 606–22.

Ellis, David Maldwyn, "The Yankee Invasion of New York, 1783–1850," *New York History* 32, no. 1 (January 1951): 3–17.

Englot, Anne Schaper, "Situating Jerusalem: Poiesis and Techne in the American Urbanism of Jemima Wilkinson and Thomas Jefferson," in *Modern Architecture and Religious Communities, 1850–1970*, Kate Jordan and Ayla Lepine, eds. (London and New York: Routledge, 2018), 159–75.

Frymer, Paul, "'A Rush and a Push and the Land Is Ours': Territorial Expansion, Land Policy, and U.S. State Formation," *Perspectives on Politics* 12 no. 1 (March 2014): 119–44.

Graymont, Barbara, "New York State Indian Policy after the Revolution," *New York History* 57, no. 4 (October 1976): 438–74.

Hanover, Lee M., "New York Oneida: Land Claims, Federal Policies, State Intervention and Casino Development" (2015), https://digitalscholarship.unlv.edu/cgi/viewcontent.cgi?article=1113&context=award.

Hendricks, Mrs. Walter P., and Arnold James Potter, "The Universal Friend: Jemima Wilkinson," *New York History* 23 (January 1942): 159–65.

Johnson, Donald F., "Occupied Newport: A Revolutionary City under British Rule," *Newport History* 84, no. 272 (Summer 2015): 1–24.

Juster, Susan, "To Slay the Beast: Visionary Women in the Early Republic," in *A Mighty Baptism: Race, Gender, and the Creation of American Protestantism*, Susan Juster and Lisa MacFarlane, ed. (Ithaca, NY: Cornell University Press, 1996), 19–37.

Kamensky, Jane, "Talk Like a Man: Speech, Power, and Masculinity in Early New England," *Gender and History* 8 (April 1996): 22–47.

Kestnbaum, Meyer, "Citizenship and Compulsory Military Service: The Revolutionary Origins of Conscription in the United States," *Armed Forces and Society* 27, no. 1 (Fall 2000): 7–36.

Koehler, Rhiannon, "Hostile Nations: Quantifying the Destruction of the Sullivan-Clinton Genocide of 1779," *American Indian Quarterly* 42, no. 4 (Fall 2018): 427–53.

Larson, Scott, "'Indescribable Being': Theological Performances of Genderlessness in the Society of the Publick Universal Friend, 1776–1819," *Early American Studies* 12, no. 3 (Fall 2014): 576–600.

Marietta, Jack D., and G. S. Rowe, "Violent Crime, Victims, and Society in Pennsylvania, 1682–1800," *Pennsylvania History: A Journal of Mid-Atlantic Studies 66, Explorations in Early American Culture* (1999): 24–54.

St. John, Robert, "Jemima Wilkinson," *Quarterly Journal of the New York State Historical Association* 11, no. 2 (April 1830): 158–75.

Taylor, Alan, "The Hungry Year: 1789 on the Northern Border of Revolutionary America", in *Dreadful Visitations: Confronting Natural Catastrophe in the Age of Enlightenment,* Alessa Johns, ed. (New York: Routledge, 1999), 145–81.

Thies, Clifford F., "The Success of American Communes," *Southern Economic Journal*, 67, no. 1 (July 2000): 186–99.

Tiro, Karim M., "We Wish to Do You Good: The Quaker Mission to the Oneida Nation, 1780–1790," *Journal of the Early Republic* 26, no. 3 (Fall 2006): 353–76.

Valeri, Mark, "The New Divinity and the American Revolution," *William and Mary Quarterly* 46, no. 4 (October 1989): 741–69.

Watkins, Susan Wareham, "Hat Honour, Self-Identity, and Commitment in Early Quakerism," *Quaker History* 103, no. 1 (Spring 2014): 1–16.

Wells, S. Spencer, "'That Everyone Should Enjoy His Sentiments': Samuel Wetherhill and the Renovation of Quaker Speech, 1780–1793," *Quaker History* 108, no. 2 (Fall 2019): 23–50.

Published Legal Records

Malin v. Malin, 1 Wend. 625, December, 1828, New York Court for the Correction of Errors, *Wendell's Reports,* 1824-1840, Vol. 1. https://cite.case.law/wend/1/625/.

Index

About the Author

Nina Sankovitch is the acclaimed author of the memoir *Tolstoy and the Purple Chair* and several works of popular history, including *American Rebels* and *The Lowells of Massachusetts.* Her writing has appeared in *The New York Times*, the *Los Angeles Times*, and *Vogue*.